Rabindrana...
Omnibus

II

Rabindranath Tagore Omnibus Contents

Volume-I

Gitanjali
Post Office
Creative Unity
Gora
My Boyhood Days
Hungry Stones & Other Stories

Volume-II

The Religion of Man
Four Chapters
Red Oleanders
The Hidden Treasure & Other Stories
Shesh Lekha
My Reminiscences

Volume-III

Creative Unity
Sādhāna
Man
Personality
Nationalism
Crisis in Civilisation & Other Essays
The Religion of Man
Greater India

Rabindranath Tagore Omnibus

II

Rupa & Co

Concept and typeset copyright © Rupa & Co. 2003

First Published 2003
Sixth Impression 2009

Published by

Rupa . Co

7/16, Ansari Road, Daryaganj
New Delhi 110 002

Sales Centres:
Allahabad Bangalooru Chandigarh
Chennai Hyderabad Jaipur Kathmandu
Kolkata Mumbai

Typeset in 11 pts. ClassicalGaramond by
Mindways Design
1410 Chiranjiv Tower
43 Nehru Place
New Delhi 110 019

Printed in India by
Rekha Printers Pvt. Ltd.
A-102/1 Okhla Industrial Area, Phase-II
New Delhi-110 020

Contents

THE RELIGION OF MAN

Preface

The chapters included in this book, which comprises the Hibbert Lectures delivered in Oxford, at Manchester College, during the month of May 1930, contain also the gleanings of my thoughts on the same subject from the harvest of many lectures and addresses delivered in different countries of the world over a considerable period of my life.

The fact that one theme runs through all only proves to me that the Religion of Man has been growing within my mind as a religious experience and not merely as a philosophical subject. In fact, a very large portion of my writings, beginning from the earlier products of my immature youth down to the present time, carry an almost continuous trace of the history of this growth. Today I am made conscious of the fact that the works that I have started and the words that I have uttered are deeply linked by a unity of inspiration whose proper definition has often remained unrevealed to me.

In the present volume I offer the evidence of my own personal life brought into a definite focus. To some of my readers this will supply matter of psychological interest; but for other I hope it will carry with it its own ideal value important for such a subject as religion.

My sincere thanks are due to the Hibbert Trustees, and especially to Dr. W.H. Drummond, with whom I have been in constant correspondence, for allowing me to postpone the delivery of these Hibbert Lectures from the year 1928, when I was too ill to proceed to Europe, until the summer of 1930. I have also to thank the Trustees for their very kind permission given to me to present the substance of the lectures in this book in an enlarged form by dividing the whole subject into chapters instead of keeping strictly to the lecture form in which they were delivered in Oxford. May I add that the great kindness of my hostess, Mrs. Drummond, in Oxford, will always remain in my memory along with these lectures as intimately associated with them?

In the Appendix I have gathered together from my own writings certain parallel passages which bring the reader to the heart of my main theme. Furthermore, two extracts, which contain historical material of great value, are from the pen of my esteemed colleague and friend, Professor Kshiti Mohan Sen. To him I would express my gratitude for the help he has given me in bringing before me the religious ideas of medieval India which touch the subject of my lectures.

Rabindranath Tagore
September 1930

The eternal Dream
Is borne on the wings of ageless Light
that rends the veil of the vague
and goes across time
weaving ceaseless patterns of Being.

The mystery remains dumb,
the meaning of this pilgrimage,
the endless adventure of existence
whose rush along the sky
flames up into innumerable rings of paths,
till at last knowledge gleams out from the dusk
in the infinity of human spirit,
and in that dim lighted dawn
she speechlessly gazes through the break in the mist
at the vision of Life and of Love
rising from the tumult of profound pain and joy.

Santiniketan
16 September 1929
[Composed for the Opening Day Celebrations of the Indian
College, Montpelier, France.]

Chapter I

Man's Universe

Light, as the radiant energy of creation, started the ring-dance of atoms in a diminutive sky, and also the dance of the stars in the vast, lonely theatre of time and space. The planets came out of their bath of fire and basked in the sun for ages. They were the thrones of the gigantic Inert, dumb and desolate, which knew not the meaning of its own blind destiny and majestically frowned upon a future when its monarchy would be menaced.

Then came a time when life was brought into the arena in the tiniest little monocycle of a cell. With its gift of growth and power of adaptation it faced the ponderous enormity of things, and contradicted the unmeaningness of their bulk. It was made conscious not of the volume but of the value of existence, which it ever tried to enhance and maintain in many-branched paths of creation, overcoming the obstructive inertia of Nature by obeying Nature's law.

But the miracle of creation did not stop here in this isolated speck of life launched on a lonely voyage to the Unknown. A multitude of cells were bound together into a larger unit, not through aggregation, but through a marvellous quality of complex inter-relationship maintaining a perfect co-ordination of functions. This is the creative principle of unity, the divine mystery of existence, that baffles all analysis. The larger co-operative units could adequately pay for a greater freedom of self-expression, and they began to form and develop in their bodies new organs of power, new instruments of efficiency. This was the march of evolution ever unfolding the potentialities of life.

But this evolution which continues on the physical plane has its limited range. All exaggeration in that direction becomes a burden that breaks the natural rhythm of life, and those creatures that encouraged their ambitious flesh to grow in dimensions have nearly all perished of their cumbrous absurdity.

Before the chapter ended Man appeared and turned the course of this evolution from an indefinite march of physical aggrandizement to a freedom of a more subtle perfection. This has made possible his progress to become unlimited, and has enabled him to realize the boundless in his power.

The fire is lighted, the hammers are working, and for laborious days and nights amidst dirt and discordance the musical instrument is being made. We may accept this as a detached fact and follow its evolution. But when the music is revealed, we know that the whole thing is a part of the manifestation of music in spite of its contradictory character. The process of evolution, which after ages has reached man, must be realized in its unity with him; though in him it assumes a new value and proceeds to a different path. It is a continuous process that finds its meaning in Man; and we must acknowledge that the evolution which Science talks of is that of Man's universe. The leather binding and title-page are parts of the book itself; and this world that we perceive through our senses and mind and life's experience is profoundly one with ourselves.

The divine principle of unity has ever been that of an inner interrelationship. This is revealed in some of its earliest stages in the evolution of multicellular life on this planet. The most perfect inward expression has been attained by man in his own body. But what is most important of all is the fact that man has also attained its realization in a more subtle body outside his physical system. He misses himself when isolated; he finds his own larger and truer self in his wide human relationship. His multicellular body is born and it dies; his multi-personal humanity is immortal. In this ideal of unity he realizes the eternal in his life and the boundless in his love. The unity becomes not a mere subjective idea, but an energizing truth. Whatever name may be given to it, and whatever form it symbolizes, the consciousness of this unity is spiritual, and our effort to be true to it is our religion. It ever waits to be revealed in our history in a more and more perfect illumination.

We have our eyes, which relate to us the vision of the physical universe. We have also an inner faculty of our own which helps us to find our relationship with the supreme self of man, the universe of personality. This faculty is our luminous imagination, which in its higher stage is special to man. It offers us that vision of wholeness which for the biological necessity of physical survival is superfluous; its purpose is to arouse in us the sense of perfection which is our true sense of immortality. For perfection dwells ideally in Man the Eternal, inspiring love for this ideal in the individual, urging him more and more to realize it.

The development of intelligence and physical power is equally necessary in animals and men for their purpose of living; but what is unique in man is the development of his consciousness which gradually deepens and widens the realization of his immortal being, the perfect, the eternal. It inspires those creations of his that reveal the divinity in him— which is his humanity—in the varied manifestations of truth, goodness and beauty, in the freedom of activity which is not for his use but for his ultimate expression. The individual man must exist for Man the great, and must express him in disinterested works, in science and philosophy, in literature and arts, in service and worship. This is his religion, which is working in the heart of all his religions in various names and forms. He knows and uses this world where it is endless and thus attains greatness, but he realizes his own truth where it is perfect and thus finds his fulfilment.

The idea of the humanity of our God, or the divinity of Man the Eternal, is the main subject of this book. This thought of God has not grown in my mind through any process of philosophical reasoning. On the contrary, it has followed the current of my temperament from early days until it suddenly flashed into my consciousness with a direct vision. The experience which I have described in one of the chapters which follow convinced me that on the surface of our being we have the ever-changing phases of the individual self, but in the depth there dwells the Eternal Spirit of human unity beyond our direct knowledge. It very often contradicts the trivialities of our daily life, and upsets the arrangements made for securing our personal exclusiveness behind the walls of individual habits and superficial conventions. It inspires in us works that are the expressions of a Universal Spirit; it invokes unexpectedly in the midst of a self-centred life a supreme sacrifice. At its call, we hasten to dedicate our lives to the cause of truth and beauty, to unrewarded service of others, in spite of our lack of faith in the positive reality of the ideal values.

During the discussion of my own religious experience I have expressed my belief that the first stage of my realization was through my feeling of intimacy with Nature—not that Nature which has its channel of information for our mind and physical relationship with our living body, but that which satisfies our personality with manifestations that make our life rich and stimulate our imagination in their harmony of forms, colours, sounds and movements. It is not that world which vanishes into abstract symbols behind its own testimony to Science, but that which lavishly displays its wealth of reality to our personal self having its own perpetual reaction upon our human nature.

I have mentioned in connection with my personal experience some songs which I had often heard from wandering village singers, belonging to a popular sect of Bengal, called Baüls,[1] who have no images, temples, scriptures, or ceremonials, who declare in their songs the divinity of Man, and express for him an intense feeling of love. Coming from men who are unsophisticated, living a simple life in obscurity, it gives us a clue to the inner meaning of all religions. For it suggests that these religions are never about a God of cosmic force, but rather about the God of human personality.

At the same time it must be admitted that even the impersonal aspect of truth dealt with by Science belongs to the human Universe. But men of Science tell us that truth, unlike beauty and goodness, is independent of our consciousness. They explain to us how the belief that truth is independent of the human mind is a mystical belief, natural to man but at the same time inexplicable. But may not the explanation be this, that ideal truth does not depend upon the individual mind of man, but on the universal mind which comprehends the individual? For to say that truth, as we see it, exists apart from humanity is really to contradict Science itself; because Science can only organize into rational concepts those facts which man can know and understand, and logic is a machinery of thinking created by the mechanic man.

---

1. See Appendix I

The table that I am using with all its varied meanings appears as a table for man through his special organ of senses and his special organ of thoughts. When scientifically analysed the same table offers an enormously different appearance to him from that given by his senses. The evidence of his physical senses and that of his logic and his scientific instruments are both related to his own power of comprehension; both are true and true for him. He makes use of the table with full confidence for his physical purposes, and with equal confidence makes intellectual use of it for his scientific knowledge. But the knowledge is his who is a man. If a particular man as an individual did not exist, the table would exist all the same, but still as a thing that is related to the human mind. The contradiction that there is between the table of our sense perception and the table of our scientific knowledge has its common centre of reconciliation in human personality.

The same thing holds true in the realm of idea. In the scientific idea of the world there is no gap in the universal law of causality. Whatever happens could never have happened otherwise. This is a generalization which has been made possible by a quality of logic which is possessed by the human mind. But this very mind of Man has its immediate consciousness of will within him which *is* aware of its freedom and ever struggles for it. Every day in most of our behaviour we acknowledge its truth; in fact, our conduct finds its best value in its relation to its truth. Thus this has its analogy in our daily behaviour with regard to a table. For whatever may be the conclusion that Science has unquestionably proved about the table, we are amply rewarded when we deal with it as a solid fact and never as a crowd of fluid elements that represent a certain kind of energy. We can also utilize this phenomenon of the measurement. The space represented by a needle when magnified by the microscope may cause us no anxiety as to the number of angels who could be accommodated on its point or camels which could walk through its eye. In a cinema-picture our vision of time and space can be expanded or condensed merely according to the different technique of the instrument. A seed carries packed in a minute receptacle a future which is enormous in its contents both in time and space. The truth, which is Man, has not emerged out of nothing at a certain point of time, even though seemingly it might have been manifested then. But the manifestation of Man has no end in itself—not even now. Neither did it have its beginning in any particular time we ascribe to it. The truth of Man is in the heart of eternity, the fact of it being evolved through endless ages. If Man's manifestation has round it a background of millions of light-years, still it is his own background. He includes in himself the time, however long, that carries the process of his becoming, and he is related for the very truth of his existence to all things that surround him.

Relationship is the fundamental truth of this world of appearance. Take, for instance, a piece of coal. When we pursue the fact of it to its ultimate composition, substance which seemingly is the most stable element in it vanishes in centres of revolving forces. These are the units, called the elements of carbon, which can further be analysed into a certain number of protons and electrons. Yet these electrical facts are what they are, not in their detachment, but in their inter-relationship, and though possibly some day they themselves may be further analysed, nevertheless the pervasive truth of inter-relation which is manifested in them will remain.

We do not know how these elements, as carbon, compose a piece of coal; all that we can say is that they build up that appearance through a unity of interrelationship, which unites them not merely in an individual piece of coal, but in a comradeship of creative co-ordination with the entire physical universe.

Creation has been made possible through the continual self-surrender of the unit to the universe. And the spiritual universe of Man is also ever claiming self-renunciation from the individual units. This spiritual process is not so easy as the physical one in the physical world, for the intelligence and will of the units have to be tempered to those of the universal spirit.

It is said in a verse of the Upanishad that this world which is all movement is pervaded by one supreme unity, and therefore true enjoyment can never be had through the satisfaction of greed, but only through the surrender of our individual self to the Universal Self.

There are thinkers who advocate the doctrine of the plurality of worlds, which can only mean that there are worlds that are absolutely unrelated to each other. Even if this were true it could never be proved. For our universe is the sum total of what Man feels, knows, imagines, reasons to be, and of whatever is knowable to him now or in another time. It affects him differently in its different aspects, in its beauty, its inevitable sequence of happenings, its potentiality; and the world proves itself to him only in its varied effects upon his senses, imagination and reasoning mind.

I do not imply that the final nature of the world depends upon the comprehension of the individual person. Its reality is associated with the universal human mind which comprehends all time and all possibilities of realization. And this is why for the accurate knowledge of things we depend upon Science that represents the rational mind of the universal Man, and not upon that of the individual who dwells in a limited range of space and time and the immediate needs of life. And this is why there is such a thing as progress in our civilization; for progress means that there is an ideal perfection which the individual sees to reach by extending his limits in knowledge, power, love, enjoyment, thus approaching the universal. The most distant star, whose faint message touches the threshold of the most powerful telescopic vision, has its sympathy with the understanding mind of man, and therefore we can never cease to believe that we shall probe further and further into the mystery of their nature. As we know the truth of the stars we know the great comprehensive mind of man.

We must realize not only the reasoning mind, but also the creative imagination, the love and wisdom that belong to the Supreme Person, whose Spirit is over us all, love for whom comprehends love for all creatures and exceeds in depth and strength all other loves, leading to difficult endeavours and martyrdoms that have no other gain than the fulfilment of this love itself.

The *Isha* of our Upanishad, the Super Soul, which permeates all moving things, is the God of this human universe whose mind we share in all our true knowledge, love and service, and whom to reveal in ourselves through renunciation of self is the highest end of life.

Chapter II

The Creative Spirit

Once, during the improvisation of a story by a young child, I was coaxed to take my part as the hero. The child imagined that I had been shut in a dark room locked from the outside. She asked me, 'What will you do for your freedom?' and I answered, ëShout for help'. But, however desirable that might be if it succeeded immediately, it would be unfortunate for the story. And thus she in her imagination had to clear the neighbourhood of all kinds of help that my cries might reach. I was compelled to think of some violent means of kicking through this passive resistance; but for the sake of the story the door had to be made of steel. I found a key, but it would not fit, and the child was delighted at the development of the story jumping over obstructions.

Life's story of evolution, the main subject of which is the opening of the doors of the dark dungeon, seems to develop in the same manner. Difficulties were created, and at each offer of an answer the story had to discover further obstacles in order to carry on the adventure. For to come to an absolutely satisfactory conclusion is to come to the end of all things, and in that case the great child would have nothing else to do but to shut her curtain and go to sleep.

The Spirit of Life began her chapter by introducing a simple living cell against the tremendously powerful challenge of the vast Inert. The triumph was thrillingly great which still refuses to yield its secret. She did not stop there, but defiantly courted difficulties, and in the technique of her art exploited an element which still baffles our logic.

This is the harmony of self-adjusting inter-relationship impossible to analyse. She brought close together numerous cell units and, by grouping them into a self-sustaining sphere of co-operation, elaborated a larger unit. It was not a mere agglomeration. The grouping had its caste system in the division of functions and yet an intimate unity of kinship. The creative life summoned a larger army of cells under her command and imparted into them, let us say, a communal spirit that fought with all its might whenever its integrity was menaced.

This was the tree which has its inner harmony and inner movement of life in its beauty, its strength, its sublime dignity of endurance, its pilgrimage to the Unknown through the tiniest gates of reincarnation. It was a sufficiently marvellous achievement to be a fit termination to the creative venture. But the creative genius cannot stop exhausted; more windows have to be opened; and she went out of her accustomed way and brought another factor into her work, that of locomotion. Risks of living were enhanced, offering opportunities to the daring resourcefulness of the Spirit of Life. For she seems to revel in the daring resourcefulness of the Spirit of Life. For she seems to revel in occasions for a fight against the giant Matter, which has rigidly prohibitory immigration laws against all new-comers from Life's shore. So the fish was furnished with appliances for moving in an element which offered its density for an obstacle. The air offered an even more difficult obstacle in its lightness; but the challenge was accepted, and the bird was gifted with a marvellous pair of wings that negotiated with the subtle laws of the air and found in it a better ally than the reliable soil of the stable earth. The Arctic snow set up is frigid sentinel; the tropical desert uttered in its scorching breath a gigantic 'No' against all life's children. But those peremptory prohibitions were defied, and the frontiers, though guarded by a death penalty, were triumphantly crossed.

This process of conquest could be described as progress for the kingdom of life. It journeyed on through one success to another by dealing with the laws of Nature through the help of the invention of new instruments. This field of life's onward march is a field of ruthless competition. Because the material world is the world of quantity, where resources are limited and victory waits for those who have superior facility in their weapons, therefore success in the path or progress for one group most often runs parallel to defeat in another.

It appears that such scramble and fight for opportunities of living among numerous small combatants suggested at last an imperialism of big bulky flesh—a huge system of muscles and bones, thick and heavy coats of armour and enormous tails. The idea of such indecorous massiveness must-have seemed natural to life's providence; for the victory in the world of quantity might reasonably appear to depend upon the bigness of dimension. But such gigantic paraphernalia of defence and attack resulted in an utter defeat, the records of which every day are being dug up from the desert sands and ancient mud flats. These represent the fragments that strew the forgotten paths of a great retreat in the battle of existence. For the heavy weight which these creatures carried was mainly composed of bones, hides, shells, teeth and claws that were non-living, and therefore imposed its whole huge pressure upon life that needed freedom and growth for the perfect expression of its own vital nature. The resources for living which the earth offered for her children were recklessly spent by these megalomaniac monsters of an immoderate appetite for the sake of maintaining a cumbersome system of dead burdens that thwarted them in their true progress. Such a losing game has now become obsolete. To the few stragglers of that party, like the rhinoceros or the hippopotamus, has been allotted a very small space on this earth, absurdly inadequate to their formidable strength and magnitude of proportions, making them look forlornly pathetic in the sublimity of their incongruousness. These and their extinct forerunners have been the biggest failures in life's experiments. And then, on some obscure dusk of dawn, the experiment entered upon a completely new phase of a disarmament proposal, when little Man made his appearance in the arena, bringing with him expectations and suggestions that are unfathomably great.

We must know that the evolution process of the world has made its progress towards the revelation of its *truth*— that is to say some inner value which is not in the extension in space and duration in time. When life came out it did not bring with it any new materials into existence. Its elements are the same which are the materials for the rocks and minerals. Only it evolved a value in them which cannot be measured and analysed. The same thing is true with regard to mind and the consciousness of self; they are revelations of a great meaning, the self-expression of a truth. In man this truth has made its positive appearance, and is struggling to make its manifestation more and more clear. That which is eternal is realizing itself in history through the obstructions of limits.

The physiological process in the progress of Life's evolution seems to have reached its finality in man. We cannot think of any noticeable addition or modification in our vital instruments which we are likely to allow to persist. If any individual is born, by chance, with an extra pair of eyes or ears, or some unexpected limbs like stowaways without passports, we are sure to do our best to eliminate them from our bodily organization. Any new chance of a too obviously physical variation is certain to meet with a determined disapproval from man, the most powerful veto being expected from his aesthetic nature, which peremptorily refuses to calculate advantage when its majesty is offended by any sudden license of form. We all know that the back of our body has a wide surface practically unguarded. From the strategic point of view this oversight is unfortunate, causing us annoyances and indignities, if nothing worse, through unwelcome intrusions. And this could reasonable justify in our minds regret for retrenchment in the matter of an original tail, whose memorial we are still made to carry in secret. But the least attempt at the rectification of the policy of economy in this direction is indignantly resented. I strongly believe that the idea of ghosts had its best chance with our timid imagination in our sensitive back—a field of dark ignorance; and yet it is too late for me to hint that one of our eyes could profitably have been spared for our burden-carrier back, so unjustly neglected and haunted by undefined fears.

Thus, while all innovation is stubbornly opposed, there is every sign of a comparative carelessness about the physiological efficiency of the human body. Some of our organs are losing their original vigour. The civilized life, within walked enclosures, has naturally caused in man a weakening of his power of sight and hearing along with subtle sense of the distant. Because of our habit of taking cooked food we give less employment to our teeth and a great deal more to the dentist. Spoilt and pampered by clothes, our skin shows lethargy in its function of adjustment to the atmospheric temperature and in its power of quick recovery from hurts.

The adventurous Life appears to have paused at a crossing in her road before Man came. It seems as if she became aware of wastefulness in carrying on her experiments and adding to her inventions purely on the physical plane. It was proved in Life's case that four is not always twice as much as two. In living things it is necessary to keep to the limit of the perfect unit within which the inter-relationship must not be inordinately strained. The ambition that seeks power in the augmentation of dimension is doomed; for that perfection which is in the inner quality of harmony becomes choked when quantity overwhelms it in a fury of extravagance. The combination of an exaggerated nose and arm that an elephant carries hanging down its front has its advantage. This may induce us to imagine that it would double the advantage for the animal if its tail also could grow into an additional trunk. But the progress which greedily allows Life's field to be crowded with an excessive production of instruments becomes a progress towards death. For Life has its own natural rhythm which a multiplication table has not; and proud progress that rides roughshod over Life's cadence kills it at the end with encumbrances that are unrhythmic. As I have already mentioned, such disasters did happen in the history of evolution.

The moral of that tragic chapter is that if the tail does not have the decency to know where to stop, the drag of this dependency becomes fatal to the body's empire.

Moreover, evolutionary progress on the physical plane inevitably tends to train up its subjects into specialists. The camel is a specialist of the desert and is awkward in the swamp. The hippopotamus which specializes in the mudlands of the Nile is helpless in the neighbouring desert. Such one-sided emphasis breeds professionalism in Life's domain, confining special efficiencies in narrow compartments. The expert training in the aerial sphere is left to the bird; that in the marine is particularly monopolized by the fish. The ostrich is an expert in its own region and would look utterly foolish in an eagle's neighbourhood. They have to remain permanently content with advantages that desperately cling to their limits. Such mutilation of the complete ideal of life for the sake of some exclusive privilege of power is inevitable; for that form of progress deals with materials that are physical and therefor necessarily limited.

To rescue her own career from such a multiplying burden of the dead and such constriction of specialization seems to have been the object of the Spirit of Life at one particular stage. For its does not take long to find out that an indefinite pursuit of quantity creates for Life, which is essentially qualitative, complexities that lead to a vicious circle. These primeval animals that produced an enormous volume of flesh had to build a gigantic system of bones to carry the burden. This required in its turn a long and substantial array of tails to give it balance. Thus their bodies, being compelled to occupy a vast area, exposed a very large surface which had to be protected by a strong, heavy and capacious armour. A progress which represented a congress of dead materials required a parallel organization of teeth and claws, or horns and hooves, which also were dead.

In its own manner one mechanical burden links itself to other burdens of machines, and Life grows to be a carrier of the dead, a mere platform for machinery, until it is crushed to death by its interminable paradoxes. We are told that the greater part of a tree is dead matter; the big stem, except for a thin covering, is lifeless. The tree uses it as a prop in its ambition for a high position and the lifeless timber is the slave that carries on its back the magnitude of the tree. But such a dependence upon a dead dependant has been achieved by the tree at the cost of its real freedom. It has to seek the stable alliance of the earth for the sharing of its burden, which it did by the help of secret underground entanglements making itself permanently stationary.

But the form of life that seeks the great privilege of movement must minimize its load of the dead and must realize that life's progress should be a perfect progress of the inner life itself and not of materials and machinery; the non-living must not continue outgrowing the living, the armour deadening the skin, the armament laming the arms.

At last, when the Spirit of Life found her form in Man, the effort she had begun completed its cycle, and the truth of her mission glimmered into suggestions which dimly pointed to some direction of meaning across her own frontier. Before the end of this cycle was reached, all the suggestions had been external. They were concerned with technique, with life's apparatus, with the efficiency of the organs. This might have exaggerated itself into an endless boredom of physical progress. It can be conceded that the eyes of the bee possessing numerous facets may have some uncommon advantage which we cannot even imagine, or the glow-worm that carries an arrangement for producing light in its person may baffle our capacity and comprehension. Very likely there are creatures having certain organs that given them sensibilities which we cannot have the power to guess.

All such enhanced sensory powers merely add to the mileage in life's journey on the same road lengthening an indefinite distance. They never take us over the border or physical existence.

The same thing may be said not only about life's efficiency, but also life's ornaments. The colouring and decorative patterns on the bodies of some of the deep sea creatures make us silent with amazement. The butterfly's wings, the beetle's back, the peacock's plumes, the shells of the crustaceans, the exuberant outbreak of decoration in plant life, have reached a standard of perfection that seems to be final. And yet if it continues in the same physical direction, then, however much variety of surprising excellence it may produce, it leaves out some great element of unuttered meaning. These ornaments are like ornaments lavished upon a captive girl, luxuriously complete within a narrow limit, speaking of a homesickness for a far away horizon of emancipation, for an inner depth that is beyond the ken of the senses. The freedom in the physical realm is like the circumscribed freedom in a cage. It produces a proficiency which is mechanical and a beauty which is of the surface. To whatever degree of improvement bodily strength and skill may be developed they keep life tied to a persistence of habit. It is closed, like a mould, useful though it may be for the sake of safety and precisely standardized productions. For centuries the bee repeats its hive, the weaver-bird its nest, the spider its web; and instincts strongly attach themselves to some invariable tendencies of muscles and nerves never being allowed the privilege of making blunders. The physical functions, in order to be strictly reliable, behave like some model schoolboy, obedient, regular, properly repeating lessons by rote without mischief or mistake in his conduct, but also without spirit and initiative. It is the flawless perfection of rigid limits, a cousin—of the inanimate.

Instead of allowing a full paradise of perfection to continue its tame and timid rule of faultless regularity the Spirit of Life boldly declared for a further freedom and decided to eat of the fruit of the Tree of Knowledge. This time her struggle was not against the Inert, but against the limitation of her own overburdened agents. She fought against the tutelage of her prudent old prime minister, the faithful instinct. She adopted a novel method of experiment, promulgated new laws, and tried her hand at moulding Man through a history which was immensely different from that which went before. She took a bold step in throwing open her gates to a dangerously explosive factor which she had cautiously introduced into her council—the element of Mind. I should not say that it was ever absent, but only that at a certain stage some curtain was removed and its play was made evident, even like the dark heat which in its glowing intensity reveals itself in a contradiction of radiancy.

Essentially qualitative, like life itself, the Mind does not occupy space. For that very reason it has no bounds in its mastery of space. Also, like Life, Mind has its meaning in freedom, which it missed in its earliest dealings with Life's children. In the animal, though the mind is allowed to come out of the immediate limits of livelihood, its range is restricted, like the freedom of a child that might run out of its room but not out of the house; or, rather, like the foreign ships to which only a certain port was opened in Japan in the beginning of her contact with the West in fear of the danger that might befall if the strangers had their uncontrolled opportunity of communication. Mind also is a foreign element for Life; its laws are different, its weapons powerful, its moods and manners most alien.

Like eve of the Semitic mythology, the Spirit of Life risked the happiness of her placid seclusion to win her freedom. She listened to the whisper of a temper who promised her the right to a new region of mystery, and was urged into a permanent alliance with the stranger. Up to this point the interest of life was the sole interest in her own kingdom, but another most powerfully parallel interest was created with the advent of this adventurer Mind from an unknown shore. Their interests clash, and complications of a serious nature arise. I have already referred to some vital organs of Man that are suffering from neglect. The only reason has been the diversion created by the Mind interrupting the sole attention which Life's functions claimed in the halcyon days of her undisputed monarchy. It is no secret that Mind has the habit of asserting its own will for its expression against life's will to live and enforcing sacrifices from her. When lately some adventurers accepted the dangerous enterprise to climb Mount Everest, it was solely through the instigation of the arch-rebel Mind. In this case Mind denied its treaty of cooperation with its partner and ignored Life's claim to help in her living. The immemorial privileges of the ancient sovereignty of Life are too often flouted by the irreverent Mind; in fact, all through the course of this alliance there are constant cases of interference with each other's functions, often because of this antagonism, the new current of Man's evolution is bringing a wealth to his harbour infinitely beyond the dream of the creatures of monstrous flesh.

The manner in which Man appeared in Life's kingdom was in itself a protest and a challenge, the challenge of Jack to the Giant. He carried in his body the declaration of mistrust against the crowding of burdensome implements of physical progress. His Mind spoke to the naked man, 'Fear not'; and he stood alone facing the menace of a heavy brigade of formidable muscles. His own puny muscles cried out in despair, and he had to invent for himself in a novel manner and in a new spirit of evolution. This at once gave him his promotion from the passive destiny of the animal to the aristocracy of Man. He began to create his further body, his outer organs— the workers which served him and yet did not directly claim a share of his life. Some of the earliest in his list were bows and arrows. Had this change been undertaken by the physical process of evolution, modifying his arms in a slow and gradual manner, it might have resulted in burdensome and ungainly apparatus. Possibly, however, I am unfair, and the dexterity and grace which Life's technical instinct possesses might have changed his arm into a shooting medium in a perfect manner and with a beautiful form. In that case our lyrical literature today would have sung in praise of its fascination, not only for a consummate skill in hunting victims, but also for a similar mischief in a metaphorical sense. But even in the service of lyrics it would show some limitation. For instance, the arms that would specialize in shooting would be awkward in wielding a pen or stringing a lute. But the great advantage in the latest method of human evolution lies in the fact that Man's additional new limbs, like bows and arrows, have become detached. They never tie his arms to any exclusive advantage of efficiency.

The elephant's trunk, the tiger's paws, the claws of the mole, have combined their best expressions in the human arms, which are much weaker in their original capacity than those limbs I have mentioned. It would have been a hugely cumbersome practical joke if the combination of animal limbs had had a simultaneous location in the human organism through some overzeal in biological inventiveness.

The first great economy resulting from the new programme was the relief of the physical burden, which means the maximum efficiency with the minimum pressure of taxation upon the vital resources of the body. Another mission of benefit was this, that it absolved the Spirit of Life in Man's case from the necessity of specialization for the sake of limited success. This has encouraged Man to dream of the possibility of combining in his single person the fish, the bird and the fleet-footed animal that walks on land. Man desired in his completeness to be the one great representative of multiform life, not through wearisome subjection of opportunities with the help of his reasoning mind. It enables the schoolboy who is given a pen-knife on his birthday to have the advantage over the tiger in the fact that it does not take him a million years to obtain its possession, nor another million years for its removal, when the instrument proves unnecessary or dangerous. The human mind has compressed ages into a few years for the acquisition of steel-made claws. The only cause of anxiety is that the instrument and the temperament which uses it may not keep pace in perfect harmony. In the tiger, the claws and the temperament which only a tiger should possess have had a synchronous development, and in no single tiger is any maladjustment possible between its nails and its tigerliness. But the human boy, who grows a claw in the form of a pen-knife, may not at the same time develop the proper temperament necessary for its use which only a man ought to have. The new organs that today are being added as a supplement to Man's original vital stock are too quick and too numerous for his inner nature to develop its own simultaneous concordance with them, and thus we see everywhere innumerable schoolboys in human society playing pranks with their own and other people's lives and welfare by means of newly acquired pen-knives which have not had time to become humanized.

One thing, I am sure, must have been noticed—that the original plot of the drama is changed, and the mother Spirit of Life has retired into the background, giving full prominence, in the third act, to the Spirit of Man—though the dowager queen, from her inner apartment, still renders necessary help. It is the consciousness in Man of his own creative personality which has ushered in this new regime in Life's kingdom. And from now onwards Man's attempts are directed fully to capture the government and make his own Code of Legislation prevail without a break. We have seen in India those who are called mystics, impatient of the continued regency of mother nature in their own body, winning for their will by a concentration of inner forces the vital regions with which our masterful minds have no direct path of communication.

But the most important fact that has come into prominence along with the change of direction in our evolution, is the possession of a Spirit which has its enormous capital with a surplus for in excess of the requirements of the biological animal in Man. Some overflowing influence led us over the strict boundaries of living, and offered to us an open space where Man's thoughts and dreams could have their holidays. Holidays are for gods who have their joy in creation. In Life's primitive paradise, where the mission was merely to live, any luck which came to the creatures entered in from outside by the donations of chance; they lived on perpetual charity, by turns petted and kicked on the back by physical Providence. Beggars never can have harmony among themselves; they are envious of one another, mutually suspicious, like dogs living upon their master's favour, showing their teeth, growling, barking, trying to tear one another. This is what Science describes as the struggle for existence. This beggar's paradise lacked peace; I am sure the suitors for special favour from fate lived in constant preparedness, inventing and multiplying armaments.

But above the din of the clamour and scramble rises the voice of the Angel of Surplus, of leisure, of detachment from the compelling claim of physical need, saying to men, 'Rejoice'. From his original serfdom as a creature Man takes his right seat as a creator. Whereas, before, his incessant appeal has been to get, now at last the call comes to him to give. His God, whose help he was in the habit of asking, now stands Himself at his door and asks for his offerings. As an animal, he is still dependent upon Nature; as a Man, he is a sovereign who builds his world and rules it.

And there, at this point, comes his religion, whereby he realizes himself in the perspective of the infinite. There is a remarkable verse in the Atharva Veda which says: 'Righteousness, truth, great endeavours, empire, religion, enterprise, heroism and prosperity, the past and the future, dwell in the surpassing strength of the surplus.

What is purely physical has its limits like the shell of an egg; the liberation is there in the atmosphere of the infinite, which is indefinable, invisible. Religion can have no meaning in the enclosure of mere physical or material interest; it is in the surplus we carry around our personality—the surplus which is like the atmosphere of the earth, bringing to her a constant circulation of light and life and delightfulness.

I have said in a poem of mine that when the child is detached from its mother's womb it finds its mother in a real relationship whose truth is in freedom. Man in his detachment has realized himself in a wider and deeper relationship with the universe. In his moral life he has the sense of his obligation and his freedom at the same time, and this is goodness. In his spiritual life his sense of the union and the will which is free has its culmination in love. The freedom of opportunity he wins for himself in Nature's region by uniting his power with Nature's forces. The freedom of social relationship he attains through owning responsibility to his community, thus gaining its collective power for his own welfare. In the freedom of consciousness he realizes the sense of his unity with his unity with his larger being, finding fulfilment in the dedicated life of an ever-progressive truth and ever-active love.

The first detachment achieved by Man is physical. It represents his freedom from the necessity of developing the power of his senses and limbs in the limited area of his own physiology, having for itself an unbounded background with an immense result in consequence. Nature's original intention was that Man should have the allowance of his sight-power ample enough for his surroundings and a little over. But to have to develop an astronomical telescope on our skull would cause a worse crisis of bankruptcy than it did to the Mammoth whose densely foolish body indulged in an extravagance of tusks. A snail carries its house on its back and therefore the material, the shape and the weight have to be strictly limited to the capacity of the body. But fortunately Man's house need not grow on the foundation of his bones and occupy his flesh. Owing to this detachment, his ambition knows no check to its daring in the dimension and strength of his dwellings. Since his shelter does not depend upon his body, it survives him.

This fact greatly affects the man who builds a house, generating in his mind a sense of the eternal in his creative work. And this background of the boundless surplus of time encourages architecture, which seeks a universal value overcoming each consisting the miserliness of the present need.

I have already mentioned a stage which Life reached when the units of single cells formed themselves into larger units, of a multitude. It was not merely an aggregation, but had a mysterious unity of interrelationship, complex in character, with differences within of forms and function. We can never know concretely what this relation means. There are gaps between the units, but they do not stop the binding force that permeates the whole. There is a future for the whole which is in its growth, but in order to bring this about each unity works and dies to make room for the next worker. While the unit has the right to claim the glory of the whole, yet individually it cannot share the entire wealth that occupies a history yet to be completed.

Of all creatures Man has reached that multicellular character in a perfect manner, not only in his body but in his personality. For centuries his evolution has been the evolution of a consciousness that tries to be liberated from the bonds of individual separateness and to comprehend in its relationship a wholeness which may be named Man. This relationship, which has been dimly instinctive, is ever struggling to be fully aware of itself. Physical evolution sought for efficiency in a perfect communication with the physical world; the evolution of Man's consciousness sought for truth in a perfect harmony with the world of personality.

There are those who will say that the idea of humanity is an abstraction, subjective in character. It must be confessed that the concrete objectiveness of this living truth cannot be proved to its own units. They can never see its entireness from outside; for they are one with it. The individual cells of our body have their separate lives; but they never have the opportunity of observing the body as a whole with its past, present and future. If these cells have the power of reasoning (which they may have for aught we know) they have the right to argue that the idea of the body has no objective foundation in fact, and though there is a mysterious sense of attraction and mutual influence running through them, these are nothing positively real; the sole reality which is provable is in the isolation of these cells made by gaps that can never be crossed or bridged.

We know something about a system of explosive atoms whirling separately in a space which is immense compared to their own dimension. Yet we do not know why they should appear to us a solid piece of radiant mineral. And if there is an onlooker who at one glance can have the view of the immense time and space occupied by innumerable human individuals engaged in evolving a common history, the positive truth of their solidarity will be concretely evident to him and not the negative fact of their separateness.

The reality of a piece of iron is not provable if we take the evidence of the atom; the only proof is that I see it as a bit of iron, and that it has certain reactions upon my consciousness. And being from, say, Orion, who has the sight to see the atoms and not the iron, has the right to say that we human beings suffer from an age-long epidemic of hallucination. We need not quarrel with him but go on using the iron as it appears to us. Seers there have been who have said *Vēdāhamētam*, 'I see', and lived a life according to that vision. And though our own sight may be blind we have ever bowed our head to them in reverence.

However, whatever name our logic may give to the truth of human unity, the fact can never be ignored that we have our greatest delight when we realize ourselves in others, and this is the definition of love. This love gives us the testimony of the great whole, which is the complete and final truth of man. It offers us the immense field where we can have our release from the sole monarchy of hunger, of the growling means, the source of cruel envy and ignoble deception, where the largest wealth of the human soul has been produced though sympathy and co-operation; through disinterested pursuit of knowledge that recognizes no limit and is unafraid of all time-honoured *taboos*; through a strenuous cultivation of intelligence for service that knows no distinction of colour and clime. The Spirit of Love, dwelling in the boundless realm of the surplus, emancipates our consciousness from the illusory bond of the separateness of self; it is ever trying to spread its illumination in the human world. This is the spirit of civilization, which in all its best endeavour invokes our supreme Being for the only bond of unity that leads us to truth, namely, that of righteousness:

Ya ēkō varnō bahudhā saktiyogāt
varnān anēkān nihitārthō dadhāti
vichaitti chānte visvamādau sa dēvah
sa nō budhyā subhayā samyunaktu

He who is one, above all colours, and who with his manifold power supplies the inherent needs of men of all colours, who is in the beginning and in the end of the world, is divine, and may he unite us in a relationship of good will.

Chapter III

The Surplus in Man

There are certain verses from the Atharva Veda in which the poet discusses his idea of Man, indicating some transcendental meaning that can be translated as follows:

Who was it that imparted form to man, gave him majesty, movement, manifestation and character, inspired him with wisdom, music and dancing? When his body was raised upwards he found also the oblique sides and all other directions in him—he who is the Person, the citadel of the infinite being.

Tasmād vai vidvān purushamidan brahmēti manyatē.
And therefore the wise man knoweth this person as Brahma.

Sanātanam ēnam āhur utādya syāt punarnavah.
Ancient they call him, and yet he is renewed even now today.

In the very beginning of his career Man asserted in his bodily structure his first proclamation of freedom against the established rule of Nature. At a creature, and the position which he made his body to assume carried with it a permanent gesture of insubordination. For there could be no question that it was Nature's own plan to provide all land-walking mammals with two pairs of legs, evenly distributed along their lengthy trunk heavily weighted with a head at the end. This was the amicable compromise made with the earth when threatened by its conservative downward force, which extorts taxes for all movements. The fact that man gave up such an obviously sensible arrangement proves his inborn mania for repeated reforms of constitution, for pelting amendments at every resolution proposed by Providence.

If we found a four-legged table stalking about upright upon two of its stumps, the remaining two foolishly dangling by its sides, we should be afraid that it was either a nightmare or some supernormal caprice of that piece of furniture, indulging in a practicl joke upon the carpenter's idea of fitness. The like absurd behaviour of Man's anatomy encourages us to guess that he was born under the influence of some comet of contradiction that forces its eccentric path against orbits regulated by Nature. And it is significant that Man should persist in his foolhardiness, in spite of the penalty he pays for opposing the orthodox rule of animal locomotion. He reduces by half the help of an easy balance of his muscles. He is ready to pass his infancy tottering through perilous experiments in making progress upon insufficient support, and followed all through his life by liability to sudden downfalls resulting in tragic or ludicrous consequences from which law-abiding quadrupeds are free. This was his great venture, the relinquishment of a secure position of his limbs, which he could comfortably have retained in return for humbly salaaming the all-powerful dust at every step.

This capacity to stand erect has given our body its freedom of posture, making it easy for us to turn on all sides and realize ourselves at the centre of things. Physically, it symbolizes the fact that while animals have for their progress the prolongation of a narrow line Man has the enlargement of a circle. As a centre he finds his meaning in a wide perspective, and realizes himself in the magnitude of his circumference.

As one freedom leads to another, Man's eyesight also found a wider scope. I do not mean any enhancement of its physical power, which in many predatory animals has a better power of adjustment to light. But from the higher vantage of our physical watch-tower we have gained our *view*, which is not merely information about the location of things but their inter-relation and their unity.

But the best means of the expression of his physical freedom gained by Man in his vertical position is through the emancipation of his hands. In our bodily organization these have attained the highest dignity for their skill, their grace, their useful activities, as well as for those that are above all uses. They are the most detached of all our limbs. Once they had their menial vocation as our carriers, but raised from their position as *shudras*, they at once attained responsible status as our helpers. When instead of keeping them underneath us we offered them their place at our side, they revealed capacities that helped us to cross the boundaries of animal nature.

This freedom of view and freedom of action have been accompanied by an analogous mental freedom in Man through his imagination, which is the most distinctly human of all our faculties. It is there to help a creature who has been left unfinished by his designer, undraped, undecorated, unarmoured and without weapons, and, what is worse, ridden by a Mind whose energies for the most part are not tamed and tempered into some difficult ideal of completeness upon a background which is bare. Like all artists he has the freedom to make mistakes, to launch into desperate adventures contradicting and torturing his psychology or physiological normality. This freedom is a divine gift lent to the mortals who are untutored and undisciplined; and therefore the path of their creative progress is strewn with debris of devastation, and stages of their perfection haunted by apparitions of startling deformities. But, all the same, the very training of creation ever makes clear an aim which cannot be in any isolated freak of an individual mind or in that which is only limited to the strictly necessary.

Just as our eyesight enables us to include the individual fact of ourselves in the surrounding view, our imagination makes us intensely conscious of a life we must live which transcends the individual life and contradicts the biological meaning of the instinct of self-preservation. It works at the surplus, and extending beyond the reservation plots of our daily life builds there the guest chambers of priceless value to offer hospitality to the world-spirit of Man. We have such an honoured right to be the host when our spirit is a free spirit not chained to the animal self. For free spirit is godly and alone can claim kinship with God.

Every true freedom that we may attain in any direction broadens our path of self-realization, which is in superseding the self. The unimaginative repetition of life within a safe restriction imposed by Nature may be good for the animal, but never for Man, who has the responsibility to outlive his life in order to live in truth.

And freedom in its process of creation gives rise to perpetual suggestions of something further than its obvious purpose. For freedom is for expressing the infinite; it imposes limits in its works, not to keep them in permanence but to break them over and over again, and to reveal the endless in unending surprises. This implies a history of constant regeneration, a series of fresh beginnings and continual challenges to the old in order to reach a more and more perfect harmony with some fundamental ideal of truth.

Our civilization, in the constant struggle for a great Further, runs through abrupt chapters of spasmodic divergences. It nearly always begins its new ventures with a cataclysm; for its changes are not mere seasonal changes of ideas gliding through varied periods of flowers and fruit. They are surprises lying in ambuscade provoking revolutionary adjustments. They are changes in the dynasty of living ideals—the ideals that are active in consolidating their dominion with strongholds of physical and mental habits, of symbols, ceremonials and adornments. But however violent may be the revolutions happening in whatever time or country, they never completely detach themselves from a common centre. They find their places in a history which is one.

The civilizations evolved in India or China, Persia or Judaea, Greece or Rome, are like several mountain peaks having different altitude, temperature, flora and fauna, and yet belonging to the same chain of hills. There are no absolute barriers of communication between them; their foundation is the same and they affect the meteorology of an atmosphere which is common to us all this is at the root of the meaning of the great teacher who said he would not seek his own salvation if all men were not saved; for well belong to a divine unity, from which our great-souled men have their direct inspiration; they feel it immediately in their own personality, and they proclaim in their life, 'I am one with the Supreme, with the Deathless, with the Perfect'.

Man, in his mission to create himself, tries to develop in his mind an image of his truth according to an idea which he believes to be universal, and is sure that any expression given to it will persist through all time. This is a mentality absolutely superfluous for biological existence. It represents his struggle for a life which is not limited to his body. For our physical life has its thread of unity in the memory of the past, whereas this ideal life dwells in the prospective memory of the future. In the records of past civilizations, unearthed from the closed records of dust, we find pathetic efforts to make their memories uninterrupted through the ages, like the effort of a child who sets adrift on a paper boat his dream of reaching the distant unknown. But why is this desire? Only because we feel instinctively that in our ideal life we must touch all men and all times through the manifestation of a truth which is eternal and universal. And in order to give expression to it materials are gathered that are excellent and a manner of execution that has a permanent value. For we mortals must offer homage to the Man of the everlasting life. In order to do so, we are expected to pay a great deal more than we need for mere living, and in the attempt we often exhaust our very means of livelihood, and even life itself.

The ideal picture which a savage imagines of himself requires glaring paints and gorgeous fineries, a rowdiness in ornaments and even grotesque deformities of over-wrought extravagance. He tries to sublimate his individual self into a manifestation which he believes to have the majesty of the ideal Man. He is not satisfied with what he is in his natural limitations; he irresistibly feels something beyond the evident fact of himself which only could give him worth. It is the principle of power, which, according to his present mental stage, is the meaning of the universal reality whereto he belongs, and it is his pious duty to give expression to it even at the cost of his happiness. In fact, through it he becomes one with his God, for him his God is nothing greater than power. The savage takes immense trouble, and often suffers tortures, in order to offer in himself a representation of power in conspicuous colours and distorted shapes, in acts of relentless cruelty and intemperate bravado of self-indulgence. Such an appearance of rude grandiosity evokes a loyal reverence in the members of his community and a fear which gives them an aesthetic satisfaction because it illuminates for them the picture of a character which, as far as they know, belongs to ideal humanity. They wish to see in him not an individual, but the Man in whom they all are represented. Therefore, in spite of their sufferings, they enjoy being overwhelmed by his exaggerations and dominated by a will fearfully evident owing to its magnificent caprice in inflicting injuries. They symbolize their idea of unlimited wilfulness in their gods by ascribing to them physical and moral enormities in their anatomical idiosyncracy and virulent vindictiveness crying for the blood of victims, in personal preferences indiscriminate in the choice of recipients and methods of rewards and punishments. In fact, these gods could never be blamed for the least wavering in their conduct owing to any scrupulousness accompanied by the emotion of pity so often derided as sentimentalism by virile intellects of the present day.

However crude all this may be, it proves that Man has a feeling that he is truly represented in something which exceeds himself. He is aware that he is not imperfect, but incomplete. He knows that in himself some meaning has yet to be realized. We do not feel the wonder of it, because it seems so natural to us that barbarism in Man is not absolute, that its limits are like the limits of the horizon. The call is deep in his mind—the call of his own inner truth, which is beyond his direct knowledge and analytical logic. And individuals are born who have no doubt of the truth of this transcendental Man. As our consciousness more and more comprehends it, new valuations are developed in us, new depths and delicacies of delight, a sober dignity of expression through elimination of tawdriness, of frenzied emotions, of all violence in shape, colour, words, or behaviour, of the dark mentality of Ku-Klux-Klanism.

Each age reveals its personality as dreamer in its great expressions that carry it across surging centuries to the continental plateau of permanent human history. These expressions may not be consciously religious, but indirectly they belong to Man's religion. For they are the outcome of the consciousness of the greater Man in the individual men of the race. This consciousness finds its manifestation in science, philosophy and the arts, in social ethics, in all things that carry their ultimate value in themselves. These are truly spiritual and they should all be consciously co-ordinated in one great religion of Man, representing his ceaseless endeavour to reach the perfect in great thoughts and deeds and dreams, in immortal symbols of art, revealing his aspiration for rising in dignity of being.

I had the occasion to visit the ruins of ancient Rome, the relics of human yearning towards the immense, the sight of which teases our mind out of thought. Does it not prove that in the vision of a great Roman Empire the creative imagination of the people rejoiced in the revelation of its transcendental humanity? It was the idea of an Empire which was not merely for opening an outlet to the pent-up pressure of over-population, or widening its field of commercial profit, but which existed as a concrete representation of the majesty of Roman personality, the soul of the people dreaming of a world-wide creation of its own for a fit habitation of the Ideal Man. It was Rome's titanic endeavour to answer the eternal question as to what Man truly was, as man. And any answer given in earnest falls within the realm of religion, whatever may be its character; and this answer, in its truth, belongs not only to any particular people but to us all. It may be that Rome did not give the most perfect answer possible when she fought for her place as a world-builder of human history, but she revealed the marvellous vigour of the indomitable human spirit which could say, *Bhumaiva sukkam*, 'Greatness is happiness itself'. Her Empire has been sundered and shattered, but her faith in the sublimity of man still persists in one of the vast strata of human geology. And this faith was the true spirit of her religion, which had been dim in the tradition of her formal theology, merely supplying her with an emotional pastime and not with spiritual inspiration. In fact this theology fell far below her personality, and for that reason it went against her religion, whose mission was to reveal her humanity on the background of the eternal. Let us seek the religion of this and other people not in their gods but in Man, who dreamed of his own infinity and majestically worked for all time, defying danger and death.

Since the dim nebula of consciousness in Life's world became intensified into a centre of self in Man, his history began to unfold its rapid chapters; for it is the history of his strenuous answers in various forms to the question rising from this conscious answers in various forms to the question rising from this conscious self of his, 'What am I?' Man is not happy or contented as the animals are; for his happiness and his peace depend upon the truth of his answer. The animal attains his success in a physical sufficiency that satisfies his nature. When a crocodile finds no obstruction in behaving like an orthodox crocodile he grins and grows and has no cause to complain. It is truism to say that Man also must behave like a man in order to find his truth. But he is sorely puzzled and asks in bewilderment: 'What is it to be like a man? What am I?' It is not left to the tiger to discover what is his own nature as a tiger, nor, for the matter of that, to choose a special colour for his coat according to his taste.

But Man has taken centuries to discuss the question of his own true nature and has not yet come to a conclusion. He has been building up elaborate religions to convince himself, against his natural inclinations, of the paradox that he is not what he is but something greater. What is significant about these efforts is that fact that in order to know himself truly Man in his religion cultivates the vision of a Being who exceeds him in truth and with whom also he has his kinship. These religions differ in details and often in their moral significance, but they have a common tendency. In them men seek their own supreme value, which they call divine, in some personality anthropomorphic in character. The Mind, which is abnormally scientific, scoffs at this; but it should know that religion is not essentially cosmic or even abstract; it finds itself when it touches the Brahma in man; otherwise it has no justification to exist.

It must be admitted that such a human element introduces into our religion a mentality that often has its danger in aberrations that are intellectually blind, morally reprehensible and aesthetically repellent. But these are wrong answers; they distort the truth of man and, like all mistakes in sociology, in economics or politics, they have to be fought against and overcome. Their truth has to be judged by the standard of human perfection and not by some arbitrary injunction that refuses to be confirmed by the tribunal of the human conscience. And great religions are the outcome of great revolutions in this direction causing fundamental changes of our attitude. These religions invariably made their appearance as a protest against the earlier creeds which had been unhuman, where ritualistic observances had become more important and outer compulsions more imperious. These creeds were, as I have said before, cults of power; they had their value for us, not helping us to become perfect through truth, but to grow formidable through possessions and magic control of the deity.

But possibly I am doing injustice to out ancestors. It is more likely that they worshipped power not merely because of its utility, but because they, in their way, recognized it as truth with which their own power had its communication and in which it found its fulfilment. They must have naturally felt that this power was the power of will behind nature, and not some impersonal insanity that unaccountably always stumbled upon correct results. For it would have been the greatest depth of imbecility on their part had they brought their homage to an abstraction, mindless, heartless and purposeless; in fact, infinitely below them in its manifestation.

Chapter IV

Spiritual Union

When Man's preoccupation with the means of livelihood became less insistent he had the leisure to come to the mystery of his own self, and could not help feeling that the truth of his personality had both its relationship and its perfection in an endless world of humanity. His religion, which in the beginning had its cosmic background of power, came to a higher stage when it found its background in the human truth of personality. It must not be thought that in this channel it was narrowing the range of our consciousness of the infinite.

The negative idea of the infinite is merely an indefinite enlargement of the limits of things; in fact, a perpetual postponement of infinitude. I am told that mathematics has come to the conclusion that our world belongs to a space which is limited. It does not make us feel disconsolate. We do not miss very much and need not have a low opinion of space even if a straight line cannot remain straight and has an eternal tendency to come back to the point from which it started. In the Hindu Scripture the universe is described as an egg; that is to say, for the human mind it has its circular shell of limitation. The Hindu Scripture goes still further and says that time also is not continuous and our world repeatedly comes to an end to begin its cycle once again. In other words, in the region of time and space infinity consists of ever-revolving finitude.

But the positive aspect of the infinite is the *advaitam*, in an absolute unity, in which comprehension of the multitude is not as in an outer receptacle but as in an inner perfection that permeates and exceeds its contents, like the beauty in a lotus which is ineffably more than all the constituents of the flower. It is not the magnitude of extension but an intense quality of harmony which evokes in us the positive sense of the infinite in our joy, in our love. For *advaitam* is *anandam*; the infinite One is infinite Love. For those among whom the spiritual sense is dull, the desire for realization is reduced to physical possession, an actual grasping in space. This longing for magnitude becomes not an aspiration towards the great, but a mania for the big. But true spiritual realization is not through augmentation of possession in dimension or number. The truth that is infinite dwells in the ideal of unity which we find in the deeper relatedness. This truth of realization is not in space, it can only by realized in one's own inner spirit.

Ekadhaivanudrashtavyam etat aprameyam dhruvam
This infinite and eternal has to be known as One.

Ākasat aja ātmā—'this birthless spirit is beyond space.' For it is *Purushah*, it is the '*Person*''.

The special mental attitude which India has in her religion is made clear by the word *Yoga*, whose meaning is to effect union. Union has its significance not in the realm of *to have*, but in that of *to be*. To *gain* truth is to admit its separateness, but to *be* true is to become one with truth. Some religions, which deal with our relationship with god, assure us of reward if that relationship be kept true. This reward has an objective value. It gives us some reason outside ourselves for pursuing the prescribed path. We have such religions also in India. But those that have attained a greater height aspire for their fulfilment in union with *Narayana*, the supreme Reality of Man, which is divine.

Our union with this spirit is not to be attained through the mind. For our mind belongs to the department of economy in the human in the human organism. It carefully husbands our consciousness for its own range of reason, within which to permit our relationship with the phenomenal world. But it is the object of *Yoga* to help us to transcend the limits built up by Mind. On the occasions when these are overcome, our inner self is filled with joy, which indicates that through such freedom we come into touch with the reality that is an end in itself and therefore is bliss.

Once man had his vision of the infinite in the universal Light, and he offered his worship to the sun. He also offered his service to the fire with oblations. Then he felt the infinite in Life, which is Time in its creative aspect, and he said, *Yat kincha yadidam sarvam prana ejati nihsritam*, 'all that there is comes out of life and vibrates in it'. He was sure of it, being conscious of Life's mystery immediately in himself as the principle of purpose, as the organized will, the source of all his activities. His interpretation of the ultimate character of truth relied upon the suggestion that Life had brought to him, and not the non-living which is dumb. And then he came deeper into his being and said '*Raso vai sah*', 'the infinite is love itself',—the eternal spirit of joy. His religion, which is in his realization of the infinite, began its journey from the impersonal *dyaus*, 'the sky', wherein light had its manifestation; then came to Life, which represented the force of self-creation in time, and ended in *purushah*, the 'Person', in whom dwells timeless love. It said, *Tam vedyam purusham vedah*, 'Know him the Person who is to be realized', *Yatha ma vo srityug parivyathah*—'So that death may not cause you sorrow'. For this Person is deathless in whom the individual person has his immortal truth. Of him it is said: *Esha devo visvakarmā mahātmā sadā janānam hridaya sannivishatah.* 'This is the divine being, the world-worker, who is the Great Soul ever dwelling inherent in the hearts of all people.'

Ya etad vidur amritas te bhavanti. 'Those who realize him, transcend the limits of mortality'—not in duration of time, but in perfection of truth.

Our union with a Being whose activity is world-wide and who dwells in the heart of humanity cannot be a passive one. In order to be united with Him we have to divest our work of selfishness and become *visvakarmā* , 'the world-worker', we must work for all. When I use the words 'for all', I do not mean for a countless number of individuals. All work that is good, however small in extent, is universal in character. Such work makes for a realization of *Visvakarmā*, 'the World-Worker' who works for all. In order to be one with this Mahatma, 'the Great Soul', one must cultivate the greatness of soul which identifies itself with the soul of all peoples all not merely with that of one's own. This helps us to understand what Buddha has described as *Brahmavihāra*, 'living in the infinite'. He says:

'Do not' deceive each other, do not despise anybody anywhere, never in anger wish anyone to suffer through your body, words or thoughts. Like a mother maintaining her only son with her own life, keep thy immeasurable loving thought for all creatures.

'Above thee, below thee, on all sides of thee, keep on all the world thy sympathy and immeasurable loving thought which is without obstruction, without any wish to injure, without enmity.

'To be dwelling in such contemplation while standing, walking, sitting or laying down, until sleep overcomes thee, is called living in Brahma'.

This proves that Buddha's idea of the infinite was not the idea of a spirit of an unbounded cosmic activity, but the infinite whose meaning is in the positive ideal of goodness and love, which cannot be otherwise than human. By being charitable, good and loving, you do not realize the infinite, in the stars or rocks, but the infinite revealed in Man. Buddha's teaching speaks of nirvana as the highest end. To understand its real character we have to know the path of its attainment, which is not merely through the negation of evil thoughts and deeds but through the elimination of all limits to love. It must mean the sublimation of self in a truth which is love itself, which unites in its bosom all those to whom we must offer our sympathy and service.

When somebody asked Buddha about the original cause of existence he sternly said that such questioning was futile and irrelevant. Did he not mean that it went beyond the human sphere as our goal—that though such a question might legitimately be asked in the region of cosmic philosophy or science, it had nothing to do with man's *dharma*, man's inner nature, in which love finds its utter fulfilment, in which all his sacrifice ends in an eternal gain, in which the putting out of the lamplight is no loss because there is the all-pervading light of the sun. And did those who listened to the great teacher merely hear his words and understand his doctrines? No, they directly felt in him what he was preaching, in the living language of his own person, the ultimate truth of Man.

It is significant that all great religions have their historic origin in persons who represented in their life a truth which was not cosmic and unmoral, but human and good. They rescued religion from the magic stronghold of demon force and brought it into the inner heart of humanity, into a fulfilment not confined to some exclusive good fortune of the individual but to the welfare of all men. This was not for the spiritual ecstasy of lonely souls, but for the spiritual emancipation of all races. They came as the messengers of Man to men of all countries and spoke of the salvation that could only be reached by the perfecting of our relationship with Man the Eternal, Man the Divine. Whatever might be their doctrines of God, or some dogmas that they borrowed from their own time and tradition, their life and teaching had the deeper implication of a Being who is the infinite in Man, the Father, the Friend, the Lover, whose service must be realized through serving all mankind. For the God in Man depends upon men's service and men's love for his own love's fulfilment.

The question was once asked in the shade of the ancient forest of India:

Kasmai devāva havishā vidhema?
Who is the God to whom we must bring our oblation?

That question is still ours, and to answer it we must know in the depth of our love and the maturity of our wisdom what man is—know him not only in sympathy but in science, in the joy of creation and in the pain of heroism; *tena tyaktena bhunjitha*, 'enjoy him through sacrifice'—the sacrifice that comes of love; *ma gridhah*, 'covet not'; for greed diverts your mind to that illusion in you which you represent the *parama purushah*, 'the supreme Person'.

Our greed diverts our consciousness to materials away from that supreme value of truth which is the quality of the universal being. The gulf thus created by the receding stream of the soul we try to replenish with a continuous stream of wealth, which may have the power to fill but not the power to unite and recreate. Therefore the gap is dangerously concealed under the glittering quicksand of things, which by their own weight cause a sudden subsidence while we are in the depths of sleep.

The real tragedy, however, does not lie in the risk of our material security but in the obscuration of Man himself in the human world. In the creative activities of his soul Man realizes his surroundings as his larger self, instinct with his own life and love. But in his ambition he deforms and defiles it with the callous handling of his voracity. His world of utility assuming a gigantic proportion, reacts upon his inner nature and hypnotically suggests to him a scheme of the universe which is an abstract system. In such a world there can be no question of *mukti*, the freedom in truth, because it is a solidly solitary fact, a cage with no sky beyond it. In all appearance our world is a closed world of hard facts; it is like a seed with its tough cover. But within this enclosure is working our silent cry of life for *mukti*, even when its possibility is darkly silent. When some huge overgrown temptation tramples into stillness this living aspiration then does civilization die like a seed that has lost its urging for germination. And this *mukti* is in the truth that dwells in the ideal man.

Chapter V

The Prophet

In my introduction I have stated that the universe to which we are related through our sense perception, reason or imagination, is necessarily Man's universe. Our physical self gains strength and success through its correct relationship in knowledge and practice with its physical aspect. The mysteries of all its phenomena are generalized by man as laws which have their harmony with his rational mind. In the primitive period of our history Man's physical dealings with the external world were most important for the maintenance of his life, the life which he has in common with other creatures, and therefore the first expression of his religion was physical— it came from his sense of wonder and awe at the manifestations of power in Nature and his attempt to win it for himself and his tribe by magical incantations and rites. In other words his religion tried to gain a perfect communion with the mysterious magic of Nature's forces through his own power of magic. Then came the time when he had the freedom of leisure to divert his mind to his inner nature and the mystery of his own personality gained for his its highest importance. And instinctively his personal self sought its fulfilment in the truth of a higher personality. In the history of religion our realization of the nature of the material world. Our method of worship has followed the course of such changes, but its evolution has been from the external and magical towards the moral and spiritual significance.

The first profound record of the change of direction in Man's religion we find in the message of the great prophet in Persia, Zarathustra, and as usual it was accompanied by a revolution. In a latter period the same thing happened in India, and it is evident that the history of this religious struggle lies embedded in the epic Mahabharata associated with the name of Krishna and the teachings of Bhagavadgita.

The most important of all outstanding facts of Iranian history is the religious reform brought about by Zarathustra. There can be hardly any question that he was the first man we know who gave a definitely moral character and direction to religion and at the same time preached the doctrine of monotheism which offered an eternal foundation of reality to goodness as an ideal of perfection. All religions of the primitive type try to keep men bound with regulations of external observances. Zarathustra was the greatest of all the pioneer prophets who showed the path of freedom to man, the freedom of moral choice, the freedom from the multiplicity of shrines which draw our worship away from the single-minded chastity of devotion.

To most of us it sounds like a truism today when we are told that the moral goodness of a deed comes from the goodness of intention. But it is a truth which once came to Man like a revelation of light in the darkness and it has not yet reached all the obscure corners of humanity. We still see around us men who fearfully follow, hoping thereby to gain merit, the path of blind formalism, which has no living moral source in the mind. This will make us understand the greatness of Zarathustra. Though surrounded by believers in magical rites, he proclaimed in those dark days of unreason that religion has its truth in its moral significance, not in external practices of imaginary value; that its value is in upholding man in his life of good thoughts, good words and goods deeds.

'The prophet', says Dr. Geiger, 'qualifies his religion as 'unheard of words' (Yasna 31.I) or as a 'mystery' (Y.48.3.) because he himself regards it as a religion quite distinct from the belief of the people hitherto. The revelation he announces is to him no longer a matter of sentiment, no longer a merely undefined presentiment and conception of the Godhead, but a matter of intellect, of spiritual perception and knowledge. This is of great importance, for there are probably not many religions of so high antiquity in which this fundamental doctrine, that religion is a knowledge or learning, a science of what is true, is so precisely declared as in the tenets of the Gathas. It is the unbelieving that are unknowing; on the contrary, the believing are learned because they have penetrated into this knowledge.'

It may be incidentally mentioned here, as showing the parallel to this in the development of Indian religious thought, that all through the Upanishad spiritual truth is termed with a repeated emphasis, *vidya*, knowledge, which has for its opposite *avidya*, acceptance of error born of unreason.

The outer expression of truth reaches its white light of simplicity through its inner realization. True simplicity is the physiognomy of perfection. In the primitive stages of spiritual growth, when man is dimly aware of the mystery of the infinite in his life and the world, when he does not fully know the inward character of his relationship with this truth, his first feeling is either of dread, or of greed of gain. This driven him into wild exaggeration in worship, frenzied convulsions of ceremonialism. But in Zarathustra's teachings, which are best reflected in his Gathas, we have hardly any mention of the ritualism of worship. Conduct and its moral motives have there received almost the sole attention.

The orthodox Persian form of worship in ancient Iran included animal sacrifices and offering of *haema* to the *daevas*. That all these should be discountenanced by Zarathustra not only shows his courage, but the strength of his realization of the Supreme Being as spirit. We are told that it has been mentioned by Plutarch that 'Zarathustra taught the Persians to sacrifice to Ahura Mazda, "vows and thanksgivings"'. The distance between faith in the efficiency of the bloodstained magical rites, and cultivation of the moral and spiritual ideals as the true form of worship is immense. It is amazing to see how Zarathustra was the first among men who crossed this distance with a certainty of realization which imparted such a fervour of faith to his life and his words. The truth which filled his mind was not a thing which he borrowed from books or received from teachers; he did not come to it by following a prescribed path of tradition, but it came to him as an illumination of his entire life, almost like a communication of his universal self to his universal self to his personal self, and he proclaimed this utmost immediacy of his knowledge when he said:

> When I conceived of Thee, O Mazda, as the very First and the Last, as the most Adorable One, as the Father of the Good Thought, as the Creator of Truth and Right, as the Lord Judge of our actions in life, then I made a place for thee in my very eyes.—*Yasna* 31.8 (Translation D.J. Irani).

It was the direct stirring of his soul which made him say:

> Thus do I announce the Greatest of all! I weave my songs of praise for him through Truth, helpful and beneficent of all that live. Let Ahura Mazda listen to them with his holy Spirit, for the Good Mind instructed me to adore Him; by his wisdom let Him teach me about what is best.—*Yasna* 45.6 (Translation D.J. Irani).

The truth which is not reached through the analytical process of reasoning and does not depend for proof on some corroboration of outward facts or the prevalent faith and practice of the people—the truth which comes like an inspiration out of context with its surroundings brings with it an assurance that it has been sent from an inner source of divine wisdom, that the individual who has realized it is specially inspired and therefore has his responsibility as a direct medium of communication of Divine Truth.

As along as man deals with his god as the dispenser of benefits only to those of His worshippers who know the secret of propitiating Him, he tries to keep Him for his own self or for the tribe to which he belongs. But directly the moral nature, that is to say, the humanity of God is apprehended, man realizes his divine self in his religion, his God is no longer an outsider to be propitiated for a special concession. The consciousness of God transcends the limitations of race and gathers together all human beings within one spiritual circle of union. Zarathustra was the first prophet who emancipated religion from the exclusive narrowness of the tribal God, the God of a chosen people, and offered it the universal Man. This is a great fact in the history of religion. The Master said, when the enlightenment came to him:

> Verily I believed Thee, O Ahura Mazda, to be the Supreme Benevolent Providence, when Sraosha came to me with the Good Mind, when first I received and became wise with your words. And though the task be difficult, though woe may come to me, I shall proclaim to all mankind Thy message, which Thou declarest to be the best.— *Yasna* 43 (Translation D.J. Irani).

He prays to Mazda:

> This I ask Thee, tell me truly, O Ahura, the religion that is best for all mankind, the religion, which

> based on truth, should prosper in all that is ours,
> the religion which establishes our actions in order
> and justice by the Divine songs of Perfect Piety,
> which has for its intelligent desire of desires, the
> desire for Thee, O Mazda.—*Yasna* 44.10
> (Translation D.J. Irani).

With the undoubted assurance and hope of one who has got
a direct vision of truth he speaks to the word:

> Hearken unto me, Ye who come form near and from
> far! Listen for I shall speak forth now; ponder well
> over all things, weigh my words with care and clear
> thought. Never shall the false teacher destroy this
> world for a second time, for his tongue stands mute,
> his creed exposed.—*Yasna* 45.1 (Translation D.J. Irani).

I think it can be said without doubt that such a high
conception of religion, uttered in such a clear note of
affirmation with a sure note of conviction that it is a truth
of the ultimate ideal of perfection which must be revealed to
all humanity, even at the cost of martyrdom, is unique in the
history of any religion belonging to such a remote dawn of
civilization.

There was a time when, along with other Aryan peoples,
the Persian also worshipped the elemental gods of Nature,
whose favour was not to be won by any moral duty performed
or service of love. That in fact was the crude beginning of
the scientific spirit trying to unlock the hidden sources of
power in nature. But through it all there must have been some
current of deeper desire, which constantly contradicted the
cult of power and indicated worlds of inner good, infinitely
more precious than material gain. Its voice was not strong at
first nor was it heeded by the majority of the people; but its
influences, like the life within the seed, were silently working.

Then comes the great prophet; and in his life and mind the hidden fire of truth suddenly bursts out into flame. The best in the people works for long obscure ages in hints and whispers till it finds its voice which can never again be silenced. For that voice becomes the voice of Man, no longer confined to a particular time or people. It works across intervals of silence and oblivion, depression and defeat, and comes out again with its conquering call. It is a call to the fighter, the fighter against untruth, against all that lures away man's spirit from its high mission of freedom into the meshes of materialism.

Zarathustra's voice is still a living voice, not alone a matter of academic interest for historical scholars who deal with the facts of the past; nor merely the guide of a small community of men in the daily details of their life. Rather, of all teachers Zarathustra was the first who addressed his words to all humanity, regardless of distance of space or time. he was not like a cave-dweller who, by some chance of friction, had lighted a lamp and, fearing lest it could not be shared with all, secured it will a miser's care for is own domestic use. But he was the watcher in the night, who stood on the lonely peak facing the East and broke out singing the paeans of light to the sleeping world when the sun came out on the brim of the horizon. The Sun of Truth is for all, he declared—its light is to unite the far and the near. Such a message always arouses the antagonism of those whose habits have become nocturnal, whose vested interest is in the darkness. And there was a bitter fight in the lifetime of the prophet between his followers and the others who were addicted to the ceremonies that had tradition on their side, and not truth.

We are told that 'Zarathustra was descended from a kingly family', and also that the first converts to his doctrine were of the ruling caste. But the priesthood, 'the Kavis and the

Karapans, often succeeded in bringing the rulers over to their side'. So we find that, in this fight, the princes of the land divided themselves into two opposite parties as we find in India in the Kurukshetra War.

It has been a matter of supreme satisfaction to me to realize that the purification of faith which was the mission of the great teachers in both communities, in Persia and in India, followed a similar line. We have already seen how Zarathustra spiritualized the meaning of sacrifice, which in former days consisted in external ritualism entailing bloodshed. The same thing we find in the Gita, in which the meaning of the word *Yajna* has been translated into a higher significance than it had in its crude form.

According to the Gita, the deeds that are done solely for the sake of self fetter our soul; the disinterested action, performed for the sake of the giving up of self, is the true sacrifice. For creation itself comes of the self-sacrifice of Brahma, which has no other purpose; and therefore, in our performance of the duty which is self-sacrificing, we realize the spirit of Brahma.

The Ideal of Zoroastrian Persia is distinctly ethical. It sends its call to men to work together with the Eternal Spirit of Good in spreading and maintaining *Kshathra*, the kingdom of righteousness, against all attacks of evil. This ideal gives us our place as collaborators with God in distributing his blessings over the world.

> Clear is this to the man of wisdom as to the man who
> carefully thinks;
> He who upholds Truth with all the might of his power,
> He who upholds Truth the utmost in his words and deed,
> He, indeed, is Thy most valued helper, O Mazda Ahura!

> *Yasna* 31.22 (Translation D.J. Irani)

It is a fact of supreme moment to us that the human world is in an incessant state of war between that which will save us and that which will drag us into the abyss of disaster. Out one hope lies in the fact that Ahura Mazda is on our side if we choose the right course.

The active heroic aspect of this religion reflects the character of the people themselves, who later on spread conquests far and wide and built up great empires by the might of their sword. They accepted this world in all seriousness. They had their zest in life and confidence in their own strength. They belonged to the western half of Asia and their great influence travelled through the neighbouring civilization of Judaea towards the Western Continent. Their ideal was the ideal of the fighter. By force of will and deeds of sacrifice they were to conquer *haurvatat*—welfare in this world, and *ameratat*—immortality in the other. This is the best ideal in the West, the great truth of fight. For paradise has to be gained through conquest. That sacred task is for the heroes, who are to take the right side in the battle, and the right weapons.

There was a heroic period in Indian history, when this holy spirit of fight was invoked by the greatest poet of the Sanskrit Literature. It is not to be wondered at that his ideal of fight was similar to the ideal that Zarathustra preached. The problem with which his poem starts is that paradise has to be rescued by the hero from its invasion by evil beings. This is the eternal problem of man. The evil spirit is exultant and paradise is lost when *Sati*, the spirit of *Sat* (Reality), is disunited from *Siva*, the Spirit of Goodness. The Real and the Good must meet in wedlock if the hero is to take his birth in order to save all that is true and beautiful. When the union was attempted though the agency of passion, the anger of god was aroused and the result was a tragedy of disappointment. At last, by purification through penance, the wedding was effected, the hero was born who fought against the forces of evil and paradise we regained. This is a poem of the ideal of the moral fight, whose first great prophet was Zarathustra.

We must admit that this ideal has taken a stronger hold upon the life of man in the West than in India—the West, where the vigour of life receives its fullest support from nature and the excess of energy finds its delight in ceaseless activities. But everywhere in the world, the unrealized ideal is a force of disaster. It gathers its strength in secret even in the heart of prosperity, kills the soul first and then drives men to their utter ruin. When the aggressive activity of will, which naturally accompanies physical vigour, fails to accept the responsibility of its ideal, it breeds unappeasable greed for material gain, leads to unmeaning slavery of things, till amidst a raging conflagration of clashing interests the tower of ambition topples down to the dust.

And for this, the prophetic voice of Zarathustra reminds us that all human activities must have an ideal goal, which is an end to itself, and therefore is peace, is immortality. It is the House of Songs, the realization of love, which comes through strenuous service of goodness.

> All the joys of life which Thou holdest, O Mazda, the joys that were, the joys that are, and the joys that shall be, Thou dost apportion all in Thy love for us.

We, on the other hand, in the tropical East, who have no surplus of physical energy inevitably overflowing in outer activities, also have our own ideal given to us. Our course is not so much through the constant readiness to fight in the battle of the good and evil, as through the inner concentration of mind, through pacifying the turbulence of desire, to reach that serenity of the infinite in our being which leads to the harmony in the all. Here, likewise, the unrealized ideal pursues us with its malediction. As the activities of a vigorous vitality may become unmeaning, and thereupon smother the soul with a mere multiplicity of material, so the peace of the extinguished desire may become the peace of death; and the inner world, in which we would dwell, become a world of incoherent dreams.

The negative process of curbing desire and controlling passion is only for saving our energy from dissipation and directing it into its proper channel. If the path of the channel we have chosen runs withinwards, it also must have its expression in action, not for any ulterior reward, but for the proving of its own truth. If the test of action is removed, if our realization grows purely subjective, then it may become like travelling in a desert in the night, going round and round the same circle, imagining all the while that we are following the straight path of purpose.

This is why the prophet of the Gita in the first place says:

Who so forsakes all desires and goeth onwards free from yearnings, selfless and without egoism, he goeth to peace.

But he does not stop here, he adds:

Surrendering all actions to me, with Thy thoughts resting on the Supreme Self, from hope and egoism freed, and of mental fever cured, engage in battle.

Action there must be, fight we must have—not the fight of passion and desire, or arrogant self-assertion, but of duty done in the presence of the Eternal, the disinterested fight of the serene soul that helps us in our union with the Supreme Being.

In this, the teaching of Zarathustra, his sacred gopel of fight finds its unity. The end of the fight he preaches is in the House of Songs, in the symphony of spiritual union. He sings:

Ye, who wish to be allied to the Good Mind, to be friend with Truth, Ye who desire to sustain the

Holy Cause, down with all anger and violence, away with all ill-will and strife! Such benevolent men, O Mazda, I shall take to the House of Songs!

The detailed facts of history, which are the battleground of the learned, are not my province. I am a singer myself, and I am ever attracted by the strains that come forth from the House of Songs. When the streams of ideals that flow from the East and from the West mingle their murmur in some profound harmony of meaning it delights my soul.

In the realm of material property men are jealously proud of their possessions and their exclusive rights. Unfortunately there are quarrelsome men who bring that pride of acquisition, the worldliness of sectarianism, even into the region of spiritual truth. Would it be sane, if the man in China should lay claim to the ownership of the sun because he can prove the earlier sunrise in his own country?

For myself, I feel proud whenever I find that the best in the world have their fundamental agreement. It is their function to unite and to dissuade the small from bristling-up, like prickly shrubs, in the pride of the minute points of their differences, only to hurt one another.

Chapter VI

The Vision

I hope that my readers have understood, as they have read these pages, that I am neither a scholar nor a philosopher. They should not expect from me fruits gathered from a wide field of studies or wealth brought by a mind trained in the difficult exploration of knowledge. Fortunately for me the subject of religion gains in interest and value by the experience of the individuals who earnestly believe in its truth. This is my apology for offering a part of the story of my life which has always realized its religion through a process of growth and not by the help of inheritance of importation.

Man has made the entire geography of the earth his own, ignoring the boundaries of climate; for, unlike the lion and the reindeer, he has the power to create his special skin and temperature, including his unscrupulous power of borrowing the skins of the indigenous inhabitants and misappropriating their fats.

His kingdom is also continually extending in time through a great surplus in his power of memory, to which is linked his immense facility of borrowing the treasure of the past from all quarters of the world. He dwells in a universe of history, in an environment of continuous remembrance. The animal occupies time only through the multiplication of its own race, but man through the memorials of his mind, raised along the pilgrimage of progress. The stupendousness of his knowledge and wisdom is due to their roots spreading into and drawing sap from the far-reaching area of history.

Man has his other dwelling place in the realm of inner realization, in the element of an immaterial value. This is a world where from the subterranean soil of his mind his consciousness often, like a seed, unexpectedly sends up sprouts into the heart of a luminous freedom, and the individual is made to realize his truth in the universal Man. I hope it may prove of interest if I give an account of my own personal experience of a sudden spiritual outburst from within me which is like the underground current of a perennial stream unexpectedly welling up on the surface.

I was born in a family which, at that time, was earnestly developing a monotheistic religion based upon the philosophy of the Upanishad. Somehow my mind at first remained coldly aloof, absolutely uninfluenced by any religion whatever. It was through an idiosyncrasy of my temperament that I refused to accept any religious teaching merely because people in my surroundings believed it to be true. I could not persuade myself to imagine that I had a religion because everybody whom I might trust believed in its value.

Thus my mind was brought up in an atmosphere of freedom—freedom from the dominance of any creed that had its sanction in the definite authority of some scripture, or in the teaching of some organized body of worshippers. And, therefore, the man who questions me has ever right to distrust my vision and reject my testimony. In such a case, the authority of some particular book venerated by a large number of men may have greater weight than the assertion of an individual, and therefore I never claim any right to preach.

When I look back upon those days, it seems to me that unconsciously I followed the path of my Vedic ancestors, and was inspired by the tropical sky with its suggestion of an uttermost Beyond. The wonder of the gathering clouds hanging heavy with the unshed rain, of the sudden sweep of storms arousing vehement gestures along the line of coconut trees, the fierce loneliness of the blazing summer noon, the silent sunrise behind the dewy veil of autumn morning, kept my mind with the intimacy of a pervasive companionship.

Then came my initiation ceremony of Brahminhood when the *Gayatri* verse of meditation was given to me, whose meaning, according to the explanation I had, runs as follows:

> Let me contemplate the adorable splendour of Him
> who created the earth, the air and the starry spheres,
> and sends the power of comprehension with our
> minds.

This produced a sense of serene exaltation in me, the daily meditation upon the infinite being which unites in one stream of creation my mind and the outer world. Though today I find no difficulty in realizing this being as an infinite personality in whom the subject and object are perfectly reconciled, at that time the idea to me was vague. Therefore the current of feeling that it aroused in my mind was indefinite, like the circulation of air—an atmosphere which needed a definite world to complete itself and satisfy me. For it is evident that my religion is a poet's religion, and neither that of an orthodox man of piety nor that of a theologian. Its touch comes to me through the same unseen and trackless channel as does the inspiration of my songs. My religious life has followed the same mysterious line of growth as has my poetical life. Somehow they are wedded to each other and, though their betrothal had a long period of ceremony, it was kept secret to me.

When I was eighteen, a sudden spring breeze of religious experience for the first time came to my life and passed away leaving in my memory a direct message of spiritual reality. One day while I stood watching at early dawn the sun sending out its rays from behind the trees, I suddenly felt as if some ancient mist had in a moment lifted from my sight, and the morning light on the face of the world revealed an inner radiance of joy. The invisible screen of the commonplace was removed from all things and all men, and their ultimate significance was intensified in my mind; and this is the definition of beauty. That which was memorable in this experience was its human message, the sudden expansion of my consciousness in the super-personal world of man. The poem I wrote on the first day of my surprise was named 'The Awakening of the Waterfall'. The waterfall, whose spirit lay dormant in its ice-bound isolation, was touched by the sun and, bursting in a cataract of freedom, it found its finality in an unending sacrifice, in a continual union with the sea. After four days the vision passed away, and the lid hung down upon my inner sight. In the dark, the world once again put on its disguise of the obscurity of an ordinary fact.

When I grew older and was employed in a responsible work in some villages I took my place in a neighbourhood where the current of time ran slow and joys and sorrows had their simple and elemental shades and lights. The day which had its special significance for me came with all its drifting trivialities of the commonplace life. The ordinary work of my morning had come to its close and before going to take my bath I stood for a moment at my window, overlooking a market place on the bank of a dry river bed, welcoming the first flood of rain along its channel. Suddenly I became conscious of a stirring of soul within me. My world of experience in a moment seemed to become lighted, and facts that were detached and dim found a great unity of meaning. The feeling which I had was like that which a man, groping through a fog without knowing his destination, might feel when he suddenly discovers that he stands before his own house.

I still remember the day in my childhood when I was made to struggle across my lessons in a first primer, strewn with isolated words smothered under the burden of spelling. The morning hour appeared to me like a once-illumined page, grown dusty and faded, discoloured into irrelevant marks, smudges and gaps, wearisome in its moth-eaten meaninglessness. Suddenly I came to a rhymed sentence of combined words, which may be translated thus—'it rains, the leaves tremble'. At once I came to a world wherein I recovered my full meaning. My mind touch the creative realm of expression, and at that moment I was no longer a mere student with his mind muffled by spelling lessons, enclosed by classroom. The rhythmic picture of the tremulous leaves beaten by the rain opened before my mind the world which does not merely carry information, but a harmony with my mind revelled in the unity of a vision. In a similar manner, on that morning in the village, the facts of my life suddenly appeared to me in a luminous unity of truth. All things that had seemed like vagrant waves were revealed to my mind in relation to a boundless sea. I felt sure that some Being who comprehended me and my world was seeking his best expression in all my experiences, uniting them into an ever-widening individuality which is a spiritual work of art.

To this being I was responsible; for the creation in me is his as well as mine. It may be that it was the same creative Mind that is shaping the universe to its eternal idea; but in me as a person it had one of its special centres of a personal relationship growing into a deepening consciousness. I had my sorrows that left their memory in a long burning track across my days, but I felt at that moment that in them I lent myself to a travail of creation that ever exceeded my own personal bounds like stars which in their individual firebursts are lighting the history of the universe. It gave me a great joy to feel in my life detachment at the idea of a mystery of a meeting of the two in a creative comradeship. I felt that I had found my religion at last, the religion of Man, in which the infinite became defined in humanity and came close to me so as to need my love and co-operation.

This idea of mine found at a later date its expression in some of my poems addressed to what I called *Jivan devata*, the Lord of my life. Fully aware of my awkwardness in dealing with a foreign language, with some hesitation I give a translation, being sure that any evidence revealed through the self-recording instrument of poetry is more authentic than answers extorted through conscious questionings:

> Thou who art the innermost Spirit of my being,
> art thou pleased, Lord of my Life?
> For I gave to thee my cup
> filled with all the pain and delight
> that the crushed grapes of my heart had
> surrendered,
> I wove with the rhythm of colours and songs the
> cover for thy bed,
> and with the molten gold of my desires
> I fashioned playthings for thy passing hours.
>
> I know not why thou chosest me for thy partner,
> Lord of my Life!
> Dist thou store my days and nights,
> my deeds and dreams for the alchemy of thy art,
> and string in the chain of thy music my songs of
> autumn and spring,
> and gather the flowers from my mature moments
> for thy crown?
>
> I see thine eyes gazing at the dark of my heart,
> Lord of my life,
> I wonder if my failures and wrongs are forgiven.
> For many were my days without service

and nights of forgetfulness;
futile were the flowers that faded in the shade not
offered to thee.
Often the tired strings of my lute
slackened at the strain of thy tunes.
And often at the ruin of wasted hours
my desolate evenings were filled with tears.

But have my days come to their end at last,
Lord of my life,
while my arms round thee grow limp,
my kisses losing their truth?
Then break up the meeting of this languid day.
Renew the old in me in fresh forms of delight;
and let the wedding come once again
in a new ceremony of life.

You will understand from this how unconsciously I had been travelling towards the realization which I stumbled upon in an idle moment on a day in July, when morning clouds thickened on the eastern horizon and a caressing shadow lay on the tremulous bamboo branches, while an excited group of village boys was noisily dragging from the bank an old fishing boat; and I cannot tell how at that moment an unexpected train of thoughts ran across my mind like a strange caravan carrying the wealth of an unknown kingdom.

From my infancy I had a keen sensitiveness which kept my mind tingling with consciousness of the world around me, natural and human. We had a small garden attached to our house; it was a fairyland to me, where miracles of beauty were of everyday occurrence.

Almost every morning in the early hour of the dusk, I would run out from my bed in a great hurry to greet the first pink flush of the dawn through the shivering branches of the palm trees which stood in a line along the garden boundary, while the grass glistened as the dew-drops caught the earliest tremor of the morning breeze. The sky seemed to bring to me the call of a personal companionship, and all my heart— my whole body in fact—used to drink in at a draught the overflowing light and peace of those silent hours. I was anxious never to miss a single morning, because each one was precious to me, more precious than gold to the miser. I am certain that I felt a larger meaning of my own self when the barrier vanished between me and what was beyond myself.

I had been blessed with that sense of wonder which gives a child his right of entry into the treasure house of mystery in the depth of existence. My studies in the school I neglected, because they rudely dismembered me from the context of my world and I felt miserable, like a caged rabbit in a biological institute. This, perhaps, will explain the meaning of my religion. This world was living to me, intimately close to my life, permeated by a subtle touch of kinship which enhanced the value of my own being.

It is true that this world also has its impersonal aspect of truth which is pursued by the man of impersonal science. The father has his personal relationship with his son; but as a doctor he may detach the fact of a son from that relationship and let the child become an abstraction to him, only a living body with its physiological functions. It cannot be said that if through the constant pursuit of his vocations he altogether discards the personal element in his relation to his son he reaches a greater truth as a doctor than he does as a father. The scientific knowledge of his son is information about a fact, and not the realization of a truth. In his intimate feeling for his son he touches an ultimate truth—the truth of relationship, the truth of a harmony in the universe, the fundamental principle of creation. It is not merely the number of protons and electrons which represents the truth of an element; it is the mystery of their relationship which cannot be analysed. We are made conscious of this truth of relationship immediately within us in our love, in our joy; and from this experience of ours we have the right to say that the Supreme One, who relates all things, comprehends the universe, is all love—the love that is the highest truth being the most perfect relationship.

I still remember the shock of repulsion I received as a child when some medical student brought to me a piece of a human windpipe and tried to excite my admiration for its structure. He tried to convince me that it was the source of the beautiful human voice. But I could not bear the artisan to occupy the throne that was for the artist who concealed the machinery and revealed the creation in its ineffable unity. God does not care to keep exposed the record of his power written in geological inscriptions, but he is proudly glad of the expression of beauty which he spreads on the green grass, in the flowers, in the play of the colours on the clouds, in the murmuring music of running water.

I had a vague notion as to who or what it was that touched my heart's chords, like the infant which does not know its mother's name, or who or what she is. The feeling which I always had was a deep satisfaction of personality that flowed into my nature through living channels of communication from all sides.

I am afraid that the scientist may remind me that to lose sight of the distinction between life and non-life, the human and the non-human, is a sign of the primitive mind. While admitting it, let me hope that it is not an utter condemnation, but rather the contrary. It may be a true instinct of Science itself, an instinctive logic, which makes the primitive mind think that humanity has become possible as a fact only because of a universal human truth which has harmony with its reason, with its will. In the details of our universe there are some differences that may be described as non-human, but not in their essence. The bones are different from the muscles, but they are organically one in the body. Our feeling of joy, our imagination, realizes a profound organic unity with the universe comprehended by the human mind. Without minimizing the differences that are in detailed manifestations, there is nothing wrong in trusting the mind, which is occasionally made intensely conscious of an all-pervading personality answering to the personality of man.

The details of reality must be studied in their differences by Science, but it can never know the character of the grand unity of relationship pervading it, which can only be realized immediately by the human spirit. And therefore it is the primal imagination of man—the imagination which is fresh and immediate in its experiences—that exclaims in a poet's verse:

> Wisdom and spirit of the universe!
> Thou soul, that art the eternity of thought,
> And giv'st to forms and images a breath
> And everlasting motion.

And in another poet's words it speaks of

> That light whose smile kindles the universe,
> That Beauty in which all things work and move.

The theologian may follow the scientist and shake his head and say that all that I have written is pantheism. But let us not indulge in an idolatry of name and dethrone living truth in its favour. When I say that I am a man, it is implied by that word that there is such a thing as a general idea of Man which persistently manifests itself in every particular human being, who is different from all other individuals. If we lazily label such a belief as 'pananthropy' and divert our thoughts from its mysteriousness by such a title it does not help us much. Let me assert my faith by saying that this world, consisting of what we call animate and inanimate things, has found its culmination in man, its best expression. Man, as a creation, represents the Creator, and this is why of all creatures it has been possible for him to comprehend this world in his knowledge and in his feeling and in his imagination, to realize in his individual spirit a union with a Spirit that is everywhere.

There is an illustration that I have made use of in which I supposed that a stranger from some other planet has paid a visit to our earth and happens to hear the sound of a human voice on the gramophone. All that is obvious to him and most seemingly active, is the revolving disc. He is unable to discover the personal truth that lies behind, and so might accept the impersonal scientific fact of the disc as final—the fact that could be touched and measured. He would wonder how it could be possible for a machine to speak to the soul. Then, if in pursuing the mystery, he should suddenly come to the heart of the music through a meeting with the composer, he would at once understand the meaning of that music as a personal communication.

That which merely gives us information can be explained in terms of measurement, but that which gives us joy cannot be explained by the facts of a mere grouping of atoms and molecules. Somewhere in the arrangement of this world there seems to be a great concern about giving us delight, which shows that, in the universe, over and above the meaning of matter and forces, there is a message conveyed through the magic touch of personality. This touch cannot be analysed, it can only be felt. We cannot prove it any more than the man from the other planet could prove to the satisfaction of his fellows the personality which remained invisible, but which, through the machinery, spoke direct to the heart.

Is it merely because the rose is round and pink that it gives me more satisfaction than the gold which could buy me the necessities of life, or any number of slaves? One may, at the outset, deny the truth that a rose gives more delight than a piece of gold. But such an objector must remember that I am not speaking of artificial values. If we had to cross a desert whose sand was made of gold, then the cruel glitter of these dead particles would become a terror for us, and the sight of a rose would bring to us the music of paradise.

The final meaning of the delight which we find in a rose can never be in the roundness of its petals, just as the final meaning of the joy of music cannot be in a gramophone disc. Somehow we feel that through a rose the language of love reached our heart. Do we not carry a rose to our beloved because in it is already embodied a message which, unlike our language of words, cannot be analysed? Through this gift of a rose we utilize a universal language of joy for own purposes of expression.

Fortunately for me a collection of old lyrical poems composed by the poets of the Vaishnava sect came to my hand when I was young. I became aware of some underlying idea deep in the obvious meaning of these love poems. I felt the joy of an explorer who suddenly discovers the key to the language lying hidden in the hieroglyphs which are beautiful in themselves. I was sure that these poets were speaking about the supreme Lover, whose touch we experience in all our relations of love—the love of nature's beauty, of the animal, the child, the comrade, the beloved, the love that illuminates our consciousness of reality. They sang of a love that ever flows through numerous obstacles between men and Man the Divine, the eternal relation which has the relationship of mutual dependence for a fulfilment that needs perfect union of individuals and the Universal.

The Vaishnava poet sings of the Lover who has his flute which, with its different stops, gives out the varied notes of beauty and love that are in Nature and Man. These notes bring to us our message of invitation. They eternally urge us to come out from the seclusion of our self-centred life into the realm of love and truth. Are we deaf by nature, or is it that we have been deafened by the claims of the world, of self-seeking, by the clamorous noise of the market-place? We miss the voice of the Lover, and we fight, we rob, we exploit the weak, we chuckle at our cleverness, when we can appropriate for our use what is due to others; we make our lives a desert by turning away from our world that stream of love which pours down from the blue sky and wells up from the bosom of the earth.

In the region of Nature, by unlocking the secret doors of the workshop department, one may come to that dark hall where dwells that mechanic and help to attain usefulness, but through it one can never attain finality. Here is the storehouse of innumerable facts and, however necessary they may be, they have not the treasure of fulfilment in them. But the hall of union is there, where dwells the Lover in the heart of existence. When a man reaches it he at once realizes that he has come to Truth, to immortality, and he is glad with a gladness which is an end, and yet which has no end.

Mere information about facts, mere discovery of power, belongs to the outside and not to the inner soul of things. Gladness is the one criterion of truth, and we know when we had touched Truth by the music it gives, by the joy of greeting it sends forth to the truth in us. That is the true foundation of all religions. It is not as ether waves that we receive light; the morning does not wait for some scientist for its introduction to us. In the same way we touch the infinite reality immediately within us only when we perceive the pure truth of love or goodness, not through the explanations of theologians, not through the erudite discussion of ethical doctrines.

I have already made the confession that my religion is a poet's religion. All that I feel about it is from vision and not from knowledge. Frankly, I acknowledge that I cannot satisfactorily answer any questions about evil, or about what happens after death. Nevertheless, I am sure that there have come moments in my own experience when my soul has touched the infinite and has become intensely conscious of it through the illumination of joy. It has been said in our Upanishad that our mind and our words come away baffled from the Supreme Truth, but he who knows truth through the immediate joy of his own soul is saved from all doubts and fears.

In the night we stumble over things and become acutely conscious of their individual separateness. But the day reveals the greater unity which embraces them. The man whose inner vision is bathed in an illumination of his consciousness at once realizes the spiritual unity reigning supreme over all differences. His mind no longer awkwardly stumbles over individual facts of separateness in the human world, accepting them as final. He realizes that peace is in the inner harmony which dwells in truth and not in any outer adjustments. He knows that beauty carries an eternal assurance of our spiritual relationship to reality, which waits for its perfection in the response of our love.

Chapter VII

The Man of My Heart

At the outburst of an experience, which is unusual, such as happened to me in the beginning of my youth, the puzzled mind seeks its explanation in some settled foundation of that which is usual, trying to adjust an unexpected inner message to an organized belief which goes by the general name of a religion. And, therefore, I naturally was glad at that time of youth to accept from my father the post of secretary to a special section of the monotheistic church of which he was the leader. I took part in its services mainly by composing hymns which unconsciously took the many-thumbed impression of the orthodox main, a composite smudge of tradition. Urged by my sense of duty I strenuously persuaded myself to think that my new mental attitude was in harmony with that of the members of our association, although I constantly stumbled upon obstacles and felt constraints that hurt me to the quick.

At last I came to discover that in my conduct I was not strictly loyal to my religion, but only to the religious institution. That latter represented an artificial average, with its standard of truth at its static minimum, jealous of any vital growth that exceeded its limits. I have my conviction that in religion, and also in the arts, that which is common to a group is not important. Indeed, very often it is a contagion of mutual imitation. After a long struggle with the feeling that I was using a mask to hide the living face of truth, I gave up my connection with our church.

About this time, one day I chanced to hear a song from a beggar belonging to the Baül sect of Bengal. We have in the modern Indian religion deities of different names, forms and mythology, some Vedic and others aboriginal. They have their special sectarian idioms and associations that give emotional satisfaction to those who are accustomed to their hypnotic influences. Some of them may have their aesthetic value to me and others philosophical significance over cumbered by exuberant distraction of legendary myths. But what struck me in this simple song was a religious expression that was neither grossly concrete, full of crude details, nor metaphysical in its rarified transcendentalism. At the same time it was alive with an emotional sincerity. It spoke of an intense yearning of the heart for the divine which is in Man and not in the temple, or scriptures, in images and symbols. The worshipper addresses his songs to the Man the ideal, and says:

Temples and mosques obstruct thy path,
and I fail to hear thy call or to move,
when the teachers and priest angrily crowd round
me.

He does not follow any tradition of ceremony, but only believes in love. According to him:

Love is the magic stone, that transmutes by its touch greed into sacrifice.

He goes on to say:

For the sake of this love heaven longs to become earth
and gods to become man.

Since then I have often tried to meet these people, and sought to understand them through their songs, which are their only form of worship. One is often surprised to find in many of these verses a striking originality of sentiment and diction; for, at their best, they are spontaneously individual in their expressions. One such song is a hymn to the Ever Young. It exclaims:

> O my flower buds, we worship the Young;
> for the Young is the source of the holy Ganges of life;
> from the Young flows the supreme bliss

And it says:

> We never offer ripe corn in the service of the Young,
> not fruit, nor seed,
> but only the lotus bud which is of our own mind.
> The young hour of the day, the morning,
> is our time for the worship of Him.
> from whose contemplation has sprung the Universe.

It calls the Spirit of the Young the *Brahma Kamal*, 'the infinite lotus'. For it is something which has perfection in its heart and yet ever grows and unfolds its petals.

There have been men in India who never wrote learned texts about the religion of Man but had an overpowering desire and practical training for its attainment. They bore in their life the testimony of their intimacy with the Person who is in all persons, of Man the formless in the individual forms of men. Rajjab, poet-saint of medieval India, says of Man:

> God-man (*nara-nārāyana*) is thy definition, it is not
> a delusion but truth. In thee the infinite sees the finite,
> the perfect knowledge seeks love, and when the form
> and the Formless (the individual and the universal) are
> united love is fulfilled in devotion.

Ravidas, another poet of the same age, sings:

> Thou seest me, O Divine Man (*narahari*), and I see thee, and our love becomes mutual.

Of this God-man a village poet of Bengal says:

> He is within us, an unfathomable reality. We know him when we unlock our own self and meet in a true love with all others.

A brother poet of his says:

> Man seeks the man in me and I lose myself and run out.

And another singer sings of the Ideal Man, and says:

> How could the scripture know the meaning of the Lord who has his play in the world of human forms? Listen, O brother man (declares Chandidas), the truth of man is the highest truth, there is no other truth above it.

All these are proofs of a direct perception of humanity as an objective truth that rouses a profound feeling of longing and love. This is very unlike what we find in the intellectual cult of humanity, which is like a body that has tragically lost itself in the purgatory of shadows.
Wordsworth says:

> We live by admiration, hope and love,
> And ever as these are well and wisely fixed
> In dignity of being we ascend.

It is for dignity of being that we aspire through the expansion of our consciousness in a great reality of man to which we belong. We realize it through admiration and love, through hope that soars beyond the actual, beyond our own span of life into an endless time wherein we live the life of all men.

This is the infinite perspective of human personality where man finds his religion. Science may include in its field of knowledge the starry world and the world beyond it; philosophy may try to find some universal principle which is at the root of all things, but religion inevitably concentrates itself on humanity, which illumines our reason, inspires our wisdom, stimulates our love, claims our intelligent service. There is an impersonal idea, which we call law, discoverable by an impersonal logic in its pursuit of the fathomless depth of the hydrogen atom and the distant virgin worlds clothed in eddying fire. But as the physiology of our beloved is not our beloved, so that impersonal law is not our God, the *Pitritamah pitrinam*, the Father who is ultimate in all fathers and mothers, of him we cannot say:

> *Tad viddhi pranipatena pariprasnena sevayā—*
> Realize him by obeisance, by the desire to know, by service—

For this can only be relevant to the God who is God and man at the same time; and if this faith be blamed for being anthropomorphic, then Man is to be blamed for being Man, and the lover for loving his dear one as a person instead of a principle of psychology. We can never go beyond Man in all that we know and fell, and a mendicant singer of Bengal has said:

> Our world is as it is in our comprehension; the thought
> and existence are commingled. Everything would
> be lost in unconsciousness if man were nought;
> and when response comes to your own call you
> know the meaning of reality.

According to him, what we call nature is not a philosophical abstraction, not cosmos, but what is revealed to *man* as a nature. In fact it is included in himself and therefore there is a commingling of his mind with it, and in that he finds his own being. He is truly lessened in humanity if he cannot take it within him and through it feel the fulness of his own existence. His arts and literature are constantly giving expression to this intimate communion of man with his world. And the Vedic poet exclaims in his hymn to the sun:

> Thou who nourishest the earth, who walkest alone,
> O Sun, withdraw thy rays, reveal thy exceeding beauty
> to me and let me realize that the Person who is there
> is the One who I am.

It is for us to realize the Person who is in the heart of the All by the emancipated consciousness of our own personality. We know that the highest mission of science is to find the universe enveloped by the human comprehension; to see man's *visvarupa*, his great mental body, that touches the extreme verge of time and space, that includes the whole world within itself.

The original Aryans who came to India had for their gods the deities of rain, wind, fire, the cosmic forces which singularly enough found no definite shapes in images. A time came when it was recognized that individually they had no separate, unrelated power of their own, but there was one infinite source of power which was named Brahma. The cosmic divinity developed into an impersonal idea; what was physical grew into a metaphysical abstraction, even as in modern science matter vanishes into mathematics. And Brahma, according to those Indians, could neither be apprehended by mind nor described by words, even as matter in its ultimate analysis proves to be.

However satisfactory that idea might be as the unknowable principle relating to itself all the phenomena that are non-personal, it left the personal man in a void of negation. It cannot be gain-said that we can never realize things in this world from inside, we can but know how they appear to us. In fact, in all knowledge we know our own self in its condition of knowledge. And religion sought the highest value of man's existence in this self. For this is the only truth of which he is immediately conscious from within. And he said:

> *Purushānna parā kinchit*
> *sā kāshthtā sā para gātih*
> Nothing is greater than the Person; he is the
> supreme, he is the ultimate goal.

It is a village poet of East Bengal who preaches in a song the philosophical doctrine that the universe has its reality in its relation to the Person, which I translate in the following lines:

> The sky and the earth are born of mine own eyes,
> The hardness and softness, the cold and the heat are
> the products of mine own body,
> The sweet smell and the bad are of my own nostrils.

This poet sings of the eternal Person within him, coming out and appearing before his eyes, just as the Vedic Rishi speaks of the Person, who is in him, dwelling also in the heart of the sun:

> I have seen the vision,
> the vision of mine own revealing itself,
> coming out from within me.

In India, there are those whose endeavour is to merge completely their personal self in an impersonal entity which is without any quality of definition; to reach a condition wherein mind becomes perfectly blank, losing all its activities. Those who claim the right to speak about it say that this is the purest state of consciousness, it is all joy and without any object or content. This is considered to be the ultimate end of *Yoga*, the cult of union, thus completely to identify one's being with the infinite Being who is beyond all thoughts and words. Such realization of transcendental consciousness accompanied by a perfect sense of bliss is a time-honoured tradition in our country, carrying in it the positive evidence which cannot be denied by any negative argument of refutation. Without disputing its truth I maintain that it may be valuable as a great psychological experience but all the same it is not religion, even as the knowledge of the ultimate state of the atom is of no use to an artist who deals in images in which atoms have taken forms. A certain condition of vacuum is needed for studying the state of things in its original purity, and the same may be said of the human spirit; but the original state is not necessarily the perfect state. The concrete form is a more perfect manifestation than the atom, and man is more perfect as a man than where he vanishes in an original indefiniteness. This is why the Ishopanishat says: 'Truth is both finite and infinite at the same time, it moves and yet moves not, it is in the distant, also in the near, it is within all objects and without them.'

This means that perfection as the ideal is immovable, but in its aspect of the real it constantly grows towards completion, it moves. And I say of the Supreme Man, that he is infinite in his essence, he is finite in his manifestation in us the individuals. As the Ishopanishat declares, a man must live his full term of life and work without greed, and thus realize himself in the Being who is in all beings. This means that he must reveal in his own personality the Supreme Person by his disinterested activities.

Chapter VIII

The Music Maker

A particle of sand would be nothing if it did not have its background in the whole physical world. This grain of sand is known in its context of the universe where we know all things through the testimony of our senses. When I say the grain of sand *is*, the whole physical world stands guarantee for the truth which is behind the appearance of the sand.

But where is that guarantee of truth for this personality of mine that has the mysterious faculty of knowledge before which the particle of sand offers its credential of identification? It must be acknowledged that this personal self of mine also has for its truth a background of personality where knowledge, unlike that of other things, can only be immediate and self-revealed.

What I mean by personality is a self-conscious principle of transcendental unity within man which comprehends all the details of facts that are individually his in knowledge and feeling, wish and will and work. In its negative aspect it is limited to the individual separateness, while in its positive aspect it ever extends itself in the infinite through the increase of its knowledge, love and activities.

And for this reason the most human of all facts about us is that we *do* dream of the limitless unattained—the dream which gives character to what *is* attained. Of all creatures man lives in an endless future. Our present is only a part of it. The ideas unborn, the unbodied spirits, tease our imagination with an insistence which makes them more real to our mind than things around us. The atmosphere of the future must always surround our present in order to make it life-bearing and suggestive of immortality. For he who has the healthy vigour of humanity in him has a strong instinctive faith that ideally he is limitless. That is why our greatest teachers claim from us a manifestation that touches the infinite. In this they pay homage to the Supreme Man. And our true worship lies in our indomitable courage to be great and thus to represent the human divine and ever to keep open the path of freedom towards the unattained.

We Indians have had the sad experience in our own part of the world how timid orthodoxy, its irrational repressions and its accumulation of dead centuries, dwarfs man through its idolatry of the past. Seated rigid in the centre of stagnation, it firmly ties the human spirit to the revolving wheels of habit till faintness overwhelms her. Like a sluggish stream choked by rotting weeds, it is divided into shallow slimy pools that shroud their dumbness in a narcotic mist of stupor. This mechanical spirit of tradition is essentially materialistic, it is blindly pious but not spiritual, obsessed by phantoms of unreason that haunt feeble minds in the ghastly disguise of religion. For our soul is shrunken when we allow foolish days to weave repeated patterns of unmeaning meshes round all departments of life. It becomes stunted when we have no object of profound interest, no prospect of heightened life, demanding clarity of mind and heroic attention to maintain and mature it. It is destroyed when we make fireworks of our animal passions for the enjoyment of their meteoric sensations, recklessly reducing to ashes all that could have been saved for permanent illumination. This happens not only to mediocre individuals hugging fetters that keep them irresponsible or hungering for lurid unrealities, but to generations of insipid races that have lost all emphasis of significance in themselves, having missed their future.

The continuous future is the domain of our millennium, which is with us more truly than what we see in or history in fragments of the present. It is in our dream. It is in the realm of the faith which creates perfection. We have seen the records of man's dreams of the millennium, the ideal reality cherished by forgotten races in their admiration, hope and love manifested in the dignity of their being through some majesty in ideals and beauty in performance. While these races pass away one after another they leave great accomplishments behind them carrying their claim to recognition as dreamers—not so much as conquerors of earthly kingdoms, but as the designers of paradise. The poet gives us the best definition of man when he says:

> We are the music-makers,
> We are the dreamers of dreams.

Our religions present for us the dreams of the ideal unity which is man himself as he manifests the infinite. We suffer from the sense of sin, which is the sense of discord, when any disruptive passion tears gaps in our vision of the One in man, creating isolation in our self from the universal humanity.

The Upanishad says, *māgridah*, 'covet not'. For coveting diverts attention from the infinite value of our personality to the temptation of materials. Our village poet sings: 'Man will brightly flash into your sight, my heart, if you shut the door of desires.'

We have seen how primitive man was occupied with his physical needs, and thus restricted himself to the present which is the time boundary of the animal; and he missed the urge of his consciousness to seek its emancipation in a world of ultimate human value.

Modern civilization for the same reason seems to turn itself back to that primitive mentality. Our needs have multiplied so furiously fast that we have lost our leisure for the deeper realization of our self and our faith in it. It means that we have lost our religion, the longing for the touch of the divine in man, the builder of the heaven, the music-maker, the dreamer of dreams. This has made it easy to tear into shreds our faith in the perfection of the human ideal, in its wholeness, as the fuller meaning of reality. No doubt it is wonderful that music contains a fact which has been analysed and measured, and which music shares in common with the braying of an ass or of a motor-car horn. But it is still more wonderful that music has a truth, which cannot be analysed into fractions; and there the difference between it and the bellowing impertinence of a motor-car horn is infinite. Men of our own times have analysed the human mind, its dreams, its spiritual aspirations,—most often caught unawares in the shattered state of madness, disease and desultory dreams—and they have found to their satisfaction that these are composed of elemental animalities tangled into various knots. This may be an important discovery; but what is still more important to realize is the fact that by some miracle of creation man infinitely transcends the component parts of his own character.

Suppose that some psychological explorer suspects that man's devotion to his beloved has at bottom our primitive stomach's hankering for human flesh, we need not contradict him; for whatever may be its genealogy, its secret composition, the complete character of our love, in its utter difference from cannibalism. The truth underlying the possibility of such transmutation is the truth of our religion. A lotus has in common with a piece of rotten flesh the elements of carbon and hydrogen. In a state of dissolution there is no difference between them, but in a state of creation the difference is immense; and it is that difference which really matters. We are told that some of our most sacred sentiments hold hidden in them instincts contrary to what these sentiments profess to be. Such disclosures have the effect upon certain persons of the relief of a tension, even like the relaxation in death of the incessant strenuousness of life.

We find in modern literature that something like a chuckle of an exultant disillusionment is becoming contagious, and the knights-errant of the cult of arson are abroad, setting fire to our time-honoured altars of worship, proclaiming that the images enshrined on them, even if beautiful, are made of mud. They say that it has been found out that the appearances in human idealism are deceptive, that the underlying mud is real. From such a point of view, the whole of creation may be said to be a gigantic deception, and the billions of revolving electric specks that have the appearance of 'you' or 'me' should be condemned as bearers of false evidence.

But whom do they seek to delude? If it be beings like ourselves who possess some inborn criterion of the real, then to them these very appearances in their integrity must represent reality, and not their component electric specks. For them the rose must be more satisfactory as an object than its constituent gases, which can be tortured to speak against the evident identity of the rose. The rose, even like the human sentiment of goodness, or ideal of beauty, belongs to the realm of creation, in which all its rebellious elements are reconciled in a perfect harmony. Because these elements in their simplicity yield themselves to our scrutiny, we in our pride are inclined to give them the best prizes as actors in that mystery-play, the rose. Such an analysis is really only giving a prize to our own detective cleverness.

I repeat again that the sentiments and ideals which man in his process of self-creation has built up, should be recognized in their wholeness. In all our faculties or passions there is nothing which is absolutely good or bad; they all are the constituents of the great human personality. They are notes that are wrong when in wrong places; our education is to make them into chords that may harmonize with the grand music of Man. The animal in the savage has been transformed into higher stages in the civilized man—in other words has attained a truer consonance with Man the divine, not through any elimination of the original materials, but through a magical grouping of them, through the severe discipline of art, the discipline of curbing and stressing in proper place, establishing a balance of lights and shadows in the background and foreground, and thus imparting a unique value to our personality in all its completeness.

So long as we have faith in this value, our energy is steadily sustained in its creative activity that reveals the eternal Man. This faith is helped on all sides by literature, arts, legends, symbols, ceremonials, by the remembrance of heroic souls who have personified it in themselves.

Our religion is the inner principle that comprehends these endeavours and expressions and dreams through which we approach Him in whose image we are made. To keep alive our faith in the reality of the ideal perfection is the function of civilization, which is mainly formed of sentiments and the images that represent that ideal. In other words, civilization is a creation of art, created for the objective realization of our vision of the spiritually perfect. It is the product of the art of religion. We stop its course of conquest when we accept the cult of realism and forget that realism is the worst form of untruth, because it contains a minimum of truth. It is like preaching that only in the morgue can we comprehend the reality of the human body—the body which has its perfect revelation when seen in life. All great human facts are surrounded by an immense atmosphere of expectation. They are never complete if we leave out from them what might be, what should be, what is not yet proven but profoundly felt, what points towards the immortal. This dwells in a perpetual surplus in the individual, that transcends all the desultory facts about him.

The realism in Man is the animal in him, whose life is a mere duration of time; the human in him is his reality which has life everlasting for its background. Rocks and crystals being complete definitely in what they are, can keep as 'mute insensate things' a kind of dumb dignity in their stolidly limited realism; while human facts grow unseemly and diseased, breeding germs of death, when divested of their creative ideal—the ideal of Man the divine. The difference between the notes as mere facts of sound and music as a truth of expression is immense. For music though it comprehends a limited number of notes yet represents the infinite. It is for man to produce the music as a truth of expression is immense. For music though it comprehends a limited number of notes yet represents the infinite. It is for man to produce the music of the spirit with all the notes which he has in his psychology and which, through inattention or perversity, can easily be translated into a frightful noise. In music man is revealed and not in a noise.

Chapter IX

The Artist

The Fundamental desire of life is the desire to exist. It claims from us a vast amount of training and experience about the necessaries of livelihood. Yet it does not cost me much to confess that the food that I have taken, the dress that I wear, the house where I have my lodging, represent a stupendous knowledge, practice and organization which I helplessly lack; for I find that I am not altogether despised for such ignorance and inefficiency. Those who read me seem fairly satisfied that I am nothing better than a poet or perhaps a philosopher—which latter reputation I do not claim and dare not hold through the precarious help of misinformation.

It is quite evident in spite of my deficiency that in human society I represent a vocation, which through superfluous has yet been held worthy of commendation. In fact, I am encouraged in my rhythmic futility by being offered moral and material incentives for its cultivation. If a foolish blackbird did not know how to seek its food, to build its nest, or to avoid its enemies, but specialized in singing, its fellow creatures, urged by their own science of genetics, would dutifully allow it to starve and perish. That I am not treated in a similar fashion is the evidence of an immense difference between the animal existence and the civilization of man. His great distinction dwells in the indefinite margin of life in him which affords a boundless background for his dreams and creations. And it is in this realm of freedom that he realizes his divine dignity, his great human truth, and is pleased when I as a poet sing victory to him, to Man the self-revealer, who goes on exploring ages of creation to find himself in perfection.

Reality, in all its manifestations, reveals itself in the emotional and imaginative background of our mind. We know it, not because we can think of it, but because we directly feel it. And therefore, even if rejected by the logical mind, it is not banished from our consciousness. As an incident it may be beneficial or injurious, but as a revelation its value lies in the fact that it offers us an experience through emotion or imagination; we feel ourselves in a special field of realization. This feeling itself is delightful when it is not accompanied by any great physical or moral risk, we love to feel even fear or sorrow if it is detached from all practical consequences. This is the reason of our enjoyment of tragic dramas, in which the feeling of pain rouses our consciousness to a white heat of intensity.

The reality of my own self is immediate and indubitable to me. whatever else affects me in a like manner is real for myself, and it inevitably attracts and occupies my attention for its own sake, blends itself with my personality, making it richer and larger and causing it delight. My friend may not be beautiful, useful, rich or great, but he is real to me; in him I feel my own extension and my joy.

The consciousness of the real within me seeks for its own corroboration the touch of the real outside me. When it fails the self in me is depressed. When our surroundings are monotonous and insignificant, having no emotional reaction upon our mind, we become vague to ourselves. For we are like pictures, whose reality is helped by the background if it is sympathetic. The punishment we suffer in solitary confinement consists in the obstruction to the relationship between the world of reality and the real in ourselves, causing the latter to become indistinct in a haze of inactive imagination: our personality is blurred, we miss the companionship of our own being through the diminution of our self. The world of our knowledge is enlarged for us through the extension of our information; the world of our personality grows in its area with a large and deeper experience of our personal self in our own universe through sympathy and imagination.

At this world, that can be known through knowledge, is limited to us owing to our ignorance, so the world of personality, that can be realized by our own personal self, is also restricted by the limit of our sympathy and imagination. In the dim twilight of insensitiveness a large part of our world remains to us like a procession of nomadic shadows. According to the stages of our consciousness we have more or less been able to identify ourselves with this world, if not as a whole, at least in fragments; and our enjoyment dwells in that wherein we feel ourselves thus united. In art we express the delight of this unity by which this world is realized as humanly significant to us. I have my physical, chemical and biological self; my knowledge of it extends through the extension of my knowledge of the physical, chemical and biological world. I have my personal self, which has its communication with our feelings, sentiments and imaginations, which lends itself to be coloured by our desires and shaped by our imageries.

Science urges us to occupy by our mind the immensity of the knowable world; our spiritual teacher enjoins us to comprehend by our soul the infinite Spirit which is in the depth of the moving and changing facts of the world; the urging of our artistic nature is to realize the manifestation of personality in the world of appearance, the reality of existence which is in harmony with the real within us. Where this harmony is not deeply felt, there we are aliens and perpetually homesick. For man by nature is an artist; he never receives passively and accurately in his mind a physical representation of things around him. There goes on a continual adaptation, a transformation of facts into human imagery, through constant touches of his sentiments and imagination. The animal has the geography of its birthplace; man has his country, the geography of his personal self. The vision of it is not merely physical; it has its artistic unity, it is a perpetual creation. In his country, his consciousness being unobstructed, man extends his relationship, which is of his own creative personality. In order to live efficiently man must know facts and their laws. In order to be happy he must establish harmonious relationship with all things with which he has dealings. Our creation is the modification of relationship.

The great men who appear in our history remain in our mind not as a static fact but as a living historical image. The sublime suggestions of their lives become blended into a noble consistency in legends made living in the life of ages. Those men with whom we live we constantly modify in our minds, making them more real to us than they would be in a bare presentation. Men's ideal of womanhood and women's ideal of manliness are creation by the imagination through a mental grouping of qualities and conducts according to our hopes and desires, and men and women consciously and unconsciously strive towards its attainment. In fact, they reach a degree of reality for each other according to their success in adapting these respective ideals to their own nature. To say that these ideals are imaginary and therefore not true is wrong in man's case. His true life is in his own creation, which represents the infinity of man. He is naturally indifferent to things that merely exist; they must have some ideal value for him, and then only his consciousness fully recognizes them as real. Men are never true in their isolated self, and their imagination is the faculty that brings before their mind the vision of their own greater being.

We can make truth ours by actively modulating its inter-relations. This is the work of art; for reality is not based in the substance of things but in the principal of relationship. Truth is the infinite pursued by metaphysics; fact is the infinite pursued by science, while reality is the definition of the infinite which relates truth to the person. Reality is human; it is what we are conscious of, by which we are affected, that which we express. When we are intensely aware of it, we are aware of ourselves and it gives us delight. We live in it, we always widen its limits. Our arts and literature represent this creative activity which is fundamental in man.

But the mysterious fact about it is that though the individuals are separately seeking their expression, their success is never individualistic in character. Men must find and feel and represent in all their creative works Man the Eternal, the creator. Their civilization is a continual discovery of the transcendental humanity. In whatever it fails it shows the failure of the artist, which is the failure is expression; and the civilization perishes in which the individual thwarts the revelation of the universal. For Reality is the truth of Man, who belongs to all times, and any individualistic madness of men against Man cannot thrive for long.

Man is eager that his feeling for what is real to him must never die; it must find an imperishable form. The consciousness of this self of mine is so intensely evident to me that it assumes the character of immortality. I cannot imagine that it ever has been or can be non-existent. In a similar manner all things that are real to me are for myself eternal, and therefore worthy of a language that has permanent meaning. We know individuals who have the habit of inscribing their names on the walls of some majestic monument of architecture. It is a pathetic way of associating their own names with some works of art which belong to all times and to all men. Our hunger for reputation comes from our desire to make objectively real that which is inwardly real to us. He who is inarticulate is insignificant, like a dark star that cannot prove itself. He ever waits for the artist to give his fullest worth, not for anything specially excellent in him but for the wonderful fact that he is what he certainly is, that he carries in him the eternal mystery of being.

A Chinese friend of mine while travelling with me in the streets of Peking suddenly exclaimed with a vehement enthusiasm: 'Look, here is a donkey!' Surely it was an utterly ordinary donkey, like as indisputable truism, needing no special introduction from him. I was amused; but it made me think. This animal is generally classified as having certain qualities that are not recommendable and then hurriedly dismissed. It was obscured to me by an envelopment of commonplace associations; I was lazily certain that I knew it and therefore I hardly saw it. But my friend, who possessed the artist mind of China, did not treat it with a cheap knowledge but could see it afresh and recognize it as real. When I say real, I mean that it did not remain at the outskirt of his consciousness tied to a narrow definition, but it easily blended in his imagination, produced a vision, a special harmony of lines, colours and life and movement, and became intimately his own. The admission of a donkey into a drawing-room is violently opposed; yet there is no prohibition against its finding a place in a picture which may be admiringly displayed on the drawing-room wall.

The only evidence of truth in art exists when it compels us to say 'I see'. A donkey we may pass by in Nature, but a donkey in art we must acknowledge even if it be a creature that disreputably ignores all its natural history responsibility, even if it resembles a mushroom in its head and a palm-leaf in its tail.

In the Upanishad it is said in a parable that there are two birds sitting on the same bough, one of which feeds and the other looks on. This is an image of the mutual relationship of the infinite being and the finite self. The delight of the bird which looks on is great, for it is a pure and free delight. There are both of these birds in man himself, the objective one with its business of life, the subjective one with its disinterested joy of vision.

A child comes to me and commands me to tell her a story. I tell her of a tiger which is disgusted with the black stripes on its body and comes to my frightened servant demanding a piece of soap. The story gives my little audience immense pleasure, the pleasure of a vision, and her mind cries out, 'It is here, for I see!' She *knows* a tiger in the book of natural history, but she can *see* the tiger in the story of mine.

I am sure that even this child of five knows that it is an impossible tiger that is out on its untigerly quest of an absurd soap. The delightfulness of the tiger for her is not in its beauty, its usefulness, or its probability; but in the undoubted fact that she can see it in her mind with a greater clearness of vision than she can the walls around her—the walls that brutally shout their evidence of certainty which is merely circumstantial. The tiger in the story is inevitable, it has the character of a complete image, which offers its testimonial of truth in itself. The listener's own mind is the eye-witness, whose direct experience could not be contradicted. A tiger must be like every other tiger in order that it may have its place in a book of Science; there it must be a commonplace tiger to be at all tolerated. But in the story it is uncommon, it can never be reduplication. We *know* a thing because it belongs to a class; we *see* a thing because it belongs to itself. The tiger of the story completely detached itself from all others of its kind and easily assumed a distinct individuality in the heart of the listener. The child could vividly see it, because by the help of her imagination it became her own tiger, one with herself, and this union of the subject and object gives us joy. Is it because there is no separation between them in truth, the separation being the *Maya*, which is creation?

There come in our history occasions when the consciousness of a large multitude becomes suddenly illumined with the recognition of a reality which rises far above the dull obviousness of daily happenings. The world becomes vivid: we see, we feel it with all our soul. Such an occasion there was when the voice of Buddha reached distant shores across physical and moral impediments. Then our life and our world found their profound meaning of reality in their relation to the central person who offered us emancipation of love. Men, in order to make this great human experience ever memorable, determined to do the impossible; they made rocks to speak, stones to sing, caves to remember; their cry of joy and hope took immortal forms along the hills and deserts, across barren solitudes and populous cities. A gigantic creative endeavour built up its triumph in stupendous carvings, defying obstacles that were overwhelming. Such heroic activity over the greater part of the Eastern continents clearly answers the question: 'What is Art?' It is the response of man's creative soul to the call of the Real.

Once there came a time, centuries ago in Bengal, when the divine love drama that has made its eternal playground in human souls was vividly revealed by a personality radiating its intimate realization of God. The mind of a whole people was stirred by a vision of the world as an instrument, through which sounded out invitation to the meeting of bliss. The ineffable mystery of God's love-call, taking shape in an endless panorama of colours and forms, inspired activity in music that overflowed the restrictions of classical conventionalism. Our Kirtan music of Bengal came to its being like a star flung up by a burning whirlpool of emotion in the heart of a whole people, and their consciousness was aflame with a sense of reality that must be adequately acknowledged.

The question may be asked as to what place music occupies in my theory that art is for evoking in our mind the deep sense of reality in its richest aspect. Music is the most abstract of all the arts, as mathematics is in the region of science. In fact these two have a deep relationship with each other. Mathematics is the logic of numbers and dimensions. It is therefore employed as the basis of our scientific knowledge. When taken out of its concrete associations and reduced to symbols, it reveals its grand structural majesty, the inevitableness of its own perfect concord. Yet there is not merely a logic but also a magic of mathematics which works at the world of appearance, producing harmony—the cadence of inter-relationship. This rhythm of harmony has been extracted from its usual concrete context, and exhibited through the medium of sound. And thus the pure essence of expressiveness in existence is offered in music. Expressiveness finds the least resistance in sound, having freedom unencumbered by the burden of facts and thoughts. This gives it a power to arouse in us an intimate feeling of reality. In the pictorial, plastic and literary arts, the object and our feelings with regard to it are closely associated, like the rose and its perfumes. In music, the feeling distilled in sound, becoming itself an independent object. It assumes a tune-form which is definite, but a meaning which is undefinable, and yet which grips our mind with a sense of absolute truth.

It is the magic of mathematics, the rhythm which is in the heart of all creation, which moves in the atom and, in its different measures, fashions gold and lead, the rose and the thorn, the sun and the planets. There are the dance-steps of numbers in the arena of time and space, which weave the *maya*, the patterns of appearance, the incessant flow of change, that ever is and is not. It is the rhythm that churns up images from the vague and makes tangible what is elusive. This is *maya*, this is the art in creation, and art in literature, which is the magic of rhythm.

And must we stop here? What we know as intellectual truth, is that also not a rhythm of the relationship of facts, that weaves the pattern of theory, and produces a sense of convincingness to a person who somehow feels sure that he knows the truth? We believe any fact to be true because of a harmony, a rhythm in reason, the process of which is analysable by the logic of mathematics, but not its result in me, just as we can count the notes but cannot account for the music. The mystery is that I am convinced, and this also belongs to the *maya* of creation, whose one important, indispensable factor is this self-conscious personality that I represent.

And the Other? I believe it is also a self-conscious personality, which has its eternal harmony with mine.

Chapter X

Man's Nature

Form The Time when Man became truly conscious of his own self he also became conscious of a mysterious spirit of unity which found its manifestation through him in his society. It is a subtle medium of relationship between individuals, which is not for any utilitarian purpose but for its own ultimate truth, not a sum of arithmetic but a value of life. Somehow Man has felt that this comprehensive spirit of unity has a divine character which could claim the sacrifice of all that is individual in him, that in it dwells his highest meaning transcending his limited self, representing his best freedom.

Man's reverential loyalty to this spirit of unity is expressed in his religion; is symbolized in the names of his deities. That is why, in the beginning, his gods were tribal gods, even gods of the different communities belonging to the same tribe. With the extension of the consiousness of human unity his God became revealed to him as one and universal, proving that the truth of human unity is the truth of Man's God.

In the Sanskrit language, religion goes by the name *dharma*, which in the derivative meaning implies the principle of relationship that holds us firm, and in its technical sense means the virtue of a thing, the essential quality of it; for instance, heat is the essential quality of fire, though in certain of its stages it may be absent.

Religion consists in the endeavour of men to cultivate and express those qualities which are inherent in the nature of Man the Eternal, and to have faith in him. If these qualities were absolutely natural in individuals, religion could have no purpose. We begin our history with all the original promptings of our brute nature which helps us to fulfil those vital needs of ours that are immediate. But deeper within us there is a current of tendencies which runs in many ways in a contrary direction, the life current of universal humanity. Religion has its function in reconciling the contradiction, by subordinating the brute nature to what we consider as the truth of Man. This is helped when our faith in the Eternal Man, whom we call by different names and imagine in different images, is made strong. The contradiction between the two natures in us is so great that men have willingly sacrificed their vital needs and courted death in order to express their *dharma*, which represents the truth of the Supreme Man.

The vision of the Supreme Man is realized by our imagination, but not created by our mind. More real than individual men, he surpasses each of us in his permeating personality which is transcendental. The procession of his ideas, following his great purpose, is ever moving across obstructive facts towards the perfected truth. We, the individuals, having our place in his composition, may or may not be in conscious harmony with his purpose, may even put obstacles in his path bringing down our doom upon ourselves. But we gain our true religion when we consciously co-operate with him, finding our exceeding joy through suffering and sacrifice. For through our own love for him we are made conscious of a great love that radiates from his being, who is MahŒtma, the Supreme Spirit.

The great Chinese sage Lao-tze has said: 'One who may die, but will not perish, has life everlasting'. It means that he lives in the life of the immortal Man. The urging for this life induces men to go through the struggle for a true survival. And it has been said in our scripture: 'Through *adharma* (the negation of *dharma*) man prospers, gains what appears desirable, conquers enemies, but he perishes at the root.' In this saying it is suggested that there is a life which is truer for men than their physical life which is transient.

Our life gains what is called 'value' in those of its aspects which represent eternal humanity in knowledge, in sympathy, in deeds, in character and creative works. And from the beginning of our history we are seeking often at the cost of everything else, the value for our life and not merely success; in other words, we are trying to realize in ourselves the immortal Man, so that we may die but not perish. This is the meaning of the utterance in the Upanishad: *Tam vedyam purusham veda, yatha ma vo mrityuh parivyathah*—'Realize the Person so that thou mayst not suffer from death.'

The meaning of these words is highly paradoxical, and cannot be proved by our senses or our reason, and yet its influence is so strong in men that they have cast away all fear and greed, defied all the instincts that cling to the brute nature, for the sake of acknowledging and preserving a life which belongs to the Eternal Person. It is all the more significant because many of they do not believe in its reality, and yet are ready to fling away for it all that they believe to be final and the only positive fact.

Our physical body has its comprehensive reality in the physical world, which may be truly called our universal body, without which our individual body would miss its function. Our physical life realizes its growing meaning through a widening freedom in its relationship with the physical world, and this gives it a greater happiness than the mere pleasure of satisfied needs. We become aware of a profound meaning of our own self at the consciousness of some ideal of perfection some truth beautiful or majestic which gives us an inner sense of completeness, a heightened sense of our own reality. This strengthens man's faith, effective even if indefinite—his faith in an objective ideal of perfection comprehending the human world. His vision of it has been beautiful or distorted, luminous or obscure, according to the stages of development that his consciousness has attained. But whatever may be the name and nature of his religious creed, man's ideal of human perfection has been based upon a bond of unity running through individuals culminating in a supreme Being who represents the eternal in human personality. In his civilization the perfect expression of this idea produces the wealth of truth which is for the revelation of Man and not merely for the success of life. But when this creative ideal which is *dharma* gives place to some overmastering passion in a large body of men civilization bursts out in an explosive flame, like a star that has lighted its own funeral pyre of boisterous brilliancy.

When I was a child I had the freedom to make my own toys out of trifles and create my own games from imagination. In my happiness my playmates had their full share, in fact the complete enjoyment of my games depended upon their taking part in them. one day, in this paradise of our childhood, entered the temptation from the market world of the adult. A toy brought from an English shop was given to one of our companious; it was perfect, it was big and wonderfully life-like. He became proud of the toy and less mindful of the game; he kept that expensive thing carefully away from us, glorying in his exclusive possession of it, feeling himself superior to his playmates whose toys were cheap. I am sure if he could use the modern language of history he would say that he was more civilized than ourselves to the extent of his owning that ridiculously perfect toy.

One thing he failed to realize in his excitement—a fact which at the moment seemed to him insignificant—that this temptation obscured something a great deal more perfect than his toy, the revelation of the perfect child which ever dwells in the heart of man, in other words, the *dharma* of the child. The toy merely expressed his wealth but not himself, not the child's creative spirit, not the child's generous joy in his play, his identification of himself with others who were his compeers in his play world. Civilization is to express Man's *dharma* and not merely his cleverness, power and possession.

Once there was an occasion for me to motor down to Calcutta from a place a hundred miles away. Something wrong with the mechanism made it necessary for us to have a repeated supply of water almost ever half-hour. At the first village where we were compelled to stop, we asked the help of a man to find water for us. It proved quite a task for him, but when we offered him his reward, poor though he was, he refused to accept it. In fifteen other villages the same thing happened. In a hot country, where travellers constantly need water and where the water supply grows scanty in summer, the villagers consider it their duty to offer water to those who need it. They could easily make a business out of it. Following the inexorable law of demand and supply. But the ideal which they consider to be their *dharma* has become one with their life. They do not claim any personal merit for possessing it.

Lao-tze, speaking about the man who is truly good, says: 'He quickens but owns not. He acts but claims not. Merit he accomplishes but dwells not in it. Since he does not dwell in it, it will never leave him.' That which is outside ourselves we can sell; but that which is one with our being we cannot sell. This complete assimilation of truth belongs to the paradise of perfection; it lies beyond the purgatory of self-consciousness. To have reached it proves a long process of civilization.

To be able to take a considerable amount of trouble in order to supply water to a passing stranger and yet never to claim merit or reward for it seems absurdly and negligibly simple compared with the capacity to produce an amazing number of things per minute. A millionaire tourist, ready to corner the food market and grow rich by driving the whole world to the brink of starvation, is sure to feel too superior to notice this simple thing while rushing through our villages at sixty miles an hour.

Yes, it is simple, as simple as it is for a gentleman to be a gentleman; but that simplicity is the product of centuries of culture. That simplicity is difficult of imitation. In a few years' time, it might be possible for me to learn how to make holes in thousands of needles simultaneously by turning a wheel, but to be absolutely simple in one's hospitality to one's enemy, or to a stranger, requires generations of training. Simplicity takes no account of its own value, claims no wages, and therefore those who are enamoured of power do not realize that simplicity of spiritual expression is the highest product of civilization.

A process of disintegration can kill this rare fruit of a higher life, as a whole race of birds possessing some rare beauty can be made extinct by the vulgar power of avarice which has civilized weapons. This fact was clearly proved to me when I found that the only place where a price was expected for the water given to us was a suburb at Calcutta, where life was richer, the water supply easier and more abundant and where progress flowed in numerous channels in all directions. It shows that a harmony of character which the people once had was lost—the harmony with the inner self which is greater in its universality than the self that gives prominence to its personal needs. The latter loses its feeling of beauty and generosity in its calculation of profit; for there is represents exclusively itself and not the universal man.

There is an utterance in the Atharva Veda, wherein appears the question as to who it was that gave Man his music. Birds repeat their single notes, or a very simple combination of them, but Man builds his world of music and establishes ever new rhythmic relationship of notes. These reveal to him a universal mystery of creation which cannot be described. They bring to him the inner rhythm that transmutes facts into truths. They give him pleasure not merely for his sense of hearing, but for his deeper being, which gains satisfaction in the ideal of perfect unity. Somehow man feels that truth finds its body in such perfection; and when he seeks for his own best revelation he seeks a medium which has the harmonious unity, as has music. Our impulse to give expression to Universal Man produces arts and literature. They in their cadence of lines, colours, movements, words, thoughts, express vastly more than what they appear to be on the surface. They open the windows of our mind to the eternal reality of man. They are the superfluity of wealth of which we claim our common inheritance whatever may be the country and time to which we belong; for they are inspired by the universal mind. And not merely in his arts, but in his own behaviour, the individual must for his excellence give emphasis to an ideal which has some value of truth that ideally belongs to all men. In other words, he should create a music of expression in his conduct and surroundings which makes him represent the supreme Personality. And civilization is the creation of the race, its expression of the universal Man.

When I first visited Japan I had the opportunity of observing where the two parts of the human sphere strongly contrasted; one, on which grew up the ancient continents of social ideal, standards of beauty, codes of personal behaviour; and the other part, the fluid element, the perpetual current that carried wealth to its shores from all parts of the world. In half a century's time Japan has been able to make her own the mighty spirit of progress which suddenly burst upon her one morning in a storm of insult and menace. China also has had her rousing, when her self-respect was being knocked to pieces through series of helpless years, and I am sure she also will master before long the instrument which hurt her to the quick. But the ideals that imparted life and body to Japanese civilization had been nourished in the reverent hopes of countless generations through ages which were not primarily occupied in an incessant hunt for opportunities. They had those large tracts of leisure in them which are necessary for the blossoming of Life's beauty and the ripening of her wisdom.

On the one hand we can look upon the modern factories in Japan with their numerous mechanical organizations and engines of production and destruction of the latest type. On the other hand, against them we may see some fragile vase, some small piece of silk, some architecture of sublime simplicity, some perfect lyric of bodily movement. We may also notice the Japanese expression of courtesy daily extracting from them a considerable amount of time and trouble. All these have come not from any accurate knowledge of things but from an intense consciousness of the value of reality which takes time for its fullness. What Japan reveals in her skilful manipulation of telegraphic wires and railway lines, of machines for manufacturing things and for killing men, is more or less similar to what we see in other countries which have similar opportunity for training. But in her art of living, her pictures, her code of conduct, the various forms of beauty which her religious and social ideals assume Japan expresses her own personality, her *dharma*, which, in order to be of any worth, must be unique and at the same time represent Man of the Everlasting Life.

Lao-tze has said: 'Not knowing the eternal causes passions to rise; and that is evil'. He has also said: 'Let us die, and yet not perish'. For we die when we lose our physical life, we perish when we miss our humanity. And humanity is the *dharma* of human beings.

What is evident in this world is the endless procession of moving things; but what is to be realized, is the supreme human Truth by which the human world is permeated.

We must never forget today that a mere movement is not valuable in itself, that it may be a sign of a dangerous form of inertia. We must be reminded that a great upheaval of spirit, a universal realization of true dignity of man once caused by Buddha's teachings in India, started a movement for centuries which produced illumination of literature, art, science and numerous efforts of public beneficence. This was a movement whose motive force was not some additional accession of knowledge or power or urging of some overwhelming passion. It was an inspiration for freedom, the freedom which enables us to realize *dharma*, the truth of Eternal Man.

Lao-tze in one of his utterances has said: 'Those who have virtue (*dharma*) attend to their obligations; those who have no virtue attend to their claims.' Progress which is not related to an inner *dharma*, but to an attraction which is external, seeks to satisfy our endless claims. But civilization, which is an ideal, gives us the abundant power to renounce which is the power that realizes the infinite and inspires creation.

This great Chinese sage has said: 'To increase life is called a blessing.' For, the increase of life realizes the eternal life and yet does not transcend the limits of life's unity. The mountain pine grows tall and great, its every inch maintains the rhythm of an inner balance, and therefore even in its seeming extravagance it has the reticent grace of self-control. The tree and its productions belong to the same vital system of cadence; the timber, the flowers, leaves and fruits are one with the tree; their exuberance is not a malady of exaggeration, but a blessing.

Chapter XI

The Meeting

O ur great prophets in all ages did truly realize in themselves the freedom of the soul in their consciousness of the spiritual kinship of man which is universal. And yet human races, owing to their external geographical condition, developed in their individual isolation a mentality that is obnoxiously selfish. In their instinctive search for truth in religion either they dwarfed and deformed it in the mould of the primitive distortions of their own race-mind, or else they shut their God within temple walls and scriptural texts safely away, especially from those departments of life where his absence gives easy access to devil-worship in various names and forms. They treated their god in the same way as in some forms of government the King is treated, who has traditional honour but no effective authority. The true meaning of God has remained vague in our minds only because our consciousness of the spiritual unity has been thwarted.

One of the potent reasons for this—our geographical separation—has now been nearly removed. Therefore the time has come when we must, for the sake of truth and for the sake of that peace which is the harvest of truth, refuse to allow the idea of our God to remain indistinct behind unrealities of formal rites and theological mistiness.

The creature that lives its life screened and sheltered in a dark cave, finds its safety in the very narrowness of its own environment. The economical providence of Nature curtails and tones down its sensibilities to such a limited necessity. But if these cave-walls were to become suddenly removed by some catastrophe, then either it must accept the doom of extinction, or carry on satisfactory negotiations with its wider surroundings.

The races of mankind will never again be able to go back to their citadels of high-walled exclusiveness. They are today exposed to one another, physically and intellectually. The shells, which have so long given them full security within their individual enclosures have been broken, and by no artificial process can they be mended again. So we have to accept this fact, even though we have not yet fully adapted our minds to this changed environment of publicity, even though through it we may have to run all the risks entailed by the wider expansion of life's freedom.

A large part of our tradition is our code of adjustment which deals with the circumstances special to ourselves. These traditions, no doubt, variegate the several racial personalities with their distinctive colours—colours which have their poetry and also certain protective qualities suitable to each different environment. We may come to acquire a strong love for our own colourful race speciality; but if that gives us fitness only for a very narrow world, then, at the slightest variation in our outward circumstances, we may have to pay for this love with our life itself.

In the animal world there are numerous instances of complete race-suicide overtaking those who fondly clung to some advantage which later on became a hindrance in an altered dispensation. In fact the superiority of man is proved by his adaptability to extreme surprised of chance—neither the torrid nor the frigid zone of his destiny offering him insuperable obstacles.

The vastness of the race problem with which we are faced to day will either compel us to train ourselves to moral fitness in the place of merely external efficiency, or the complications arising out of it will fetter all our movements and drag us to our death.[1]

When our necessity becomes urgently insistent, when the resources that have sustained us so long are exhausted, then our spirit puts forth all its force to discover some other source of sustenance deeper and more permanent. This leads us from the exterior to the interior of our store-house. When muscle does not fully serve us, we come to awaken intellect to ask for its help and are then surprised to find in it a greater source of strength for us than physical power. When, in their turn, our intellectual gifts grow perverse, and only help to render our suicide gorgeous and exhaustive, our soul must seek an alliance with some power which is still deeper, yet further removed from the rude stupidity of muscle.

It is well known that when greed has for its object material gain then it can have no end. It is like the chasing of the horizon by a lunatic. To go on in a competition multiplying millions becomes a steeplechase of insensate futility that has obstacles but no goal. It has for its parallel the fight with material weapons—weapons which must perpetually be multiplied, opening us new vistas of destruction and evoking new forms of insanity in the forging of frightfulness. Thus seems now to have commenced the last fatal adventure of drunken Passion riding on an intellect of prodigious power.

Today, more than ever before in our history, the aid of spiritual power is needed. Therefore, I believe its resources will surely be discovered in the hidden depths of our being. Pioneers will come to take up this adventure and suffer, and

1. See Appendix III.

through suffering open out a path to that higher elevation of life in which lies our safety.

Let me, in reference to this, give an instance from the history of Ancient India. There was a noble period in the early days of India when, to a band of dreamers, agriculture appeared as a great idea and not merely useful fact. The heroic personality of Ramachandra, who espoused its cause, was sung in popular ballads, which in a later age forgot their original message and were crystallized into an epic merely extolling some domestic virtues of its hero. It is quite evident, however, from the legendary relics lying entombed in the story, that a new age ushered in by the spread of agriculture came as a divine voice to those who could hear. It lifted up the primeval screen of the wilderness, brought the distant near, and broke down all barricades. Men who had formed separate and antagonistic groups in their sheltered seclusions were called upon to form a united people.

In the Vedic verses, we find constant mention of conflicts between the original inhabitants of Ancient India and the colonists. There we find the expression of a spirit that was one of mutual distrust and a struggle in which was sought either wholesale slavery or extermination for the opponents carried on in the manner of animals who live in the narrow segregation imposed upon them by their limited imagination and imperfect sympathy. This spirit would have continued in all its ferocious vigour of savagery had men failed to find the opportunity for the discovery that man's highest truth was in the union of co-operation and love.

The progress of agriculture was the first external step which led to such a discovery. It not only made a settled life possible for a large number of men living in close proximity, but it claimed for its very purpose a life of peaceful co-operation. The mere fact of such a sudden change from a nomadic to an agricultural condition would not have benefited

Man if he had not developed therewith his spiritual condition would not have benefited Man if he had not developed therewith his spiritual sensitiveness to an inner principle of truth. We can realize, from our reading of the Ramayana, the birth of idealism among a section of the Indian colonists of those days, before whose mind's eye was opened a vision of emancipation rich with the responsibility of a higher life. The epic represents in its ideal the change of the people's aspiration from the path of conquest to that of reconciliation.

At the present time, as I have said, the human world has been overtaken by another vast change similar to that which had occurred in the epic age of India. So long men had been cultivating, almost with a religious fervour, that mentality which is the product of racial isolation; poets proclaimed, in a loud pitch of bragging, the exploits of their popular fighters; money-makers felt neither pity nor shame in the unscrupulous dexterity of their pocket-picking; diplomats scattered lies in order to reap concessions from the devastated future of their own victims. Suddenly the walls that separated the different races are seen to have given way, and we find ourselves standing face to face.

This is a great fact of epic significance. Man, suckled at the wolf's breast, sheltered in the brute's den, brought up in the prowling habit of depredation, suddenly discovers that he is Man, and that his true power lies in yielding up his brute power for the freedom of spirit.

The God of humanity has arrived at the gates of the ruined temple of the tribe. Though he has not yet found his altar, I ask the men of simple faith, wherever they may be in the world, to bring their offering of sacrifice to him, and to believe that it is far better to be wise and worshipful than to be clever and supercilious. I ask them to claim the right of manhood to be friends of men, and not the right of a particular proud race or nation which may boast of the fatal quality of being the rulers of men. We should know for certain that such rulers will no longer be tolerated in the new world, as it basks in the open sunlight of mind and breathes life's free air.

In the geological ages of the infant earth the demons of physical force had their full sway. The angry fire, the devouring flood, the fury of the storm, continually kicked the earth into frightful distortions. These titans have at last given way to the reign of life. Had there been spectators in those days who were clever and practical they would have wagered their last penny on these titans and would have waxed hilariously witty at the expense of the helpless living speck taking its stand in the arena of the wrestling giants. Only a dreamer could have then declared with unwavering conviction that those titans were doomed because of their very exaggeration, as are, today, those formidable qualities which, in the parlance of schoolboy science, are termed Nordic.

I ask once again, let us, the dreamers of the East and the West, keep our faith firm in the Life that creates and not in the Machine that constructs—in the power that hides its force and blossoms in beauty, and not in the power that bares its arms and chuckles at its capacity to make itself obnoxious. Let us know that the Machine is good when it helps, but not so when it exploits life; that Science is great when it destroys evil, but not when the two enter into unholy alliance.

Chapter XII

The Teacher

I have already described how the nebulous idea of the divine
essence condensed in my consciousness into a human
realization. It is definite and finite at the same time, the
Eternal Person manifested in all persons. It may be one of the
numerous manifestations of God, the one in which is
comprehended Man and his Universe. But we can never know
or imagine him as revealed in any other inconceivable universe
so long as we remain human beings. And therefore, whatever
character our theology may ascribe to him, in reality he is
the infinite ideal of Man towards who men move in their
collective growth, with whom they seek their union of love
as individuals, in whom they find their ideal of father, friend
and beloved.

I am sure that it was this idea of the divine Humanity
unconsciously working in my mind, which compelled me to
come out of the seclusion of my literary career and take my
part in the world of practical activities. The solitary enjoyment
of the infinite in meditation no longer satisfied me, and the
texts which I used for my silent worship lost their inspiration
without my knowing it. I am sure I vaguely felt that my need
was spiritual self-realization in the life of Man through some
disinterested service. This was the time when I founded an

educational institution for our children in Bengal. It has a special character of its own which is still struggling to find its fulfilment; for it is a living temple that I have attempted to build for my divinity. In such a place education necessarily becomes the preparation for a complete life of man which can only become possible by living that life, through knowledge and service, enjoyment and creative work. The necessity was my own, for I felt impelled to come back into a fulness of truth from my exile in a dream-world.

This brings to my mind the name of another poet of ancient India, Kalidasa, whose poem of Meghaduta reverberates with the music of the sorrow of an exile.

It was not the physical home-sickness from which the poet suffered, it was something far more fundamental, the home-sickness of the soul. We feel from almost all his works the oppressive atmosphere of the kings' palaces of those days, dense with things of luxury, and also with the callousness of self-indulgence, albeit an atmosphere of refined culture based on an extravagant civilization.

The poet in the royal court lived in banishment— banishment from the immediate presence of the eternal. He knew it was not merely his own banishment, but that of the whole age to which he has born, the age that had gathered its wealth and missed its well-being, built its storehouse of things and lost its background of the great universe. What was the form in which his desire for perfection persistently appeared in his drama and poems? It was the form of the *tapovana*, the forest-dwelling of the patriarchal community of ancient India. Those who are familiar with Sanskrit literature will know that this was not a colony of people with a primitive culture and mind. They were seekers after truth, for the sake of which they lived in an atmosphere of purity but not of Puritanism, of the simple life but not the life of self-mortification. They never advocated celibacy and they had constant intercommunication with other people who lived the life of worldly interest. Their aim and endeavour have briefly been suggested in the Upanishad in these lines:

Tesarvagam sarvatah prapya dhira
yuktatmanah sarvamevavisanti.

Those men of serene mind enter into the All, having realized and being in union everywhere with the omnipresent Spirit.

It was never a philosophy of renunciation of a negative character, but a realization completely comprehensive. How the tortured mind of Kalidasa in the prosperous city of Ujjaini, and the glorious period of Vikramaditya, closely pressed by all-obstructing things and all-devouring self, let his thoughts hover round the vision of a *tapovana* for his inspiration of life!

It was not a deliberate copy but a natural coincidence that a poet of modern India also had the similar vision when he felt within him the misery of a spiritual banishment. In the time of Kalidasa the people vividly believed in the ideal of *tapovana*, the forest colony, and there can be no doubt that even in the late age there were communities of men living in the heart of nature, not ascetics fiercely in love with a lingering suicide, but men of serene sanity who sought to realize the spiritual meaning of their life. And, therefore, when Kalidasa sang of the *tapovana*, his poems found their immediate communion in the living faith of his hearers. But today the idea has lost any definite outline of reality, and has retreated into the far away phantom-land of legend. Therefore the Sanskrit word in a modern poem would merely be poetical, its meaning judged by a literary standard of appraisement. Then, again, the spirit of the forest-dwelling in the purity of its original shape would be a fantastic anachronism in the present age, and therefore, in order to be real, it must find its reincarnation under modern conditions of life. It must be the same in truth, but not identical in fact. It was this which made the modern poet's heart crave to compose his poem in a language of tangible words.

But I must give the history in some detail. Civilized man has come far away from the orbit of his normal life. He has gradually formed and intensified some habits that are like those of the bees for adapting himself to his hive-world. We often see men suffering from ennui, from world-weariness, from a spirit of rebellion against their environment for no reasonable cause whatever. Social revolutions are constantly ushered in with a suicidal violence that has its origin in our dissatisfaction with our hive-wall arrangement—the too exclusive enclosure that deprives us of the perspective which is so much needed to give us the proper proportion in our art of living. All this is an indication that man has not been moulded on the model of the bee and therefore he becomes recklessly anti-social when his freedom to be more than social is ignored.

In our highly complex modern condition mechanical forces are organized with such efficiency that materials are produced that grow far in advance of man's selective and assimilative capacity to simplify them into harmony with his nature and needs.

Such an intemperate overgrowth of things, like rank vegetation in the tropics, creates confinement for man. The nest is simple, it has an early relationship with the sky; the cage is complex and costly; it is too much itself excommunicated from whatever lies outside. And man is building his cage, fast developing his parasitism on the monster Thing, which he allows to envelop him on all sides. He is always occupied in adapting himself to its dead angularities, limits himself to its limitations, and merely becomes a part of it.

This may seem contrary to the doctrine of those who believe that a constant high pressure of living, produced by an artificially cultivated hunger of things, generates and feeds the energy that drives civilization upon its endless journey. Personally, I do not believe that this had ever been the principal driving force that had led to eminence any great civilization of which we know in history.

I was born in what was once the metropolis of British India. My own ancestors came floating to Calcutta upon the earliest tide of the fluctuating fortune of the East India Company. The unconvential code of life for our family has been a confluence of three cultures, the Hindu, Mohammedan and British. My grandfather belonged to that period when the amplitude of dress and courtesy and a generous leisure were gradually being clipped and curtailed into Victorian manners, economical in time, in ceremonies, and in the dignity of personal appearance. This will show that I came to a world in which the modern citybred spirit of progress had just begun driving its triumphal car over the luscious green life of our ancient village community. Though the trampling process was almost complete round me, yet the wailing cry of the past was still lingering over the wreckage.

Often I had listened to my eldest brother describing with the poignancy of a hopeless regret a society hospitable, sweet with the old-world aroma of natural kindliness, full of simple faith and the ceremonial-poetry of life. But all this was a vanishing shadow behind me in the dusky golden haze of a twilight horizon—the all-pervading fact around my boyhood being the modern city newly built by a company of western traders and the spirit of the modern time seeking its unaccustomed entrance into our life, stumbling against countless anomalies.

But it always is a surprise to me to think that through this closed-up hardness of a city was my only experience of the world, yet my mind was constantly haunted by the home-sick fancies of an exile. It seems that the sub-conscious remembrance of a primeval dwelling-place, where, in our ancestor's minds, were figured and voiced the mysteries of the inarticulate rocks, the rushing water and the dark whispers of the forest, was constantly stirring my blood with its call. Some shadow-haunting living reminiscence in me seemed to ache for the pre-natal cradle and playground it shared with the primal life in the illimitable magic of the land, water and air. The shrill, thin cry of the high-flying kite in the blazing sun of the dazed Indian midday sent to a solitary boy the signal of a dumb distant kinship. The few coconut plants growing by the boundary wall of our house, like some war captives from an older army of invaders of this earth, spoke to me of the eternal companionship which the great brotherhood of trees has even offered to man.

Looking back upon those moments of my boyhood days, when all my mind seemed to float poised upon a large feeling of the sky, of the light, and to tingle with the brown earth in its glistening grass, I cannot help believing that my Indian ancestry had left deep in my being the legacy of its philosophy—the philosophy which speaks of fulfilment through our harmony with all things. The founding of my school had its origin in the memory of that longing for the freedom of consciousness, which seems to go back beyond the skyline of my birth.

Freedom in the mere sense of independence has no content, and therefore no meaning. Perfect freedom lies in a perfect harmony of relationship, which we realize in this world not through our response to it in knowing, but in being. Objects of knowledge maintain an infinite distance from us who are the knowers. For knowledge is not union. Therefore the further world of freedom awaits us there where we reach truth, not through feeling it by our senses or knowing it by our reason, but through the union of perfect sympathy.

Children with the freshness of their senses come directly to the intimacy of this world. This is the first great gift they have. They must accept it naked and simple and must never again lose their power of immediate communication with it. For our perfection we have to be vitally savage and mentally civilized; we should have the gift to be natural with nature and human with human society. My banished soul sitting in the civilized isolation of the town-life cried within me for the enlargement of the horizon of its comprehension. I was like the torn-away line of a verse, always in a state of suspense, while the other line, with which it rhymed and which could give it fulness, was smudged by the mist away in some undecipherable distance. The inexpensive power to be happy which, along with other children, I brought to this world, was being constantly worn away by friction with the brick-and-mortar arrangement of life, by monotonously mechanical habits and the customary code of respectability.

In the usual course of things I was sent to school, but possibly my suffering was unusually greater than that of most other children. The non-civilized in me was sensitive; it had the great thirst for colour, for music, for movement of life. Our city-built education took no heed of that living fact. It had its luggage-van waiting for branded bales of marketable result. The relative proportion of the non-civilized to the civilized in man should be in the proportion of the water and the land in our globe, the former predominating. But the school had for its object a continual reclamation of he civilized. Such a drain in the fluid element causes an aridity which may not be considered deplorable under city conditions. But my nature never got accustomed to those conditions, to the callous decency of the pavement. The non-civilized triumphed in me only too soon and drove me away from school when I had just entered my teens. I found myself stranded on a solitary island of ignorance, and had to rely solely upon my own instincts to build up my education from the very beginning.

This reminds me that when I was young I had the great good fortune of coming upon a Bengali translation of *Robinson Crusoe*. I still believe that it is the best book for boys that has ever been written. There was a longing in me when young to run away from my own self and be one with everything in Nature. This mood appears to be particularly Indian, the outcome of a traditional desire for the expansion of consciousness. One has to admit that such a desire to too subjective in its character; but this inevitable in the geographical circumstances which we have to endure. We live under the extortionate tyranny of the tropics, paying heavy toll every moment for the barest right of existence. The heat, the damp, the unspeakable fecundity of minute life feeding upon big life, the perpetual sources of irritation, visible and invisible, leave very little margin of capital for extravagant experiments. Excess of energy seeks obstacles for its self-realization. That is why we find so often in Western literature a constant emphasis upon the malignant aspect of Nature, in whom the people of the West seem to be delighted to discover an enemy for the sheer enjoyment of challenging her to fight. The reason which made Alexander express his desire to find other worlds to conquer, when his conquest of he world was completed, makes the enormously vital people of the West desire, when they have some respite in their sublime mission of fighting against objects that are noxious, to go out of their way to spread their coat-tails in other people's thoroughfares and to claim indemnity when these are trodden upon. In order to make the thrilling risk of hurting themselves they are ready to welcome endless trouble to hurt others who are inoffensive, such as the beautiful birds which happen to know how to fly away, the timid beasts, which have the advantage of inhabiting inaccessible regions, and—but I avoid the discourtesy of mentioning higher races in this connection.

Life's fulfilment finds constant contradictions in its path; but those are necessary for the sake of its advance. The stream is saved from the sluggishness of its current by the perpetual opposition of the soil through which it must cut its way. It is this soil which forms its banks. The spirit of fight belongs to the genius of life. The tuning of an instrument has to be done, not because it reveals a proficient perseverance in the face of difficulty, but because it helps music to be perfectly realized. Let us rejoice that in the West life's instrument is being tuned in all its different chords owning to the great fact that the West has triumphant pleasure in the struggle with obstacles. The spirit of creation in the heart of the universe will never allow, for its own sake, obstacles to be completely removed. It is only because positive truth lies in that ideal of perfection, which has to be won by our own endeavour in order to make it our own, that the spirit of fight is great. But this does not imply a premium for the exhibition of a muscular athleticism or a rude barbarism of ravenous rapacity.

In *Robinson Crusoe*, the delight of the union with Nature finds its expression in a story of adventure in which the solitary Man is face to face with solitary Nature, coaxing her, co-operating with her, exploring her secrets, using all his faculties to win her help.

This is the heroic love-adventure of the West, the active wooing of the earth. I remember how, once in my youth, the feeling of intense delight and wonder followed me in my railway journey across Europe from Brindisi to Calais, when I realized the chaste beauty of this continent everywhere blossoming in a glow of health and richness under the age-long attention of her chivalrous lover, Western humanity. He had gained her, made her his own, unlocked the inexhaustible generosity of her heart. And I had intently wished that the introspective vision of the universal soul, which an Eastern devotee realizes in the solitude of his mind, could be united with this spirit of its outward expression in service, the exercise of will in unfolding the wealth of beauty and well-being from its shy obscurity to the light.

I remember the morning when a beggar woman in a Bengal village gathered in the loose end of her *sari* the stale flowers that were about to be thrown away from the vase on my table; and with an ecstatic expression of tenderness buried her face in them, exclaiming., 'Oh, beloved of my Heart!' her eyes could easily pierce the veil of the outward form and reach the realm of the infinite in these flowers, where she found the intimate touch of her Beloved, the great, the universal Human. But in spite of it all she lacked that energy of worship, that Western form of direct divine service, the service of man, which helps the earth to bring out her flowers and spread the reign of beauty on the desolate dust. I refuse to think that the twin spirits of the East and the West, the Mary and Martha, can never meet to make perfect the realization of truth. And in spite of our material poverty in the east and the antagonism of time I wait patiently for this meeting.

Robinson Crusoe's island comes to my mind when I think of some institution where the first great lesson in the perfect union of Man and Nature, not only through love, but through active communication and intelligent ways, can be had unobstructed. We have to keep in mind the fact that love and action are the only intermediaries through which perfect knowledge can be obtained; for the object of knowledge is not pedantry but wisdom. The primary object of an institution should not be merely to educate one's limbs and mind to be in efficient readiness for all emergencies, but to be in perfect tune in the symphony of response between life and world, to find the balance of their harmony which is wisdom. The first important lesson for children in such a place would be that of improvization, the constant imposition of the ready-made having been banished from here. It is to give occasions to explore one's capacity through surprises of achievement. I must make it plain that this means a lesson not in simple life, but in creative life. For life may grow complex, and yet if there is a living personality in its centre, it will still have the unity of creation; it will carry its own weight in perfect grace, and will not be a mere addition to the number of facts that only goes to swell a crowd.

I wish I could say that I had fully realized my dream in my school. I have only made the first introduction towards it and have given an opportunity to the children to find their freedom in Nature by being able to love it. For love is freedom; it gives us that fulness of existence which saves us from paying with our soul for objects that are immensely cheap. Love lights up this world with its meaning and makes life feel that it has that 'enough' everywhere which truly is its 'feast'. I know men who preach the cult of simple life by glorifying the spiritual merit of poverty. I refuse to imagine any special value in poverty when it is a mere negation. Only when the mind has the sensitiveness to be able to respond to the deeper all of reality is it naturally weaned away from the lure of the fictitious value of things. It is callousness which robs us of our simple power to enjoy, and dooms us to the indignity of a snobbish pride in furniture and the foolish burden of expensive things. But the callousness of asceticism pitted against the callousness of luxury is merely fighting one evil with the help of another, inviting the pitiless demon of the desert in place of the indiscriminate demon of the jungle.

I tried my best to develop in the children of my school the freshness of their feeling for Nature, a sensitiveness of soul in their relationship with their human surroundings, with the help of literature, festive ceremonials and also the religious teaching which enjoins us to come to the nearer presence of the world through the soul, thus to gain it more than can be measured—like gaining an instrument in truth by bringing out its music.

Chapter XIII

Spiritual Freedom

There are injuries that attack our life; they hurt the harmony of life's functions through which is maintained the harmony of our physical self with the physical world; and these injuries are called diseases. There are also factors that oppress our intelligence. They injure the harmony of relationship between our rational mind and the universe of reason; and we call them stupidity, ignorance of insanity. They are uncontrolled exaggerations of passions that upset all balance in our personality. They obscure the harmony between the spirit of the individual man and the spirit of the universal Man; and we give them the name sin. In all these instances our realization of the universal Man, in his physical, rational and spiritual aspects, is obstructed, and our true freedom in the realms of matter, mind and spirit is made narrow or distorted.

All the higher religions of India speak of the training for *Mukti*, the liberation of the soul. In this self of ours we are conscious of individuality, and all its activities are engaged in the expression and enjoyment of our finite and individual nature. In our soul we are conscious of the transcendental truth in us, the Universal, the Supreme Man; and this soul, the spiritual self, has its enjoyment in the renunciation of the individual self for the sake of the supreme soul. This renunciation is not in the negation of self, but in the dedication of it. The desire for it comes from an instinct which very often knows its own meaning vaguely and gropes for a name that would define its purpose. This purpose is in the realization of its unity with some objective ideal of perfections, some harmony of relationship between the individual and the infinite man. It is of this harmony, and not of a barren isolation that the Upanishad speaks, when it says that truth no longer remains hidden in him who finds himself in the All.

Once when I was on a visit to a remote Bengali village, mostly inhabited by Mahomedan cultivators, the villagers entertained me with an operatic performance the literature of which belonged to an obsolete religious sect that had wide influence centuries ago. Though the religion itself is dead, its voice still continues preaching its philosophy to a people, who, in spite of their different culture, are not tired of listening. It discussed according to its own doctrine the different elements, material and transcendental, that constitute human personality, comprehending the body, the self and the soul. Then came a dialogue, during the course of which was related the incident of a person who wanted to make a journey to Brindaban, the Garden of Bliss, but was prevented by a watchman who startled him with an accusation of theft. The thieving was proved when it was shown that inside his clothes he was secretly trying to smuggle into the garden the self, which only finds its fulfilment by its surrender. The culprit was caught with the incriminating bundle in his possession which barred for him his passage to the supreme goal. Under a tattered canopy, supported on bamboo poles and lighted by a few smoking kerosene lamps, the village crowd, occasionally interrupted by howls of jackals in the neighbouring paddy fields, attended with untired interest, till the small hours of the morning, the performance of a drama the discussed the

ultimate meaning of all thing in a seemingly incongruous
setting of dance, music and humorous dialogue.

This illustration will show how naturally, in India, poetry
and philosophy have walked hand in hand, only because the
latter has claimed its right to guide men to the practical path
of their life's fulfilment. What is that fulfilment? It is our
freedom in truth, which has for its prayer:

Lead us from the unreal to reality.
For *satyam* is *anandam*, the Real is Joy.

In the world of art, our consciousness being freed from
the tangle of self interest, we gain an unobstructed vision of
unity, the incarnation of the real, which is a joy for ever.

As in the world of art, so in the spiritual world, our soul
waits for its freedom from the ego to reach that disinterested
joy which is the source and goal of creation. It cries for its
mukti, its freedom in the unity of truth. The idea of *mukti*
has affected our lives in India, touched the springs of pure
emotions and supplications; for its soars heavenward on the
wings of poesy. We constantly hear men of scanty learning
and simple faith singing in their prayer to Tara, the Goddess
Redeemer:

'For what sin should I be compelled to remain in this
dungeon of the world of appearance?'

They are afraid of being alienated from the world of truth,
afraid of perpetual drifting amidst the froth and foam of
things, of being tossed about by the tidal waves of pleasure
and pain and never reaching the ultimate meaning of life. Of
these men, one may be a carter driving his cart to market,
another a fisherman playing his net. They may not be prompt
with an intelligent answer if they are questioned about the
deeper import of the song they sing, but they have no doubt
in their mind, that the abiding cause of all misery is not so
much in the lack of life's furniture as in the obscurity of life's

significance. It is a common topic with such to decry an undue emphasis upon 'me' and 'mine', which falsifies the perspective the truth. For have they not often seen men, who are not above their own level in social position or intellectual acquirement, going out to seek truth, leaving everything that they have behind them?

They know that the object of these adventurers is not betterment in worldly wealth and power—it is *mukti*, freedom. Thy possibly know some poor fellow villager of their own craft, who remains in the world carrying on his daily vocation and yet has the reputation of being emancipated in the heart of the Eternal. I myself have come across a fisherman singing with an inward absorption of mind, while fishing all day in the Ganges, who was pointed out to me by my boatman, with awe, as a man of liberated spirit. He is out of reach of the conventional prices that are set upon men by society, and which classify them like toys arranged in the shop-windows according to the market standard of value.

When the figure of this fisherman comes to my mind, I cannot but think that their number is not small who with their lives sing to epic of the unfettered soul, but will never be known in history. These unsophisticated Indian peasants know that an Emperor is merely a decorated slave, remaining chained to his Empire, that a millionaire is kept pilloried by his fate in the golden cage of his wealth, while this fisherman is free in the realm of light. When, groping in the dark, we stumble against objects, we cling to them believing them to be our only hope. When light comes, we slacken our hold, finding them to be mere parts of the All to which we are related. The simple man of the village knows what freedom is—freedom from the isolation of self, from the isolation of things, which imparts a fierce intensity to our sense of possession. He knows that this freedom is not the mere negation of bondage, in the bareness of our belongings, but in some positive realization which gives pure joy to our being, and he sings: 'To him who sinks into the deep, nothing remains unattained.' He says again:

> Let my two minds meet and combine,
> And lead me to the city Wonderful.

When that one mind of ours which wanders in search of things in the outer region of the varied, and the other which seeks the inward vision of unity, are no longer in conflict, they help us to realize the *ajab*, the *anirvachaniya*, the ineffable. The poet saint Kabir has also the same message when he sings:

> By saying that Supreme Reality only dwells in the inner realm of spirit, we shame the outer world of matter; and also when we say that he is only in the outside, we do not speak the truth.

According to these singers, truth is in unity, and therefore freedom is in its realization. The texts of our daily worship and meditation are for training our mind to overcome the barrier of separateness from the rest of existence and to realize *advaitam*, the Supreme Unity which is *anantam*, infinitude. It is philosophical wisdom, having its universal radiation in the popular mind in India, that inspires our prayer, our daily spiritual practices. It has its constant urging for us to go beyond the world of appearances, in which facts as facts are alien to us, like the mere sounds of foreign music; it speaks to us of an emancipation in the inner truth of all things, where the endless *Many* reveal the *One*.

Freedom in the material world has also the same meaning expressed in its own language. When nature's phenomena appeared to us as irrelevant, as heterogeneous manifestations of an obscure and irrational caprice, we lived in an alien world never dreaming of our *swaraj* within its territory. Through the discovery of the harmony of its working with that of our reason, we realize our unity with it, and therefore our freedom.

Those who have been brought up in a misunderstanding of this world's process, not knowing that it is one with themselves through the relationship of knowledge and intelligence, are trained as cowards by a hopeless faith in the ordinance of a destiny darkly dealing its blows. They submit without struggle when human rights are denied them, being accustomed to imagine themselves born as outlaws in a world constantly thrusting upon them incomprehensible surprises of accidents.

Also in the social or political field, the lack of freedom is based upon the spirit of alienation, on the imperfect realization of the One. There our bondage is in the tortured link of union. One may imagine that an individual who succeeds in dissociating himself from his fellow attains real freedom, inasmuch as all ties of relationship imply obligation to others. But we know that, thought it may sound paradoxical, it is true that in the human world only a perfect arrangement of interdependence gives rise to freedom. The most individualistic of human beings who own no responsibility are the savages who fail to attain their fulness of manifestation. They live immersed in obscurity, like an ill-lighted fire that cannot liberate itself from its envelope of smoke. Only those may attain their freedom from the segregation of an eclipsed life who have the power to cultivate mutual understanding and co-operation. The history of the growth of freedom is the history of the perfection of human relationship.

It has become possible for men to say that existence is evil, only because in our blindness we have missed something wherein our existence has its truth. If a bird tries to soar with only one of its wings, it is offended with the wind for buffeting it down to the dust. All broken truths are evil. They hurt because they suggest something they do not offer. Death does not hurt us, but disease does, because disease constantly reminds us of health and yet withholds it from us. And life in a halfworld is evil because it feigns finality when it is obviously incomplete, giving us the cup but not the draught of life. All tragedies result from truth remaining a fragment, its cycle not being completed. That cycle finds its end when the individual realize the universal and thus reaches freedom.

But because this freedom is in truth itself and not in an appearance of it, no hurried path of success, forcibly cut out by the greed of result, can be a true path. And an obscure village poet, unknown to the world of recognized respectability, sings:

> O cruel man of urgent need, must you scorch with fire the mind which still is a bud? You will burst it into bits, destroy its perfume in your impatience. Do you not see that my Lord, the Supreme Teacher, takes ages to perfect the flower and never is in a fury of haste? But because of your terrible greed, you only rely on force, and what hope is there for you, O man of urgent need? 'Prithi', says Madan the poet, 'Hurt not the mind of my Teacher. Know that only he who follows the simple current and loses himself, can hear the voice, O man of urgent need.'

This poet knows that there is no external means of taking freedom by the throat. It is the inward process of losing ourselves that leads to it. Bondage in all its forms has its stronghold in the inner self and not in the outside world; it is in the dimming of our consciousness, in the narrowing of our perspective, in the wrong valuation of things.

Let me conclude this chapter with a song of the Baül sect in Bengal, over a century old, in which the poet sings of the eternal bond of union between the infinite and the finite soul, from which there can be no *mukti*, because love is ultimate, because it is an inter-relation which makes truth complete, because absolute independence is the blankness of utter servility. The song runs thus:

> It goes on blossoming for ages, the soul-lotus, in which I am bound, as well as thou, without escape. There is no end to the opening of its petals, and the honey in it has so much sweetness that thou, like an enchanted bee, canst never desert it, and therefore thou art bound, and I am, and *mukti* is nowhere.

Chapter XIV

The Four Stages of Life

I have expressly said that I have concentrated my attention upon the subject of religion which is solely related to man, helping him to train his attitude and behaviour towards the infinite in its human aspect. At the same time it should be understood that the tendency of the Indian mind has ever been towards that transcendentalism which does not hold religion to be ultimate but rather to be a means to a further end. This end consists in the perfect liberation of the individual in the universal spirit across the furthest limits of humanity itself.

Such an extreme form of mysticism may be explained to my Western readers by its analogy in science. For science my truly be described as mysticism in the realm of material knowledge. It helps us to go beyond appearances and reach the inner reality of things in principles which are abstractions; it emancipates our mind from the thraldom of the senses to the freedom of reason.

The commonsense view of the world that is apparent to us has its vital importance for ourselves. For all our practical purposes the earth *is* flat, the sun *does* set behind the western horizon and whatever may be the verdict of the great mathematician about the lack of consistency in time's dealings we should fully trust it in setting our watches right. In questions relating to the arts and our ordinary daily avocations we must treat material objects as they seem to be and not as they are in essence. But the revelations, of science even when they go far beyond man's power of direct perception give him the purest feeling of disinterested delight and a supersensual background to his world. Science offers us the mystic knowledge of matter which very often passes the range of our imagination. We humbly accept it following those teachers who have trained their reason to free itself from the trammels of appearance of personal preferences. Their mind dwells in an impersonal infinity where there is no distinction between good and bad, high and low, ugly and beautiful, useful and useless, where all things have their one common right of recognition, that of their existence.

The final freedom of spirit which India aspires after has a similar character of realization. It is beyond all limits of personality, divested of all moral, or aesthetic distinctions; it is the pure consciousness of Being, the ultimate reality which has an infinite illumination of bliss. Though science brings our thoughts to utmost limit of mind's territory it cannot transcend its own creation made of a harmony of logical symbols. In it the chick has come out of its shell but not out of the definition of its own chickenhood. But in India it has been said by the *yogi* that through an intensive process of concentration and quietude our consciousness *does* reach that infinity where knowledge ceases to be knowledge, subject and object become one, a state of existence that cannot be defined.

We have our personal self. It has its desires which struggle to create a world where they could have their unrestricted activity and satisfaction. While it goes on we discover that our self-realization reaches its perfection in the abnegation of self. This fact has made us aware that the individual finds his meaning in a fundamental reality comprehending all individuals—the reality which is the moral and spiritual basis of the realm of human values. This belongs to our religion. As science is the liberation of our knowledge in the universal reason which cannot be other than human reason, religion is the liberation of our individual personality in the universal Person who is human all the same.

The ancient explorers in psychology in India who declare that our emancipation can be carried still further into a realm where infinity is not bounded by human limitations, are not content with advancing this as a doctrine; they advocate its pursuit for the attainment of the highest goal of man. And for its sake the path of discipline has been planned which should be opened out across our life through all its stages helping us to develop our humanity to perfection so that we may surpass it in a finality of freedom.

Perfection has its two aspects in man which can to some extent be separated, the perfection in being, and perfection in doing. It can be imagined that through some training or compulsion good works may possibly be extorted from a man who personally may not be good. Activities that have fatal risks are often undertaken by cowards even though they are conscious of the danger. Such works may be useful and may continue to exist beyond the lifetime of the individual who produced them. And yet where the question is not that of utility but of moral perfection we hold it important that the individual should be true in his goodness. His outer good work may continue to produce good results but the inner perfection of his personality has its own immense value which for him is spiritual freedom and for humanity is an endless asset though we may not know it. For goodness represents the detachment of our spirit from the exclusiveness of our egoism; in goodness we identify ourselves with the universal humanity. Its value is not merely in some benefit for our fellow beings but in its truth itself through which we realize within us that man is not merely an animal bound by his individual passions and appetites but a spirit that has its unfettered perfection. Goodness is the freedom of our self in the world of man, as is love. We have to be true within, not for worldly duties but for that spiritual fulfilment, which is harmony with the Perfect, in union with the eternal. If this were not true, then mechanical perfection would be considered to be of higher value than the spiritual. In order to realize his unity with the universal, the individual man must live his perfect life which alone gives him the freedom to transcend it.

Doubtless Nature, for its own biological purposes, has created in us a strong faith in life, by keeping us unmindful of death. Nevertheless, not only our physical existence, but also the environment which it builds up around itself, may desert us in the moment of triumph, the greatest prosperity comes to its end, dissolving into emptiness; the mightiest empire is overtaken by stupor amidst the flicker of its festival lights. All this is none the less true because its truism bores us to be reminded of it.

And yet it is equally true that, though all our mortal relationships have their end, we cannot ignore them with impunity while they last. If we behave as if they do not exist, merely because they will not continue forever, they will all the same exact their dues, with a great deal over by way of penalty. Trying to ignore bonds that are real, albeit temporary, only strengthens and prolongs their bondage. The soul is great, but the self has to be crossed over in order to reach it. We do not attain our goal by destroying our path.

Our teachers in ancient India realized the soul of man as something very great indeed. They saw no end to its dignity, which found its consummation in Brahma himself. Any limited view of man would therefore be an incomplete view. He could not reach his finality as a mere citizen or Patriot, for neither

City nor Country not the bubble called the World, could contain his eternal soul.

Bhartrihari, who was once a king, has said:

> What if you have secured the fountain-head of all desires; what if you have put your foot on the neck of your enemy, or by your good fortune gathered friends around you? What, even, if you have succeeded in keeping mortal bodies alive for ages—*tatah kim*, what then?

That is to say, man is greater than all these objects of his desire. He is true in his freedom.

But in the process of attaining freedom one must bind his will in order to save its forces from distraction and wastage, so as to gain for it the velocity which comes from the bondage itself. Those also, who seek liberty in a purely political plane, constantly curtail it and reduce their freedom of thought and action to that narrow limit which is necessary for making political power secure, very often at the cost of liberty of consciousness.

India had originally accepted the bonds of her social system in order to transcend society, as the rider puts reins on his horse and stirrups on his own feet in order to ensure greater speed towards his goal.

The Universe cannot be so madly conceived that desire should be an interminable song with no finale. And just as it is painful to stop in the middle of the turn, it should be as pleasant to reach its final cadence.

India has not advised us to come to a sudden stop while work is in full swing. It is true that the unending procession of the world has gone on, through its ups and downs, from the beginning of creation till to-day; but it is equally obvious that each individual's connection therewith *does* get finished. Much he necessarily quit it without any sense of fulfilment?

So, in the divisions of man's world-life which we had in India, work came in the middle, and freedom at the end. As the day is divided into morning, noon, afternoon and evening, so India had divided man's life into four parts, following the requirements of his nature. The day has the waxing and waning of its light; so has man the waxing and waning of his bodily powers. Acknowledging this, India gave a connected meaning to his life from start to finish.

First came *brahmacharya*, the period of discipline in education; then *grahasthya*, that of that world's work; then *vanaprasthya*, the retreat for the loosening of bonds; and finally *pravrajya*, the expectant awaiting of freedom across death.

We have come to look upon life as a conflict with death,—the intruding enemy, not the natural ending,—in impotent quarrel with which we spend ever stage of it. When the time comes for youth to depart, we would hold it back by main force. When the fervour of desire slackens, we would revive it with fresh fuel of our own devising. When our sense organs weaken, we urge them to keep up their efforts. Even when our grip has relaxed we are reluctant to give up possession. We are not trained to recognize the inevitable as natural, and so cannot give up gracefully that which has to go, but needs must wait till it is snatched from us. The truth comes as conqueror only because we have lost the art of receiving it as guest.

The stem of the ripening fruit becomes loose, its pulp soft, but its seed hardens with provision for the next life. Our outward losses, due to age, have likewise corresponding inward gains. But, in man's inner life, his will plays a dominant part, so that these gains depend on his own disciplined striving; that is why, in the case of undisciplined man, who has omitted to secure such provision for the next stage, it is so often seen that his hair is grey, his mouth toothless, his muscles slack, and yet his stem-hold on life has refused to let go its grip, so much so that he is anxious to exercise his will in regard to worldly details even after death.

But renounce we must, and through renunciation gain,— that is the truth of the inner world.

The flower must shed its petals for the sake of fruition, the fruit must drop off for the re-birth of the tree. The child leaves the refuge of the womb in order to achieve the further growth of body and mind in which consists the whole of the child life; next, the soul has to come out of this self-contained stage into the fuller life, which has varied relations with kinsman and neighbour, together with whom it forms a larger body; lastly comes the decline of the body, the weakening of desire, and, enriched with its experiences, the soul now leaves the narrower life for the universal life, to which it dedicates its accumulated wisdom and itself enters into relationship with the Life Eternal; so that, when finally the decaying body has come to the very end of its tether, the soul views its breaking away quite simply and without regret, in the expectation of its own entry into the Infinite.

From individual body to community, from community to universe, from universe to Infinity,—this is the soul's normal progress.

Our teachers, therefore, keeping in mind goal of this progress, did not, in life's first stage of education, prescribe merely the learning of books of things, but *brahmacharya*, the living in discipline, whereby both enjoyment and its renunciation would come with equal ease to the strengthened character. Life being a pilgrimage, with liberation in Brahma as its object, the living of it was as a spiritual exercise to be carried through its different stages, reverently and with a vigilant determination. And the pupil, from his very initiation, had this final consummation always kept in his view.

Once the mind refuses to be bound by temperate requirements, there ceases to be any reason why it should cry halt at any particular limit; and so, like trying to extinguish fire with oil, its acquisitions only make its desires blaze up all the fiercer. That is why it is so essential to habituate the mind, form the very beginning, to be conscious of, keeping within the natural limits; to cultivate the spirit of enjoyment which is allied with the spirit of freedom, the readiness for renunciation.

After the period of such training comes the period of world-life,—the life of the householder. Manu tells us:

It is not possible to discipline ourselves so effectively if out of touch with the world, as while pursuing the world-life with wisdom.

That is the say, wisdom does not attain completeness except through the living of life; and discipline divorced from wisdom is not true discipline, but merely the meaningless following of custom, which is only a disguise for stupidity.

Work, especially good work, becomes easy only when desire has learnt to discipline itself. Then alone does the householder's state become a centre of welfare for all the world, and instead of being an obstacle, helps on the final liberation.

The second stage of life having been thus spent, the decline of the bodily powers must be taken as a warning that it is coming to its natural end. This must not be taken dismally as a notice of dismissal to one still eager to stick to his post, but joyfully as maturity may be accepted as the stage of fulfilment.

After the infant leaves the womb, it still has to remain close to its mother for a time, remaining attached in spite of its detachment, until it can adapt itself to its new freedom. Such is the case in the third stage of life, when man though aloof from the world still remains in touch with it while preparing himself for the final stage of complete freedom. He still gives to the world from his store of wisdom and accepts its support; but this inter-change is not of the same intimate character as in the stage of the householder, there being a new sense of distance.

Then at last comes a day when even such free relations have their end, and the emancipated soul steps out of all bonds to face the Supreme Soul.

Only in this way can man's world-life be truly lived from one end to the other, without being engaged at ever step in trying conclusions with death, not being overcome, when death comes in due course, as by a conquering enemy.

For this fourfold way of life India attunes man to the grand harmony of the universal, leaving no room for untrained desires of a rampant individualism to pursue their destructive career unchecked, but leading them on to their ultimate modulation in the Supreme.

If we really believe this, then we must uphold an ideal of life in which everything else,—the display of individual power, the might of nations,—must be counted as subordinate and the soul of man must triumph and liberate itself form the bond of personality which keeps it in an ever revolving circle of limitation.

If that is not to be, *tatah kim*, what then?

But such an ideal of the utter extinction of the individual separateness has not a universal sanction in India. There are many of us whose prayer is for dualism so that for them the bond of devotion with god may continue forever. For them religion is a truth which is ultimate and they refuse to envy those who are ready to sail for the further shore of existence across humanity. They know that human imperfection is the cause of our sorrow but there is a fulfilment in love within the range of our limitation which accepts all sufferings and yet rises above them.

Chapter XV

Conclusion

In the Sanskrit Language the bird is described as 'twice-born'—once in its limited shell and then finally in the freedom of the unbounded sky. Those of our community who believe in the liberation of man's limited self in the freedom of the spirit retain the same epithet for themselves. In all departments of life man shows this dualism—his existence within the range of obvious facts and his transcendence of it in a realm of deeper meaning.

Having this instinct inherent in his mind which ever suggests to him the crossing of the border, he has never accepted what is apparent as final and his incessant struggle has been to break through the shell of his limitations. In this attempt he often goes against the instincts of his vital nature, and even exults in his defiance of the extreme penal laws of the biological kingdom. The best wealth of his civilization has been achieved by his following the guidance of this instinct in his ceaseless adventure of the Endless Further. His achievement of truth goes far beyond his needs and the realization of his self strives across the frontier of its individual interest. This proves to him his infinity and makes his religion real to him by his own manifestation in truth and goodness. Only for man there can be religion because his evolution is form efficiency in nature towards the perfection of spirit.

According to some interpretations of the Vedanta doctrine Brahman is the absolute Truth, the impersonal It, in which there can be no distinction of this and that, the good and the evil, the beautiful and its opposite, having no other quality except its ineffable blissfulness in the eternal solitude of its consciousness utterly devoid of all things and all thoughts. But, as our religion can only have its significance in this phenomenal world comprehended by our human self, this absolute conception of Brahman is outside the subject of my discussion. What I have tried to bring out in this book is the fact that whatever name may have been given to the divine Reality it has found its highest place in the history of our religion owing to its human character, giving meaning to the idea of sin and sanctity, and offering an eternal background to all the ideals of perfection which have their harmony with man's own nature.

We have the age-long tradition in our country, as I have already stated, that through the process of *yoga* man can transcend the utmost bounds of his humanity and find himself in a pure state of consciousness of his undivided unity with Parabrahman. There is none who has the right to contradict this belief; for it is a matter of direct experience and not of logic. It is widely known in India that there are individuals who have the power to attain temporarily the state of *Samadhi*, the complete merging of the self in the infinite, a state which is indescribable. While accepting their testimony as true, let us at the mean time have faith in the testimony of others who have felt a profound love, which is the intense feeling of union, for a Being who comprehends in himself all things that are human in knowledge, will and action. And he is God, who is not merely a sum total of facts, but the goal that lies immensely beyond all that is comprised in the past and the present.

Appendix I

The Baul Singers of Bengal

[*The following account of the Baüls in Northern India has been given in the Visvabharati Quarterly by my friend and fellow-worker, Professor Kshiti Mohun Sen of Santiniketan, to whom I am grateful for having kindly allowed me to reproduce what he has written in this Appendix.—Editor*]

Baül means madcap, from *bayu* (Skt. Vayu) in its sense of nerve current, and has become the appellation of a set of people who do not conform to established social usage. This derivation is supported by the following verse of Narahari:

That is why, brother, I became a madcap Baül.
No master I obey, nor injunctions, canons or custom.
Now no men-made distinctions have any hold on me,
And I revel only in the gladness of my own welling love.
In love there's no separation, but commingling always.
So I rejoice in song and dance with each and all.

These lines also introduce us to the main tenets of the cult. The freedom, however, that the Baüls seek form all forms of outward compulsion goes even further, for among such are recognized as well the compulsions exerted by our desires and antipathies. Therefore, according to this cult, in order to gain real freedom, one has first to die to the life of the world whilst still in the flesh—for only then can one be rid of all extraneous claims. Those of the Baüls who have Islamic leanings call such 'death in life' *fana*, a term used by the Sufis to denote union with the Supreme Being. True love, according to the Baüls, is incompatible with any kind of compulsion. Unless the bonds of necessity are overcome, liberation is out of the question. Love represents the wealth of life which is in excess of needÉ From hard, practical politics touching our earth to the nebulous regions of abstract metaphysics, everywhere India expressed the power of her genius equally well....And yet none of these, neither severally nor collectively, constituted her specific genius; none showed the full height to which she could raise herself, none compassed the veritable amplitude of her inner-most reality. It is when we come to the domain of the Spirit, of God-realization, that we find the real nature and stature and genius of the Indian people; it is here that India lives and moves as in her own home of Truth.

The Baüls cult is followed by householders as well as homeless wanderers, neither of whom acknowledge class or caste, special deities, temples or sacred places. Though they congregate on the occasion of religious festivals, mainly of the Vaishnavas, held in special centres, they never enter any temple. They do not set up any images of divinities, or religious symbols, in their own places of worship of mystic realization. True, they sometimes maintain with care and reverence spots sacred to some esteemed master or devotee, but they perform no worship there. Devotees from the lowest strata of the Hindu and Moslem communities are welcomed into their ranks, hence the Baüls are looked down upon by both. It is possible that their own contempt for temples had its origin in the denial of admittance therein to their low class brethren. What need, say they, have we of other temples, is not this body of ours the temple where the Supreme Spirit has His abode? The human body, despised by most other religions, is thus for them the holy of holies, wherein the Divine is intimately enshrined as the Man of the Heart. And in this wise is the dignity of Man upheld by them.

Kabir, Nanak, Ravidas, Dadu and his followers have also called man's body the temple of God—the microcosm in which the cosmic abode of the all-pervading Supreme Being is represented.

Kabir says:

In this body is the Garden of Paradise; herein are comprised the seven seas and the myriad stars; here is the Creator manifest. (I. 101.)

Dadu says:

This body is my scripture; herein the All-Merciful has written for me His message.

Rajjab (Dadu's chief Moslem disciple) says:

Within the devotee is the paper on which the scriptures are written in letters of Life. But few care to read them; they turn a deaf ear to the message of the heart.

Most Indian sects adopt some distinct way of keeping the hair of head and face as a sign of their sect or order. Therefore, so as to avoid being dragged into any such distinctions, the Baüls allow hair and beard and moustache to grow freely. Thus do we remain simple, they say. The similar practice of the Sikhs in this matter is to be noted. Neither do the Baüls believe that lack of clothing or bareness of body conduce to religious merit. According to them the whole body should be kept decently covered. Hence their long robe, for which, if they cannot afford a new piece of cloth, they gather rags and make it of patches. In this they are different from the ascetic *sanyasins*, but resemble rather the Buddhist monks.

The Baüls do not believe in aloofness from, or renunciation of, any person or thing; their central idea is *yoga*, attachment to and communion with the divine and its manifestations, as the means of realization. We fail to recognize the temple of God in the bodily life of man, they explain, because its lamp is not alight. The true vision must be attained in which this temple will become manifest in each and every human body, whereupon mutual communion and worship will spontaneously arise. Truth cannot be communion and worship will spontaneously arise. Truth cannot be communicated to those on whom you look down. You must be able to see the divine light that shines within them, for it is your own lack of vision that makes all seem dark.

Kabir says the same thing:

> In every abode the light doth shine; it is you who are blind that cannot see. When by dint of looking and looking and looking you at length can discern it, the veils of this world will be torn asunder. (II. 33.)

> It is because the devotee is not in communion that he says the goal is far away. (II. 34).

Many such similarities are to be observed between the sayings of the Baüls and those of the Upper Indian devotees of the Middle Ages, but, unlike the case of the followers of the latter, the Baüls did not become crystallized into any particular order or religious organization. So, in the Baüls of Bengal, there is to be found a freedom and independence of mind and spirit that resists all attempt at definition. Their songs are unique in courage and felicity of expression. But under modern conditions they are becoming extinct, or at best holding on to external features bereft of their original speciality. It would be a great pity if no record of their achievements should be kept before their culture is lost to the world.

Though the Baül count amongst their following a variety of sects and castes, both Hindu and Moslem, chiefly coming from the lower social ranks, they refuse to give any other account of themselves to the questioner than that they are Baüls. They acknowledge none of the social or religious formalities, but delight in the ever-changing play of life, which cannot be expressed in mere words but of which something may be captured in song, through the ineffable medium of rhythm and tune.

Their songs are passed on from Master to disciple, the latter when competent adding others of his own, but, as already mentioned, they are never recorded in book form. Their replies to questions are usually given by singing appropriate selections from these songs. If asked the reason why, they say: 'We are like birds. We do not walk on our legs, but fly with our wings.'

There was a Brahmin of Bikrampur, known as Chhaku Thakur, who was the disciple of a Baül of the Namasudra caste (accounted one of the lowest) and hence had lost his place in his own community. When admonished to be careful about what he uttered, so as to avoid popular odium, he answered with the song:

Let them relieve their minds by saying what they will,
I pursue my own simple way, fearing none at all.
The Mango seed will continue to produce Mango trees, no Jambolans.
This seed of mine will produce the real *me*—all glory to my Master!

Love being the main principle according to the Baüls, a Vaishnava once asked a Baül devotee whether he was aware of the different kinds of love as classified in the Vaishnava scriptures. 'What should an illiterate ignoramus like me know of the scriptures?' was the reply. The Vaishnava then offered to read and explain the text, which he proceeded to do, while the Baül listened with such patience as he could muster. When asked for his opinion, after the reading was over, he sang:

> A goldsmith, methinks, has come into the flower garden.
> He would appraise the lotus, forsooth,
> By rubbing it on his touchstone!

Recruits from the higher castes are rare amongst the Baüls. When any such do happen to come, they are reduced to the level of the rest. Are the lower planks of a boat of any lesser importance than the upper? say they.

Once in Vikrampur, I was seated on the river bank by the side of a Baül. 'Father', I asked him, 'why is it that you keep no historical record of yourselves for the use of posterity?' 'We follow the *sahaj* (simple) way', he replied, 'and so leave no trace behind us.' The tide had then ebbed, and there was but little water in the river bed. Only a few boatmen were to be seen pushing their boats along the mud. The Baül continued: 'Do the boats that sail over the flooded river leave any mark? What should these boatmen of the muddy track, urged on by their need, know of the *sahaj* (simple) way? The true endeavour is to keep oneself simple afloat in the stream of devotion that flows through the lives of devotees—to mingle one's own devotion with theirs. There are many classes of men amongst the Baüls, but they are all Baül—they have no other achievement or history. All the streams that fall into the Ganges become the Ganges. So must we lose ourselves in the common stream, else will it cease to be living.'

On another Baül being asked why they did not follow the scriptures, 'Are we dogs', he replied, 'that we should lick up the leavings of others? Brave men rejoice in the output of their own energy, they create their own festivals. These cowards who have not the power to rejoice in themselves have to rely on what others have left. Afraid lest the world should lack festivals in the future, they save up the scraps left over by their predecessors for later use. They are content with glorifying their forefathers because they know not how to create for themselves.'

> If you would know the Man,
> Simple must be your endeavour.
> To the region of the simple must you fare.
> Pursuers of the path of man's own handiwork,
> Who follow the crowd, gleaning their false
> leavings,
> What news can they get of the Real?

It is hardly to be wondered at that people who think thus should have no use for history!

We have already noticed that, like all the followers of the simple way, the Baül have no faith in specially sacred spots or places of pilgrimage, but that they nevertheless congregate on the occasion of religious festivals. If asked why, the Baül says:

> We would be within hail of the other Boatmen, to
> hear their calls,
> That we may make sure our boat rightly floats on the
> *sahaj* stream.

Not what men have said or done in the past, but the living human touch is what they find helpful. Here is a song giving their ideas about pilgrimage:

> I would not go, my heart, to Mecca or Medina,
> For behold, I ever abide by the side of my Friend.
> Mad would I become, had I dwelt afar, not knowing
> Him.

There's no worship in Mosque or Temple or special
holy day.
At ever step I have my Mecca and Kashi; sacred is
every moment.

If a Baül is asked the age of his cult—whether it comes before
or after this one or that, he says, 'Only the artificial religions
of the world are limited by time. our *sahaj* (simple, natural)
religion is timeless, it has neither beginning nor end, it is of
all time.' The religion of the Upanishads and Puranas, even
that of the Vedas, is, according to them, artificial.

The followers of the *sahaj* cult believe only in living
religious experience. Truth, according to them, has two aspects,
inert and living. Confined to itself truth has no value for man.
It becomes priceless when embodied in a living personality.
The conversion of the inert into living truth by the devotee
they compare to the conversion into milk by the cow of its
fodder, or the conversion by the tree of dead matter into fruit.
He who has this power of making truth living, is the Guru
or Master. Such Gurus they hold in special reverence, for the
eternal and all-pervading truth can only be brought to man's
door by passing through his life.

The Baül say that emptiness of time and space is required
for a playground. That is why god has preserved an emptiness
in the heart of man, for the sake of His own play of Love. Our
wise and learned ones were content with finding in Brahma
the *tat* (lit. 'that'—the ultimate substance). The Baül, not being
Pandits, do not profess to understand all this fuss about *thatness*,
they want a Person. So their god is the Man of the Heart (*maner
manush*) sometimes simply the Man (*purush*). Whilst He is
revealed within, no worldly pleasures can give satisfaction.
Their sole anxiety is the finding of this Man.

The Baül sings:

Ah, where am I to find Him, the Man of my Heart?

> Alas, since I lost Him, I wander in search of Him,
> Thro' lands near and far.

The agony of separation from Him cannot be mitigated for them by learning or philosophy:

> Oh, these words and words, my mind would none of them,
> The Supreme Man it must and shall discover.
> So long as Him I do not see, these mists slake not my thirst.
> Mad am I; for lack of that Man I madly run about;
> For his sake the world I've felt; for Bisha naught else will serve.

This Bisha was a *bhuin-mali*, by caste, disciple of Bala, the Kaivarta.

This cult of the Supreme Man is only to be found in the Vedas hidden away in the Purushasukta (A.V. 19.6). It is more freely expressed by the Upper Indian devotees of the Middle Ages. It is all in all with the Baüls. The God whom these illiterate outcastes seek so simply and naturally in their lives is obscured by the accredited religious leaders in philosophical systems and terminology, in priestcraft and ceremonial, in institutions and temples.

Not satisfied with the *avatars* (incarnations of God) mentioned in the scriptures, the Baül sings:

> As we look on ever creature, we find each to be His *avatar*. What can you teach us of His ways? In ever-new play He wondrously revels.

And Kabir also tells us:

> All see the Eternal One, but only the devotee, in his solitude, recognizes him.

A friend of mine was once much impressed by the reply of a Baül who was asked why his robe was not tinted with ascetic ochre:

Can the colour show outside, unless the inside is first
tinctured? Can the fruit attain ripe sweetness by the
painting of its skin?

This aversion of the Baül from outward marks of distinction
is also shared by the Upper Indian devotees, as I have elsewhere
noticed.

The age-long controversy regarding *dvaita* (dualism) and
advaita (monism) is readily solved by these wayfarers on the
path of Love. Love is the simple striving, love the natural
communion, so believe the Baüls. 'Ever two and ever one, of
this the name of Love', say they. In love, oneness is achieved
without any loss of respective self-hood.

The same need exists for the reconcilement of the
antagonism between the outer all of the material world and
the inner call of the spiritual world, as for the realization of
the mutual love of the individual and Supreme Self. The god
who is Love, say the Baül, can alone serve to turn the currents
of the within and the without in one and the same direction.

Kabir says:

If we say He is only within then the whole
Universe is shamed.
If we say he is only without, then that is false.
He, whose feet rest alike on the sentient and on
the inert,
fills the gap between the inner and the outer
world.

The inter-relations of man's body and the Universe have to
be realized by spiritual endeavour. Such endeavour is called
Kaya Sadhan (Realization through the body).

One process in this *Kaya Sadhan* of Baül is known as
Urdha-srota (the elevation of the current). Waters flow
downwards according to the ordinary physical law. But with

the advent of Life the process is reversed. When the living seed sprouts the juices are drawn upwards, and on the elevation that such flow can attain depends the height of the tree. It is the same in the life of man. His desires ordinarily flow downward towards animality. The endeavour of the expanding spirit is to turn their current upwards towards the light. The currents of *Shiva* (animal life) must be converted into the current of *Shiva* (God life). They form a centre round the ego; they must be raised by the force of love.

> Says Dadu's daughter, Nanimata:
> My life is the lamp afloat on the stream.
> To what bourne shall it take me?
> How is the divine to conquer the carnal,
> The downward current to be upward turned?
> As when the wick is lighted the oil doth upward flow,
> So simply is destroyed the thirst of the body.

The *Yoga* Vasistha tells us:

> Uncleansed desires bind to the world, purified desires give liberation.

References to this reversal of current are also to be found in the Atharva Veda (X. 2.9; 2.34). This reversal is otherwise considered by Indian devotees as the conversion of the *sthula* (gross) in the sukshma (fine).

The Baül sings:

> Love is my golden touch—it turn desire into service:
> Earth seeks to become Heaven, man to become god.

Another aspect of the idea of reversal has been put thus by Rabindranath Tagore in the *Broken Ties*:

> If I keep going in the same direction along which He comes to me, then I shall be going further and further

away from Him. If I proceed in the opposite direction, then only can we meet. He loves form, so He is continually descending towards form. We cannot live by form alone, so we must ascend towards His formlessness. He is free, so His play is within bonds. We are bound, so we find our joy in freedom. All our sorrow is because we cannot understand this. He who sings, proceeds from his joy to the tune; he who hears, from the tune to joy. one comes from freedom into bondage, the other goes from bondage into freedom; only thus can they have their communion. He sings and we hear. He ties the bonds as He sings to us, we untie them as we listen to Him.

This idea also occurs in our devotees of the Middle Ages.

The 'sahaj' folk endeavour to seek the bliss of divine union only for its own sake. Mundane desires are therefore accounted the chief obstacles in the way. But for getting rid of them, the wise Guru, according to the Baül, does not advise renunciation of the good things of the world, but the opening of the door to the higher self. Thus guided, says Kabir,

I close not my eyes, stop not my ears, nor torment my body.
But ever path I then traverse becomes a path of pilgrimage, whatever work I engage in becomes service.
This simple consummation is the best.

The simple way has led its votaries easily and naturally to their living conception of Humanity.

Rajjab says:

All the world is the Veda, all creations the Koran.
Why read paper scriptures, O Rajjab.
Gather ever fresh wisdom from the Universe.

The eternal wisdom shines within the concourse of
the millions of Humanity.

The Baül sings:

The simple has its thirty million strings whose
mingled symphony ever sounds.
Take all the creatures of the World into yourself.
Drown yourself in that eternal music.

I conclude with a few more examples of Baül songs,
esoteric and otherwise, from amongst many others of equal
interest.

By Gangaram, the Namasudra:
Realize how finite and unbounded are One,
As you breathe in and out.
Of all ages, then you will count the moments,
In every moment find the ages,
The drop in the ocean, the ocean in the drop.
If your endeavour be but *sahaj*, beyond argument and
cogitation,
You will taste the precious quintessence.
Blinded are you by over-much journeying from bourne
to bourne,
O Gangaram, by simple! Then alone will vanish all
your doubts.

By Bisha, the disciple of Bala:

The Simple Man was in the Paradise of my heart,
Alas, how and when did I lose Him,
That now no peace I know, at home or abroad?
By meditation and telling of beads, in worship and
travail,
The quest goes on for ever;
But unless the Simple Man comes of Himself,
Fruitless is it all;

For he yields not to forgetfulness of striving.
Bisha's heart has understood right well,
That by His own simple way alone is its door
unlocked.

'Listen, O brother man', declares Chandidas, 'the Truth
of Man is the highest of truths; there is no other truth above
it.'

Appendix II

Dadu and the
Mystery of Form

[*From an article in the Visva-Bharati Quarterly by Professor Kshiti Mohan Sen.*]

The Language of man has been mainly occupied with telling us about the elements into which the finite world has been analysed; nevertheless, now and again, it reveals glimpses of the world of the Infinite as well; for the spirit of man has discovered rifts in the wall of Matter. Our intellect can count the petals, classify the scent, and describe the colour of the rose, but its unity finds its expression when we rejoice in it.

The intellect at best can give us only a broken view of things. The marvellous vision of the Seer, in spite of the scoffing in which both Science and Metaphysics so often indulge, can alone make manifest to us the truth of a thing in its completeness. When we thus gain a vision of unity, we are no longer intellectually aware of detail, counting, classifying, or distinguishing—for them we have found admittance into the region of the spirit, and there we simply measure the truth of our realization by the intensity of our joy.

What is the meaning of this unutterable joy? That which we know by intellectual process is something outside ourselves. But the vision of anything in the fulness of its unity involves the realization of the unity of the self within, as well as of the relation between the two. The knowledge of the *many* may make up proud, but it makes us glad when our kinship with the *One* is brought home to us. Beauty is the name that we give to this acknowledgment of unity and of its relationship with ourselves.

It is through the beauty of Nature, or of Human Character, or Service, that we get out glimpses of the Supreme Soul whose essence is bliss. Or rather, it is when we become conscious of Him in Nature, or Art, or Service, that Beauty flashes out. And whenever we thus light upon the Dweller-within, all discord disappears and Love and Beauty are seen inseparable from truth. It is really the coming of Truth to us as kinsman which floods our being with Joy.

This realization in Joy is immediate, self-sufficient, ultimate. When the self experiences Joy within, it is completely satisfied and has nothing more to ask from the outside world. Joy, as we know it, is a direct, synthetic measure of Beauty and neither awaits nor depends upon any analytical process. In our Joy, further, we behold not only the unity, but also the origin, for the Beauty which tells us of Him can be nothing but radiance reflected, melody re-echoed, from Him; else would all this have been unmeaning indeed—Society, Civilization, Humanity. The progress of Man would otherwise have ended in an orgy of the gratification of his animal passions.

The power of realization, for each particular individual, is limited. All do not attain the privilege of directly apprehending the universal Unity. Nevertheless, a partial vision of it, say in a flower, or in a friend, is a common experience; moreover, the potentiality is inherent in ever individual soul, by dint of disciplined striving, to effect its own expansion and thereupon eventually to achieve the realization of the Supreme Soul.

By whom, meanwhile, are these ineffable tidings from the realm of the Spirit, the world of the Infinite, brought to us? Not by potentates or philosophers, but by the poor, the untutored, the despised. And with what superb assurance do they lead us out of the desert of the intellect into the paradise of the Spirit!

When our metaphysicians, dividing themselves into rival schools of Monism, Dualism or Monistic-Dualism, had joined together in dismissing the world as *Maya*, then, up from the depths of their social obscurity, rose these cobblers, weavers, and sewers of bags, proclaiming such theorems of the intellect to be all nonsense; for the metaphysicians had not seen with their own inner vision how the world overflowed with truth and Love, Beauty and Joy.

Dadu, Ravidas, Kabir and Nanak were not ascetics; they bore no message of poverty, or renunciation, for their own sake; they were poets who had pierced the curtain of appearances and had glimpses of the world of Unity, where god himself is a poet. Their words cannot stand the glare of logical criticism; they babble, like babes, of the joy of their vision of Him, of the ecstasy into which His music has thrown them.

Nevertheless, it is they, not the scientists or philosophers, who have taught us of reality. On the one side the Supreme Soul is alone on the other my individual soul is alone. If the two do not come together, then indeed there befalls the greatest of all calamities, the utter emptiness of chaos. For all the abundance of His inherent joy, God is in want of my joy of Him; and Reality in its perfection only blossoms where we meet.

'When I look upon the beauty of this Universe', says Dadu, 'I cannot help asking: "How, O Lord, did you come to create it? What sudden wave of joy coursing through your being compelled its own manifestation? Was it really due to desire for self-expression, or simply on the impulse of emotion? Or was it perhaps just your fancy to revel in the play of form? Is this play then so delightful to you; or is it that you would see your own inborn delight thus take shape?" Oh, how can these questions be answered in words?' cries Dadu. 'Only those who know will understand.'

'Why not go to him who has wrought this marvel', says Dadu elsewhere, 'and ask: "Cannot your own message make clear this wondrous making of the One into the many?" When I look on creation as beauty of form. I see only Form and Beauty. When I look on it as life, every where I see Life. When I look on it as Brahma, then indeed is Dadu at a loss for words. When I see it in relation, it is of bewildering variety. When I see it in my own soul, all its variousness is merged in the beauty of the Supreme Soul. This eye of mine then becomes also the eye of Brahma, and in this exchange of mutual vision does Dadu behold Truth.'

The eye cannot see the face—for that purpose a mirror is necessary. That is to say, either the face has to be put at a distance from the eye, or the eye moved away from the face—in any case what was one has to be made into two. The image is not the face itself, but how else is that to be seen?

So does God mirror Himself in Creation; and since He cannot place Himself outside His own Infinity, He can only gain a vision of Himself—and get a taste of His own joy—through my joy in Him and in His Universe. Hence the anxious striving of the devotee to keep himself thoroughly pure—not through any pride of puritanism, but because his soul is the playground where God would revel in Himself. Had not God's radiance, His beauty, thus found its form in the Universe, its joy in the devotee, He would have remained mere formless, colourless Being in the nothingness of infinity.

This is what makes the Mystery so profound, so inscrutable. Whether we say that only Brahma is true, or only the universe is true, we are equally far from the truth, which can only be expressed as both *this* and *that*, or neither *this* nor *that*.

And Dadu can only hint at it by saying: 'Neither death nor life is He; He neither goes out, nor does He come in; nor sleeps, nor wakes; nor wants, nor is satisfied. He is neither I nor you, neither One nor Two. For no sooner do I say that all is One, than I find us both; and when I say there are two, I see we're One. So, O Dadu, rest content to look on Him just as He is, in the deep of your heart, and give up wrestling with vain imaginings and empty words.'

'Words shower', Dadu goes on, 'when spouts the fount of the intellect; but where realization grows, there music has its seat.' When the intellect confesses defeat, and words fail, then, indeed, from the depth of the heart wells up the song of the joy of realization. What words cannot make clear, melody can; to its strains one can revel in the vision of God in His revels.

'That is why', cries Dadu, 'your universe, this creation of yours, has charmed me so—your waters and your breezes, and this earth which holds them, with its ranges of mountains, its great oceans, its snow-capped poles, its blazing sun, because, through all the three regions of earth, sky and heaven, amidst all their multifarious life, it is your ministration, your beauty, that keeps me enthralled. Who can know you, O Invisible, Unapproachable, Unfathomable! Dadu has no desire to know; he is satisfied to remain enraptured with all this beauty of yours, and to rejoice in it will you.'

To look upon Form as the play of His love is not to belittle it. In creating the senses God did not intend them to be starved. 'And so', says Dadu, 'the eye is feasted with colour, the ear with music, the palate with flowers, wondrously provided.' And we find that the body longs for the spirit, the spirit for the body; the flower for the scent, the scent for the flower; our words for truth, the Truth for words; form for its ideal, the ideal for form; all thus mutual worship is but the worship of the ineffable Reality behind, by whose Presence everyone of them is glorified. And Dadu struggles not, but simply keeps his heart open to this shower of love and thus rejoices in perpetual Springtime.

Every vessel of form the Formless fills with Himself, and in their beauty He gains them in return. With His love the Passionless fulfils ever devoted heart and sets it a-dance, and their love streams back to the Colourless, variegated with the tints of each. Beauteous Creation yields up her charms, in all their purity, to her Lord. Need she make further protestation, in words of their mutual love? So Dadu surrenders his heart, mind and soul at the feet of his Beloved. His one care is that they be not sullied.

If any one should object that evanescent Form is not worthy to represent the Eternal, Dadu would answer that it is just because Form is fleeting that it is a help, not a hindrance, to His worship. While returning back to its Origin, it captures our mind all takes it along with itself. The call of Beauty tells us of the Unthinkable, towards whom it lies. In passing over us, death assures us of the truth of Life.

Appendix III

Night and Morning

[*An address in the Chapel of Manchester College, Oxford, on Sunday, May 25, 1930, by Rabindranath Tagore.*]

In his early youth, stricken with a great sorrow at the death of his grandmother, my father painfully groped for truth when his world had darkened, and his life lost its meaning. At this moment of despair a torn page of a manuscript carried by a casual wind was brought to his notice. The text it contained was the first verse of the Ishopanishad:

Īśāvāsyam idam sarvam
Yat Kincha jagatyām jagat.
tēna tyaktena bhunjīthā
Mā gṛdhah Kasyasvitdhanam.

It may be thus translated:

Thou must know that whatever moves in this moving world is enveloped by god. And therefore find thy enjoyment in renunciation, never coveting what belongs to others.

In this we are enjoined to realize that all facts that move and change have their significance in their relation to one everlasting truth. For then we can be rid of the greed of acquisition, gladly dedicating everything we have to that Supreme Truth. The change in our mind is immense in its generosity of expression when an utter sense of vanity and vacancy is relieved at the consciousness of a pervading reality.

I remember once while on a boat trip in a strange neighbourhood I found myself unexpectedly at the confluence of three great rivers as the daylight faded and the night darkened over a desolation dumb and inhospitable. A sense of dread possessed the crew and an oppressive anxiety burdened my thoughts, with its unreasonable exaggeration all through the dark hours. The morning came and at once the brooding obsession vanished. Everything remained the same only the sky was filled with light.

The night had brought her peace, the peace of a black ultimatum in which all hope ceased in an abyss of nothingness, but the peace of the morning appeared like that of a mother's smile, which in its serene silence utters, 'I am here'. I realized why birds break out singing in the morning, and felt that their songs are their own glad answers to the emphatic assurance of a Yes in the morning light in which they find a luminous harmony of their own existence. Darkness drives our being into an isolation of insignificance and we are frightened because in the dark the sense of our own truth dwindles into a minimum. Within us we carry a positive truth, the consciousness of our personality, which naturally seeks from our surroundings its response in a truth which is positive, and then in this harmony we find our wealth or reality and are gladly ready to sacrifice. That which distinguishes man from the animal is the fact that he expresses himself not in his claims, in his needs, but in his sacrifice, which has the creative energy that builds his home, his society, his civilization. It proves that his instinct acknowledges the inexhaustible wealth of a positive truth which gives highest value to existence. In whatever we are mean, greedy and unscrupulous, there are the dark bands in the spectrum of our consciousness; they prove chasms of bankruptcy in our realization of the truth that the world moves, not in a blank sky of negation, but in the bosom of an ideal spirit of fulfilment.

Most often crimes are committed when it is night. it must not be thought that the only reason for this is that in the dark they are likely to remain undetected. But the deeper reason is that in the dark the negative aspect of time weakness the positive sense of our own humanity. Our victims, as well as we ourselves, are less real to us in the night, and that which we miss within we desperately seek outside us. Wherever in the human world the individual self forgets its isolation, the light that unifies is revealed the light of the Everlasting Yes, whose sound-symbol in India is 'OM'. Then it becomes easy for man to be good not because his badness is restrained, but because of his joy in the positive background of his own reality, because his mind no longer dwells in a fathomless night of an anarchical world of denial.

Man finds an instance of this in the idea of his own country, which reveals to him a positive truth, the idea that has not the darkness of negation which is sinister, which generates suspicion, exaggerates fear, encourages uncontrolled greed; for his own country is an indubitable reality to him which delights his soul. in such intense consciousness of reality we discover our own greater self that spreads beyond our physical life and immediate present, and offers us generous opportunities of enjoyment in renunciation.

In the introductory chapter of our civilization individuals by some chance found themselves together within a geographic enclosure. But a mere crowd without an inner meaning of inter-relation is negative, and therefore it can easily be hurtful. The individual who is a mere component part of an unneighbourly crowd, who in his exclusiveness represents only himself, is apt to be suspicious of others, with no inner control in hating and hitting his fellow-beings at the very first sight. This savage mentality is the product of the barren spirit of negation that dwells in the spiritual night. but when the morning of mutual recognition broke out, the morning of co-operative life, that divine mystery which is the creative spirit of unity, imparted meaning to individuals in a larger truth named 'people'. These individuals gladly surrendered themselves to the realization of their true humanity, the humanity of a great wholeness composed of generations of men consciously and unconsciously building up a perfect future. They realized peace according to the degree of unity which they attained in their mutual relationship, and within that limit they found the one sublime truth which pervades time that moves, the things that change, the life that grows, the thoughts that flow onwards. They united with themselves the surrounding physical nature in her hills and rivers, in the dance of rhythm in all her forms and colours, in the blue of her sky, the tender green of her corn shoots.

In gradual degrees men became aware that the subtle intricacies of human existence find their perfection in the harmony of interdependence, never in the vigorous exercise of elbows by a mutually pushing multitude, in the arrogant assertion of independence which fitly belongs to the barren rocks and deserts grey with the pallor of death.

For rampant individualism is against what is truly human— that is to say spiritual—it belongs to the primitive poverty of the animal life, it is the confinement of a cramped spirit, of restricted consciousness.

The limited boundaries of a race or a country within which the supreme truth of humanity has been more or less realized in the past are crossed today from the outside. The countries are physically brought closer to each other by science. But science has not brought with it the light that helps understanding. On the contrary science on its practical side has raised obstacles among them against the development of a sympathetic knowledge.

But I am not foolish enough to condemn science as materialistic. No truth can be that. Science means intellectual probity in our knowledge and dealings with the physical world and such conscientiousness has a spiritual quality that encourages sacrifice and martyrdom. But in science the oft-used half-truth that honesty is the best policy is completely made true and our mind's honesty in this field never fails to bring us the best profit for our living. Mischief finds its entry through this back-door of utility, tempting the primitive in man, arousing his evil passions. And through this the great meeting of races has been obscured of its great meaning. When I view it in my mind I am reminded of the fearful immensity of the meeting of the three mighty rivers where I found myself unprepared in a blackness of universal menace. Over the vast gathering of peoples the insensitive night darkly broods, the night of unreality. The primitive barbarity of limitless suspicion and mutual jealousy fills the world's atmosphere today—the barbarity of the aggressive individualism of nations, pitiless in its greed, unashamed of its boastful brutality.

Those that have come out for depredation in this universal night have the indecent audacity to say that such conditions are eternal in man, that the moral ideals are only for individuals but that the race belongs to the primitive nature of the animal.

But when we see that in the range of physical power man acknowledges no limits in his dreams, and is not even laughed at when he hopes to visit the neighbouring planet; must he insult his humanity by proclaiming that human nature has reached its limit of moral possibility? We must work with all our strength for the seemingly impossible; we must be sure that faith in the perfect builds the path for the perfect—that the external fact of unity which has surprised us must be sublimated in an internal truth of unity which would light up the Truth of Man the Eternal.

Nations are kept apart not merely by international jealousy, but also by their *Karma*, their own past, handicapped by the burden of the dead. They find it hard to think that the mentality which they fondly cultivated within the limits of a narrow past has no continuance in a wider future, they are never tired of uttering the blasphemy that warfare is eternal, that physical might has its inevitable right of moral cannibalism where the flesh is weak. The wrong that has been done in the past seeks to justify itself by its very perpetuation, like a disease by its chronic malignity, and it sneers and growls at the least proposal of its termination. Such an evil ghost of a persistent past, the dead that would cling to life, haunts the night today over mutually alienated countries, and men that are gathered together in the dark cannot see each other's faces and features.

We in India are unfortunate in not having the chance to give expression to the best in us in creating intimate relations with the powerful nations, whose preparations are all leading to an enormous waste of resources in a competition of brow-beating and bluff. Some great voice is waiting to be heard which will usher in the sacred light of truth in the dark hours of the nightmare of politics, the voice which will proclaim that 'God is over all', and exhort us never to covet, to be great in renunciation that gives us the wealth of spirit, strength of truth, leads us from the illusion of power to the fullness of perfection, to the *Sāntam*, who is peace eternal, to the *Advaitam* who is the infinite One in the heart of the manifold. But we in India have not yet had the chance. Yet we have our own human voice which truth demands. The messengers of truth have ever joined hands across centuries, across the seas, across historical barriers, and they help to raise up the great continent of human brotherhood from *avidyā*, from the slimy bottom of spiritual apathy. We individuals, however small may be our power and whatever corner of the consciousness that comprehends all humanity. And for this cause I ask your co-operation, not only because co-operation gives us strength in our work, but because co-operation itself is the best aspect of the truth we represent; it is an end and not merely the means.

Let us keep our faith firm in the objectivity of the source of our spiritual ideal of unity, though it cannot be proved by any mathematical logic. Let us proclaim in our conduct that it has already been given to us to be realized, like a song which has only to be mastered and sung, like the morning which has only to be welcomed by raising the screens, opening the doors.

The idea of a millennium is treasured in our ancient legends. The instinct cradled and nourished in them has profound meaning. It is like the instinct of a chick which dimly feels that an infinite world of freedom *is* already given to it, truer than the narrow fact of its immediate life within the egg. An agnostic chick has the rational right to doubt it, but at the same time it cannot help pecking at its shell. The human soul, confined in its limitation, has also dreamt of millennium, and striven for a spiritual emancipation which seems impossible of attainment, and yet it feels its reverence for some ever-present source of inspiration in which all its experience of the true, the good and beautiful finds its reality.

And therefore it has been said by the Upanishad: 'Thou must know that God pervades all things that move and change in this moving world; find thy enjoyment in renunciation, covet not what belongs to others.'

Ya ēkō varnō bahudhā saktiyogāt
Varnān anēkān nihitārthō dadhāti.
Vichaiti chāntē vi·vamādau sa dēvah
Sa nō buddhyā subhayā samyunaktu

He who is one, and who dispenses the inherent needs of all peoples and all times, who is in the beginning and the end of all things, may he unite us with the bond of truth, of common fellowship, of righteousness.

FOUR CHAPTERS

Author's Note

Much of the controversy over my *Four Chapters* falls outside the province of literary criticism. This is only natural, for the background to the story is vividly coloured by the passions aroused by the political struggle and turmoil in modern Bengal. Not only are we too close to that scene; there is, still, a constant radiation of its heat through our minds. It is for this reason that to many readers the setting of the story appears more important than the story itself. I can only hope that when the present agitation of spirit recedes into the distant past and becomes merely the subject of dispassionate historical research, the imagination of the reader will be free to accept the story in a spirit of detachment. In other words, it will be possible, then, to look at it solely as literature.

I should like to set down what, as its author, I have to say about the story. I know what was in my mind when I sat down to write it and I can, therefore, supply that particular bit of personal information; what it has turned out to be, it is for the reader and the critic to judge in the light of their own taste and ability. It is natural for taste and ability to vary with individuals; so that their criticisms are also likely to be various in kind and quality. The writer should be indifferent to them, depending on time alone for the correct assessment.

What might be called the only theme of the book is the love of Ela and Atindra. The nature and course of the love between man and woman is determined not only by the individual characters of the lovers; it is influenced also by the impact of their circumstances on them. The river brings down its gushing nature from the mountain-top that gives it birth, but it acquires its distinctiveness from the contour of the land through which it flows. The same is the case with love. On the one hand, there is the inner feeling, on the other, the conflict with outward circumstances. It is the combination of these two factors that gives the complete picture its individuality. I have tried in this story to body forth that individuality in the love of Ela and Atindra. I have had to show the capital asset of their natures, as well as to render an account of their transactions with the outside world with which they had to deal to the last.

Much of this world produced by the play of events in our political struggle, I have naturally seen according to my own lights, though fringes of it have actually touched my experience. Its appeal is likely to be different to different persons, just as direct experience of it must necessarily be of many kinds. But if the story is to be regarded as a piece of literature, controversy over its political context is uncalled-for, for my picture of that context must be accepted as authentic. If even a Christian were to read *Kumarasambhavam*, he must be prepared to accept without question Kalidasa's account of the Hara-Parvati story, and not bring in theological discussions about its validity. Whether this Puranic story is in strict accordance with the tenets of the Sankhya philosophy or not is a question that does not even merit a reply; for in Kalidasa's treatment of this theme the main emphasis is on the love and union of Hara and Parvati. So much so, that Kalidasa seems to treat with indifference even the story of Kumara's birth.

If a reader should remark that the back-ground to my story is mainly or partly a figment of my imagination, as a story-teller there would be no harm in my pleading guilty to the charge. Nowhere in the book is there any indication of the final outcome of the movement directed by Indranath or of what happened to Batu or Kanai. The end of the story is solely concerned with the love of Atindra and Ela, and this conclusion gives a completeness to the picture of that love.

There is another bone of contention. In the course of the story the different characters have voiced their views about the revolutionary movement. If these comments on the movement had been entirely absent, the context would have lost all meaning. It must be assumed that the opinions expressed serve only to support and confirm the characterization of the speakers. Should anyone suspect that some of these opinions tally with my own, then I would submit that such speculation is irrelevant and extraneous to the matter in hand and, so far as the story is concerned, equally valueless whether valid or otherwise. If the views expressed by a speaker were to be found inconsistent with his character, then only could the author be charged with a serious defect in his writing.

If any learned professor should succeed some day in proving beyond the shadow of a doubt, that in the words he speaks, as well as in his attitude and behaviour, Hamlet is Shakespeare himself – true or not, this would neither enhance nor lower the value of *Hamlet* as a piece of dramatic art. Similarly, it would be saying nothing about the quality of the play if one were to make the incredible statement that nowhere in it does Shakespeare reveal himself.

To sum up:

It is unnecessary in any literary appraisal of *Four Chapters* to discuss whether it propagates a particular creed or moral. It is obvious that its main interest centres round the story of two modern Bengali lovers. The revolutionary movement in Bengal has provided their love with its special dramatic setting.

Descriptions of the movement are of secondary importance: what matters as literature is the portrayal of the poignance and pain of their love against the stormy background of the revolution. Controversy and moral preaching are fit material for articles in periodicals, not for literature.

Chapter One

The scene is a Calcutta tea-shop. On one side is a little room in which a few school and college text-books, mostly second-hand, are displayed for sale. Among them are some English translations of modern Continental stories and plays. These the students read, so far as they may, as they turn over the pages. To this no objection is offered by the owner of the shop, Kanai Gupta, a retired sub-inspector of police.

For those who want to have their tea in comparative privacy, a portion of the front room is partitioned off by a screen of tattered sacking. This part of the shop shows to-day signs of special preparation. The inadequacy of chairs and stools has been made good by sundry packing cases marked 'Darjeeling Tea'. The tea-service also lacks uniformity, of course; blue enamel cups and saucers supplement white porcelain. In a broken-handled milk-jug on the table is a bunch of flowers.

It is nearly three in the afternoon. The boys, when they had invited Ela, had set two-thirty as the exact time, and had specially requested her not to be a minute late. The reason for fixing this untimely hour was that only then would the shop be empty. Ela had come exactly on time, but not one of the boys was to be seen anywhere. As she sat alone, wondering whether she had mistaken the date, she was startled to see Indranath coming into the room—surely the last place where he could have been expected to appear.

Indranath had spent many years in Europe, and had made a name for himself in scientific circles. He was qualified to hold the highest positions. But, while in Europe, he had happened on a few rare occasions to meet an Indian political suspect, on which ground he found, when he came back home, that every door to advancement was closed against him. At last, through the special recommendation of a distinguished English scientist, he secured the post of a teacher, but under a far less competent superior. Incompetency and intense envy go hand in hand, so that all kinds of obstacles were placed in the way of his attempts to continue his scientific researches, until, finally, he was transferred to a college in which there was no laboratory.

The bitter realization at length dawned on Indranath that in his own country it was hopeless for him to dream of rising to the height of his powers, although he felt sure that elsewhere he could have won recognition and honour. Here he stood condemned to turn the mill of routine teaching to the end of his working days, after which a meagre pension would carry him on somehow to the end of life itself. To such prostitution of his talents he was utterly unprepared to submit. Eventually he started a small class for teaching French and German, and also helped science students with their botany and geology. In some fissure in the depths of this little institution of his, there lodged a seed of secret purpose, which spread its underground ramifications, across prison yards, far and wide through the country.

'You here, Ela?' remarked Indranath.

'You forbade the boys to come to my house,' replied Ela, 'so they asked me to a tea here.'

'That I know already. So I found urgent work for them elsewhere. I have now come to apologize to you on their behalf, and to settle their bill.'

'Why was it so necessary to break up our party?'

'To suppress the fact that your relations with the boys are cordial. You'll see in the newspapers to-morrow that I've also sent in an article over your signature.'

'If it has been written by you, no one will believe my signature to be genuine. Your style can't so easily be palmed off on another.'

'I've not only disguised my handwriting but seen to it that the article shows little of intelligence and much of moral sentiment.'

'In what way?'

'Well, you have written that our boys are going to ruin the country by their untimely attempts to rouse it. You have piteously appealed to the women of Bengal to do their best to cool the overheated heads of these impossible jackanapes. But, you have pointed out, that can't be done by good counsel offered from afar. The women must go amongst them, must go into their very dens of intoxication, even at the risk of being themselves laid open to the fate of political suspects. You women are of the mother sex, you have said, and if you can save these hapless misguided boys by taking their punishment on yourselves, such sacrifice, even unto death, would be worth while. You know, Ela, how often you put forward your claim to belong to the mother sex. I've only soaked those words in salt tears and put them into the writing; when the mother-loving reader reads them his eyes will brim over. After this, if, you were a man, it wouldn't have been impossible for you to get the title of Rai Bahadur.'

'I'll not deny,' said Ela, after a pause, 'that what you've made me say could have been my real sentiments. I do so love these horrid boys—where can you find their equals? I've been with them since we were in college together and I lost my parents. At first, I must confess, they used to write all kinds of things about the girl students on the blackboard. Their pranks made some of the girls angry, but I always sided with the boys. I knew it was because they were unused to meet our sex in these surroundings that they couldn't behave properly. When they got used to us their whole tone softened down to naturalness—occasionally perhaps, to an even softer note. But what of that? I know from my own experience how easy it is to get on with the boys, if only the girl doesn't turn huntress, consciously or unconsciously. Then I saw them rushing off, one by one, the best of them, who had no touch of vulgarity in them, whose true manhood knew how to respect women—'

'You mean,' interjected Indranath with a smile, 'those whose finer emotions have not turned into unsavoury ferment, like those of the average town boy?'

'Yes, I mean just those like myself, who come from the country. It's they that I've seen desperately running after the messenger of death. Am I to remain safely living in my corner while they rush to their doom? Let me tell you the truth, Master. The more we go on, the more does our purpose cease to be purpose, and becomes mere intoxication. These splendid boys are being sacrificed at the altar of some blind, monstrous idol. It's breaking my heart!'

'My child,' said Indranath, 'such revulsion of spirit is common on the eve of a great battle. The *Mahabharata* tells us how the peerless warrior, Arjuna himself, was thus afflicted at the outset of the Kurukshetra war. As for me, I nearly fainted with horror when as a medical student I had to dissect my first corpse. This kind of revulsion is itself revolting. In the struggle for power, the cult of cruelty comes first, to be followed at last, it may be, by that of mercy. You take pride in belonging to the mother sex. But that's nothing to glory in. The mother instinct is one of nature's devices, found in the lower animals too. Much the bigger thing is that your sex is the embodiment of power. You have to prove this. Give strength, give men strength.'

'It's with these big words that you keep us deluded. You claim far more than we have in us to give.'

'The very force of the claim brings about its fulfilment. What we persist in believing you to be, that you shall become. You, also, must so believe in us, that our strivings may come true.'

'I love to hear you talk. But no more to-day. Now I've something to say to you.'

'Very well, then,' agreed Indranath, 'let's go into the back room.'

They passed out together into the dimness of the room behind. Its only furniture was an old table and some benches and a map of India on the wall.

'I can't help telling you,' began Ela, 'that you have done a grievous wrong!' Only Ela could venture to say such a thing straight to Indranath, and, even for her, it was not easy; her voice betrayed a strain.

To say that Indranath was handsome would be to leave much unsaid. From him radiated a tense, inflexible attraction. It was as if there was a thunderbolt in the depths of his being, of which the rumblings could not be heard, but only the cruel flashes sometimes seen. In his looks there was a polished urbanity like a sharpened knife. Harsh words were not difficult for him to speak, but he spoke them with a smile. Anger never raised his voice, but only changed the quality of his laugh. He took just so much care of his appearance as was necessary for his dignity, and no more. His short-clipped hair needed no special attention to be kept in place. His complexion was almond, with just a touch of colour in his face. In his glance was the glint of keen insight, in his compressed lips unyielding resolve. He could make the most impossible claims without a qualm, secure in the conviction that they could not be lightly disregarded. Some believed that his intelligence was unusual, others that his power was super natural; so that some had limitless veneration for him, others an unaccountable dread. Students all over the country looked on him as an uncrowned king.

'What is the wrong I have done?' asked Indranath, smiling.

'You have laid on Uma the command to get married when she doesn't at all want to.'

'Who says she doesn't?'

'She says so herself.'

'It's possible she doesn't know her own mind, or won't speak it.'

'Didn't she swear to you that she would never marry?'

'The promise was truly meant then, but it is no longer true now. Truth cannot be created by word of mouth. She herself would have broken her pledge. I am saving her from that disgrace by letting it be done under compulsion.'

'The responsibility for keeping or not keeping her word was hers alone—what if she decided to break it and accept the consequences?'

'Once breaking is started, one never knows how far it will spread, and the losses would fall on all of us.'

'The poor girl is weeping her heart out.'

'In that case I'll shorten the period of her tribulation till the day after to-morrow.'

'What of the rest of her life that will be left over after the day after to-morrow?'

'The tears shed by girls before marriage are like the proverbial morning clouds that disperse on the rising of the sun.'

'Oh, you are cruel!'

'That's because God, who loves man, is Himself cruel. His indulgence is for the lower animals.'

'Surely you know that Sukumar is the one whom Uma loves?'

'That's just why I am separating them.'

'As a punishment for their love?'

'Punishment for love is nonsense. You might as well talk of punishing a person for getting smallpox. All the same, it's better to send the sufferer out of the house to the hospital.'

'Why not let Uma marry Sukumar, then?'

'What crime has poor Sukumar committed—one of the best of our boys?'

'Suppose he himself wants to marry Uma—'

'Not at all unlikely. That's why I am in such a hurry. It's so easy for a girl to turn the head of a gallant fellow like Sukumar. A few teardrops, duly shed, would be enough to convince him that his civility was tantamount to encouragement. Are you vexed at my bluntness?'

'Why should I be vexed? Do I not know from experience with what silent skill women have often continued to bring about this encouragement, and how the men have had to bear the brunt of it afterwards! The time has come for dealing equal justice to the sexes; and the girls cannot bear me because I try to do that. Any how, what has the victim, to whom Uma is to be married, to say to it?'

'He's one of those spineless good fellows who have no such worries as opinions of their own. Every woman of Bengal is for him a special masterpiece of the Creator. This kind of human rubbish has to be thrown out of the inner circle, and the most suitable dustbin for them is marriage.'

'If these mutual attractions cause you so much misgiving, why group the sexes together at all?'

'Because I've no use either for ascetics who mortify their bodies with sackcloth and ashes or for self-immolators who reduce to ashes their natural passions. We want fire-worshippers, but if any of these kindle the fire within themselves, they have to be got rid of. Our conflagration must rage throughout the land, and that cannot be achieved with those whose fire has gone out, or those who cannot control their own flame.'

Ela had been gravely listening to his words. Now she dropped her eyes and murmured, 'Let me leave you, then.'

'How can you expect me to put up with such a loss?'

'I suspect you do not know me.'

'Who says I don't? Did I not notice it the very day a tinge of colour crept into your white *khadi* homespun? That told me of the rosy dawn within. Am I blind to how your ears are astrain for the first sound of certain footsteps? When I came into your room last Friday, could I not feel that it was someone else you were expecting?'

Ela kept silent, reddening to the tips of her ears.

'You love someone,' pursued Indranath. 'What of it? Your heart's not made of stone. I know who it is you love. In that also I see nothing to be ashamed of.'

Ela was remembering the day five years ago, when, at a gathering at her uncle's house, she had first casually met Indranath. Overcoming her natural reserve, she had begged him to give her some of his work to do, and he had offered to put her in charge of a high school for girls, just started in Calcutta. He had said: 'The only promise I ask of you is never to become entangled in any social relationship. You are not for society, but for your country alone!'

'I promise,' she had answered simply.

'You gave us the injunction exclusively to devote ourselves to our duties. Is that possible in all circumstances?' she now asked.

'It mayn't be possible for every one. But you're not the girl to sink your pledge by overloading it with a love affair.'

'But—' ·

'There's no "But". You simply can't be let off.'

'And yet you know I do practically no work for you.'

'I never expected you would. It's not work I want of you.

Of course, it is hardly possible for you yourself to know of
the glory that lights up the hearts of the boys at the touch
of your fingers when you anoint their foreheads with the red
sandal-paste of initiation. How can the dry rewards I have
to offer evoke the same quality of work? Where sex works
I put woman on a pedestal.'

'I'll not keep anything from you. This love of mine is day
by day overshadowing my love for all else.'

'Love as much as you like. Only the incurably immature
revel in calling their country "Mother". Our country is not
the Mother of senile infants. She is half God and half Goddess.
Her fitting worship is in the coming together of man and
woman, but such union should not be enervated by
imprisonment within the bars set up by society.'

'Why then is poor Uma—?'

'Uma! Kalu! Are they fit to bear unscathed the scorching
flame of the larger love? There's nothing for it but to pack
them off to the cremation ground of matrimony. But enough
of this. Did I not hear that a burglar entered your room night
before last?'

'Yes, a man suddenly came in.'

'Did your *jiujutsu* training stand you in good stead?'

'Well, I sent him off with a dislocated wrist.'

'You felt no pricks of sympathy when you did that to him?'

'I might have, had I not been afraid of being assaulted.
I couldn't have given the final twist if I'd seen any signs of
retreat.'

'Did you recognize him?'

'No, it was too dark to see his face.'

'Had you seen it, you'd have found him to be Anadi.'

'Oh, what a shame! Our Anadi? But he's a mere boy.'

'I sent him.'

'You! What on earth for?'

'To test both you and him.'

'What a horrible thing to do!'

'I was in a room below, and set his wrist for him then and there. You plume yourself on your sympathy with suffering. I wanted to show you how out of place that is in a situation of danger. When I asked you to shoot a kid the other day, you said you couldn't. The other girl, your cousin, did it— to show off. She laughed when the kid rolled over with a broken leg, to make out that she didn't care. But her laugh was hysterical, and she had no sleep that night. Had it been a tiger coming after you, would you have hesitated to shoot to kill? It's because I can clearly visualize the tiger that I have ceased to have any use for pity or compunction. The advice given by Sri Krishna to Arjuna, in the *Gita,* to fight, did not mean that he was to be cruel, but simply to be undeterred by softer sentiments in carrying out his high purpose. You see the point?'

'I do.'

'If you do, let me ask you a question. You love Atin, do you not?'

Ela made no reply.

'Well, suppose he became a source of danger to our cause, could you kill him?'

'I can say "yes" without hesitation, because I know that to be impossible.'

'But if it did become possible?'

'Whatever I may say now, can one really know oneself to the end?'

'It's with just such certainty that you'll have to know yourself.'

'I know one thing for certain. You've selected me by mistake.'

'On the contrary, I'm certain I made no mistake.'

'I humbly beg of you, Master, at least release Atin.'

'Who am I to release him? He remains bound by his own resolve. I know he'll never be rid of his doubts. At every step his finer feelings will be hurt. And yet his self-respect will keep him on till the end.'

A deep voice called out from outside, 'Is that you, brother?'

'Come in, Kanai, come in!' cried Indranath.

Kanai Gupta entered the room. He was a short thickset man of middle age. His forehead was bald. His face bristled with a week's growth of beard which he had been too busy to shave. It was long since his homespun *dhoti* and wrap had been washed. The chief purpose of his tea-shop was the feeding of the organization.

Ela rose to depart. Indranath turned to her, saying: 'Ela, let me tell you just one thing more before you go. I constantly speak disparagingly of you to the members of our band. I've gone to the length of warning them that some day it may become necessary to cause you to disappear without a trace! I've complained that you're making Atin break away from us, and that one break will break something else.'

'Why help to make this true,' replied Ela, 'by continually saying it? Who knows, I may be a misfit here.'

'In spite of that, I don't mistrust you, and yet I disparage you before them. Rumour has it that you have no enemy. But I've found most of your professed admirers eager to hear all I say against you.'

'They listen to you, Master, on account of their liking for this kind of talk, not because of any dislike for me.'

'Enough of this for the present,' broke in Kanai. 'Sister Ela, if I've been at the bottom of the breaking up of your tea-party, I ask your pardon. The time is near when my tea-shop itself will have to be padlocked. Perhaps it may reappear as a barber's shop two or three hundred miles away.'

As she left the room Ela paused at the door to turn and say: 'I shall remember your words, Master, and keep myself ready. Should the day come for causing me to disappear, I will silently vanish.'

'Why so disturbed, Kanai?' asked Indranath when Ela had gone.

'The other day,' said Kanai, 'some ruffianly youths were talking heroics, sitting at that table facing the street. The very tone of their voices proclaimed them to be pet calves of John Bull himself. I promptly made a report to the police, with quotations of their seditious talk.'

'You're sure you didn't misread them, Kanai?'

'They were loud in their demand for drowning the Satanic Government in torrents of blood. If they were mere fools, they were bound to get into trouble sooner or later; if they were pure knaves, no one can hurt a hair of their heads—my report will but get them promotion. Another evening, when I was counting my till, up comes a dusty fellow in tattered clothes, asking me in a whisper for twenty-five rupees for going to our centre at Dinajpur; and he actually mentioned our Uncle Mathur's name. I jumped up shouting, "How dare you, you impudent scoundrel! I'll hand you over to the police this minute." Had I the time, I'd have completed the farce by dragging him to the police station. Your boys who were drinking tea in the other room were furiously indignant with me. They started to go through their pockets to raise a subscription for the fellow, but couldn't collect more than thirteen annas among them. By then he had made himself scarce.'

'I see that the smell of the mess you've been cooking has escaped through some hole in the lid, and the flies have begun to buzz around.'

'No doubt about it. Now, brother, is the time to scatter your boys and, moreover, to provide each of them with some ostensible means of livelihood.'

'True enough, but have you made any plans?'

'Long ago. I've not only devised means, but also gathered materials. Madhab Kaviraj, the Indian physician, sells a lot of his 'Fever Destroyer Pellets'—mostly made up of quinine.

I have taken over his stock and changed the label to 'Malaria-killer Tablets.' The quinine must be supplemented by plenty of verbiage. Let Pratul Sen, that glib orator, carry them about in a canvas bag in the capacity of salesman. Your medical doctor, Tarini, can proceed to make life miserable for his acquaintances by touting for subscriptions to build a temple to Sitala, goddess of smallpox. The point is, you must hide your boys under some kind of trashy work or other.'

Indranath laughed. 'Your eloquence,' he said, 'makes me want to take up some business myself, if only to get acquainted with the methods and psychology of insolvency.'

'The business you have already in hand, brother,' retorted Kanai, 'is making for bankruptcy, sure enough. But what's the use of discussing that now? A question has occurred to me which I should like to ask you. You admit, I suppose, that beauty like Ela's is not to be seen every day?'

'Of course I do.'

'Then how is it you're not afraid of keeping her amongst your boys?'

'My dear Kanai, you should have known me better by this time. One who fears fire cannot use fire. I can't afford to leave fire out of my work.'

'That's to say, you don't care whether the fire you play with burns up your work or not!'

'The Creator Himself plays with fire. He doesn't count on certainties. This boy, Atin, has joined us for love of Ela. He holds within him dynamite that may at any time explode disastrously. That's why I'm so curious to see how he shapes.'

'Look here, brother, we only do the sweeping and dusting in your terrible laboratory. If any of your gases should burst its bottle, it's our fate that will be torn to pieces.'

'Why, then, don't you resign and leave us?'

'Because it was some agent of yours who taught us to believe that it's the Elixir of Life you're after, and we poor fools are here because we still have expectations of tangible results. You look on the work as a gambler, we as sober businessmen. I pray you, don't end up with the practical joke of making a bonfire of our carefully kept books of account. Every pice entered there, I tell you, means a drop of our heart's blood.'

'It's not possible for me to hold on to any blind belief, Kanai. I've long given up thinking in terms of victory and defeat. As leader in a grand enterprise I'm here because it becomes me; either victory or defeat will be equally great. They tried to make me petty by closing the doors on every side. I'm determined to show them that I'm great, even if that entails disaster at every step. You can see for yourself, Kanai, how these followers have come round me at my call, recking nothing of life or death. Why? Because I know how to call. That's what I want to make clear to myself and to others; and, after that, I don't care what happens. You, also, Kanai, once looked very ordinary on the outside, but I've brought out your extraordinary self. I've put the force of fire in you— that's what my laboratory is for. What more can you want? On a historical view, the epic may seem to end in a vast burial ground of defeat. Still it would be an epic. For the curtailed manhood of this slave-ridden country, isn't it the greatest of opportunities to be able to die the death of a hero?'

'I don't know, brother, how you led me, a plain, unimaginative, practical man, into the thick of this madhouse dance of yours. It's a mystery to me.'

'This power I have over all of you, because I never came to you as a beggar. I didn't ask you to come in under any delusion, nor lure you by any prospect of gain. I called on you to join my forlorn hope, not to show any particular results, but to prove your valour. My temperament is impersonal, so that I can submit cheerfully to the inevitable. And of whom am I to beg and pray that India may be spared its fate while it continues to worship with sandal-paste and vermilion the very germs of its own ruination? Mine is the dispassionate scientific attitude which tells me that if the reasons for decay are left uncured, death must ensue. Yet even in the face of all the signs of impending death, I will not allow dejection to enter my soul.'

'But what about the rest of us?'

'Are the rest of you so many children? If your ship has split her bottom in mid-ocean, do you suppose you can save her by wailing and supplication?'

'What's to happen to us if we can't?'

'But was it not you yourselves who, knowing her condition, set full sail into the storm, without a tremor in your hearts? With the few of you who will stay on with me to the last, I'll count sinking a victory. Doesn't the *Gita* tell us our concern is with the doing of our duty, not with the results?'

'Are you so impersonal that you never feel anger?'

'Anger against whom?'

'Against the British.'

'I've travelled all over the continent of Europe, and also known the people of England. I feel that the Britishers are the greatest of Westerners. I don't say they never commit atrocities under the influence of greed or lust for power, but they cannot do so whole-heartedly. They are ashamed when they do it. Their worst fear is that they'll have to explain their conduct to their great men at home. So they try to delude themselves, as well as their masters. That's why I can't raise my anger against them to the pitch that will generate steam.'

'You are a strange man!'

'They had the power completely to crush out our manhood, but their better nature did not allow them to do it. For that I cannot but admire their manhood. No doubt that manhood is deteriorating by the continued exercise of irresponsible power all over their empire, and in such deterioration are being sown the seeds of their own downfall.'

'If you don't hate your opponents as enemies, I can't understand how you can raise your hand to smite them.'

'Just as I lift my pickaxe to hit a stone that blocks my way without getting into a passion over it. It's not the question whether the British are good or bad. Their rule is one of foreign exploitation, killing our very souls within us. I only show human intelligence by trying to get rid of this unnatural situation.'

'And yet you've no hope of certain success.'

'But need I, therefore, lower myself, even if before me there is nothing certain save death? Rather should the prospect of defeat impel us at least to assert our manhood. To my mind that is our first and last duty.'

Chapter Two

Ela was sitting in a lounge chair by the window, a cushion supporting her back, one knee over the other, busy writing. She had on a purple *sari* of homespun, tolerated as a useful working garment for domestic use. On her wrists were bangles of red-lacquered conchshell, round her neck a chain of gold. Her body, with its ivory sheen, was taut and trim in its shapeliness. She looked very young indeed, but her expression was one of grave maturity. Along one of the walls there was a narrow iron cot, with a green homespun counterpane over the bed. The floor was covered with a coarse cotton carpet. On a small table near her chair were an inkstand and a small brass bowl with a sprig of gardenia.

Darkness came on, and she was on the point of rising to light the lamp, when the curtain in the doorway was violently thrust aside, with a shout of 'Elie!' and Atin burst into the room like a gust of wind.

Startled into sudden gladness, Ela chided him: 'Oh, you barbarian! How dare you come in so?'

Atin dropped down at Ela's feet as he replied, 'Life is too short, and etiquette too long.'

'I'm not yet really dressed.'

'So much the better. That makes you fit in with my state. Once I was a gentleman, immaculately attired. It was you who stripped me of my trimmings. How do you like my present dress?'

'I can't find any word for it. Is that zig-zag pattern down the front of your tunic an advertisement of your own needlework?'

'No. I didn't dare give this tunic to a tailor, for he, at least, can't have lost all self-respect.'

'Why didn't you give it to me?'

'Aren't you busy enough repairing the new age, not to be burdened with a tunic besides?'

'What makes you cleave to this particular garment?'

'Why does a man cleave to his wife? Because it's the only one he has.'

'Whatever do you mean, Ontu! Have you only this one tunic left?'

'Well, in my previous style of living, I used to have tunics large in number and varied in pattern. Then came the flood in our country. Do you remember your speech? You said: "In this tear-flooded day of disaster when so many of our countrywomen lack even a single piece of cloth to cover their shame, the shame is theirs who keep for themselves clothes in excess of their needs." I hadn't then the courage to laugh openly. I merely smiled to myself, for I knew that in your wardrobe you had clothes far beyond your actual needs. But, of course, if a girl has fifty dresses of fifty hues, each one is an absolute necessity. When I laid at your feet a trunk filled with all my clothes, you clapped your hands in delight.'

'What a shame, Ontu! You should have told me.'

'Don't you worry. The situation is not so tragic. I kept two coloured tunics for everyday use, which I wear and wash in turn. I have two others put away for emergencies.'

Ela playfully pushed away Atin's head as she said, 'What is this madness come over you these days?'

'It's been coming on ever since that day we met. The days that do not rise to the height of fulfilment are doomed to such ghöstly wanderings on the horizon of the might-have-been. There lies the mirage of a bridal chamber in which our union was to be. I've come to invite you to it. Your work may be disturbed.'

'Bother the work!' said Ela, letting her writing-board slide to the floor as she started to rise. 'I'll light the lamp.'

'No, don't. Light can only show reality. I want to take you along the unlighted road to the yet-unrealized. It's now almost four years since I was crossing the river at Mokameh Ghat on the ferry steamer. I was still holding on to the remnants of my ancestral fortune, full of debt-made holes. Luxurious tastes still clung to me like the cloud colours of declining day. Clad in a silk tunic, a scarf of old-gold *muga* neatly folded on my shoulder, I was sitting alone in a cane chair on the first-class deck. You had cast in your lot with "the people" as a deck passenger. All of a sudden, you came up and stood right in front of me. The golden brown of your *sari* is still vivid in my mind. The end was drawn up over the back of your head, fixed to the coil of your hair with a pin, swelling to the breeze on either side of your face. With strained naturalness you asked me, "Why don't you wear *khadi*?" Do you remember?'

'Very clearly.'

'I want to recall the whole of that day—you'll have to listen.'

'Only too gladly. It is the refrain of my new life. My heart wants to go back to it over and over again.'

'The music of your voice thrilled me through and through. It struck me like a sudden shaft of light. Could I have become indignant at this unheard-of impertinence from a strange girl, I'd have followed the usual path of fashionable society to the end of my days. But vanity is the best part of my nature; so I jumped to the conclusion that, if the girl hadn't specially liked me, she would never have come to reprove me. Tell me, wasn't I right?'

'Haven't I told you often enough, you greedy boy, how I had been gazing and gazing at you from my corner of the third-class deck, regardless of whether anybody was watching me or not? That was a most wonderful experience of life-long intimacy felt at first sight. "Whence comes this strange being," asked my heart, "so much bigger than his surroundings, a lotus flower amongst water weeds?" I was at once filled with the determination to draw near to me this rare creature—not only near to me, but near to all of us.'

'It was my evil fate that made your resolve plural.'

'I had no choice, Ontu. I had already sworn to devote myself to my country, not to keep anything for myself alone. My betrothal was to my country.'

'This pledge of yours was a crime and, every day you keep it, you commit a fresh outrage against your own nature. To crush under the heels of your party a feeling which is of the purest, which comes by command of the Creator Himself, is a sin for which you'll have to take punishment.'

'There is no end of this, Ontu! It tortures me day and night. Supreme good fortune, not to be won by any striving, an unmasked gift of the gods, was vouchsafed to me, and I could not accept it. Heart linked to heart, and yet the unbearable pangs of widowhood—may fate never inflict this suffering on any other woman! I had been from my childhood spell-bound within conventional barriers, but at the very first sight of you my heart said, "Let all barriers be broken". I could never have imagined such a revolution within myself. I used to be proud of my success in controlling my feelings. That pride I have lost. Look within me and you'll see my surrender. You are the hero, I your captive.'

'I also have owned defeat at the hands of my captive, a defeat not yet come to an end. At every moment there is my struggle and my defeat.'

'When I had that first wonderful vision of you, Ontu, on the first-class deck, I was still full of the newly-born patriotic pride in going third-class. On changing into the train you took a second-class ticket. My whole being was drawn to the same class. A trick even occurred to me. I would board your compartment at the last moment, and say I was led into the mistake in my hurry. In our old poems it's the woman who always goes to keep tryst with her lover. The poets have done us this favour out of pity, knowing how impossible that is in society-ridden real life. Our unsanctioned desires go round and round in the darkness of their confinement within us, knocking their heads against the walls. Such desires women do not acknowledge except to themselves. You have made me acknowledge them to you.'

'Why have you done so?'

'I haven't been able to give you anything else.'

Atin suddenly clasped both of Ela's hands in his own, and asked bitterly: 'Why couldn't you? What prevented you from accepting me? society? caste?'

'For shame, Ontu, never think of such a thing! There was nothing outside. The obstacle was within me.'

'Does that mean that you do not love me enough?'

'"Enough" has no meaning here, Ontu. Don't despise me for being weak if I can't move mountains. I had sworn not to marry. Even if I hadn't sworn it, marriage wouldn't have been possible for me.'

'Why not?'

'Don't be angry with me, Ontu! My love itself would have stood in the way. So destitute am I, I feel I have not enough to offer you.'

'Tell me more plainly.'

'I've told you so often!'

'Tell me once more. I want to finish all our telling to-night. I'll never ask again.'

A voice outside called, 'Sister, dear!'

'Is that you, Akhil? Come in,' said Ela.

A boy entered. A handsome, obstinate-looking, mischievous face; dishevelled curly hair; light-brown complexion of an infantile softness; restless eyes aglow. He wore a khaki jacket unbuttoned at the neck, and khaki shorts, their pockets bulging with all kinds of litter, including a horn-handled jack-knife.

Akhil was an orphan, a distant cousin of Ela's. As he entered, he made a shamefaced attempt to salute her formally by touching her feet.

'Aren't you going to greet your brother Atin, too?' admonished Ela.

Akhil turned his back on Atin, without reply. Atin laughed as he patted Akhil's shoulder. 'Well done!' he said. 'If you must bend your head, let it be before a single divinity.'

'Don't listen to him, Akhil,' said Ela ; 'go on with what you want to say.'

'To-morrow is the day of mother's death.'

'So it is. Do you wish to invite any one to the rites of observance?'

'No.'

'Then what is it you want?'

'I want three days off from my studies.'

'What will you do with your holiday?'

'I want to make a rabbit hutch.'

'You haven't any rabbits left, why bother about a hutch?'

Atin smiled as he interposed: 'Rabbits can be imagined. The real thing is the making of the hutch.'

'All right, Akhil, you may have three days off,' said Ela.

Without another word Akhil was out of the room at a run.

'I've been quite unable to tame him,' said Atin. There's a third party dividing us. But let that be. Now for your explanation. What made you keep me at a distance?'

'Why can't you remember one simple thing—that I am older than you?'

'Because I can't forget the simple thing that you are twenty-eight, and I am a few months over twenty-eight.'

'My twenty-eight is far more than yours. At your age all the wicks of the lamp of youth are burning brightly. You still have your window open to unrealized, unthought-of possibilities.'

'Elie, you don't understand me simply because you won't. Don't go on saying that the unrealized is yet to come in my life. It has already come—it is you. And yet it's still unrealized. Shall I have to keep my window expectantly open forever? Through its emptiness only the wail of my yearning heart goes forth, "I want you, only you!" And no reply comes.'

'Oh, ungrateful! How can you say that you've had no reply? I also want you, you, you! And there's nothing I want more in all the world. Only, our meeting happened at a time when it could not be auspiciously carried further.'

'Why, what harm would it have done to carry it on to union?'

'My life, indeed, would have been fulfilled, but what a trifle that is! You aren't like the others, but ever so much above them. And it's because I kept my distance that I was privileged to see this wonderful greatness of yours. I'm mortally afraid even to think of swathing you round with my smallness, of bringing you down to the pettinesses which make up my little household. There may be women who would have no compunction in smothering you under the number-less details of their lives. I know of so many tragedies which such women have brought about—monarchs of the forest stunted under a tangle of clinging creepers—as if their embraces are all-sufficient.'

'Elie! Only he who receives can say what is, or is not, all-sufficient.'

'I refuse to live in a false paradise, I know you, Ontu, better than you do yourself. Pent in the narrow cage of my love, you'd soon have begun to beat your wings. The little of satisfaction I have in me to offer, you'd have by now drained to the dregs. Then you'd have found out my utter destitution. That's why I gave up all my personal claims on you and surrendered you completely at the shrine of our country. There your gifts will not lack full scope.'

Atin's eyes flashed. He got up and began to pace up and down the room. Then, standing in front of Ela, he said: 'The time has come to talk to you straight and hard. What right have you, let me ask, to deliver me up to the country, or to any one else? Your offering to me could have been something beautiful—call it service, call it favour, as you will—and according to your mood I'd have come to you, proudly if you had allowed pride, humbly if such had been your pleasure. But you cut down your gift to paltriness. Your woman's glory you had to bestow, but that you cast aside and offered instead to place the country in my hands! That you can't do, positively cannot—no one can. The country cannot be passed from hand to hand like this.'

Ela winced at this blow to her self-assurance. 'What are you talking about?' she murmured.

'I'm saying that the realm of sweetness and light which has woman for its centre may appear small on an outward view, but, within, its depth is immeasurable. It's by no means a cage. But the place you've assigned me, calling it country—which after all is nothing but a country of your band's own make—whatever it may mean to others, it's nothing but a cage for me. My natural powers do not find full scope in it; they are becoming unhealthy and perverted. I'm ashamed of what I'm doing, but I find the way out blocked. You don't seem to realize how my wings have been clipped, my limbs shackled. I had the responsibility, as well as the capacity, to take my own true place in my country's service. You made me forget it.'

'What did I do to make you forget, Ontu?'

'I'll admit a thousand times that you can make me forget all else but you; had it not been so, I'd have doubted my own manliness.'

'Why then reproach me?'

'After making me forget myself, you should have taken me into your own realm, your own world. Instead of that you merely echoed the words of your band and showed me "the one and only way!" And, going round and round in the pursuit of my official duties over that cement road of yours, the whole current of my life is being stirred into muddiness.'

'Official duties?'

'Yes, the duty of pulling at the car of Juggernaut's. Our Supreme Counsellor decreed that our whole duty was to take hold of a thick rope and keep pulling with closed eyes. Thousands of boys caught hold of the ropes. Some were crushed under the wheels, others crippled for life. Then came the order to turn back. The car began its return journey. But the broken bones did not become whole, and the cripples were swept out of the way on to the dust heaps. Independent thinking was knocked on the head from the very start and the boys came strutting up, ready and proud to be moulded into puppets. When they all began to dance to the same tune, at the wire-pulling of the Master, they were struck with admiration at their own performance. "Verily the dance of *Sakti* (Power)!"—thought they. But, whenever the Master slackens his pull, thousands of the puppet-boys fall out of the dance.'

'The boys themselves spoil it by trying to do their own steps, out of time.'

'They should have known from the first that live men cannot play the puppet for long. To ignore man's nature by trying to make him a puppet is folly. Had you respected me for my own individuality you would have drawn me not to your group, but to your heart!'

'Why, oh, why, Ontu, didn't you drive me away at the very beginning? Why did you make me guilty of doing you this injury?'

'That is what I've been trying to tell you. I desired union with you—a very simple desire, a most ungovernable desire. I found the usual way closed. I desperately entrusted my life to a crooked way. I have now come to know that it will lead me to my death. When at last I am dead to my real self, your outstretched arms will beseech me, by day and by night, to return to the equally dead emptiness of your bosom... I am talking like a fool, I know, a romantic fool. As if the getting of a shadow, without body or substance, is getting at all. As if your agony at our separation then, could pay the price of our frustrated union to-day!'

'The intoxication of words has got hold of you, now, Ontu!'

'Got hold of me now? It has always possessed me. Such a word-ridden creature has this Atin of yours always been! But I've lost all hope that you'll ever know him for what he really is—now that you've gone and made him one of the pawns in the game started by your precious band.'

Ela slipped down from her chair and laid her head on Atin's feet. Atin drew her up beside him as he continued: 'With words have I decorated this slim, dainty body of yours in my own mind—my joy and my sorrow in one—what have I not called you! I'm surrounded by an invisible atmosphere, an atmosphere of words—they come down around me from the Elysium of literature to save me from the crowd. Ever aloof am I, and that your Master knows. Why, then, does he trust me, I wonder!'

'He trusts you for that very reason. To mingle with the crowd one has to come down to the crowd. But come down you cannot. That's why I, too, trust you. No woman ever so trusted any man. Had you been an ordinary man, then like an ordinary woman I'd have been afraid of you. But there's no place for fear in your company.'

'A curse upon such fearlessness! You can't know a man unless you fear him. You claim desperate courage for winning the country, why not for winning your glorious self? Oh, why did I not desperately snatch you away long ago, while there was yet time! Good breeding? But love is barbarous. Its barbarity is for cutting a way through mountainous obstacles. It's a wild torrent, not a tame water-pipe—'

Ela suddenly rose to her feet. 'Come, Atin,' said she, 'let's go down to the other room.'

'Afraid!' cried Atin, as he also stood up. 'So at last you're afraid! Then the victory is mine. In the depths of me I'm a man, an impetuous barbarian. Had I not lost my opportunity, I'd have crushed you in my embrace, making your ribs ache: I'd not have given you the time to think—not left the breath in you to sob out a protest; I'd have pitilessly dragged you along the road to my own fastness! But the road on which I've actually arrived is narrow as a razor's edge, with no room for two, side by side—'

'Oh, my barbarian! You won't have to snatch me—take me, take me, take me!' cried Ela. With outstretched arms she flung herself on his breast and raised her face to his. As suddenly she recoiled. Through the window her glance fell on the street below. 'Oh, look!' she whispered with a shudder. 'He's there!'

'Who? Where?' asked Atin.

'There, at the corner. It's Batu. He's sure to be coming here. My whole being shrinks in disgust when I come across this odious creature—there's something so fleshy, so slimy about him. The look in his eyes insults me from a distance.'

'Don't worry about him, Ela. Why not dismiss him from your thoughts altogether?'

'I can't, I'm so afraid of him. And it's not only for myself— my fears are more for you, for I know that his jealousy has its snake's hood raised to strike.'

'These beasts have no courage, Ela. Only a bad smell. At bottom the fellow's afraid of me; not for anything he thinks I may do to him, but because he feels I belong to a different species.'

'Ontu, I have imagined all kinds of evil and suffering that may come upon me, and am prepared for everything except falling, by some trick of fate, into this man's clutches. I'd die any death first.' Ela clung to Atin's arm, as though need for rescue was imminent. 'Listen! here he is, coming right up.'

Atin went out on the landing, saying loudly: 'Not here, Batu. Let's go down to the sitting room. Sister Ela's dressing now.'

'I want just one word with her.'

'She told me she doesn't want any one to come to her room till she's ready.'

'Except you—?'

'Except me.'

Batu smiled a derisive smile. 'We old boys,' said he, 'have all this time been kept doing the ordinary chapters of grammar. You, the newcomer, get on at one jump to Poetic License! Exceptions are slippery things; their vogue, let me warn you, doesn't last long.' With this, Batu quickly ran downstairs.

A moment later Akhil came up, swinging a small saw in one hand and holding out the other. 'A letter,' he said. 'I was told to put it in your own hands.'

'Who told you?'

'I don't know him.' The letter delivered, Akhil was off.

Opening the envelope, Atin saw a note written on red paper—a danger signal. It was in code. He deciphered it to read: 'Don't stay any longer in Ela's house. Come away at once, without a word to her.'

Atin in self-respect could not disregard the command of one whose authority he had acknowledged. According to rule he tore the note into little pieces. For a moment he lingered; then he was out of the house with rapid strides, and with a bound boarded a passing tram-car.

Chapter Three

A verdant mass of trees, creepers and undergrowth, the light green, dark green, yellow green and brown green of their foliage jostling one another; in their shade a pool of water, choked with rotting leaves; along its edge a winding village lane, deeply rutted by cart wheels. The lane is fringed with cactus, yam and wild flowering shrubs, with occasional palisades of live *seora* stakes. Through gaps, here and there, glimpses of fields are to be seen, the young rice shoots just showing through the water held by mud embankments. Here, at some little distance beyond, overgrown by jungle, is a long-deserted hundred-and-fifty-year-old house, popularly believed to have come under a curse, and to be haunted by the ghost of some matricide. No living claimant has since ventured to dispute its ownership with this bodiless possessor. Our scene is the *puja dalan*—the room set apart for family worship and religious ceremonies—of this tumbledown house.

Into this secluded retreat of Atin's there entered, towards the close of the day, old Kanai Gupta. Atin was startled at the sight of him, for Kanai was not supposed even to be aware of his whereabouts. 'You here,' he stammered.

'I've come a-spying,' returned Kanai.

'Please explain the joke,' said Atin, mystified.

'There's no joke. When my tea-shop fell under Saturn's baleful influence, I, your humble purveyor, had to fare forth.

But the baleful eyes of the authorities did not cease to follow me wherever I went. As a last resort, I had to enter my name in their Spy Register. Those of us with no way left but to the cremation ground, find in this line a grand trunk road from one end of the country to the other.'

'So, instead of making tea, you're making news.'

'This profession can't be carried on with made-up news. You have to supply the real article. But I tighten the knot only when the prey is already netted. After they got ninety-nine per cent of information about your Haren, I supplied the superfluous remainder. He's now reposing in the Government Rest House at Jalpaiguri.'

'My turn this time, I suppose?'

'Very near it. Batu has advanced it most of the way. The little that remains in my hands may get you some respite. You remember how you lost your diary in your old quarters?'

'Remember? I should think I do!'

'It was sure to fall into the hands of the police some day, so I had to steal it.'

'So it was you!'

'Yes, fortune favours him whose cause is just. You were writing in it one day, as I came in. On some pretext I managed to get you away for five minutes. That was enough for me.'

'You read the whole of it!' cried Atin, with a gesture of despair.

'Certainly I did. It took me upto one o'clock in the morning. I must admit I didn't know before what force and charm there is in the Bengali language. Secrets there were, to be sure, but they didn't touch the British Government.'

'Was it right of you—?'

'I can't tell you how right it was! You have the literary gift, and, though you gave no names or details, your disillusionment and contempt came out in letters of fire. Had it come from the pen of any government favour-seeker he would straightway have attained the heaven of advancement. Had not Batu been after you, this document might have averted the evil eye of the authorities. I honestly feel that brother Indranath has deprived the country by entangling you in his band.'

'Does the band know of your latest profession?'

'Not one of them.'

'Not even the Master?'

'He's clever, and may have some inkling of it. But neither has he asked me, nor have I told him.'

'What made you tell me then?'

'That's the strange part of it. Those who have to make their livelihood out of mistrust would get choked if they couldn't get some one at least to confide in. I am not a fool, neither am I sentimental, so I don't keep a diary. Had I done so, nothing would have relieved my feelings like placing it in your hands.'

'Don't you confide in the Master?'

'To him one can make reports, but not open one's heart. I may be Indranath's chief adviser, but I don't know all about what he's doing. There are things I don't even dare guess at. It's my belief that when Indranath wishes to get rid of any one of his own traitors he gets him buried in the police refuse heap. That may be a betrayal, but not a crime. I warn you, if you ever come to find the handcuffs on you, that'll either be my doing or his—anyway I hope you'll take it in good part! The news of your transfer here was first hinted to the whispering department of Law and Order by Batu. So I had to go one better by furnishing them with a photograph of the place.'

'Now to business. All I can get you is twenty-four hours' time to clear out. If after that you're still here, I myself will have to put you on the road to the police station. I've written out for you in full how to get to your next destination. You know the code. Commit the directions to memory and tear up the paper. Here's a sketch map of the place. On this side of the road is the room you'll live in—it's in one corner of the schoolhouse. On the opposite side of the road is the police station. The Head Constable in charge is some sort of grandnephew of mine. His name is Raghubir. I call him Raghab, the killer fish. You've been appointed a teacher of Bengali. This Raghab will come over, now and then, and rummage your things; he may also give you a poke or two with his baton. Take it all as God's own mercy. His people have lived for generations in the upper provinces, and this fellow lets his contempt for the Bengal-born find unrestrained expression in his adopted language. Don't you make the faintest attempt to talk back, and for the life of you don't try to return home. I'm leaving my bicycle outside. When you hear the signal, jump on it in the twinkling of an eye. Now, my child, a last embrace.'

They embraced, and Kanai vanished.

Atin sat awhile in silent thought, looking withinwards. The last act of his life's drama had been brought on out of its time; the curtain would soon be rung down, the lights put out. His start had been made in the clear light of dawn, since when he had travelled very far. The vision of a woman's beauty that had been revealed to him at the bend of the road by the goddess of his fortunes, was not of this world. It was the inspiration of history working within him that had made Atin, like Dante, throw himself into the vortex of political revolt. But where was the truth, the valour, the glory in it? From the mire of masked robberies and murder into which the movement had progressively been drawn, no pillar of light would ever rise to illumine the pages of history. With his God-given gifts destroyed, Atin could now see no prospect of fruition before him, but rather the certain vanquishment of his self. Defeat has its value, but not the defeat of soul that brings in its train ghastly doings underground; unmeaning, unending ...

The daylight waned. The cicadas shrilled in the courtyard. The wheels of a distant cart creaked their agony.

Suddenly into his room came Ela, with rapid steps, in a blind hurry, like that of a suicide taking the final plunge. As Atin jumped up, she threw herself on his breast, sobbing, 'Ontu, Ontu, I couldn't keep away any longer!'

Atin gently disengaged her arms and, placing her before him, silently gazed at her tearful face, as he said, 'What's this you've done, Elie?'

'I don't know—I didn't know what I was doing.'

'But how did you come to know where I am?'

'*You* didn't tell me,' said Ela, with a world of reproach in her voice.

'He who has told you is no friend of yours.'

'Of that I've no doubt either; but to live in the emptiness of not knowing the way to you became so unbearable, I cared not whether I got it from friend or foe. What ages have passed since I saw you last!'

'Elie, you are wonderful!'

'It's you who are wonderful, Ontu. How easily could you obey the mandate to cease to see me!'

'That was my ingrained pride. Tremendous longing crushed me in its coils day and night, but I wouldn't give in. They had put me down as sentimental; they were so certain that in the day of trial I'd be found to be made of clay! It was beyond them to understand that in my sentiments lay my strength.'

'The Master understands, Ontu.'

'But Elie, you've broken the rules by coming here.'

'I know, Ontu. I admit my weakness. Yet it wasn't for my own need alone, but for yours, too. Every day my heart told me you were calling me. Not to respond to your call would

have suffocated me. Tell me, Ontu, aren't you glad that
I came?'

'So glad am I that I'm ready to risk punishment for it!'

Ela took a turn round the room. A blanket spread on the
floor, with a mat over it, served as a bed. A canvas bag filled
with books had taken the place of a pillow. A packing case
did duty as a writing desk. In a corner was a water jar with
an earthen pot for a lid. A tattered basket contained a bunch
of bananas and an enamel-ware goblet with the enamel chipped
off in places, which could be used as a tea-cup on the rare
occasions when any tea was to be had. At the other end of
the room was a huge wooden chest with a clay image of the
elephant-headed Ganesha resting on it. A musty smell of
dampness pervaded the stagnant atmosphere of the whole
room.

She found it quite impossible to adjust her mind to the
idea of Atin doomed to these squalid, unclean surroundings.

Atin laughed outright. 'The sight of my wealth,' said he,
'seems to amaze you. We have to keep ourselves thoroughly
mobile. Neither man nor thing must be there to clog our steps
when the time comes for us to run. A little way off there are
the quarters of the jute mill operatives. They call me Master
Babu. I read for them the letters they get, put the address on
the letters they write, and see to it that their mutual accounts
of debts and dues are in order. I get frequent gifts of milk
and fruit and vegetables.'

'Whose is that big box on the other side, Ontu?'

'One is more conspicuous in a place like this, if alone;
so I have let in a Marwari tradesman who was swept into the
streets by the goddess of misfortune. He is a discharged
insolvent for the third time. I'm inclined to think that becoming
bankrupt is his chief business. He looks on this dilapidated
dalan as a training academy for his nephew. After breakfasting
on roasted barley meal, they turn up here. They dye cheap
cloths for the village women, and out of the proceeds pay the

interest on the capital they've borrowed, and a part of the principal as well. Those big pots you see over there are not used by us for cooking feasts, but are for boiling the dye-stuff. The dyed cloth is kept in that box, which also contains trinkets suitable for the wives of the mill hands—glass bangles, brass bangles, combs and hand mirrors. They go out at three o'clock in the afternoon and return the next morning. Meanwhile I and the ghost act as custodians.'

'How long are you to be here?'

'Twenty-four hours, I expect.'

'What's your next address?'

'It's forbidden to tell.'

Ela had taken out the books from the canvas bag. They were mostly poetry in English and Bengali.

'I've been carrying these about all this time,' said Atin, 'so that I may not altogether forget my caste. My original abode was in the dream-land of their making; if you turn over their pages you'll find its highways and byways marked in pencil. And where am I to-day? Look around you.'

Ela sank to the ground and clasped Atin's feet. 'Forgive me, Ontu, forgive me,' she wailed.

'What have I to forgive you for, Elie? If there be a God, and if He be all-merciful, may He forgive *me!*'

'I brought you to this pass when I didn't know you for what you are.'

'My own folly brought me to the place which is not mine,' said Atin with a bitter laugh. 'Why grudge me even that much credit? I'm not in the mood to put up with your trying to make me out a minor needing your guardianship. Come down, rather, from your height; look me in the face and say, "Come, my lover, come and sit close by me, on the half of my Sari's end spread for you."'

'Maybe I would have said that, but why this mad mood of yours?'

'What can I do but flare up when you dare suggest that your lotus-stem arms dragged me forth on this road?'

'Why be angry with me for telling the truth?'

'You call that the truth! The urge within me flung me out—you were only the passive object.'

'For heaven's sake, Ontu, stop this wild talk. I'll never be able to forgive myself for drawing you away from your own way of living, uprooting you from your normal life. Why were you led to make your mistake, merely because I had made mine? Why did you risk the degradation of ceasing to earn your own living?'

'Had I not accepted suffering, you'd have turned away from me and never understood how much I loved you. Now don't try to twist this to mean love of country.'

'Had our country nothing to do with it, Ontu?'

'What I was doing for the country I was doing for you. The opportunity came to me to brave death for your sake. This you forget, and reserve all your remorse for my lost livelihood—you incorrigible housewife!'

'Yes, we women cannot bear the idea of want. Grant me at least one prayer. I inherited my father's house and I have some money put by. I beseech you to take some of it from me. I know you are in great need.'

'Had I been so hard put to it, all kinds of ways were open to me, from writing coaching manuals to clearing dustbins.'

'I admit, Ontu, that my resources should have been spent in the service of my country. But the road to earning is blocked for us women; that's why our necessity to save is so imperative. The little store that we lay up is not only for the needs of our living, but of our love as well. Oh, could I but persuade you that whatever I have is for you!'

'On that point you'll never persuade me. The only gift I could unhesitatingly ask of you, you held back behind the bars of your pledge.'

'One day you were busy casting up the accounts of the Narayanee School. I came and dropped into a seat by your side, sorely wounded at heart, as a kite, buffeted by storm, drops to the dust. I came with a mind already defeated. You didn't even look at me. I kept my longing eyes on you all the time, hoping against hope that a touch of those flowerlike fingers might be vouchsafed to heal my pangs of body and mind. But no sympathy stirred within you. Miser, even so little you were unable to give!'

Ela's eyes filled. 'You're quite impossible, Ontu,' she interrupted. 'Why need you have waited for my response? Why didn't you snatch away my account book? Couldn't you understand how your diffidence made me diffident?'

She drew Atin's head to her breast and laid her own on his, passing her fingers lightly through his hair.

After a while Atin raised his head and sat upright. Taking Ela's hand in his, he said: 'When we were on the ferry steamer from Mokameh Ghat, I hadn't understood that Grandmother Fate had merely given a mischievous tweak to my ears as she passed me by. My mind has ever since been building castles in the sky of my memory...

'My servant had taken off my heavy luggage, stowed on the lower deck, to the railway station. A leather suitcase remained in my cabin. I was looking about for a coolie to carry it. Demurely you came up to me. "Waiting for a coolie?" you asked, without the suspicion of a smile. "Why? Let me carry your suitcase." And before I could make the wild protest I felt, you had caught it up. Then, with a show of compunction for my awkward plight, you added: "If you're feeling embarrassed, I'll tell you what you can do. There's my trunk on the other deck. You may take that. Then we'll cancel each other's debt." There was nothing else to do. It was seven times heavier than mine! I kept shifting it from one hand to the other as I staggered all the way to the railway station, till I managed to put it into a third-class compartment. There was I, wet through with perspiration, my breath coming in gasps; and you with mischievous laughter in your eyes. Pity might have been lurking somewhere in your composition, but you wouldn't show it; for you had taken on yourself the burden of making a man of me!'

'Oh, stop, please stop! I feel so ashamed to think of what I then was, how silly, how ridiculous. I wonder you could tolerate me.'

'You came to me that day in a halo of illusion. The sun was setting. The lightly clouded sky was filled with the rare diffused radiance that our womenfolk call the "bride-viewing light". The smooth-flowing Ganges glowed back like a mirror. And your slim, supple figure remains forever painted in my mind against that radiant background. What happened after? I heard your call. But where did it lead me? So far, so very far away from you. You do not even know how far.'

'Why did you not tell me, Ontu?'

'There are injunctions I have to obey. Not only that. What would be the good of telling you all? The light is getting dim, Elie. Come nearer to me. These truant, wayward locks of yours, constantly straying over your eyes, which you keep putting into place with your deft fingers; this black-bordered *tussar* sari, hanging loosely over your shoulder, with its edge over the back of your head, pinned to your hair; the trace of fatigue in your eyes, the touch of entreaty on your lips; the waning light that sinks into the vagueness of its ending. All this that I see is truth, miraculous truth.'

'What is all this you're saying, Ontu?'

'It's mostly imagination. It brings back to me how you once wanted me to go and live amongst the labouring folk. It must have been your idea to level to the dust my pride of birth. Your great enterprise amused me. I entered into the spirit of the democratic picnic. I wandered about amongst the carters, from one buffalo shed to another. I called some of them brother, others uncle. But they could see as well as I that these affectionate relations wouldn't stand wear. There are, no doubt, great-souled men in whose voice such words strike the right note, whatever be the instrument on which they play. But our attempts at imitation sound miserably out of tune.'

'But, Ontu, I'm not yet able to understand why, when you discovered your mistake, you didn't turn back from the road which wasn't yours.'

'Before I took this road there was much I wasn't aware of, much I didn't even suspect. Then I came to know the boys, one after another—boys the dust of whose feet I'd have taken, had not they been so much younger than I! What have they not seen since, what have they not suffered, what insults they have not borne—the whole story will never see the light of day. It was the torment of all this that drove me mad. Many times have I vowed to myself: I will not be vanquished by fear or torment; I will die striking my head against the heartless stone wall, but, snapping my fingers at it, I will ignore the wall.'

'Have you then changed your mind now?'

'Listen. One who openly fights a more powerful foe, even if his be a hopeless struggle, is in the same class as his opponent; his honour remains unsullied. I had imagined that at least that honour would be mine. But, as the days went by, I saw with my own eyes how even the most high-minded of the boys began to lose their manhood. What greater loss could there be? I knew for certain they'd only laugh at me, perhaps get angry with me, and yet I had to tell them that the worst of all defeats was to come down to the wrong-doer's level. It was for us, before we were knocked out, before we met our death, to prove ourselves the greater, as men—why else this play of pitting ourselves against immeasurably superior forces? Some of them understood me, but how few!'

'Why even then didn't you leave them?'

'How could I? The net of punishment was then closing round them. Every bit of their career had passed before my eyes. I had felt with them each heart-rending experience. So, however revolted my feelings, however strong my hate of the movement, I simply could not desert them in the moment of their greatest danger. One thing had become clear to me. To oppose overwhelming strength by brute force can but brutalize in the end one's very soul.'

'I must confess, Ontu, that lately the terrible tragedy of it has been revealed to me also. I had entered the lists at the call of glory, but the shame of it is enveloping me more and more. Tell me, what can we do now?'

'Every man and woman is called upon to fight the great fight in the field of righteousness, where to die is to earn the highest heaven. But for us, the way to that battlefield is closed. We must now reap to the end the fruits of our past *karma,* our past deeds.'

'I understand you, Ontu, and yet the cynical way in which you talk of our patriotic movement hurts me deeply.'

'I'll confess to you for the first time to-day: what you call a patriot, that I am not. The patriotism of those who have no faith in that which is above patriotism is like a crocodile's back used as a ferry to cross the river. Meanness, unfaithfulness, mutual mistrust, secret machination, plotting for leadership—sooner or later these drag them into the mud at the bottom. That, the life of the country can be saved by killing its soul, is the monstrously false doctrine that nationalists all over the world are bellowing forth stridently. My heart groans to give it effective contradiction. I had it in me, perhaps, to express it in words burning with truth, words that would have remained great through the ages. But that has been denied me in this life. That is why the pain at my heart sometimes becomes so cruel.'

'Turn back yet, Ontu, turn back,' cried Ela, with a deep sigh.'

'The way is closed.'

'But why?'

'Even if I'm on the wrong road, it has its own responsibilities to the bitter end.'

Ela put her arms round Atin's neck as she implored him: 'Turn back, Ontu. You have broken down the foundation of my faith, my refuge all these years. Now that I'm adrift I have nothing but wreckage to cling to. Rescue me and take me back with you.'

'There's no way out now. The arrow can miss the mark, but it cannot return to the quiver.'

'I offer you my hand in marriage, Ontu, as the princesses of old used to do. Take me. There's no time to lose. Let us pledge our troth by exchange of vows. Then take me as helpmate along your path.'

'Had it been a path of danger, I'd have taken you. But how can truth be pledged when Truth itself has been wrecked? But no more of this. Something true may still be left, even in this day of shipwreck. That I would hear from your lips.'

'What am I to tell you?'

'Tell me that you love me.'

'I tell you, I do love you.'

'Tell me that you'll remember I loved you, even when I have ceased to live.'

Ela's face was wet with tears. After a long pause she said: 'Take something at least from me, Ontu. Take this necklace.'

'Never! I'll not take alms of you.'

'Then take me as your companion on your own terms!'

'Don't tempt me, Ela. My way is not yours.'

'Neither is it yours, then. Turn back.'

'The way is not mine—it's I who belong to the way. No one calls the noose round his neck an ornament.'

'Know for certain, Ontu, if you cease to live, so will I. I've no one else but you. If you doubt that now, it's my own hope that somewhere, somehow, after our death, such doubt will be removed forever.'

With a sudden start Atin sprang to his feet. The thin, keen sound of a whistle, like the whine of an arrow in flight, came from the distance.

'I'm off,' he said.

'Stay—' pleaded Ela, as she held him in her arms.

'No.'

'Where are you going?'

'I don't know.'

Ela slipped to the ground, still clasping him. 'I am your slave,' she moaned, 'yours to command. For mercy's sake don't leave me behind.'

Atin hesitated, but only for a moment. A second blast on the whistle was heard.

'Let me go!' he shouted. Then, tearing himself free, he disappeared.

The evening darkness had deepened. Ela lay prone on the floor, her eyes tearless, her very heart dried up, how long she knew not. A flash of light brought her to herself. A grave voice sounded in her ears. 'Ela!'

She sat up, startled. There was Indranath, electric torch in hand. She jumped up. 'Bring Atin back to me!' she cried.

'Why are you here?' said Indranath curtly.

'I knew I was facing danger when I came.'

'It's not your danger that matters,' Indranath sternly rebuked her. 'Who told you of this place?'

'Batu.'

'And you couldn't see why he told you?'

'I was unfit to understand anything.'

'Had it been wise to kill you, I'd have done so here and now. Go back to your rooms at once! There's a taxi on the road outside.'

Chapter Four

'You here again, Akhil, escaped from the boarding-house as usual! It's bad of you. How often have I told you not to be coming over here these days. You'll get into some terrible trouble if you go on like this.'

Akhil made no answer, but, dropping his voice, he said: 'Just now a man with a bushy beard climbed over the back wall into the garden. So I locked your door as I came in. Listen—you'll hear footsteps.' With this he pulled open the biggest blade of his clasp knife and stood on guard.

'Put away that knife, O you hero! Here, give it to me,' said Ela, and she took the knife from him.

'There's nothing to be afraid of, Akhil, came a voice from the landing. It's I, Atin.'

Ela turned pale as she cried, 'Open the door!'

'Where's the bearded man?' asked Akhil, as he let Atin in.

'The beard's somewhere in the garden, the man's here,' replied Atin. 'Run away, Akhil, and see if you can find that beard.'

As Akhil left the room, Ela stood stiff for a moment, as if turned to stone. Then she cried: 'What have you done to yourself, Ontu? How awful you look!'

'Not exactly bewitching?'

'Then it's true! that you've been seriously ill.'

'Doctors differ, so they needn't be believed.'

'You couldn't have had any dinner, either.'

'That can wait. Let's not waste our time.'

'Oh, what made you come here, Ontu?' Ela burst out, clasping Atin's hand in dismay. 'Don't you know they're after you?'

'I don't want to disappoint them.'

'Why, Ontu, do you court certain danger like this? What is to be done now?'

'Why I've come, you shall know just before I leave. Meanwhile that's the one thing I want to forget. First let me go downstairs and lock the doors.'

Atin came back presently and said: 'It's all right. I've taken out the electric bulbs from the lamp sockets below. Now let's go up to the terrace.'

They went up the winding stairs together to the roof terrace. Closing the door after him, Atin sat on the floor with his back against it. Ela sat beside him.

'Try to feel natural, Elie,' said Atin, 'as if nothing has happened, as if we're still in the chapter before the great war begins. Why, your hands are ice-cold, they're actually trembling! Let me warm them.' He took her hands in his own and pressed them to his heart. The faint sound of wedding music came to them from some distant house.

'Are you still afraid, Elie?'

'Afraid of what?'

'Oh, of everything, of every moment.'

'I'm afraid for you, Ontu—of nothing else.'

'Try to think, Elie,' he went on, keeping her hands in his, 'that we're here on such a night as this, fifty or a hundred years hence. The present rings us round too narrowly. What we desire so passionately is ticketed with a high price by the tricky pen of the present. What we mourn so inconsolably is labelled "Eternal Sorrow" with vanishing ink. All lies! Life, the forger, imitates the writing of eternity ; death comes and makes away with the false document, smiling—not a cruel nor a mocking smile, but a smile benign as Shiva's with all the beauty of the great peace of dawn after a nightmare of illusion. Have you, Elie, in the stillness of the night ever felt the freedom of the depths that is given by death, with its eternal forgiveness?'

'I haven't the power, like you, of seeing things in their bigness. And yet, when my heart is tortured with anxiety for all of you, I try to feel, with conviction, that death is easy.'

'It is cowardly to look on death as a means of escape. It's the only certainty, the sea into which flow all the courses of life, in which the opposites of truth and falsity, good and bad, find their final solution. This very night, this very moment, we two are in the embrace of its immensity. You remember those four little lines of Ibsen?

'Upwards
Towards the peaks,
Towards the stars,
Towards the vast silence.'

Ela with her hands pressed in Atin's sat still in silent thought.

Atin suddenly laughed out, saying: 'There, behind us, hangs motionless the black pall of death stretching back to the infinite. In front of it the play of our life dances along to its last act. Let me bring before you one of its earlier scenes. Three years ago you celebrated my birthday on this very terrace—you remember?'

'Very well, indeed!'

'Your devoted "boys" were all there. The feast was simple enough. Parched rice fried, boiled green peas peppered and salted, also fritters if I remember right. The boys scrambled for these dainties and finished them to the last pea. Then of a sudden Matilal, with a flourish of his arms, started to declaim: "On this day of brother Atin's new birth into the new age—." I jumped up and clapped my hand over his mouth. "If you persist in making this speech," said I, "the days of your old birth will end here." The new birth, the new age, the gate of death—all these tags sicken me so! The members of the band have tried their best to paint me with their brush, but I've not been able to take their colour.'

'The folly was mine, Ontu. It was I who thought of making you one of us pawns by putting on you the same livery.'

'That's why, I suppose, you vigorously played the loving elder sister. Perhaps you thought a touch of jealousy would help in my reformation. What a delightful trayful you handed out to them—of gushing hospitality, tender inquiry and needless solicitude. I can still hear your honeyed accents, "Oh, why are you looking so flushed, Nandalal?" And before the poor bashful fellow could stammer out, for truth's sake, that nothing was the matter with him, you bustled about to minister to his imaginary headache with a wet compress. I had my own illusions then, but still I could see that only some immaculate, dream-land ideal of country prompted this display of pure, patriotic sisterliness.'

'Oh, please stop, Ontu, for goodness' sake!'

'You yourself will admit, Elie, that your pose in those days savoured of the ludicrous.'

'I'll admit it, a thousand times. It's you who washed me clean of it. Why then so cruelly remind me of all that to-day?'

'Some heartache impels me, Elie. You asked my forgiveness the other day for drawing me away from my own way of living. But what of my being drawn away from the fullness of life, and yet denied the price I was entitled to? I broke my very nature; but, convention-blinded, you couldn't even break your pledge, devoid of truth as it was—remorse for *this* wouldn't have been so superfluous! I know what stood in your way. You couldn't bring yourself to believe that so much as all this had happened to me.'

'True, Ontu. Even now I can't help wondering how so much power could ever have been mine.'

'How could you know? It's not your own power, but the enchantment of *Maya*, Mother Nature. So magical is the melody of your voice, it flings burning whirls of music through the firmament of my mind. And this hand, these fingers of yours, they have the golden touch, making every trifle, true or false, seem priceless. How tremendous was the attraction which impelled me to accept the insult of my fall from grace, even as I reviled myself at every step. I have read of such a thing happening, but in the pride of my keen intellect I never thought it could happen to me. Now that the time has come to rend the net of illusion, I am telling you the truth so relentlessly.'

'Go on, then, go on with all you have to say. Have no pity on me, who have been so blind, so foolish, so heartless, unable at any time to understand you truly. The incomparable came to me offering itself with outstretched hands; unworthy was I, I could not pay its price. Unimaginable good fortune came to my door, and was turned away, unclaimed, never to return. If yet more punishment be my due, punish me.'

'Let's not talk of punishment. I want to forgive you, with the infinite forgiveness of death itself. That's why I'm here to-day.'

'That's why?'

'Yes, only for that.'

'Wouldn't it have been less cruel not to forgive, rather than step right into this trap of fire, before my very eyes? I know too well you've no desire to live on. If that be so, give me your few remaining days, give me the right to serve you to the end. That's all I beg at your feet.'

'What good will your service do me? You would pour nectar into the broken pitcher of my life! You can't even realize the intolerable gnawing at my heart of the might-have-been. What can your service do for that? What can it avail one who has lost his truth?'

'You haven't lost your truth, Ontu. Every bit of it is there, within you, still.'

'I have lost it. Oh, I've hopelessly lost it!'

'Don't say that!'

'Did you but know what I now am, you'd shiver from head to foot.'

'Look here, Ontu, you're imagining all kinds of horrid things about yourself. What you've done without any thought of self, however wrong, it can't stain your soul.'

'I've slain my soul, the biggest sin of all. Not a single evil have I been able to uproot from our country—I've only uprooted myself. For that sin I'm condemned not to take you even when you're giving yourself. Accept your hand? With this hand! But why all this? All stains will be washed away by the waters of Lethe, on whose brink we now stand. At such a time let us talk of light things, laughingly. Let me finish the story of my birthday party. Shall I?'

'I'm afraid I can't put my mind on all that, Ontu.'

'The only things in our life worth calling to mind are just such trivialities scattered ·over a few lightsome days. The ponderous days deserving of oblivion are only too many. My birthday feast being over, Nirod took it into his head to recite Nabin Sen's epic. In the style favoured by the favourite actor of those days he ranted: "Why dost depart, O lord of a thousand rays! look back but once, thou ornament of day—." Good fellow that, Nirod, simple and straight, but with a merciless memory! While I was pining and fretting for the party to come to an end, they needs must ask Bhabesh for a song. He fortunately protested he couldn't even open his mouth without a harmonium to accompany him—an instrument of torture you didn't happen to possess. So the crisis passed. At last the end, thought I—but no! Apropos of nothing, Satu started an argument whether the anniversary of one's birth properly fell on the same date of the month, or the same day of the moon. I tried to stop it, but signally failed. Pungent patriotism invaded the discussion; voices were raised, friendships were threatened. I felt furious with you. My birthday was but an excuse, I felt sure, for a patriotic orgy.'

'Don't try to judge from the outside, Ontu, which was the excuse and which the real object. I may deserve punishment, but not unjust punishment. Don't you remember, that was the day Mr. Atindra became Ontu for me? Was that such a small thing? Now go on with the story of your pet-name-giving.'

'Then listen, my friend. When I was four or five years old, I was short in stature, of few words, with a stupid look, I'm told, in my eyes. My father's elder brother, on coming home from the upper provinces, saw me for the first time. Taking me on his knee, he facetiously remarked: "Who's responsible for giving this little pigmy the name of Atindra, Great Indra? Call him rather the opposite, Anatindra. In rhetoric, exaggeration often has the reverse effect"—your pet name of Ontu was really short and affectionate for Anatin. I came to you great. For your sake I cut myself down small—'

Atin stopped short with a start. 'Is that the sound of footsteps?' he muttered as he rose.

'It's only Akhil,' said Ela.

'Sister dear!' came his voice.

'What is it?' asked Ela as she opened the door.

'Your dinner,' announced Akhil.

Ela did no cooking in the house. Her meals came from a restaurant nearby. 'Come along, Ontu, have some food,' she said.

'Don't talk of food now. It takes man quite a long time to die for lack of it, otherwise India wouldn't now have been a land of the living. Akhil, old chap, don't be annoyed with me. Go straight down and begin by eating my share of the dinner; then finish with a run—run right away.'

Akhil ruefully departed.

The two of them sat down as before. Atin began again: 'To go back to that celebration. It seemed it would go on for ever. Not one of them would budge. I kept looking at my watch, hoping in vain that it might prove a hint to those time-blind youths. At last I had to say to you: "Hadn't you better go off to bed? You're only just up from your influenza." "What's the time?" then arose the question from all sides. It was half-past ten. Yawns here and there indicated the approaching dispersal. "Aren't you coming?" Batu pointedly asked me. "Let's go together." "Where to?" It appeared that he wanted us to pay a surprise visit to the sweepers' quarters, catch them at their drinking, and stop it. I felt angry all over. "What if you stop their drink?" I said roughly. "Have you anything to give them instead?" As the only result of my meaningless excitement, those who were on the point of going, stopped to join in. "Do you then mean to say—" some one began. "I don't mean anything at all!" I shouted back. Then realizing that my outburst was quite uncalled for, I dropped my voice and with a meaning look toward you out of the corner of my eyes, I begged your leave to depart. By the time we had reached the door of your room below, my legs refused to carry me farther. A device occurred to me. I slapped my breast pocket saying, "I must have dropped my fountain pen on the terrace." "Let me fetch it for you," offered the irrepressible Batu, and he immediately ran up the stairs. After him I had to go, to find him making a great show of a search. On seeing me he said with a smile: "Will you go through all your pockets, brother Atin? It may be in one of them." I knew well enough that, to find my pen, nothing short of a voyage of discovery into my rooms would serve. So I had to come forth with, "I want a word with sister Ela."

"Very well," he rejoined, nothing daunted, "I'll wait for you."
"Oh, get along with you," I blurted out, having come to the
end of my patience. "Don't be hanging about me like this!"
"I'm going. But what means this loss of temper?" was his
parting shot.'

Once more Atin stopped to listen, as some one was heard
coming up. It was again Akhil who came out onto the terrace
with a slip of paper. 'Here's a message for brother Atin,' he
said; 'I've kept the man waiting in the street.'

Ela's heart sank within her. 'Who is it?' she whispered.

'Show him into the sitting-room,' Atin told him.

As Akhil doggedly went off, Ela asked, 'Is it Batu?'

'No, it's not.'

'Why don't you tell me who it is? I'm not feeling at all
easy.'

'It doesn't matter. I want to finish what I was telling you.'

'It's quite impossible for me to attend to all that now,
Ontu.'

'Elie, you really must allow me to come to the end of my
story. There's not much left. You came up to the terrace, after
Batu had left, bringing with you a faint perfume. You had kept
by a special bouquet of tuberoses, till the party was over, for
you wanted to put them into my hands when we should be
alone. That was the moment of Ontu's new birth, ushered
in by these shy flowers. And little by little all Mr. Atindra's
gravity, learning and logic were drowned in profound self-
forgetfulness. For the first time, that day, you put your arms
round my neck, saying, "Here's your birthday present." That
was our first kiss. The last kiss is what I've now come to
claim.'

Akhil came up once more and reported: 'I locked him in
the sitting room. He's now started thumping on the door. He
says it's very important. He'll be breaking the door at this rate.'

'It's all right, Akhil,' said Atin. 'I'll see that he's calmed down before the door gives way. You needn't mount guard over him. Leave him alone and clear out. I'll look after your sister Ela.'

Ela drew Akhil to herself and, kissing him on the forehead, entreated him: 'Akhil dear, my own little brother, you really must go away from here. Take this money. I've been keeping it tied up in a corner of my *sari* for your birthday. Now touch my feet and promise me you'll leave at once.'

'Look here, Akhil,' said Atin. 'You'll have to follow the advice I'm giving you. If anybody asks you, tell him exactly what happened. Say that at eleven o'clock tonight it was I who turned you out of this house. Now come along with me, let's make these words true.'

Ela once more drew Akhil near and said: 'Don't worry about me, Akhil darling. Your brother, Atin, is with me, there's no fear.'

When Atin, tucking Akhil's arm under his own, was marching him off, Ela, unable to contain herself, cried, 'Let me come down with you, too!'

'You can't do that!' commanded Atin.

Ela remained leaning over the low parapet of the terrace, trying hard to suppress the sobs rising in her breast. She somehow felt that this was her last parting with Akhil.

Atin came back. 'Akhil's gone,' he said. 'I've bolted the front and back doors.'

'And the man in the sitting-room?'

'I've let him out, too. He thought that, engrossed in our talk, I'd forgotten all about his message. He was beginning to get afraid that another *Arabian Nights* story had been started. Arabian Nights is the word! It's all been a story, an absurd marvel of a story. Are you feeling afraid, Elie—aren't you afraid of me?'

'Afraid of you, Ontu? What an idea!'

'Is there anything I'm incapable of doing? I've come down to the last rung of my degradation. The other day our band robbed a helpless old widow of all she had. Our Manmatha belonged to the same village and was on friendly terms with her. It was he who told of her hoard and showed the way. She made him out through his mask, and tried to plead with him. "Manu, my son, how could you have the heart—?" They didn't let her live to say any more. For the purposes of what we call the country's need—the need for murdering our own souls!—that widow's money passed through my hands to headquarters. Part of that money helped to break my recent fast. I end my career branded as a thief—receiver and user of stolen property. Batu has got the charge laid against robber Atindra. He has made it practically certain that I'll be arrested tomorrow. Meanwhile, fear me, for I myself fear that tainted ghost of my dead self. There's no one with you to-day.'

'But you're here yourself!'

'Who'll save you from me?'

'I don't care if I'm not saved from you!'

'The word has gone forth from your own band—your beloved, patriotic brothers, whom you've anointed with sandal-paste on each Brothers' Day—that you're not fit to live any longer.'

'How am I more unworthy than they?'

'You're supposed to know too much, and liable to give out what you know under torture.'

'Never.'

'What if the man who came just now brought this order? You know what an order means with us!'

Ela started up. 'Is this true, Ontu, is it really true?'

'We've got a piece of news.'

'What's that?'

'At the end of this very night, at dawn, the police will come for you.'

'I was certain they'd do so one of these days.'

'What made you think so?'

'I had a letter from Batu yesterday, telling me, and offering to save me.'

'How?'

'He says if I marry him, he'll stand surety for me and get me off.'

Atin's face darkened. 'And what was your reply?' he asked.

'I simply wrote the word "Monster" on it, and returned the letter.'

'Well, our information is that Batu himself will lead the police here. If he can get your consent, he'll come to terms with the tiger and benevolently offer you refuge in the crocodile's hole. After all, he has a soft heart!'

Ela seized Atin's feet, begging him: 'Kill me, Ontu, kill me with your own hands. I couldn't wish for a happier end.' She got up from the floor and, throwing her arms round him, kissed him again and again as she repeated, 'Kill me, Atin, kill me now!' She tore open the front of her blouse.

Atin stood rigid as a statue.

'Don't have any qualms,' Ela continued. 'Am I not yours, wholly yours, even in death? Take me. Don't let their unclean hands touch my body, for this body belongs to you.'

'Go to bed,' commanded Atin in a hard voice. 'I order you, go at once.'

But, clasping Atin to her, Ela went on: 'Ontu, my Ontu, my king, my god! I've not to this day been able to show you how much I love you. By this love I charge you—kill me, kill me!'

Atin took hold of her arm and drew her down with him to her bedroom. 'Get into bed at once,' he repeated, 'and go off to sleep.'

'I can't, sleep won't come.'

'I've brought medicine that'll put you to sleep.'

'What's the use of that Ontu? Let the last bit of my consciousness be for you. Is it chloroform that you have? Throw it away. I'm not a coward. Let me die awake, in your arms. Let our last kiss be eternal, Ontu, my Ontu.'

From afar came the thin sound of a whistle.

RED OLEANDERS

A DRAMA IN ONE ACT

The curtain rises on a window covered by a network of intricate pattern in front of the Palace.

(*Nandini* and *Kishôr,* a digger boy, come in.)

Kishôr. Have you enough flowers, Nandini? Here, I have brought some more.

Nandini. Run away, Kishôr, do,—back to your work, quick! You'll be late again.

Kishôr. I must steal some time from my digging and digging of nuggets to bring out flowers to you.

Nandini. But they'll punish you, my boy, if they know.

Kishôr. You said you *must* have red oleanders. I am glad they're hard to find in this place, Only one tree I discovered after days of search, nearly hidden away behind a rubbish heap.

Nandini. Show it me. I'll go and gather the flowers myself.

Kishôr. Don't be cruel, Nandini. This tree is my one secret which none shall know. I've always envied Bishu, he can sing to you songs that are his own. From now I shall have flowers which you'll have to take only from my hands.

Nandini. But it breaks my heart to know that those brutes punish you.

Kishôr. It makes these flowers all the more preciously mine. They come from my pain.

Nandini. It pains me to accept anything which brings you
    hurt.

Kishôr. I dream of dying one day for your sake, Nandini.

Nandini. Is there nothing I can give you in return?

Kishôr. Promise that you will accept flowers only from me
    every morning.

Nandini. I will. But do be careful.

Kishôr. No, no, I shall be rash and defy their blows. My
    homage shall be my daily triumph. (*Goes.*)

(*Professor* comes in.)

Professor. Nandini!

Nandini. Yes, Professor!

Professor. Why do you come and startle one, now and again,
    and then pass by? Since you awaken a cry in our hearts,
    what harm if you stop a moment in answer to it? Let
    us talk a little.

Nandini. What need have you of me?

Professor. If you talk of need, look over there!—You'll see our
    tunnel-diggers creeping out of the holes like worms,
    with loads of things of need. In this Yaksha Town all
    our treasure is of gold, the secret treasure of the dust.
    But the gold which is you, beautiful one, is not of the
    dust, but of the light which never owns any bond.

Nandini. Over and over again you say this to me. What makes
    you wonder at me so, Professor?

Professor. The sunlight gleaming through the forest thickets
    surprises nobody, but the light that breaks through a
    cracked wall is quite a different thing. In Yaksha Town,
    you are this light that startles. Tell me, what d'you think
    of this place?

Nandini. It puzzles me to see a whole city thrusting its head
    underground, groping with both hands in the dark. You

dig tunnels in the underworld and come out with dead
wealth that the earth has kept buried for ages past.

Professor. The *Jinn* of that dead wealth we invoke. If we can
enslave him the whole world lies at our feet.

Nandini. Then again, you hide your king behind a wall of
netting. Is it for fear of people finding out that he's a
man?

Professor. As the ghost of our dead wealth is fearfully potent
so is our ghostly royalty, made hazy by this net, with
its inhuman power to frighten people.

Nandini. All you say is a kind of made-up talk.

Professor. Of course made-up. The naked is without a
credential, it's the made-up clothes that define us. It
delights me immensely to discuss philosophy with
you.

Nandini. That's strange! You who burrow day and night in
a mass of yellow pages, like your diggers in the bowels
of the earth,—why waste your time on me?

Professor. The privilege of wasting time proves one's wealth
of time. We poor drudges are insects in a hole in this
solid toil, you are the evening star in the rich sky of
leisure. When we see you, our wings grow restless.
Come to my room. For a moment allow me to be
reckless in my waste of time.

Nandini. No, not now. I have come to see your king, in *his*
room.

Professor. How can you enter through the screen?

Nandini. I shall find my way through the net-work.

Professor. Do you know, Nandini, I too live behind a network
of scholarship. I am an unmitigated scholar, just as our
king is an unmitigated king.

Nandini. You are laughing at me, Professor. But tell me, when
they brought me here, why didn't they bring my Rañjan
also?

244 ❖ RABINDRANATH TAGORE OMNIBUS II

Professor. It's their way to snatch things by fractions. But why should you want to drag your life's treasure down amongst this dead wealth of ours?

Nandini. Because I know he can put a beating heart behind these dead ribs.

Professor. Your own presence is puzzling enough for our governors here; if Rañjan also comes they will be in despair.

Nandini. They do not know how comic they are,—Rañjan will bring God's own laughter in their midst and startle them into life.

Professor. Divine laughter is the sunlight that melts ice, but not stones. Only the pressure of gross muscle can move our governors.

Nandini. My Rañjan's strength is like that of your river, Sankhini,—it can laugh and yet it can break. Let me tell you a little secret news of mine. I shall meet Rañjan to-day.

Professor. Who told you that?

Nandini. Yes, yes, we shall meet. The news has come.

Professor. Through what way could news come and yet evade the Governor?

Nandini. Through the same way that brings news of the coming Spring.

Professor. You mean it's in the air,—like the rumours which flush in the colour of the sky, or flutter in the dance of the wind?

Nandini. I won't say more now. When Rañjan comes you'll see for yourself how rumours in the air come down on earth.

Professor. Once she begins to talk of Rañjan there's no stopping Nandini's mouth! Well, well, I have my books, let me take my shelter behind them,—I dare not go on with this. (*Coming back after going a little way.*) Nandini.

Let me ask you one thing. Aren't you frightened of our
Yaksha Town?

Nandini. Why should I feel afraid?

Professor. All creatures fear an eclipse, not the full sun. Yaksha
Town is a city under eclipse. The Shadow Demon, who
lives in the gold caves, has eaten into it. It is not whole
itself, neither does it allow any one else to remain
whole. Listen to me, don't stay here. When you go,
these pits will yawn all the wider for us, I know,—yet
I say to you, fly; go and live happily with Rañjan where
people in their drunken fury don't tear the earth's veil
to pieces. (*Going a little way and then coming back.*)
Nandini, will you give me a flower from your chain of
red oleanders?

Nandini. Why, what will you do with it?

Professor. How often have I thought that there is some omen
in these ornaments of yours.

Nandini. I don't know of any.

Professor. Perhaps your fate knows. In that red there is not
only beauty, but also the fascination of fear.

Nandini. Fear! Even in me?

Professor. I don't know what event you have come to write
with that crimson tint. There was the gardenia and the
tuberose, there was white jasmine,—why did you leave
them all and choose this flower? Do you know, we
often choose our own fate thus, without knowing it!

Nandini. Rañjan sometimes calls me Red Oleander. I feel that
the colour of his love is red,—that red I wear on my
neck, on my breast, on my arms.

Professor. Well, just give me one of those flowers,—a moment's
gift,—let me try to understand the meaning of its colour.

Nandini. Here, take it. Rañjan is coming to-day,—out of my
heart's delight I give it to you. (*Professor goes.*)

(*Gôkul*, a digger, comes in.)

Gôkul. Turn this way, woman! Who are you? I've never yet been able to understand you.

Nandini. I'm nothing more than what you see. What need have you to understand me?

Gôkul. I don't trust what I can't understand. For what purpose has the King brought you here?

Nandini. Because I serve no purpose of his.

Gôkul. You know some spell, I'm sure. You're snaring everybody here. You're a witch! Those who are bewitched by your beauty will come to their death.

Nandini. That death will not be yours, Gôkul, never fear! You'll die digging.

Gôkul. Let me see, let me see, what's that dangling over your forehead?

Nandini. Only a tassel of red oleanders.

Gôkul. What does it mean?

Nandini. It has no meaning at all.

Gôkul. I don't believe you, one bit! You're up to some trickery. Some evil will befall us before the day is out. That's why you have got yourself up like this. Oh you terrible, terrible witch!

Nandini. What makes you think me so terrible?

Gôkul. You're looking like an ominous torch.

Nandini. The autumn song:
> *Hark, 'tis Autumn calling:*
> *'Come, O, come away!'*—
> *Her basket is heaped with corn.*

Don't you see the September sun is spreading the glow of the ripening corn in the air?
> *Drunken with the perfumed wine of wind,*
> *the sky seems to sway among the*

shivering corn,
  its sunlight trailing on the fields

You too come out, King!—out into the fields.

Voice. Fields! What could I do there?

Nandini. The work there is much simpler than your work in Yaksha Town.

Voice. It's the simple which is impossible for me. A lake cannot run out dancing, like a frolicsome waterfall. Leave me now, I have no time.

Nandini. The day you let me into your store-house the blocks of gold did not surprise me,—what amazed me was the immense strength with which you lifted and arranged them. But can blocks of gold ever answer to the swinging rhythm of your arms in the same way as fields of corn? Are you not afraid, King, of handling the dead wealth of the earth?

Voice. What is there to fear?

Nandini. The living heart of the earth gives itself up in love and life and beauty, but when you rend its bosom and disturb the dead, you bring up with your booty the curse of its dark demon, blind and hard, cruel and envious. Don't you see everybody here is either angry, or suspicious, or afraid?

Voice. Curse?

Nandini. Yes, the curse of grabbing and killing.

Voice. But we bring up strength. Does not my strength please you, Nandini?

Nandini. Indeed it does. Therefore I ask you, come out into the light, step on the ground, let the earth be glad.

Voice. Do you know, Nandini, you too are half-hidden behind an evasion,—you mystery of beauty! I want to pluck you out of it, to grasp you within my closed fist, to handle you, scrutinise you,—or else to break you to pieces.

Nandini. Whatever do you mean?

Voice. Why can't I strain out the tint of your oleanders and build a dream out of it to keep before my eyes? Those few frail petals guard it and hinder me. Within you there is the same hindrance, so strong because so soft. Nandini, will you tell me what you think of me?

Nandini. Not now, you have no time. Let me go.

Voice. No, no, don't go. Do tell me what you think of me.

Nandini. Have I not told you often enough? I think you are wonderful. Strength swelling up in your arms, like rolling clouds before a storm,—it makes my heart dance within me.

Voice. And when your heart dances to see Rañjan, is that also—

Nandini. Let that be,—you have no time.

Voice. There is time,—for this; only tell me, then go.

Nandini. That dance rhythm is different, you won't understand.

Voice. I will, I must understand.

Nandini. I can't explain it clearly. Let me go.

Voice. Tell me, at least, whether you like me.

Nandini. Yes, I like you.

Voice. The same as Rañjan?

Nandini. Again the same question! I tell you, you don't understand these things.

Voice. I *do* understand, a little. I know what the difference is between Rañjan and me. In me there is only strength, in Rañjan there is magic.

Nandini. What d'you mean by magic?

Voice. Shall I explain? Underground there are blocks of stone, iron, gold,—there you have the image of strength. On the surface grows the grass, the flower blossoms,— there you have the play of magic. I can extract gold from the fearsome depths of secrecy, but to wrest that magic from the near at hand I fail.

Nandini. You have no end of things, yet why always covet?

Voice. All I possess is so much dead weight. No increase of gold can create a particle of a touchstone, no increase of power can ever come up to youth. I can only guard by force. If I had Rañjan's youth I could leave you free and yet hold you fast. My time is spent in knotting the binding rope, but alas, everything else can be kept tied, except joy.

Nandini. It is you who entangle yourself in your own net, then why keep on fretting?

Voice. You will never understand. I, who am a desert, stretch out my hand to you, a tiny blade of grass, and cry: I am parched, I am bare, I am weary. The flaming thirst of this desert licks up one fertile field after another, only to enlarge itself,—it can never annex the life of the frailest of grasses.

Nandini. One would never think you were so tired.

Voice. One day, Nandini, in a far off land, I saw a mountain as weary as myself. I could not guess that all its stones were aching inwardly. One night I heard a noise, as if some giant's evil dream had moaned and moaned and suddenly snapped asunder. Next morning I found the mountain had disappeared in the chasm of a yawning earthquake. That made me understand how overgrown power crushes itself inwardly by its own weight. I see in you something quite opposite.

Nandini. What is it you see in me?

Voice. The dance rhythm of the All.

Nandini. I don't understand.

Voice. The rhythm that lightens the enormous weight of matter. To that rhythm the bands of stars and planets go about dancing from sky to sky, like so many minstrel boys. It is that rhythm, Nandini, that makes you so

simple, so perfect. How small you are compared to me,
yet I envy you.

Nandini. You have cut yourself off from everybody and so
deprived yourself.

Voice. I keep myself apart, that it may be come easy for me
to plunder the world's big treasure-houses. Nevertheless
there are gifts that your little flower-like fingers can
easily reach, but not all the strength of my body,—gifts
hidden in God's closed hand. That hand I must force
open some day.

Nandini. When you talk like that, I don't follow you. Let me
go.

Voice. Go then; but here, I stretch out this hand of mine from
my window, place your hand on it for a moment.

Nandini. Only a hand, and the rest of you hidden? It frightens
me!

Voice. Everybody flies from me because they only see my
hand. But if I wished to hold you with all of me, would
you come to me, Nandini?

Nandini. Why talk like this when you wouldn't even let me
come into your room?

Voice. My busy time, overloaded with work, dragged along
against obstruction, is not for you. On the day when
you can arrive, full sail before the wind, into the bosom
of my full.

Phágulal. Isn't it our holiday? Yesterday was the fast day of
the War Goddess. To-day they worship the Flag.

Chandrá. Must you drink just because it's a holiday? In our
village home, on feast days, you never—

Phágulal. Freedom itself was enough for the holidays in our
village. The caged bird spends its holiday knocking
against the bars. In Yaksha Town holidays are more of
a nuisance than work.

Chandrá. Let's go back home, then.

Phágulal. The road to our home is closed for ever.

Chandrá. How's that?

Phágulal. Our homes don't yield them any profit.

Chandrá. But are we closely fitted to their profits only,—like husks to grains of corn,—with nothing of us left over?

Phágulal. Our mad Bishu says: to remain whole is useful only for the lamb itself; those who eat it prefer to leave out its horns and hooves, and even object to its bleating when butchered.

There's the madcap, singing as he goes.

Chandrá. It's only the last few days that his songs have burst forth.

Phágulal. That's true.

Chandrá. He's been possessed by Nandini. She draws his heart and his songs too.

Phágulal. No wonder.

Chandrá. Indeed! You'd better be careful. She'll next be bringing out songs from *your* throat,—which would be rough on our neighbours. The witch is up to all kinds of tricks, and is sure to bring misfortune.

Phágulal. Bishu's misfortune is nothing recent, he knew Nandini long before coming here.

Chandrá (calling out). I say, Bishu, come this way. Maybe you'll find somebody here also to listen to your singing,— it won't be altogether thrown away.

(*Bishu* comes in, singing.)

Bishu (sings).
    Boatman of my dreams,
    The sail is filled with a boisterous breeze
    and my mad heart sings

> to the lilt of the rocking of thy boat,
> at the call of the far away landing.

Chandrá. I know who the boatman of your dreams is.

Bishu. How should you know from outside? You haven't seen from inside my boat.

Chandrá. Your boat is going to get wrecked one of these days, let me tell you,—by that pet Nandini of yours.

(*Gôkul,* the digger, comes in.)

Gôkul. I say, Bishu, I don't quite trust your Nandini.

Bishu. Why, what has she done?

Gôkul. She does nothing, that's the rub. I don't understand the way she goes on.

Chandrá. To see her flaunting her prettiness all over the place makes me sick.

Gôkul. We can trust features that are plain enough to understand.

Bishu. I know the atmosphere of this place breeds contempt for beauty. There must be beauty even in hell; but nobody there can understand it, that's their cruellest punishment.

Chandrá. Maybe we are fools, but even our Governor here can't stand her—d'you know that?

Bishu. Take care, Chandrá, lest you catch the infection of our Governor's eyes—then perhaps yours too will redden at the sight of us. What say you, Phágulal?

Phágulal. To tell you the truth, brother, when I see Nandini, I feel ashamed to think of myself. I can't utter a word when she's there.

Gôkul. The day will come when you'll know her to your cost.—perhaps too late. (*Goes.*)

Phágulal. Bishu, your friend Chandrá wants to know why we drink.

Bishu. God in his mercy has everywhere provided a liberal allowance of drink. We men with our arms supply the output of our muscles, you women with yours supply the wine of embraces. In this world there is hunger to force us to work; but there's also the green of the woods, the gold of the sunshine, to make us drunk with their holiday-call.

Chandrá. You call these things *drink?*

Bishu. Yes, drinks of life, an endless stream of intoxication. Take my case. I come to this place; I am set to work burgling the underworld; for me nature's own ration of spirits is stopped; so my inner man craves the artificial wine of the market place. (*Sings.*)

My life, your sap has run day,
Fill then the cup with the wine of death,
That flushes all emptiness with its laughter.

Chandrá. Come, brother, let us fly from here.

Bishu. To that boundless tavern, underneath the blue canopy? Alas, the road is closed, and we seek consolation in the stolen wine of the prison house. No open sky, no leisure for us; so we have distilled the essence of all the song and laughter, all the sunlight of the twelve hours' day into one draught of liquid fire. (*Sings.*)

Thy sun is hidden amid a mass of murky cloud.
Thy day has smudged itself black in dusty toil.
Then let the dark night descend
     the last comrade of drunken oblivion,
Let it cover thy tired eyes with the mist
     that will help thee desperately to lose thyself.

Chandrá. Well, well, Bishu, you men have gone to the dogs in Yaksha Town, if you like, but we women haven't changed at all.

Bishu. Haven't you? Your flowers have faded, and you are all slavering for gold.

Chandrá. No, never!

Bishu. I say, yes. That Phágulal toils for hours over and above the twelve,—why? For a reason unknown to him, unknown even to you. But I know. It's your dream of gold that lashes him on to work, more severely than the foreman's whip.

Chandrá. Very well. Then why don't we fly from here, and go back home?

Bishu. Your Governor has closed the way as well as the will to return. If you go there to-day you will fly back here to-morrow, like a caged bird to its cage, hankering for its drugged food.

Phágulal. I say, Bishu, once upon a time you came very near spoiling your eyesight poring over books; how is it they made you ply the spade along with the rest of us stupid boors?

Chandrá. All this time we've been here, we haven't got from Bishu the answer to this particular question.

Phágulal. Yet we all know it.

Bishu. Well, out with it then!

Phágulal. They employed you to spy on us.

Bishu. If you knew that, how is it you let me off alive?

Phágulal. But, we knew also, that game was not in your line.

Chandrá. How is it you couldn't stick to such a comfortable job, brother?

Bishu. Comfortable job? To stick to a living being like a carbuncle on his back?

I said: 'I must go home, my health is failing.'

'Poor thing,' said the Governor, 'how can you go home in such a state? However, there's no harm in your trying.'

Well, I did try. And then I found that, as soon as one enters the maw of Yaksha Town, its jaws shut fast, and the one road that remains open leads withinwards. Now I am swamped in that interior without hope and

without light, and the only difference between you and
me is, that the Governor looks down upon me even
worse than upon you. Man despises the broken pot of
his own creation more than the withered leaf fallen
from the tree.

Phágulal. What does that matter, Bishu? You have risen high
in our esteem.

Bishu. Discovery only means death. Where you favour falls
there falls the Governor's glance. The more noisily the
yellow frogs welcome the black toad, the sooner their
croaking points him out to the boa-constrictor.

Chandrá. But when will your work be finished?

Bishu. The calendar never records the last day. After the first
day comes the second, after the second the third. There's
no such thing as getting finished here. We're always
digging—one yard, two yards, three yards. We go on
raising gold nuggets,—after one nugget another, then
more and more and more. In Yaksha Town figures
follow one another in rows and never arrive at any
conclusion. That's why we are not men to them, but
only numbers.—Phagu, what's yours?

Phágulal. I'm No. 47 V.

Bishu. I'm 69 Ng.

Chandrá. Brother, they've hoarded such heaps of gold, can't
they stop digging now?

Bishu. There's always an end to things of need, no doubt; so
we stop when we've had enough to eat. But we don't
need drunkenness, therefore there's no end to it. These
nuggets are the drink—the solid drink—of our Gold
King. Don't you see?

Chandrá. No, I don't.

Bishu. Cups in hand, we forget that we are chained to our
limits. Gold blocks in hand, our master fancies he's

freed from the gravitation of the commonplace, and is soaring in the rarest of upper heights.

Chandrá. In this season the villages are preparing for their harvest festival. Let's go home.

Phágulal. Don't worry me, Chandrá. A thousand times over have I told you that in these parts there are high roads to the market, to the burning ground, to the scaffold,— everywhere except to the homeland.

Chandrá. If we were to go to the Governor, and just tell him—

Bishu. Hasn't your woman's wit seen through the Governor yet?

Chandrá. Why, he seems to be so nice and—

Bishu. Yes, nice and polished, Like the crocodile's teeth, which fit into one another with so thorough a bite that the King himself can't unlock the jaw, even if he wants to.

Chandrá. There comes the *Governor.*

Bishu. Then it's all up with us. He's sure to have overheard—

Chandrá. Why, we haven't said anything so very—

Bishu. Sister, we can only say the words,—they put in the meaning.

(The *Governor* comes in.)

Chandrá. Sir Governor!

Governor. Well, my child?

Chandrá. Grant us leave to go home for a little.

Governor. Why, aren't the rooms we have given you excellent, much better than the ones at home? We have even kept a state watchman for your safety.

Hullo, 69 Ng, to see you amongst these people reminds one of a heron come to teach paddy birds how to cut capers.

Bishu. Sir, your jesting does not reassure me. Had my feet the strength to make others dance, would I not have run away from here, first thing? Especially after the striking examples I've seen of the fate that overtakes dancing masters in this country. As things are, one's legs tremble even to walk straight.

Chandrá. Give us leave, Sir Governor, do give us leave. Let us go just for once, and see our waving fields of barleycorn in the ear, and the ample shade of our banian tree with its hanging roots. I cannot tell you how our hearts ache. Don't you see that your men here work all day in the dark, and in the evening steep themselves in the denser dark of drunkenness? Have you no pity for them?

Governor. My dear child, surely you know of our constant anxiety for their welfare. That is exactly why I have sent for our High Preacher, Kenarám Gosain himself, to give moral talks to the men. Their votive fees will pay for his upkeep. Every evening the Gosain will come and—

Phágulal. That won't do, sir! Now, at worst, we get drunk of an evening, but if we are preached to every night, there'll be manslaughter!

Bishu. Hush, hush, Phágulal.

(Preacher *Gosain* comes in.)

Governor. Talk of the Preacher and he appears. Your Holiness, I do you reverence. These workmen of ours sometimes feel disturbed in their weak minds. Deign to whisper in their ears some texts of peace. The need is urgent.

Gosain. These people? Are they not the very incarnation of the sacred Tortoise of our scripture, that held up the sinking earth on its back? Because they meekly suppress themselves underneath their burden, the upper world can keep its head aloft. The very thought sends a thrill through my body!

Just think of it, friend 47 V̌, yours is the duty of

supplying food to this mouth which chants the holy name. With the sweat of your brow have you woven this wrap printed with the holy name, which exalts this devoted body. Surely that is no mean privilege. May you remain for ever undisturbed, is my benediction, for then the grace of God will abide with you likewise.

My friends, repeat aloud the holy name of Hari, and all your burdens will be lightened. The name of Hari shall be taken in the beginning, in the middle, and at the end,—so say the scriptures.

Chandrá. How sweet! It's long since I have heard such words! Give, oh give me a little dust off your feet!

Phágulal. Stop this waste of money, Governor. If it's our offerings you want, we can stand it, but we're fairly sick of this cant.

Bishu. Once Phágulal runs amok it's all over with the lot of you. Hush, hush, Phágulal!

Chandrá. Are you bent on spoiling your chances both in this world and the next, you wretched man? You were never like this before. Nandini's ill wind has blown upon you,—and no mistake.

Gosain. What charming naiveté, Sir Governor! What's in their heart is always on their lips. What can we teach them?—it's they who'll teach us a lesson. You know what I mean.

Governor. I know where the root of the trouble is. I'll have to take them in hand myself, I see. Meanwhile, pray go to the next parish and chant them the holy name,— the sawyers there have taken to grumbling, somewhat.

Gosain. Which parish did you say?

Governor. Parish T-D. No. 71 T is headman there. It ends to the left of where No. 65 of Row M lives.

Gosain. My son, though Parish T-D may not yet be quieted, the whole Row of M's have lately become steeped in a beautiful spirit of meekness. Still it is better to keep an extra police force posted in the parish some time longer. Because, as you know our scripture says—pride is our greatest foe. After the strength of the police has helped to conquer pride, then comes our turn. I take my leave.

Chandrá. Forgive these men, Your Holiness, and give them your blessing, that they may follow the right path.

Gosain. Fear not, good woman, they'll all end thoroughly pacified.

(*The* Gosain *goes.*)

Governor. I say, 69 Ng, the temper of your parish seems to be somewhat strained.

Bishu. That's nothing strange. The Gosain called them the incarnation of the Tortoise. But, according to scripture, incarnations change; and, when the Tortoise gave place to the Boar, in place of hard shell came out aggressive teeth, so that all-suffering patience was transformed into defiant obstinacy.

Chandrá. But, Sir Governor, don't forget my request.

Governor. I have heard it and will bear it in mind.

(*He goes.*)

Chandrá. Ah now, didn't you see how nice the Governor is? How he smiles every time he talks!

Bishu. Crocodile's teeth begin by smiling and end by biting.

Chandrá. Where does his bite come in?

Bishu. Don't you know he's going to make it a rule not to let the workmen's wives accompany them here.

Chandrá. Why?

Bishu. We have a place in their account book as numbers, but women's figures do not mate with figures of arithmetic.

Chandrá. O dear! but have they no women-folk of their own?

Bishu. Their ladies are besotted with the wine of gold, even worse than their husbands.

Chandrá. Bishu, you had a wife at home,—what's become of her?

Bishu. So long as I filled the honoured post of spy, they used to invite her to those big mansions to play cards with their ladies. Ever since I joined Phágulal's set, all that was stopped, and she left me in a huff at the humiliation.

Chandrá. For shame! But look, brother Bishu, what a grand procession! One palanquin after another! Don't you see the sparkle of the jewelled fringes of the elephant-seats? How beautiful the out-riders on horseback look, as if they had bits of sunlight pinned on the points of their spears!

Bishu. Those are the Governor's and Deputy Governor's ladies, going to the Flag-worship.

Chandrá. Bless my soul, what a gorgeous array and how fine they look!

I say, Bishu, if you hadn't given up that job, would you have gone along with that set in this grand style?— and that wife of yours surely—

Bishu. Yes, we too should have come to just such a pass.

Chandrá. Is there no way going back,—none whatever?

Bishu. There is,—through the gutter.

A Distant Voice. Bishu, my mad one!

Bishu. Yes, my mad girl!

Phágulal. There's Nandini. There'll be no more of Bishu for us, for the rest of the day.

Chandrá. Tell me, Bishu, what does she charm you with?

Bishu. The charm of sorrow.

Chandrá. Why do you talk so topsy-turvy?

Bishu. She reminds me that there are sorrows, to forget which is the greatest of sorrow.

Phágulal. Please to speak plainly, Bishu, otherwise it becomes positively annoying!

Bishu. The pain of desire for the near belongs to the animal, the sorrow of aspiration for the far belongs to man. That far away flame of my eternal sorrow is revealed through Nandini.

Chandrá. Brother, we don't understand these things. But one thing I do understand and that is,—the less you men can make out a girl, the more she attracts you! We simple women,—our price is not so high, but we at least keep you on the straight path. I warn you, once for all, that girl with her noose of red oleanders will drag you to perdition.

(Chandrá *and* Phágulal *go.*)

(*Nandini* comes in.)

Nandini. My mad one, did you hear their autumn songs this morning?

Bishu. Is my morning like yours that I should hear singing? Mine is only a swept-away remnant of the weary night.

Nandini. In my gladness of heart I thought I'd stand on the rampart and join in their song. But the guards would not let me, so I've come to you.

Bishu. I am not a rampart.

Nandini. You are *my* rampart. When I come to you I seem to climb high, I find the open light.

Bishu. Ever since coming to Yaksha Town the sky has dropped out of my life. I felt as if they had pounded me in the same mortar with all the fractions of men here, and rolled us into a solid lump.

Then you came and looked into my face in a way that made me sure some light could still be seen through me.

Nandini. In this closed fort a bit of sky survives only between you and me, my mad one.

Bishu. Through that sky my songs can fly towards you. (*Sings.*)

You keep me awake that I may sing to you,
O Breaker of my sleep!
And so my heart you startle with your call,
O Waker of my grief!
The shades of evening fall,
    the birds come to their nest.
The boat arrives ashore,
    yet my heart knows no rest,
O Waker of my grief!

Nandini. The waker of your grief, Bishu?

Bishu. Yes, you are my messenger from the unreachable shore. The day you came to Yaksha Town a guest of salt air knocked at my heart.

Nandini. But I never had any message of this sorrow of which you sing.

Bishu. Not even from Rañjan?

Nandini. No, he holds an oar in each hand and ferries me across the stormy waters; he catches wild horses by the mane and rides with me through the woods; he shoots an arrow between the eyebrows of the tiger on the spring, and scatters my fear with loud laughter. As he jumps into our Nagai river and disturbs its current with his joyous splashing, so he disturbs me with his tumultuous life. Desperately he stakes his all on the game and thus has he won me.

You also were there with us, but you held aloof, and at last something urged you one day to leave our gambling set. At the time of your parting you looked at my face in a way I could not quite make out. After that I've had no news of you for long. Tell me where you went off to then.

Bishu. My boat was tied to the bank; the rope snapped; the wild wind drove it into the tackles unknown.

Nandini. But who dragged you back from there to dig for nuggets here in Yaksha Town?

Bishu. A woman. Just as a bird on the wing is brought to the ground by a chance arrow, so did she bring me down to the dust. I forgot myself.

Nandini. How could she touch you?

Bishu. When the thirsty heart despairs of finding water it's easy enough for it to be deluded by a mirage, and driven in barren quest from desert to desert.

One day, while I was gazing at the sunset clouds, she had her eye upon the golden spire of the Governor's palace. Her glance challenged me to take her over there. In my foolish pride I vowed to do so. When I did bring her here, under the golden spire, the spell was broken.

Nandini. I've come to take you away from here.

Bishu. Since you have moved even the king of this place, what power on earth can prevent you? Tell me, don't you feel afraid of him?

Nandini. I did fear him from outside that screen. But now I've seen him inside.

Bishu. What was he like?

Nandini. Like a man from the epics,—his forehead like the gateway of a tower, his arms the iron bolts of some inaccessible fortress.

Bishu. What did you see when you went inside?

Nandini. A falcon was sitting on his left wrist. He put it on the perch and gazed at my face. Then, just as he had been stroking the falcon's wings, he began gently to stroke my hand. After a while he suddenly asked: 'Don't you fear me, Nandini?'

'Not in the least,' said I.

Then he buried his fingers in my unbound hair and sat long with closed eyes.

Bishu. How did you like it?

Nandini. I liked it. Shall I tell you how? It was as if he were a thousand-year-old banyan tree, and I a tiny little bird; when I lit on a branch of his and had my little swing, he needs must have felt a thrill of delight to his very marrow. I loved to give that bit of joy to that lonely soul.

Bishu. Then what did he say?

Nandini. Starting up and fixing his spear-point gaze on my face, he suddenly said: 'I want to know you.'

I felt a shiver run down my body and asked: 'What is there to know?—I am not a manuscript!'

'I know all there is in manuscripts,' said he, 'but I don't know you.' Then he became excited and cried: 'Tell me all about Rañjan. Tell me how you love him.'

I talked on: 'I love Rañjan as the rudder in the water might love the sail in the sky, answering its rhythm of wind in the rhythm of waves.'

He listened quietly, staring like a big greedy boy. All of a sudden he startled me by exclaiming: 'Could you die for him?'

'This very moment,' I replied.

'Never,' he almost roared, as if in anger.

'Yes, I could,' I repeated.

'What good would that do you?'

'I don't know,' said I.

Then he writhed and shouted: 'Go away from my room, go, go at once, don't disturb me in my work.' I could not understand what that meant.

Bishu. He gets angry when he can't understand.

Nandini. Bishu, don't you feel pity for him?

Bishu. The day when God will be moved to pity for him, he will die.

Nandini. No, no, you don't know how desperately he wants to live.

Bishu. You will see this very day what his living means. I don't know whether you'll be able to bear the sight.

Nandini. There, look, there's a shadow. I am sure the Governor has secretly heard what we've been saying.

Bishu. This place is dark with the Governor's shadow, it is everywhere. How do you like him?

Nandini. I have never seen anything so lifeless,—like a cane stick cut from the cane bush,—no leaves, no roots, no sap in the veins.

Bishu. Cut off from life, he spends himself in repressing life.

Nandini. Hush, he will hear you.

Bishu. He hears even when you are silent, which is all the more dangerous. When I am with the diggers I am careful in my speech, so much so that the Governor thinks I'm the sorriest of the lot, and spares me out of sheer contempt. But, my mad girl, when I am with you my mind scorns to be cautious.

Nandini. No, no, you must not court danger. There comes the Governor.

(The *Governor* comes in.)

Governor. Hallo, 69 Ng! you seem to be making friends with everybody, without distinction.

Bishu. You may remember that I began by making friends even with you, only it was the distinction that stood in the way.

Governor. Well, what are we discussing now?

Bishu. We are discussing how to escape from this fortress of yours.

Governor. Really? So recklessly, that you don't even mind confessing it?

Bishu. Sir Governor, it doesn't need much cleverness to know that when a captive bird pecks at the bars it's not in the spirit of caress. What does it matter whether that's openly confessed or not?

Governor. The captives' want of love we were aware of, but their not fearing to admit it has become evident only recently.

Nandini. Won't you let Rañjan come?

Governor. You will see him this very day.

Nandini. I knew that; still, for your message of hope I wish you victory. Governor, take this garland of *kunda* flowers.

Governor. Why throw away the garland thus, and not keep it for Rañjan?

Nandini. There is a garland for him.

Governor. Aha, I thought so! I suppose it's the one hanging round your neck. The garland of victory may be of *kunda* flowers. The gift of the hand; but the garland of welcome is of red oleanders, the gift of the heart. Well, let's be quick in accepting what comes from the hand, for that will fade; as for the heart's offering, the longer it waits the more precious it grows. (*The* Governor *goes.*)

Nandini (*knocking at the window*). Do you hear? Let me come into your room.

Voice. (*from behind the scenes*). Why always the same futile request? Who is that with you? A pair to Rañjan?

Bishu. No, King, I am the obverse side of Rañjan, on which falls the shadow.

Voice. What use has Nandini for you?

Bishu. The use which music has for the hollow of the flute.

Voice. Nandini, what is this man to you?

Nandini. He's my partner in music. My heart soars in his voice, my pain cries in his tunes,—that's what he tells me.   (*Sings.*)

 'I love, I love,'—*'Tis the cry that breaks out*
 from the bosom of earth and water.

Voice. So that's your partner! What if I dissolved your partnership this very minute?

Nandini. Why are you so cross? Haven't you any companion yourself?

Voice. Has the mid-day sun any companion?

Nandini. Well, let's change the subject. What's that? What's that in your hand?

Voice. A dead frog.

Nandini. What for?

Voice. Once upon a time this frog got into a hole in a stone, and in that shelter it existed for three thousand years. I have learnt from it the secret of continuing to exist, but to live it does not know. To-day I felt bored and smashed its shelter. I've thus saved it from existing for ever. Isn't that good news?

Nandini. Your stone walls will also fall away from around me to-day,—I shall meet Rañjan.

Voice. I want to see you both together.

Nandini. You won't be able to see from behind your net.

Voice. I shall let you sit inside my room.

Nandini. What will you do with us?

Voice. Nothing, I only want to know you.

Nandini. When you talk of knowing, it frightens me.

Voice. Why?

Nandini. I feel that you have no patience with things that cannot be known, but can only be felt.

Voice. I dare not trust such things lest they should play me false. Now go away, don't waste my time.—No, no, wait a little. Give me that tassel of red oleanders which hangs from your hair.

Nandini. What will you do with it?

Voice. When I look at those flowers it seems to me as if the red light of my evil star has appeared in their shape. At times I want to snatch them from you and tear them to pieces. Again I think that if Nandini were ever to place that spray of flowers on my head, with her own hands, then—

Nandini. Then what?

Voice. Then perhaps I might die in peace.

Nandini. Someone loves red oleanders and calls me by that name. It is in remembrance of him that I wear these flowers.

Voice. Then, I tell you, they're going to be *his* evil star as well as *mine.*

Nandini. Don't say such things for shame! I am going.

Voice. Where?

Nandini. I shall go and sit near the gate of your fort.

Voice. Why?

Nandini. When Rañjan comes he'll see I am waiting for him.

Voice. I should like to tread hard on Rañjan and grind him in the dust.

Nandini. Why pretend to frighten me?

Voice. Pretend, you say? Don't you know I am really fear-some?

Nandini. You seem to take pleasure in seeing people frightened at you. In our village plays Srikantha takes the part of a demon; when he comes on the stage, he is delighted

if the children are terrified. You are like him. Do you
know what I think?

Voice. What is it?

Nandini. The people here trade on frightening others. That's
why they have put you behind a network and dressed
you fantastically. Don't you feel ashamed to be got up
like a bogeyman?

Voice. How dare you!

Nandini. Those whom you have scared all along will one day
feel ashamed to be afraid. If my Rañjan were here, he
would have snapped his fingers in your face, and not
been afraid even if he died for it.

Voice. Your impudence is something great. I should like to
stand you up on the top of a heap of everything I've
smashed throughout my life. And then—

Nandini. Then what?

Voice. Then, like a squeezed bunch of grapes with its juice
running out from between the gripping fingers, if I
could but hold you tight with these two hands of mine,—
and then—go, go, run away, at once, at once!

Nandini. If you shout at me so rudely, I'll stay on, do what
you will!

Voice. I long savagely to prove to you how cruel I am. Have
you never heard moans from inside my room?

Nandini. I have. Whose moaning was it?

Voice. The hidden mystery of life, wrenched away by me,
bewails its torn ties. To get fire from a tree you have
to burn it. Nandini, there is fire within you too, red
fire. One day I shall burn you and extract that also.

Nandini. Oh, you are cruel!

Voice. I must either gather or scatter. I can feel no pity for
what I do not get. Breaking is a fierce kind of getting.

Nandini. But why thrust out your clenched fist like that?

Voice. Here, I take away my fist. Now fly, as the dove flies
from the shadow of a hawk.

Nandini. Very well, I will go, and not vex you any more.

Voice. Here, listen, come back, Nandini!

Nandini. What is it?

Voice. On your face, there is the play of life in your eyes and
lips; at the back of you flows your black hair, the silent
fall of death. The other day when my hands sank into
it they felt the *soft calm of dying.* I long to sleep with
my face hidden inside those thick black clusters. You
don't know how tired I am!

Nandini. Don't you ever sleep?

Voice. I feel afraid to sleep.

Nandini. Let me sing you the latest song that I've learnt.
(*Sings.*)

'I love, I love' is the cry that breaks out from
the bosom of earth and water.

The sky broods like an aching heart, the horizon is
tender like eyes misted with tears.

Voice. Enough! Enough! stop your singing!

Nandini. (*sings on*).

A lament heaves and bursts
on the shore of the sea,

The whispers of forgotten days
are born in new leaves to die again.

See, Bishu, he has left the dead frog there and disappeared.
He is afraid of songs.

Bishu. The old frog in his heart yearns to die when it hears
singing, that's why he feels afraid. My mad girl, why
is there a strange light on your face to-day, like the glow
of a distant torch in the sky?

Nandini. News has reached me, Rañjan is coming to-day.

Bishu. How?

Nandini. Let me tell you. Every day a pair of blue-throats come and sit on the pomegranate tree in front of my window. Every night, before I sleep, I salute the pole star and say: Sacred star of constancy, if a feather from the wings of the blue-throats finds its way into my room, then I will know my Rañjan is coming. This morning, as soon as I woke, I found a feather on my bed. See, here it is under my breast-cloth. When I meet him I shall put this feather on his crest.

Bishu. They say blue-throats' wings are an omen of victory.

Nandini. Rañjan's way to victory lies through my heart.

Bishu. No more of this; let me go to my work.

Nandini. I shan't let you work to-day.

Bishu. What must I do then.

Nandini. Sing that song of waiting.

Bishu. (*sings*).

> *He who ever wants me through the ages,—*
> *is it not he who sits to-day by my wayside?*
> *I seem to remember a glimpse I had of his face,*
> *in the twilight dusk of some ancient year.*
> *Is it not he who sits to-day by the wayside?*

Nandini. Bishu, when you sing I cannot help feeling that I owe you much, but have never given anything to you.

Bishu. I shall decorate my forehead with the mark of your never-giving, and go my way. No little-giving for me, in return for my song! Where will you go now?

Nandini. To the wayside by which Rañjan is coming. (*They go*).

(The *Governor* and a *Headman* come in.)

Governor. No, we can't possibly allow Rañjan to enter this parish.

Headman. I put him to work in the tunnels of Vajragarh.

Governor. Well, what happened?

Headman. He said he was not used to being made to work. The Headman of Vajragarh came with the police, but the fellow doesn't know what fear is. Threaten him, he bursts out laughing. Asked why he laughs, he says solemnity is the mask of stupidity and he has come to take it off.

Governor. Did you set him to work with the diggers?

Headman. I did, I thought that pressure would make him yield. But on the contrary it seemed to lift the pressure from the diggers' minds also. He cheered them up, and asked them to have a digger's dance!

Governor. Digger's dance! What on earth is that?

Headman. Rañjan started singing. Where were they to get drums?— they objected. Rañjan said, if there weren't any drums, there were spades enough. So they began keeping time with the spades, making a joke of their digging up of nuggets.

The Headman himself came over to reprimand them. 'What style of work is this?' he thundered.

'I have unbound the work,' said Rañjan. 'It won't have to be dragged out by main force any more, it will run along of itself, dancing.'

Governor. The fellow is mad, I see.

Headman. Hopelessly mad. 'Use your spade properly,' shouted I. 'Much better give me a guitar,' said he, smiling.

Governor. But how did he manage to escape from Vajragarh and come up here?

Headman. That I do not know. Nothing seems to fasten on to him. His boisterousness is infectious. The diggers are getting frisky.

Governor. Hallo, isn't that Rañjan himself,—going along the road, thrumming on an old guitar? Impudent rascal! He doesn't even care to hide.

Headman. Well, I never! Goodness alone knows how he broke through the wall!

Governor. Go and seize him instantly! He must not meet Nandini in this parish, for anything.

(Enters *Assistant Governor.*)

Governor. Where are you going?

Assistant Governor. To arrest Rañjan.

Governor. Where is the Deputy Governor?

Assistant Governor. He is so much amused by this fellow that he doesn't want to lay hands on him. He says the man's laugh shows us what queer creatures we governors have grown into.

Governor. I have an idea. Don't arrest Rañjan. Send him on to the King's sanctum.

Assistant Governor. He refuses to obey our call, even in the King's name.

Governor. Tell him the King has made a slave-girl of his Nandini.

Assistant Governor. But if the King—

Governor. Don't you worry. Come on, I'll go with you myself.

(*They go.*)

(Enter *Professor* and *Antiquarian.*)

Antiquarian. I say, what is this infernal noise going on inside?

Professor. The king, probably in a temper with himself, is engaged in breaking some of his own handiwork.

Antiquarian. It sounds like big pillars crashing down one after another.

Professor. There was a lake, at the foot of our hill over there, in which the waters of this Sankhini river used to gather. One day, suddenly, the rock to its left gave way, and the stored-up water rushed out laughing like mad. To see the King now-a-days, it strikes me that his treasure lake has grown weary of its rock wall.

Antiquarian. What did you bring me here for, Professor?

Professor. Latterly he has begun to get angry with my science. He says it only burgles through one wall to reveal another behind it, and never reaches the inner chamber of the Life spirit. I thought that, perhaps in the study of antiquity, he might explore the secret of Life's play. My knapsack has been rifled empty, now he can go on pocket-picking history.

Antiquarian. A girl wearing a grass-green robe.

Professor. She has for her mantle the green joy of the earth. That is our Nandini. In this Yaksha Town there are governors, foremen, headmen, tunnel-diggers, scholars like myself; there are policemen, executioners, and undertakers,—altogether a beautiful assortment! Only *she* is out of element. Midst the clamour of the market place she is a tuned-up lyre. There are days when the mesh of my studies is torn by the sudden breeze of her passing by, and through that rent my attention flies away *swish,* like a bird.

Antiquarian. Good heavens, man! Are even your well-seasoned bones subject to these poetic fits?

Professor. Life's attraction, like the tidal wave, tears away mind from its anchorage of books.

Antiquarian. Tell me, where am I to meet the King?

Professor. There's no means of meeting him. You'll have to talk to him from outside this network.

Antiquarian. We're to converse with this net between us?

Professor. Not the kind of whispered talk that may take place through a woman's veil, but solidly concentrated conversation. Even the cows in his stall don't dare to give milk, they yield their butter straight off!

Antiquarian. Admirable! To extract the essential from the diluted, is what scholars aim at.

Professor. But not what God is His creation aims at. He respects the fruit stones that are hard, but rejoices in the pulp that is sweet.

Antiquarian. Professor, I see that your grey science is galloping fast towards grass-green. But I wonder how you can stand this King of yours.

Professor. Shall I tell you the truth? I love him.

Antiquarian. You don't mean to say so?

Professor. He is so great that even what is wrong with him will not be able to spoil him.

(The *Governor* comes in.)

Governor. I say, man of science, so this is the person you volunteered to bring here. Our King flew into a passion at the very mention of his special subject.

Antiquarian. May I ask why?

Governor. The King says there is no age of history which may be called old. It is always an eternal extension of the present.

Antiquarian. Can the front exist without the back?

Governor. What he said was: 'Time proceeds by revealing the new on his front; but the men of learning, suppressing that fact, will have it that Time ever carries the burden of the old on his back.'

(*Nandini* comes in hurriedly.)

Nandini. What is happening? Who are they?

Governor. Hallo, Nandini, is that you? I shall wear your

kunda chain late in the evening. When three-quarters of me can hardly be seen for the dark, then perchance a flower garland might become even me.

Nandini. Look over there—what a piteous sight! Who are those people, going along with the guards, filing out from the backdoor of the King's apartments?

Governor. We call them the King's leavings.

Nandini. What does that mean?

Governor. Some day you too will know its meaning; let it be for today.

Nandini. But are these men? Have they flesh and marrow, life and soul?

Governor. Maybe they haven't.

Nandini. Had they never any?

Governor. Maybe they had.

Nandini. Where then is it all gone now?

Governor. Man of science, explain it if you can, I'm off. (*He goes.*)

Nandini. Alas, alas! I see amongst these shadows faces that I know. Surely that is our Anup and Upamanyu?

Professor, they belong to our neighbouring village. Two brothers as tall as they were strong. They used to come and race their boats in our river on the fourteenth day of the moon in rainy June. Oh, who has brought them to this miserable plight?

See, there goes Shaklu,—in sword play he used to win the prize garland before all the others. Anu-up! Sha-klu-u! look this way; it's I, you're the principle underlying all rise to greatness.

Nandini. It's a fiendish principle!

Professor. It's no use getting annoyed with a principle. Principles are neither good nor bad. That which happens *does* happen. To go against it, is to knock your head against the law of being.

Nandini. If this is the way of man's being, I refuse to *be,* I
want to depart with those shadows,—show me the way.

Professor. When the time comes for showing us out, the great
ones themselves will point the way. Before that, there's
no such nuisance as a way at all! You see how our
Antiquarian has quietly slipped off, thinking he'll fly
and save himself. After going a few steps, he'll soon
discover that there's a wire network stretched from
post to post, from country to country.

Nandini, I see, your temper is rising. The red oleanders
against your flaming cheek are beginning to look like
evening storm clouds gathering for a night of terror.

Nandini (knocking at the net window). Listen, listen!

Professor. Whom are you calling?

Nandini. That King of yours, shrouded in his mist of netting.

Professor. The door of the inner room has been closed. He
won't hear you.

Nandini. (calling out). Bishu, mad brother mine!

Professor. What d'you want with *him?*

Nandini. Why hasn't he come back yet? I feel afraid.

Professor. He was with you only a little while ago.

Nandini. The Governor said he was wanted to identify Rañjan.
I tried to go with him, but they wouldn't let me. Whose
groaning is that?

Professor. It must be that wrestler of ours.

Nandini. What wrestler?

Professor. The world-famous Gajju, whose brother, Bhajan, had
the bravado to challenge the King to a wrestling match,
since when not even a thread of his loin cloth is anywhere
to be seen. That put Gajju on his mettle, and he came
on with great sound and fury. I told him at the outset
that, if he wanted to dig in the tunnels underneath this
kingdom, he was welcome,—he could at least drag on
a dead and alive existence for some time. But if he

wanted to make a show of heroics, that would not be tolerated for a moment.

Nandini. Does it at all make for their well-being thus to keep watch and ward over these man-traps night and day?

Professor. Well-being! There's no question of 'well' in it at all,— only 'being.' That *being* of theirs has expanded so terribly that, unless millions of men are pressed into service, who's going to support its weight? So the net is spreading farther and farther. They must exist, you see.

Nandini. Must they? If it is necessary to die in order to live like men, what harm in dying?

Professor. Again that anger, the wild cry of red oleander? It is sweet, no doubt, yet what is true is true. If it gives you pleasure to say that one must die to live, well, say so by all means; but those who say that others must die that they themselves may live,—it's only they who are actually alive. You may cry out that this shows a lack of humanity, but you forget, in your indignation, that this is what humanity itself happens to be. The tiger does not feed on the tiger, it's only man who fattens on his fellow-man.

(The *Wrestler* totters in)

Nandini. Oh poor thing, see how he comes, staggering. Wrestler, lie down here. Professor, do see where he's hurt.

Professor. You won't see any outward sign of a wound.

Wrestler. All-merciful God, grant me strength once more in my life, if only for one little day!

Professor. Why, my dear fellow?

Wrestler. Just to wring that Governor's neck!

Professor. What has the Governor done to you?

Wrestler. It's he who brought about the whole thing. I never wanted to fight. Now, after egging me on, he goes about saying it's my fault.

Professor. Why, what interest had he in your fighting?

Wrestler. They only feel safe when they rob the whole world of strength. Lord of Mercy, grant that I may be able to gouge his eyes out some day, to tear asunder his lying tongue!

Nandini. How do you feel now, Wrestler?

Wrestler. Altogether hollowed out! These demons know the magic art of sucking away not only strength but hope. If only once I could somehow,—O good God, but once,—everything is possible to Thy mercy,—if only I could fasten my teeth for once in the Governor's throat!

Nandini. Professor, help me to raise him.

Professor. That would be a crime, Nandini, according to the custom of this land.

Nandini. Wouldn't it be a crime to let the man perish?

Professor. That which there is none to punish may be a sin, but never a crime. Nandini, come away, come right away out of this. The tree spreads its root-fingers and does its grabbing underground, but there it does not bring forth its flowers. Flowers bloom on the branches which reach towards the light. My sweet Red Oleander, don't try to probe our secrets in the depths of their dust. Be for us swaying in the air above, that we may gaze upwards to see you.

There comes the Governor. He hates to see me talk to you. So I must go.

Nandini. Why is he so dead against me?

Professor. I can guess. You have touched his heart-strings. The longer it takes to tune them up, the more awful the discord meanwhile.

(The *Professor* goes, the *Governor* comes in.)

Nandini. Sir Governor!

Governor. Nandini, when our Gosain saw that *kunda* garland
of yours in my room, both his eyes,—but here he
comes—(The *Gosain* comes in.)
Your Holiness, accept my reverence. That garland was
given to me by our Nandini here.

Gosain. Ah indeed! the gift of a pure heart! God's own white
kunda flowers! Their beauty remains unsullied even in
the hands of a man of the world. This is what gives one
faith in the power of virtue, and hope for the sinners'
redemption.

Nandini. Please do something for this man, Your Reverence.
There's very little life left in him.

Gosain. The Governor is sure to keep him as much alive as
it is necessary for him to be. But, my child, these
discussions ill become your lips.

Nandini. So in this kingdom you follow some calculation in
apportioning life?

Gosain. Of course,—for mortal life has its limits. Our class
of people have their great burden to bear, therefore we
have to claim a larger portion of life's sustenance for
our share. That's according to Almighty God's own
decree.

Nandini. Reverend Sir, may I know what good God has so
heavily charged you to do to these people?

Gosain. The life that is unlimited gives no provocation to fight
for its distribution. We Preachers have the charge of
turning these people towards this unlimited life. So
long as they remain content with that, we are their
friends.

Nandini. Let me come over to the Headman's quarters to help you.

Wrestler. No. Don't add to my troubles, I beg of you. (The *Wrestler* goes.)

Nandini. Governor, stay, tell me, whither have you taken my Bishu?

Governor. Who am I that I should take him? The wind carries off the clouds,—if you think that to be a crime, make enquiries as to who is behind the wind.

Nandini. Dear me, what an awful place! You are not men, and those you drive are not men, either,—you are winds and they are clouds!

Reverend Gosain, I am sure, *you* know where my Bishu is.

Gosain. I know, for sure, that wherever he is, it's for the best.

Nandini. For whose best?

Gosain. That you won't understand—

Oh, I say, leave off, let go of that, it's my rosary.—Hallo, Governor, what wild girl is this you have—

Governor. The girl has somehow managed to ensconce herself in a niche, safe from the laws of this land, and we can't lay hands on her. Our King himself—

Gosain. Good heavens, now she'll tear off my wrap of the Holy Name too. What unspeakable outrage! (The *Gosain* flies.)

Nandini. Governor, you *must* tell me where you have taken Bishu.

Governor. They have summoned him to the court of judgement. That's all that there is to tell you. Let me go.

Nandini. Because I am a woman, you are not afraid of me? God sends His thunderbolt through His messenger, the lightning spark—that bolt I have borne here with me; it will shatter the golden spire of your mastery.

Governor. Then let me tell you the truth before I go. It's you who have dragged Bishu into danger.

Nandini. I?

Governor. Yes, you! He was so long content to be quietly burrowing away underground like a worm. It's you who taught him to spread the wings of death. O fire of the gods, you'll yet draw forth many more to their fate.—Then at length will you and I come to our understanding, and that won't be long.

Nandini. So may it be. But tell me one thing before you go. Will you not let Rañjan come and see me?

Governor. No, never.

Nandini. Never, you say! I defy you to do your worst. This very day I am sure, absolutely sure, that he and I will meet! (Governor *goes.*)

Nandini (*knocking and tugging at the network*). Listen, listen, King! Where's your court of judgement? Open its door to me. (*Kishôr comes in.*)

Who is that? My boy, Kishôr! Do you know where Bishu is?

Kishôr. Yes, Nandini, be ready to see him. I don't know how it was, the Chief of the Guard took a fancy to my youthfulness and yielded to my entreaties. He has consented to take him along by this path.

Nandini. Guard! Take him along? Is he then—

Kishôr. Yes, here they come.

Nandini. What! Handcuffs on your wrists? Friend of my heart, where are thy taking you like that?

(*Bishu* comes in under arrest.)

Bishu. It's nothing to be anxious about!—Guards, please wait a little, let me say a few words to her.—My wild girl, my heart's joy, at last I am free.

Nandini. What do you mean, Singer of my heart? I don't understand your words.

Bishu. When I used to be afraid, and try to avoid danger at every step, I seemed to be at liberty; but that liberty was the worst form of bondage.

Nandini. What offence have you committed that they should take you away thus?

Bishu. I spoke out the truth to-day, at last.

Nandini. What if you did?

Bishu. No harm at all!

Nandini. Then why did they bind you like this?

Bishu. What harm in that either? These chains will bear witness to the truth of my freedom.

Nandini. Don't they feel ashamed of themselves to lead you along the road chained like a beast? Aren't they men too?

Bishu. They have a big beast inside them, that's why their heads are not lowered by the indignity of man, rather the inner brute's tail swells and wags with pride at man's downfall.

Nandini. O dear heart! Have they been hurting you? What are these marks on your body?

Bishu. They have whipped me, with the whips they use for their dogs. The string of that whip is made with the same thread which goes to the stringing of their Gosain's rosary. When they tell their beads they don't remember that; but probably their God is aware of it.

Nandini. Let them bind me like that too, and take me away with you, my heart's joy! Unless I share some of your punishment I shan't be able to touch food from to-day.

Kishôr. I'm sure I can persuade them to take me in exchange for you. Let me take your place, Bishu.

Bishu. Don't be silly!

Kishôr. Punishment won't hurt me. I am young. I shall bear it with joy.

Nandini. No, no, do not talk like that.

Kishôr. Nandini, my absence has been noticed, their
bloodhounds are after me. Allow me to escape the
indignity awaiting me by taking shelter in a punishment
I joyfully accept.

Bishu. No, it won't do for you to be caught—not for a while
yet. There's work for you, dear boy, and dangerous
work too. Rañjan has come. You must find him out.

Kishôr. Then I bid you farewell, Nandini. What is your message
when I meet Rañjan?

Nandini. This tassel of red oleanders. (*Hands it to him.*)

(*Kishôr goes.*)

Bishu. May you both be united once again.

Nandini. That union will give me no pleasure now. I shall
never be able to forget that I sent you away empty-
handed. And what has that poor boy, Kishôr, got from
me?

Bishu. All the treasure hidden in his heart has been revealed
to him by the fire you have lighted in his life. Nandini,
I remind you, it's for you to put that blue-throat's
feather on Rañjan's crest.—There, do you hear them
singing the harvest song?

Nandini. I do, and it wrings my heart, to tears.

Bishu. The play of the fields is ended now, and the field-
master is taking the ripe corn home. Come on, Guards,
let's not linger any more.

(*Sings.*)

Mow the corn of the last harvest,
    bind it in sheaves.
The remainder, let it return
    as dust unto the dust.

(*They go.*)

(The *Governor* and a *Doctor* come in.)

Doctor. I've seen him. I find the King.

Governor. My wife will be driving out to-day. The post will
be changed near your village, and you must see that
she's not detained.

Headman. There's a plague on the cattle of our parish, and
not a single ox can be had to draw the car. Never mind,
we can press the diggers into service.

Governor. You know where you have to take her? To the
garden-house, where the feast of the Flag-worship is to
be held.

Headman. I'll see to it at once, but let me tell you one thing
before I go. That 69 Ng, whom they call mad Bishu,—
it's high time to cure his madness.

Governor. Why, how does he annoy you?

Headman. Not so much by what he says or does, as by what
he implies.

Governor. There's no need to worry about him any further.
You understand!

Headman. Really! That's good news, indeed! Another thing.
That 47 V, he's rather too friendly with 69 Ng.

Governor. I have observed that.

Headman. Your Lordship's observation is ever keen. Only, as
you have to keep an eye on so many things, one or two
may perchance escape your notice. For instance, there's
our No. 95, a distant connection of mine by marriage,
ever ready to make sandals for the feet of Your Lordship's
sweeper out of his own ribs,—so irrepressibly loyal is
he that even his wife hangs her head for very shame,—
and yet up to now—

Governor. His name has been entered in the High Register.

Headman. Ah, then his lifelong service will at last receive its
reward! The news must be broken to him gently, because
he gets epileptic fits, and supposing suddenly—

Governor. All right, we'll see to that. Now be off, there's no time.

Headman. Just a word about another person,—though he's my own brother-in-law. When his mother died, my wife brought him up with her own hands; yet for my master's sake—

Governor. You can tell me about him another time. Run away now.

Headman. There comes His Honour the Deputy Governor. Please speak a word to him on my behalf. He doesn't look upon me with favour. I suspect that when 69 Ng used to enjoy the favour of free entry into the palace, he must have been saying things against me.

Governor. I assure you, he never even mentioned your name.

Headman. That's just his cleverness! What can be more damaging than to suppress the name of a man, whose name is his best asset? These schemers have their different ways. No. 33 of our parish has an incurable habit of haunting Your Lordship's private chamber. One is always afraid of his inventing goodness knows what calumnies about other people. And yet if one knew the truth about his own—

Governor. There's positively no time to-day. Get away with you, quick!

Headman. I make my salute. (*Coming back.*) Just one word more lest I forget. No. 88 of our neighbouring parish started work on a miserable pittance, and before two years are out his income has run into thousands, not to speak of extras! Your Lordship's mind is like that of the gods—a few words of hypocritical praise are enough to draw down the best of your boons.

Governor. All right, all right,—that can keep for to-morrow.

Headman. I'm not so mean as to suggest taking away the bread from his mouth. But Your Lordship should seriously consider whether it's wise to keep him on at the Treasury. Our Vishnu Dutt knows him inside out. If you send—

Governor. I shall send for him this very day. But begone,— not another word!

Headman. Your Lordship, my third son is getting to be quite a big boy. He came the other day to prostrate himself at your feet. After two days of dancing attendance outside, he had to go away without gaining admission to you. He feels it very bitterly. My daughter-in-law has made with her own hands an offering of sweet pumpkin for Your Lordship—

Governor. Oh confound you! Tell him to come day after to-morrow, he will be admitted. *Now, will you—*

(*Headman* goes. The *Deputy Governor* comes in.)

Deputy Governor. I've just sent on the dancing girls and musicians to the garden.

Governor. And that little matter about Rañjan,—how far—?

Deputy Governor. That kind of work is not in my line. The Assistant Governor has taken it upon himself to do the job. By this time his—

Governor. Does the King—?

Deputy Governor. The King can't possibly have understood. Some lie told by our men has goaded Rañjan to frenzy, and he's rushing to the usual fate of—I detest the whole business. Moreover, I don't think it right to deceive the King like this.

Governor. That responsibility is mine. Now then, that girl must be—

Deputy Governor. Don't talk of all that to me. The Headman who has been put on duty is the right man,—he doesn't stick at any dirtiness whatever.

Governor. Does that man Gosain know about this affair?

Deputy Governor. I'm sure he can guess, but he's careful not to know for certain.

Governor. What's his object?

Deputy Governor. For fear of there being no way left open for saying: 'I don't believe it.'

Governor. But what makes him take all this trouble?

Deputy Governor. Don't you see? The poor man is really two in one, clumsily joined,—Priest on the skin, Governor at the marrow. He has to take precious care to prevent the Governor part of him coming up to the surface, lest it should clash too much with his telling of beads.

Governor. He might have dropped the beads altogether.

Deputy Governor. No, for whatever his blood may be, his mind, in a sense, is really pious. If only he can tell his beads in his temple, and revel in slave-driving in his dreams, he feels happy. But for him, the true complexion of our God would appear too black. In fact, Gosain is placed here only to help our God to feel comfortable.

Governor. My friend, I see the instinct of the Ruler doesn't seem to match with the colour of your own blood, either!

Deputy Governor. There's hope still. Human blood is fast drying up. But I can't stomach your No. 321 yet. When I'm obliged to embrace him in public, no holy water seems able to wash out the impurity of his touch.

Here comes Nandini.

Governor. Come away, I don't trust you. I know the spell of Nandini has fallen on your eyes.

Deputy Governor. I know that as well as you do. But you don't seem to know that a tinge of her oleanders has got mixed with the colour of duty in *your* eyes too—that's what makes them so frightfully red.

Governor. That may be. Fortunately for us, our mind knows not its own secret. Come away.

(They go.)

(*Nandini* comes in.)

Nandini (*knocking and pushing at the network*). Listen, listen, listen!

(The *Gosain* comes in.)

Gosain. Whom are you prodding like that?

Nandini. That boa-constrictor of yours, who remains in hiding and swallows men.

Gosain. Lord, lord! When Providence wishes to destroy the small, it does so by putting big words into their little mouths.

See here, Nandini, believe me when I tell you that I aim at your welfare.

Nandini. Try some more real method of doing me good.

Gosain. Come to my sanctuary, let me chant you the Holy Name for a while.

Nandini. What have I to do with the name?

Gosain. You will gain peace of mind.

Nandini. Shame, shame on me if I do! I shall sit and wait here at the door.

Gosain. You have more faith in men than in God?

Nandini. Your God of the Flagstaff,—he will never unbend. But the man who is lost to sight behind the netting, will he also remain bound in his network for ever? Go, go. It's your trade to delude men with words, after filching away their lives.

(*The* Gosain *goes*.)

(Enter *Phágulal* and *Chandrá*.)

Phágulal. Our Bishu came away with you, where is he now?
Tell us the truth.

Nandini. He has been made prisoner and taken away.

Chandrá. You witch, you must have given information against
him. You are their spy.

Nandini. You don't really believe that!

Chandrá What else are you doing here?

Phágulal. Every person suspects every other person in this
cursed place. Yet I have always trusted you, Nandini.
In my heart I used to—However, let that pass. But today it looks very very strange, I must say.

Nandini. Perhaps it does. It may really be even as you say.
Bishu has got into trouble for coming with me. He used
to be quite safe in your company, he said so himself.

Chandrá. Then why did you decoy him away, you evil-omened
creature?

Nandini. Because he said he wanted to be free.

Chandrá. A precious kind of freedom you have given him!

Nandini. I could not understand all that he said. Chandrá.
Why did he tell me that freedom could only be found
by plunging down to the bottom of danger?—Phágulal,
how could I save him who wanted to be free from the
tyranny of safety?

Chandrá. We don't understand all this. If you can't bring him
back, you'll have to pay for it. I'm not to be taken in
by that coquettish prettiness of yours.

Phágulal. What's the use of idle bickering? Let's gather a big
crowd from the workmen's lines, and then go and
smash the prison gate.

Nandini. I'll come with you.

Phágulal. What for?

Nandini. To join in the breaking.

Chandrá. As if you haven't done quite enough breaking already, you sorceress!

(*Gôkul* comes in.)

Gôkul. That witch must be burnt alive, before everything else.

Chandrá. That won't be punishment enough. First knock off that beauty of hers, with which she goes about ruining people. Weed it out of her face as the grass is weeded with a hoe.

Gôkul. That I can do. Let this hammer just have a dance on her nose tip—

Phágulal. Beware! If you dare touch her—

Nandini. Stop, Phágulal. He's coward; he wants to strike me because he's afraid of me. I don't fear his blows one bit.

Gôkul. Phágulal, you haven't come to your senses yet. You think the Governor alone is your enemy. Well, I admire a straightforward enemy. But that sweet-mouthed beauty of yours—

Nandini. Ah, so you too admire the Governor, as the mud beneath his feet admires the soles of his shoes!

Phágulal. Gôkul, the time has at length come to show your prowess, but not by fighting a girl. Come along with me. I'll show you what to fight. (*Phágulal, Chandrá, and* Gôkul *go.*)

(A band of *Men* come in.)

Nandini. Where are you going, my good men?

First Man. We carry the offering for the Flag-worship.

Nandini. Have you seen Rañjan?

Second Man. I saw him once, five days ago, but not since. Ask those others who follow us.

Nandini. Who are they?

Third Man. They are bearing wine for the Governors' feast.

(The first batch goes, another comes in.)

Nandini. Look here, red-caps, have you seen Rañjan?

First Man. I saw him the other day at the house of Headman Sambhu.

Nandini. Where is he now?

Second Man. D'you see those men taking the ladies' dresses for the feast? Ask them. They hear a lot of things that don't reach our ears.

(Second batch goes, a third come in.)

Nandini. Do *you* know, my men, where they have kept Rañjan?

First Man. Hush, hush!

Nandini. I am sure you know. You *must* tell me.

Second Man. What enters by our ears doesn't come out by our mouths, that's why we are still alive. Ask one of the men who are carrying the weapons.

(They go, others come in.)

Nandini. Oh do stop a moment and listen to me. Tell me, where is Rañjan?

First Man. The auspicious hour draws near. It's time for the King himself to come for the Flag-worship. Ask him about it when he steps out. We only know the beginning, not the end.

(*They go.*)

Nandini (*shaking the network/violently*). Open the door. The time has come.

Voice (*behind the scenes*). But not for you. Go away from here.

Nandini. You must hear *now* what I have to say. It cannot wait for another time.

Voice. You want Rañjan, I know. I have asked the Governor to fetch him at once. But don't remain standing at the door when I come out for the worship, for then you'll run great risk.

Nandini. I have cast away all fear. You can't drive me away. Happen what may, I'm not going to move till your door is opened.

Voice. To-day's for the Flag-worship. Don't distract my mind. Get away from my door.

Nandini. The gods have all eternity for their worship, they're not pressed for time. But the sorrows of men cannot wait.

King. Deceived! These traitors have deceived me,—perdition take them! My own machine refuses my sway! Call the Governor—bring him to me handcuffed—

Nandini. King, they all say you know magic. Make him wake up for my sake.

King. My magic can only put an end to waking.—Alas! I know not how to awaken.

Nandini. Then lull me to sleep,—the same sleep! Oh, why did you work this havoc? I cannot bear it any more.

King. I have killed youth. Yes, I have indeed killed youth,— all these years, with all my strength. The curse of youth, dead, is upon me.

Nandini. Did he not take my name?

King. He did,—in such a way that every vein in my body was set on fire.

Nandini (*to* Rañjan). My love, my brave one, here do I place this blue-throat's feather in your crest. Your victory has begun from today, and I am its bearer. Ah, here is that tassel of my flowers in his hand. Then Kishôr must have met him—

But where is he? King, where is that boy?

King. Which boy?

Nandini. The boy who brought these flowers to Rañjan.

King. That absurd little child! He came to defy me with his girlish face.

Nandini. And then? Tell me! Quick!

King. He burst himself against me, like a bubble.

Nandini. King, the Time is indeed now come!

King. Time for what?

Nandini. For the last fight between you and me.

King. But I can kill you in no time,—this instant.

Nandini. From that very instant that death of mine will go on killing you every single moment.

King. Be brave, Nandini, trust me. Make me your comrade to-day.

Nandini. What would you have me do?

King. To fight against me, but with your hand in mine. That fight has already begun. There is my flag. First I break the Flagstaff,—thus! Next it's for you to tear its banner. Let your hand unite with mine to kill me, utterly kill me. That will be my emancipation.

Guards (rushing up). What are you doing, King? You dare break the Flagstaff, the holiest symbol of our divinity? The Flagstaff which has its one point piercing the heart of the earth and the other that of heaven? What a terrible sin,—on the very day of the Flag-worship! Comrades, let us go and inform our Governors. (*They run off.*)

King. A great deal of breaking remains to be done. You will come with me, Nandini?

Nandini. I will.

(Phágulal *comes in.*)

Phágulal. They won't hear of letting Bishu off. I am afraid,
they'll— Who is this? The King!
Oh you wicked witch,—conspiring with the King himself! O
vile deceiver!

King. What is the matter with you? What is that crowd out
for?

Phágulal. To break the prison gate. We may lose our lives,
but we shan't fall back.

King. Why should you fall back? I too am out for breaking.
Behold the first sign—my broken Flagstaff!

Phágulal. What! This is altogether beyond us simple folk.
Be merciful, Nandini, don't deceive me. Am I to
believe my eyes?

Nandini. Brother, you have set out to win death. You have
left no chance for deception to touch you.

Phágulal. You too come along with us, our own Nandini!

Nandini. That is what I'm still alive for, Phágulal. I wanted
to bring my Rañjan amongst you. Look there, he has
come, my hero, braving death!

Phágulal. Oh, horror! Is that Rañjan lying there, silent?

Nandini. Not silent. He leaves behind him in death his
conquering call. He will live again, he cannot die.

Phágulal. Ah, my Nandini, my beautiful one, was it for this
you were waiting all these eager days?

Nandini. I *did* await his coming, and he *did* come. I still wait
to prepare for his coming again, and he *shall* come
again. Where is Chandrá?

Phágulal. She has gone with her tears and prayers to the
Governor, accompanied by Gôkul. I'm afraid Gôkul is
seeking to take up service with the Governor. He will
betray us.

King, are you sure you don't mistake us? We are out
to break your own prison, I tell you!

King. Yes, it is my *own* prison. You and I must work together,
for you cannot break it alone.

Phágulal. As soon as the Governor hears of it, he will march
will all his forces to prevent us.

King. Yes, my fight is against them.

Phágulal. But the soldiers will not obey you.

King. *You* will be on my side!

Phágulal. Shall we be able to win through?

King. We shall at least be able to die! At last I have found
the meaning of death. I am saved!

Phágulal. King, do you hear the tumult?

King. There comes the Governor with his troops. How could
he be so quick about it? He must have been prepared
beforehand. They have used my own power against me.

Phágulal. My men have not yet turned up.

King. They will never come. The Governor is sure to get
round them.

Nandini. I had my last hope that they would bring my Bishu
to me. Will that never be?

King. No hope of that, I'm afraid.

Phágulal. Then come along, Nandini, let us take you to a safe
place first. The Governor will see red, if he but catches
sight of you.

Nandini. You want to banish me into the solitary exile of
safety? (*Calling out*) Governor! Governor!—He has
swung up my garland of *kunda* flowers on his spear-
head. I will dye that garland the colour of my oleanders
with my heart's blood.— Governor! He has seen me!
Victory to Rañjan! (*Runs off.*)

King (*calling after her*). Nandini! (*Follows her.*)

(*The* Professor *comes in.*)

Phágulal. Where are *you* hurrying to, Professor?

Professor. Some one said that the King has at last had tidings of the secret of Life, and has gone off in quest of it. I have thrown away my books to follow him.

Phágulal. The King has just gone off to his death. He has heard Nandini's call.

Professor. The network is torn to shreds! Where is Nandini?

Phágulal. She has gone before them all. We can't reach her any more.

Professor. It is only now that we shall reach her. She won't evade us any longer.

(*Professor* rushes out, *Bishu* comes in.)

Bishu. Phágulal, where is Nandini?

Phágulal. How did you get here?

Bishu. Our workmen have broken into the prison. There they are,—running off to fight. I came to look for Nandini. Where is she?

Phágulal. She has gone in advance of us all.

Bishu. Where?

Phágulal. To the last freedom. Bishu, do you see who is lying there?

Bishu. Rañjan!

Phágulal. You see the red streak?

Bishu. I understand,—then red marriage.

Phágulal. They are united.

Bishu. Now it is for me to take my last lonely journey.— Perhaps we may meet.—Perhaps she may want me to sing.—My mad girl, O my mad girl!—

Come, brother, on to the fight!

Phágulal. To the fight! Victory to Nandini!

Bishu. Victory to Nandini!

Phágulal. Here is her wristlet of red oleanders. She has bared her arm to-day,—and left us.

Bishu. Once I told her I would not take anything from her hand. I break my word and take this. Come along!

(*They go.*)

(Song in the distance.)

Hark 'tis Autumn calling,—
Come, O come away!
The earth's mantle of dust is filled with ripe corn!
O the joy! the joy!

THE HIDDEN TREASURE & OTHER STORIES

The Hidden Treasure

It was a moonless night, and Mrityunjaya was seated before the ancestral image of the goddess Kali. As he finished his devotions the cawing of an early morning crow was heard from a neighbouring mango grove.

First seeing that the door of the temple was shut, he bowed once more before the image and, shifting its pedestal, took from under it a strong wooden box. This he opened with a key which hung on his sacred thread, but the moment he had looked inside he started in dismay. He took up the box and shook it several times. It had not been broken open, for the lock was uninjured. He groped all round the image a dozen times, but could find nothing.

Mrityunjaya's little temple stood on one side of his inner garden which was surrounded by a wall. It was sheltered by the shade of some tall trees. Inside there was nothing but the image of Kali, and it had only one entrance. Like a mad man Mrityunjaya threw open the door, and began to roam round on all sides in search of a clue, but in vain. By this time daylight had come. In despair he sat on some steps and with his head buried in his hands began to think. He was just beginning to feel sleepy after his long sleepless night when suddenly he heard someone say: "Greeting, my son!" Looking up he saw in the courtyard before him a long-haired sannyasi. Mrityunjaya made a deep obeisance to him and the ascetic placed his hand on his head, saying: "My son, your sorrow is vain."

Mrityunjaya, in astonishment, replied: "Can you read people's thoughts? How do you know about my sorrow? I have spoken of it to no one."

The sannyasi answered: "My son, instead of sorrowing over what you have lost, you ought to rejoice."

Clasping his feet Mrityunjaya exclaimed: "Then you know everything? Tell me how it got lost and where I can recover it."

The sannyasi replied: "If I wanted you to suffer misfortune then I would tell you. But you must not grieve over that which the goddess has taken from you out of pity."

But Mrityunjaya was not satisfied and in the hope of pleasing his visitor he spent the whole of that day serving him in different ways. But when early next morning he was bringing him a bowl of fresh milk from his own cow he found that the sannyasi had disappeared.

2

When Mrityunjaya had been a child his grandfather, Harihar, was sitting one day on those same steps of the temple, smoking his *hookah,* when a sannyasi came into the courtyard and greeted him. Harihar invited him into his home and for several days treated him as an honoured guest.

When about to go the sannyasi said to him: "My son, you are poor, are you not?", to which Harihar replied: "Father, I am indeed. Only hear what my condition is. Once our family was the most prosperous in the village but now our condition is so miserable that we can hardly hold up our heads. I beg you to tell me how we can restore ourselves to prosperity again."

The sannyasi laughing slightly said: "My son, why not be satisfied with your present position? What's the use of trying to become wealthy?"

But Harihar persisted and declared that he was ready to undertake anything that would restore his family to their proper rank in society.

Thereupon the sannyasi took out a roll of cloth in which an old and stained piece of paper was wrapped. It looked like a horoscope. The sannyasi unrolled it and Harihar saw that it had some signs in cypher written within circles, and below these was a lot of doggerel verse which commenced thus:

> For attainment of your goal
> Find a word that rhymes with soul.
> From the 'rādhā' take its 'dhā',
> After that at last put 'rā'.
> From the tamarind-banyan's mouth
> Turn your face towards the south.
> When the light is in the East
> There shall be of wealth a feast.

There was much more of the same kind of rigmarole.

Harihar said: "Father, I can't understand a single word of it."

To this the sannyasi replied: "Keep it by you. Make your *puja* to the goddess Kali and by her grace you, or some descendant of yours, will gain the untold wealth of which this writing tells the secret hiding place."

Harihar entreated him to explain the writing, but the sannyasi said that only by the practice of austerity could its meaning be discovered.

Just at this moment Harihar's youngest brother, Shankar, arrived on the scene and Harihar tried to snatch the paper away before it could be observed. But the sannyasi, laughing, said: "Already, I see, you have started on the painful road to greatness. But you need not be afraid. The secret can only be discovered by one person. If anyone else tries a thousand times he will never be able to solve it. It will be a member of your family, so you can show this paper to anyone without fear."

The sannyasi having left them, Harihar could not rest until he had hidden the paper. Fearful lest anyone else should profit by it, and above all lest his young brother Shankar should enjoy this hidden wealth, he locked the paper in a strong wooden box and hid it under the seat of the household goddess Kali. Every month, at the time of the new moon, he would go in the dead of night to the temple and there he would offer prayers to the goddess in the hope that she would give him the power to decipher the secret writing.

Some time after this Shankar came to his brother and begged him to show him the paper.

"Go away, you idiot!" shouted Harihar, "that paper was nothing. That rascal of a sannyasi wrote a lot of nonsense on it simply to deceive me. I burnt it long ago."

Shankar remained silent, but some weeks afterwards he disappeared from the house and was never seen again.

From that time Harihar gave up all other occupations, and spent all his waking moments in thinking about the hidden treasure.

When he died he left this mysterious paper to his eldest son, Shyamapada, who, as soon as he got possession of it, gave up his business and spent his whole time in studying the secret cypher and in worshipping the goddess in the hope of goodluck coming to him.

Mrityunjaya was Shyamapada's eldest child, so he became the owner of this precious heirloom on his father's death. The worse his condition became the greater the eagerness he showed in trying to solve the secret. It was about this time that the loss of the paper occurred. The visit of the long-haired sannyasi coinciding with its disappearance, Mrityunjaya determined that he would try to find him, feeling sure he could discover everything from him. So he left his home on the quest.

3

After spending a year in going from place to place Mrityunjaya one day arrived at a village named Dharagole. There he stayed at a grocer's shop, and as he was sitting absent-mindedly smoking and thinking, a sannyasi passed along the edge of a neighbouring field. At first Mrityunjaya did not pay much attention, but after a few minutes he came to himself and it flashed across his mind that that was the very sannyasi for whom he had been searching. Hurriedly laying aside his *hookah* he rushed past the startled storekeeper and dashed from the shop into the street. But the sannyasi was nowhere to be seen.

As it was dark and the place was strange to him he gave up the idea of searching further and returned to the shop. There he asked the storekeeper what lay beyond the village in the great forest near by. The man replied:

"Once a great city was there, but owing to the curse of the sage Agastya, its king and all his subjects died of some dreadful pestilence. People say that enormous wealth and piles of jewels are still hidden there, but no one dares to enter that forest even at midday. Those who have done so have never returned."

Mrityunjaya's mind became restless, and all night long he lay on his mat tormented by mosquitoes and by thoughts of the forest, the sannyasi, and his lost secret. He had read the verses so often that he could almost repeat them by heart, and hour after hour the opening lines kept ringing through his mind, until his brain reeled:

> For attainment of your goal
> Find a word that rhymes with soul.
> From the 'rādhā' take its 'dhā'
> After that at last put 'rā'.

He could not get the words out of his head. At last when dawn came he fell asleep and in a dream the meaning of the verse became as clear as day-light. Taking the 'dhā' from 'rādhā' and at the end of that putting 'rā' you get 'dhārā', and 'gole' rhymes with soul! The name of the village in which he was staying was 'Dhārāgole'! He jumped up from his mat sure that he was at last near the end of his search.

4

The whole of that day Mrityunjaya spent roaming about the forest in the hope of finding a path. He returned to the village at night half dead with hunger and fatigue, but next day he took a bundle of parched rice and started off again. At midday he arrived at the side of a lake round which there were traces of a path. The water was clear in the middle but near the banks it was a tangle of weeds and water-lilies. Having soaked his rice in the water by some broken stone steps on the bank he finished eating it and began to walk slowly round the lake looking carefully everywhere for signs of buildings. Suddenly when he had reached the west side of the lake he stood stock still, for there before him was a tamarind tree growing right in the centre of a gigantic banyan. He immediately recalled the lines:

> From the tamarind-banyan's mouth
> Turn your face towards the south.

After walking some distance towards the south he found himself in the middle of a thick jungle through which it was impossible to force a way. He however determined not to lose sight of the tamarind tree.

Turning back he noticed in the distance through the branches of the tree the pinnacles of a building. Making his way in that direction he came upon a ruined temple, by the side of which were the ashes of a recent fire. With great caution Mrityunjaya made his way to a broken door and peeped in. There was no one there, not even an image, only a blanket, and a water pot with a sannyasi's scarf lying beside it.

Evening was approaching, the village was far off, and it would be difficult to find a path back by night, so Mrityunjaya was pleased at seeing signs of a human being. By the door lay a large piece of stone which had fallen from the ruin. On this he seated himself and was deep in thought when he suddenly noticed what appeared to be written characters on the surface of the stone. Looking closely he saw a circular symbol which was familiar to him. It was partly obliterated, it is true, but it was sufficiently distinct for him to recognize the design as that which had appeared at the top of his lost piece of paper. He had studied it so often that it was clearly printed on his brain. How many times had he begged the goddess to reveal to him the meaning of that mystic sign as he sat at midnight in the dimly lit temple of his home with the fragrance of incense filling the night air. Tonight the fulfilment of his long cherished desire seemed so near that his whole body trembled. Fearing that by some slight blunder he might frustrate all his hopes, and above all dreading lest the sannyasi had been beforehand in discovering his treasure he shook with terror. He could not decide what to do. The thought came to him that he might even at that very moment be sitting above untold wealth without knowing it.

As he sat repeating the name of Kali, evening fell and the sombre darkness of the forest resounded with the continual chirping of crickets.

5

Just as he was wondering what to do he saw through the thick foliage the distant gleam of a fire. Getting up from the stone on which he was seated he carefully marked the spot he was leaving and went off in the direction of the light.

Having progressed with great difficulty a short way he saw from behind the trunk of a tree the very sannyasi he had been seeking with the well-known paper in his hand. He had opened it and, by the light of the flames, he was working out its meaning in the ashes with a stick.

There was the very paper which belonged to Mrityunjaya and which had belonged to his father and his grandfather before him, in the hands of a thief and a cheat! It was for this then that this rogue of a sannyasi had bidden Mrityunjaya not to sorrow over his loss!

The sannyasi was calculating the meaning of the signs, and every now and then would measure certain distances on the ground with a stick. Sometimes he would stop and shake his head with a disappointed air, and then he would go back and make fresh calculations.

In this way the night was nearly spent and it was not until the cool breeze of daybreak began to rustle in the leafy branches of the trees that the sannyasi folded up the paper and went away.

Mrityunjaya was perplexed. He was quite sure that without the sannyasi's help it would be impossible for him to decipher the mystery of the paper. But he was equally certain that the covetous rascal would not knowingly assist him. Therefore to watch the sannyasi secretly was his only hope; but as he could not get any food without going back to the village, Mrityunjaya decided he would return to his lodgings that morning.

When it became light enough he left the tree behind which he had been hiding and made his way to the place where the sannyasi had been making his calculations in the ashes. But he could make nothing of the marks. Nor, after wandering all round, could he see that the forest there differed in any way from other parts of the jungle.

As the sunlight began to penetrate the thick shade of the trees Mrityunjaya made his way towards the village, looking carefully on every side as he went. His chief fear was lest the sannyasi should catch sight of him.

That morning a feast was given to Brahmins at the shop where Mrityunjaya had taken shelter, so he came in for a sumptuous meal. Having fasted so long he could not resist eating heavily, and after the feast he soon rolled over on his mat and fell sound asleep.

Although he had not slept all night, Mrityunjaya had made up his mind that he would that day take his meals in good time and start off early in the afternoon. What happened was exactly the opposite, for when he woke the sun had already set. But although it was getting dark, he could not refrain from entering the forest.

Night fell suddenly and so dense was the darkness that it was impossible for him to see his way through the deep shadows of the thick jungle. He could not make out which way he was going and when day broke he found that he had been going round and round in one part of the forest quite near the village.

The raucous cawing of some crows from near by sounded to Mrityunjaya like mockery.

6

After many miscalculations and corrections the sannyasi had at length discovered the path to the entrance of a subterranean tunnel. Lighting a torch he entered. The brick walls were mouldy with moss and slime, and water oozed out from the many cracks. In some places sleeping toads could be seen piled up in heaps. After proceeding over slippery stones for some distance the sannyasi came to a wall. The passage was blocked! He struck the wall in several places with a heavy iron bar but there was not the least suspicion of a hollow sound. There was not a crack anywhere; without a doubt the tunnel ended there.

He spent the whole of that night studying the paper again, and next morning having finished his calculations, he entered the underground passage once more. This time, carefully following the secret directions, he loosened a stone from a certain place and discovered a branch turning. This he followed, but once more he came to a stop where another wall blocked all further progress.

But finally, on the fifth night, the sannyasi as he entered exclaimed: "Tonight I shall find the way without the shadow of a doubt!"

The passage was like a labyrinth. There seemed no end to its branches and turnings. In some places it was so low and narrow that he had to crawl on hands and knees. Carefully holding the torch he arrived at length at a large circular room, in the middle of which was a wide well of solid masonry. By the light of his torch the sannyasi was unable to see how deep it was, but he saw that from the roof there descended into it a thick heavy iron chain. He pulled with all his strength at this chain and it shook very slightly. But there rose from the depth of the well a metallic clang which reverberated through that dark dismal chamber. The sannyasi called out in excitement: "At last I have found it!"

Next moment a huge stone rolled through the hole in the broken wall through which he had entered and someone fell on the floor with a loud cry. Startled by this sudden sound the sannyasi let his torch fall to the ground and the room was plunged in darkness.

7

He called out "Who is there?" but there was no answer. Putting out his hand he touched a man's body. Shaking it. he asked, "Who are you?" Still he got no reply. The man was unconscious.

Striking a flint he at last found his torch and lighted it. In the meantime the man had regained consciousness and was trying to sit up though he was groaning with pain.

On seeing him the sannyasi exclaimed: "Why, it is Mrityunjaya! What are you doing here?"

Mrityunjaya replied: "Father, pardon me. God has punished me enough. I was trying to roll that stone on you when my foot slipped and I fell. My leg must be broken."

To this the sannyasi answered: "But what good would it have done you to kill me?"

Mrityunjaya exclaimed: "What good indeed! Why did you steal into my temple and rob me of that secret paper? And what are you doing in this underground place yourself? You are a thief, and a cheat! The sannyasi who gave that paper to my grandfather told him that one of his family was to discover the secret of the writing. The secret is mine by rights and it is for this reason that I have been following you day and night like your shadow, going without food and sleep all these days. Then today when you exclaimed 'At last I have found it!' I could restrain myself no longer. I had followed you and was hiding behind the wall where you had made the hole, and I tried to kill you. I failed because I am weak and the ground was slippery and I fell. Kill me if you wish, then I can become a guardian spirit to watch over this treasure of mine. But if I live, you will never be able to take it. Never! Never! Never! If you try, I will bring the curse of a Brahmin on you by jumping into this well and committing suicide. Never will you be able to enjoy this treasure. My father, and his father before him, thought of nothing but this treasure and they died thinking of it. We have become poor for its sake. In search of it I have left wife and children, and without food or sleep have wandered from place to place like a maniac. Never shall you take this treasure from me while I have eyes to see!"

8

The sannyasi said quietly: "Mrityunjaya, listen to me. I will tell you everything. You remember that your grandfather's youngest brother was called Shankar?"

"Yes," replied Mrityunjaya, "he left home and was never heard of again."

"Well," said the sannyasi, "I am that Shankar!"

Mrityunjaya gave a gasp of despair. He had so long regarded himself as the sole owner of this hidden wealth that, now that this relative had turned up and proved his equal right, he felt as if his claim were destroyed.

Shankar continued: "From the moment that my brother got that paper from the sannyasi he tried every means in his power to keep it hidden from me. But the harder he tried the greater became my curiosity, and I soon found that he had hidden it in a wooden box under the seat of the goddess. I got hold of a duplicate key, and by degrees, whenever the opportunity occurred, I copied out the whole of the writing and the signs. The very day I had finished copying it I left home in quest of the treasure. I even left my wife and only child neither of whom is now living. There is no need to describe all the places I visited in my wanderings. I felt sure that as the paper had been given to my brother by a sannyasi I would be able to find out its meaning from one, so I began to serve sannyasis whenever I had the chance. Many of them were impostors and tried to steal the writing from me. In this way many years passed, but not for a single moment did I have any peace or happiness.

"At last in my search, by virtue of some right action in a previous birth, I had the good fortune to meet in the mountains Swami Rupananda. He said to me: 'My child, give up desire, and the imperishable wealth of the whole universe will be yours.'

"He cooled the fever of my mind. By his grace the light of the sky and the green verdure of the earth seemed to me equal to the wealth of kings. One winter day at the foot of the mountain I lit a fire in the brazier of my revered *Guru* and offered up the paper in its flames. The Swami laughed slightly as I did it. At the time I did not understand that laugh. But now I do. Doubtless he thought it is easy enough to burn a piece of paper, but to burn to ashes our desires is not so simple!

"When not a vestige of the paper remained it seemed as if my heart had suddenly filled with the rare joy of freedom. My mind at last realized the meaning of detachment. I said to myself, 'Now I have no more fear, I desire nothing in the world.'

"Shortly after this I parted from the Swami and although I have often sought for him since, I have never seen him again.

"I then wandered as a sannyasi with my mind detached from worldly things. Many years passed and I had almost forgotten the existence of the paper, when one day I came to the forest near Dharagole and took shelter in a ruined temple. After a day or two I noticed that there were inscriptions on the walls, some of which I recognized. There could be no doubt that here was a clue to what I had spent so many years of my life in trying to discover. I said to myself: 'I must not stay here. I must leave this forest.'

"But I did not go. I thought there was no harm in staying to see what I could find out, just to satisfy my curiosity. I examined the signs carefully, but without result. I kept thinking of the paper I had burnt. Why had I destroyed it? What harm would there have been in keeping it?

"At last I went back to the village of my birth. On seeing the miserable condition of my ancestral home I thought to myself: 'I am a sannyasi, I have no need of wealth for myself, but these poor people have a home to keep up. There can be no sin in recovering the hidden treasure for their benefit.'

"I knew where the paper was, so it was not difficult for me to steal it.

"For a whole year since then I have been living in this lonely forest searching for the clue. I could think of nothing else. The oftener I was thwarted the greater did my eagerness become. I had the unflagging energy of a mad man as I sat night after night concentrating on the attempt to solve my problem.

"When it was that you discovered me I do not know. If I had been in an ordinary frame of mind you would never have remained concealed, but I was so absorbed in my task that I never noticed what was going on around me.

"It was not until today that I discovered at last what I had been so long searching for. The treasure hidden here is greater than that of the richest king in the world, and to find it the meaning of only one more sign had to be deciphered.

"This secret is the most difficult of all, but in my mind I had come even to its solution. That was why I cried out in my delight, 'At last I have found it!' If I wish I can in a moment enter that hidden storehouse of gold and jewels."

Mrityunjaya fell at Shankar's feet and exclaimed:

"You are a sannyasi, you have no use for wealth—but take me to that treasure. Do not cheat me again!"

Shankar replied: "Today the last link of my fetters is broken! That stone which you intended should kill me did not indeed strike my body but it has shattered forever the folly of my infatuation. Today I have seen how monstrous is the image of desire. That calm and incomprehensible smile of my saintly *Guru* has at last kindled the inextinguishable lamp of my soul."

Mrityunjaya again begged pitifully: "You are free, but I am not. I do not even want freedom. You must not cheat me of this wealth."

The sannyasi answered: "Very well, my son, take this paper of yours, and if you can find this treasure, keep it."

Saying this the sannyasi handed the paper and his staff to Mrityunjaya and left him alone. Mrityunjaya called out in despair: "Have pity on me. Do not leave me. Show me the treasure!" But there was no answer.

Mrityunjaya dragged himself up and with the help of the stick tried to find his way out of the tunnels, but they were such a maze that he was again and again completely puzzled. At last worn out he lay down and fell asleep.

When he awoke there was no means of telling whether it was night or day. As he felt hungry he ate some parched rice, and again began to grope for the way out. At length in despair he stopped and called out: "Oh! Sannyasi, where are you?" His cry echoed and re-echoed through the tangled labyrinth of those underground tunnels, and when the sound of his own voice had died away, he heard from close by a reply, "I am near you—what is it you want?"

Mrityunjaya answered: "Have pity on me and show me where the treasure is."

There was no answer, and although he called again and again all was silent.

After a time Mrityunjaya fell asleep again in this underground realm of perpetual darkness where there was neither night nor day. When he woke up and found it still dark he called out beseechingly: "Oh! Sannyasi, tell me where you are."

The answer came from near at hand: "I am here. What do you want?"

Mrityunjaya answered: "I want nothing now but that you should rescue me from this dungeon."

The sannyasi asked: "Don't you want the treasure?"

Mrityunjaya replied: "No."

There was the sound of a flint being struck and the next moment there was a light. The sannyasi said: "Well Mrityunjaya, let us go."

Mrityunjaya: "Then, father, is all my trouble to be in vain? Shall I never obtain that wealth?"

Immediately the torch went out. Mrityunjaya exclaimed "How cruel!', and sat down in the silence to think. There was no means of measuring time and the darkness was without end. How he wished that he could with all the strength of his mind and body shatter that gloom to atoms. His heart began to feel restless for the light, for the open sky, and for all the varied beauty of the world, and he called out: "Oh! Sannyasi, cruel sannyasi, I do not want the treasure. I want you to rescue me."

The answer came: "You no longer want the treasure? Then take my hand, and come with me."

This time no torch was lighted. Mrityunjaya holding his stick in one hand and clinging to the sannyasi with the other slowly began to move. After twisting and turning many times through the maze of tunnels they came to a place where the sannyasi said, "Now stand still."

Standing still Mrityunjaya heard the sound of an iron door opening. The next moment the sannyasi seized his hand, and said: "Come!"

Mrityunjaya advanced into what appeared to be a vast hall. He heard the sound of a flint being struck and then the blaze of the torch revealed to his astonished eyes the most amazing sight that he had ever dreamed of. On every side thick plates of gold were arranged in piles. They stood against the walls glittering like heaped rays of solid sunlight stored in the bowels of the earth. Mrityunjaya's eyes began to gleam. Like a mad man he cried: "All this gold is mine—I will never part with it!"

"Very well," replied the sannyasi, "here is my torch, some barley and parched rice, and this large pitcher of water for you. Farewell."

And as he spoke the sannyasi went out, clanging the heavy iron door behind him.

Mrityunjaya began to go round and round the hall touching the piles of gold again and again. Seizing some small pieces he threw them down on the floor, he lifted them into his lap, striking them one against another he made them ring, he even stroked his body all over with the precious metal. At length, tired out, he spread a large flat plate of gold on the floor, lay down on it, and fell asleep.

When he woke he saw the gold glittering on every side. There was nothing but gold. He began to wonder whether day had dawned and whether the birds were awake and revelling in the morning sunlight. It seemed as though in imagination he could smell the fragrant breeze of daybreak coming from the garden by the little lake near his home. It was as if he could actually see the ducks floating on the water, and hear their contented cackle as the maidservant came from the house to the steps of the ghat, with the brass vessels in her hand to be cleaned.

Striking the door Mrityunjaya called out: "Oh, Sannyasi, listen to me!"

The door opened and the sannyasi entered. "What do you want?" he asked.

"I want to go out," replied Mrityunjaya, "but can't I take away a little of this gold?"

Without giving any answer the sannyasi lighted a fresh torch, and placing a full water pot and a few handfuls of rice on the floor went out closing the door behind him.

Mrityunjaya took up a thin plate of gold, bent it and broke it into small fragments. These he scattered about the room like lumps of dirt. On some of them he made marks with his teeth. Then he threw a plate of gold on the floor and trampled on it. He asked himself, 'How many men in the world are rich enough to be able to throw gold about as I am doing!' Then he became oppressed with a fever for destruction. He was seized with a longing to crush all these heaps of gold into dust and sweep them away with a broom. In this way he could show his contempt for the covetous greed of all the kings and maharajahs in the world.

At last he became tired of throwing the gold about in this way and fell asleep. Again he saw on awakening those heaps of gold, and rushing to the door he struck at it with all his strength and called out: "Oh Sannyasi, I do not want this gold. I do not want it!"

But the door remained closed. Mrityunjaya shouted till his throat was hoarse and still the door did not open. He threw lump after lump of gold against it, but with no effect. He was in despair. Would the sannyasi leave him there to shrivel up and die, inch by inch, in that golden prison?

As Mrityunjaya watched the gold fear gripped him. Those piles of glittering metal surrounded him on all sides with a terrifying smile, hard, silent, without tremor or change, until his body began to tremble, his mind to quake. What connection had he with these heaps of gold? They could not share his feelings—they had no sympathy with him in his sorrows. They had no need of the light, or the sky. They did not long for the cool breezes, they did not even want life. They had no desire for freedom. In this eternal darkness they remained hard and bright for ever.

On earth perhaps sunset had come with its golden gift of limpid light—that golden light which cools the eyes as it bids farewell to the fading day, falling like tears on the face of darkness. Now the evening star would be gazing serenely down on the courtyard of his home where his young wife had tended the cows in the meadow and lit the lamp in the corner of the house, while the tinkling of the temple bell spoke of the closing ceremony of the day.

Today the most trifling events of his home and his village shone in Mrityunjaya's imagination with overpowering lustre. Even the thought of his old dog lying curled up asleep in front of the stove caused him pain. He thought of the grocer in whose shop he had stayed while he was at Dharagole and imagined him putting out his lamp, shutting up his shop and walking leisurely to some house in the village to take his evening meal, and as he thought of him he envied him his happiness. He did not know what day it was, but if it were Sunday he could picture to himself the villagers returning to their homes after market, calling their friends from over the fields and crossing the river together in the ferry boat. He could see a peasant, with a couple of fish dangling in his hand and a basket on his head, walking through the meadow paths, or making his way along the dikes of the paddy fields, past the bamboo fences of the little hamlets, returning to his village after the day's work in the dim light of the star-strewn sky.

The call came to him from the world of men. But layers of earth separated him from the most insignificant occurrences of life's varied and unceasing pilgrimage. That life, that sky, and that light appeared to him now as more priceless than all the treasures of the universe. He felt that if only he could for one moment again lie in the dusty lap of mother earth in her green clad beauty, beneath the free open spaces of the sky, filling his lungs with the fragrant breeze laden with the scents of mown grass and of blossoms, he could die feeling that his life was complete.

As these thoughts came to him the door opened, and the sannyasi entering asked: "Mrityunjaya, what do you want now?"

He answered: "I want nothing further. I want only to go out from this maze of darkness. I want to leave this delusive gold. I want light, and the sky; I want freedom!"

The sannyasi said: "There is another storehouse full of rarest gems of incalculable value, tenfold more precious than all this gold. Do you not wish to go there?"

Mrityunjaya answered: "No."

"Haven't you the curiosity just to see it once?"

"No, I don't want even to see it. If I have to beg in rags for the rest of my life I would not spend another moment here."

"Then come," said the sannyasi, and taking Mrityunjaya's hand he led him in front of the deep well. Stopping here he took out the paper and asked: "And what will you do with this?"

Taking it Mrityunjaya tore it into fragments and threw them down the well.

Cloud and Sun

It had rained the previous day. But this morning there was no sign of rain and the pale sunlight and scattered clouds between them were painting the nearly-ripe autumnal corn-fields alternately with their long brushes; the broad green landscape was now being touched with light to a glittering whiteness, and again smeared over the next moment with the deep coolness of shadow.

While these two actors, sun and cloud, were playing their own parts by themselves with the whole sky for a stage, innumerable plays were being enacted down below in various places on the stage of the world.

In the particular place on which we are about to raise the curtain on one of life's little plays, a house can be seen by the side of a village lane. Only one of the outer rooms is brick-built, and on either side of it a dilapidated brick wall runs to encircle a few mud huts. From the lane one can discover through the grated window a young man with the upper half of his body uncovered, sitting on a plank bed, trying every now and then to drive away both heat and mosquitoes with a palm-leaf fan held in his left hand and reading attentively a book held in his right. Out in the village lane, a girl wearing a striped *sāri* with some black plums tied in a corner thereof, which she was engaged in demolishing one by one, kept passing again and again in front of the said grated window.

From the expression of her face it could be clearly perceived that the young girl was on terms of intimacy with the person sitting and reading on the bed inside and that she was bent on attracting his attention somehow or other and letting him know by her silent contempt: 'Just now I am busily engaged in eating black plums and don't care a fig for you.'

Unfortunately, the man engaged in reading inside the room was short-sighted and the silent scorn of the girl could not touch him from afar. The girl herself knew this, so that after many fruitless journeyings to and fro, she was obliged to use pellets of plumstones in lieu of silent scorn. So difficult is it to preserve the purity of disdain when one has to deal with the blind.

When three or four stones thrown at random, as it were, every now and again rapped against the wooden door, the reader raised his head and looked out. When the designing young person came to know this, she began to choose succulent black plums from her *sāri*-knot with redoubled attention. The man, puckering his brows and straining his eyes, recognized the girl at last and putting down his book came up to the window and smilingly called out "Giribala!"

Giribala, while keeping her attention fixed steadily and wholly upon the task of examining the black plums tied in her *sāri*-end, proceeded to walk on slowly step by step.

Upon this it was brought home to the myopic young man that he was being punished for some unknown misdeed. Hurriedly coming outside he asked, "I say, how is it you haven't given me any plums today?" Turning a deaf ear to this question Giribala chose a plum after much searching and deliberation, and proceeded to eat it with the utmost composure.

These plums came from Giribala's home-garden, and were the daily perquisite of the young man. But for some reason or other Giribala seemed to have forgotten this fact, and her behaviour went to indicate that she had gathered them for herself alone. However, it was not clear what the idea was of plucking fruit from one's own garden and coming and eating it ostentatiously in front of another's door. Hence the youth came out and caught hold of her hand. At first Giribala turned and twisted and tried to wriggle out of his grasp, but suddenly she burst into a flood of tears and scattering the plums from her *sāri* on to the ground, rushed away.

The restless sunlight and shadows of the morning had become tired and tranquil in the afternoon. White swollen clouds lay massed in a corner of the sky and the fading evening light glimmered upon the leaves of the trees, the water in the ponds, and every nook and corner of the rain-washed landscape. Again we see the girl in front of the grated window, and the young man sitting inside the room, the only difference being that there are no plums now in the girl's *sāri*-end, neither does the youth hold any book in his hand. There may have been certain other deeper and more serious differences also.

It is difficult to say what particular need has brought the girl again this afternoon to this particular spot. Whatever other grounds she may have had, it is quite apparent from her behaviour that talking to the man inside the room is not one of them. Rather it would appear as if she has come to see whether the plums she had scattered upon the ground this morning had sprouted in the afternoon.

But one of the principal reasons for their not sprouting was that the fruits were lying heaped up at present in front of the young man on the wooden bed; and whilst the girl was occupied in bending low every now and then in search of some imaginary object, the youth, suppressing his inward laughter, was gravely eating the plums one after another, after carefully selecting them. At length, when one or two stones came and fell by chance near the girl's feet or even upon them, she realized that the young man was paying her back for her fit of pique. But was this fair! When she had thrown overboard all the pride of her little heart and was seeking for some means of surrendering herself, wasn't it cruel of him to place an obstacle in her very difficult path? As the girl came to realize with a blush that she had been caught in the attempt of giving herself up, and began to seek some means of escape, the youth came out and caught hold of her hand.

This time too the girl turned and twisted and made several attempts to shake off his grasp and run away as she had done this morning; but she did not cry. On the other hand she flushed and, turning her head aside, hid her face on her tormentor's back and laughed profusely and, as if compelled by outward force alone, entered the iron-barred cell like a conquered captive.

Like the light play of sun and cloud in the sky, the play of these two human beings in a corner of the earth was equally trivial and equally transient. Again as the play of sun and cloud in the sky is not really unimportant and not really a game but only looks like it, so the humble history of an idle rainy day spent by these ordinary folk may seem to be of no account amidst the hundreds of events happening in this world; but as a matter of fact it was not so. The ancient and stupendous Fate that eternally weaves one age into another with unchanging sternness of countenance, that same Ancient was causing the seeds of grief and joy throughout the girl's whole life to sprout amidst the trivial tears and laughter of this morning and evening. And yet the uncalled-for grievance of the girl seemed altogether incomprehensible, not only to the onlookers, but also to the young man—the hero of this little play. Why the girl should get annoyed one day and lavish unbounded affection on another, why she should increase the rations one day and on another stop them altogether, was not easy to understand. Some day it was as if all her powers of imagination and thought and skill were concentrated on giving pleasure to the young man; again on another day she would muster all her limited stock of energy and hardness to try and hurt him. When she failed to wound him her hardness was redoubled; when she succeeded, it was dissolved in profuse showers of repentant tears and flowed in a thousand streams of affection.

The first part of the trivial history of this trivial play of sun and shadow is briefly narrated in the following chapter.

2

All the other people in the village were occupied with factions, plotting against one another, sugarcane planting, false lawsuits and trade in jute; the only ones interested in ideas and literature were Sashibhushan and Giribala.

There was no call for anybody to be curious or anxious on this account. Because Giribala was ten years old and Sashibhushan was a newly-fledged M.A., B.L. They were neighbours only.

Giribala's father Harakumar was at one time the sub-landlord of his village. Falling on evil days, he had sold everything and accepted the post of manager of their absentee landlord. He had to superintend the same *pargana* in which he lived, so that he was not obliged to move from his home.

Sashibhushan had taken his M.A. degree and also passed his examination in law, but he did not take up any work for a living. He could not bring himself to mix with people or speak even a few words at a meeting. Because of his short sight he could not recognize his acquaintances, hence he had to resort to frowning, which people considered a sign of arrogance.

It is all very well to keep oneself to oneself in the sea of humanity of a city like Calcutta; but in a village such behaviour is looked upon as haughtiness. When after many unsuccessful efforts, Sashibhushan's father at length sent his good-for-nothing son to look after their small village estate, Sashibhushan had to put up with a lot of ill-treatment, harassment and ridicule from his village neighbours. There was another reason for this persecution; peace-loving Sashibhushan was unwilling to marry—hence the worried parents of marriageable girls looked upon this unwillingness of his as intolerable pride and could not find it in their hearts to forgive him.

The more Sashibhushan was persecuted the more he hid himself in his den. He used to sit on a plank bed in a corner room with some bound English volumes before him and read whichever one he liked. This was all the work he did, and how the property managed to exist, the property alone knew.

We have already seen that Giribala was the only human being with whom he had any contact.

Giribala's brothers used to go to school and on their return would ask their silly little sister some day what the shape of the earth was; another day they would want to know which was bigger, the sun or the earth. And when she made mistakes, they corrected her with infinite contempt. If in the absence of proof to the contrary, Giribala considered the belief that the sun was bigger than the earth to be groundless, and if she had the boldness to express her doubts, then her brothers would declare with redoubled scorn, "Indeed! it is written in our books, and you—".

When Giribala heard that this fact was recorded in printed books, she was completely silenced and did not think any other proof necessary.

But she felt a great desire to be able to read books like her brothers. Some days she would sit in her own room with an open book before her, and go on muttering to herself as if she were reading, and keep turning over the pages quickly one after another. The small black unknown letters seemed to be keeping guard at the lion's gate of some great hall of mystery in endless serried rows, with bayonets of vowels raised aloft on their shoulders, and gave no reply to the questions put by Giribala. The Book of Fables revealed not a single word of its tigers, foxes, horses and donkeys to the curiosity-tormented girl, and the Book of Tales with all its tales remained gazing dumbly as if under a vow of silence.

Giribala had suggested taking lessons from her brothers, but they had not paid the slightest heed to her request. Sashibhushan was her sole ally.

Like the Fables and The Book of Tales, Sashibhushan also at first seemed to Giribala to be full of inscrutable mystery. The young man used to sit alone in the small sitting-room with iron-grated windows by the roadside, on a plank bed surrounded by books. Standing outside and catching hold of the bars Giribala would fix a wondering gaze upon this strange figure with bent back, absorbed in reading; and comparing the number of books, would decide in her own mind that Sashibhushan was much more learned than her brothers. She could conceive of nothing more wonderful than this.

She had not the slightest doubt that Sashibhushan had read through all the world's greatest books, such as the Book of Fables, etc. Hence when Sashibhushan turned over the pages, she stood stock-still, unable to measure the depths of his learning.

At length this wonderstruck girl came to attract the attention even of the short-sighted Sashibhushan. One day he opened a glittering bound volume and said, "Giribala, come and look at the pictures." Giribala immediately ran away.

This is how their acquaintance started, and it would require some historical research to determine the exact date on which it ripened into intimacy and the girl, entering Sashibhushan's room from outside the grating, obtained a seat amongst the bound books on the plank bed.

Giribala began taking lessons from Sashibhushan. My readers will laugh when they hear that this teacher taught his little pupil not only her letters, spelling and grammar, but translated and read out many great poems to her and asked her opinion of them. God alone knows what the girl understood but that she liked it, there is no doubt. She drew many imaginary and wonderful pictures in her child-mind made up of a mixture of understanding and non-understanding, and she listened intently and silently with wide-open eyes, asked one or two altogether foolish questions now and then, and sometimes veered off suddenly to an irrelevant subject. Sashibhushan never objected to this, but derived a particular pleasure from hearing this tiny little critic praise and blame and comment on famous poems. Giribala was his only discerning friend in the whole neighbourhood.

When Sashibhushan first came to know her, Giri was eight years old; now she was ten. In these two years, she had learnt the English and Bengali alphabet, and finished reading three or four easy books. At the same time Sashi-bhushan also had not felt these two years of village life to be altogether lonely and uninteresting.

3

But Sashibhushan had not been able to get on well with Giribala's father Harakumar. Harakumar used to come and ask this M.A., B.L. to advise him about his lawsuits. The said M.A., B.L., however, did not show much interest, nor did he hesitate to confess his ignorance of law to the Manager Babu, who considered this to be pure evasion. In this way two years passed.

At about this time, it had become imperative to punish a recalcitrant tenant. The Manager Babu earnestly entreated Sashibhushan to advise him with regard to his intention of prosecuting the said tenant in different districts on different charges and claims. But far from advising him, Sashibhushan said certain things to him quietly yet firmly, which did not strike him as being at all pleasant.

On the other hand Harakumar was unable to win a single case against this tenant, so he became firmly convinced that Sashibhushan had been helping the unfortunate man and vowed that the village should be rid of such a person without delay.

Sashibhushan found that cows kept straying into his fields, his pulse-stores were catching fire, his boundaries were being disputed, his tenants were making difficulties about paying their rents and not only that, were trying to bring false cases against him. There were even rumours that he would get a beating if he went out in the evenings, and his house would be set on fire some night.

At last the harmless peace-loving Sashibhushan prepared to leave the village and escape to Calcutta.

Whilst he was making his preparations, the Joint Magistrate Sahib's tents were pitched in the village, which thereupon became astir with constables, *khansamas,* dogs, horses, syces and sweepers. Batches of small boys began to wander about the outskirts of the Sahib's camp with fearful curiosity, like packs of jackals on a tiger's trail.

The Manager Babu proceeded to supply fowls, eggs, *ghee* and milk to the Sahib under the heading of hospita-lity, according to custom. He freely and unquestioningly supplied a much larger quantity of food than was actually required by the Joint Sahib; but when the Sahib's sweeper came one morning and demanded four seers of *ghee* at once for the Sahib's dog, then, as ill-luck would have it, Harakumar felt this was the limit and explained to the sweeper that though the Sahib's dog could doubtlessly digest much more *ghee* than a country dog without fear of consequences, still such a large quantity of fat was not good for its health; and he refused to supply the *ghee*.

The sweeper went and told the Sahib that he had gone to enquire from the Manager Babu where dog's meat could be had, but because he belonged to the sweeper caste the Manager had driven him away with contempt before everybody, and had not even hesitated to show disrespect to the Sahib.

As a rule Sahibs are easily offended by the Brahmin's pride of caste, moreover, they had dared to insult his sweeper; so that he found it impossible to control his temper, and immediately ordered his *chaprassi* to send for the Manager Babu.

The trembling Manager came and stood before the Sahib's tent, inwardly muttering the name of the goddess Durga. Coming out of the tent with loud creaking of boots, the Sahib shouted at the Manager in Bengali with a foreign accent: "Why have you driven away my sweeper?"

The flurried Harakumar hastened to assure the Sahib with folded hands that he could never dare to be so insolent as to drive away the Sahib's sweeper, but since the latter had asked for four seers of *ghee* at once for the dog, he (the Manager) had at first entered a mild protest in the interests of the said quadruped, and then sent out messengers to various places for procuring the *ghee*.

The Sahib enquired who had been sent out and where.

Harakumar promptly mentioned some names haphazard as they occurred to him.

The Sahib despatched messengers at once to enquire whether the aforesaid persons had been sent to the aforesaid villages to procure *ghee* and meanwhile kept the Manager Babu waiting in his tent.

The messengers came back in the afternoon and informed the Sahib that nobody had been sent anywhere for the *ghee*. This left no doubt in his mind that everything the Manager had said was false and his sweeper had spoken the truth. Whereupon, roaring with rage, the Joint Sahib called the sweeper and said, "Catch hold of this swine by the ear and race him round the tent", which command the sweeper executed in front of the crowd of spectators, without waste of time.

The report of this event spread like wild fire through the village and Harakumar came home and lay down like one half dead, without touching a morsel of food.

The Manager had made many enemies in connection with his *zemindari* work. They were overjoyed at the news, but when the departing Sashibhushan heard it, his blood boiled within him, and he could not sleep the whole night.

Next morning he went to Harakumar's house; the latter caught hold of his hand and began to weep bitterly. Sashibhushan said, "A case for libel must be brought against the Sahib, and I will fight it as your counsel."

At first Harakumar was frightened to hear that a suit must be filed against the Magistrate Sahib himself, but Sashibhushan strongly insisted upon it.

Harakumar asked for time to think it over. But when he found that the rumour had spread throughout the village and his enemies were openly expressing their jubilation, he hesitated no longer, and appealed to Sashibhushan, saying "My boy, I hear you are preparing to go to Calcutta for no ostensible reason—but you can't possibly do so. It is such a tower of strength for us to have a person like you in the village! Anyhow you must deliver me from this terrible indignity."

4

That Sashibhushan who had hitherto always tried to lead a
guarded and secluded life screened from the public eye, it was
that same Sashibhushan who now presented himself in court.
On hearing his case, the Magistrate took him into his private
chamber, and treated him with the utmost courtesy, saying
"Sashi Babu, wouldn't it be better to compromise this case
privately?"

Keeping his short-sighted frowning gaze fixed very steadily
upon the cover of a law-book lying on the table Sashi Babu
replied, "I cannot advise my client to do so. How can he make
a compromise privately when he has been insulted publicly?"

After exchanging a few words, the Sahib realized that this
myopic and laconic young man was not to be easily moved
and said, "All right Babu, let's see how it turns out in the end."

Saying which, the Magistrate adjourned the case and went
on tour to the moffussil.

On the other hand, the Joint Sahib wrote as follows to
the Zemindar: "Your Manager has insulted my servants and
shown disrespect to me. I trust you will take necessary action."

The Zemindar was thoroughly upset and sent for
Harakumar at once. The Manager recounted the whole affair
in detail, from beginning to end. The Zemindar got extremely
annoyed and said, "When the Sahib's sweeper asked for four
seers of *ghee,* why didn't you give it to him at once without
any question? Would it have cost you your father's money?"

Harakumar couldn't deny that his paternal property would
not have suffered any loss thereby. Admitting he was to blame,
he said, "It was my bad luck that made me act so foolishly."

"Then again, who told you to prosecute the Sahib", asked
the Zemindar.

"O Incarnation of Righteousness", replied Harakumar,
"I had no wish to prosecute: it was that young fellow Sashi

of our village, who never gets a single brief—who got me into this mess by insisting upon it, almost without my permission."

Whereupon the Zemindar became highly incensed with Sashibhushan. He gathered that the aforesaid youth was a worthless new pleader, who was trying to attract the public eye by creating a sensation. He ordered the Manager to withdraw the case, and appease the pair of magistrates, elder and younger, immediately.

The Manager presented himself at the Joint Magistrate's quarters with a peace-offering of fruits and sweets calculated to cool the atmosphere. He informed the Sahib that it was altogether foreign to his nature to bring a case against him; it was only that green young duffer of a pleader known as Sashibhushan of their village who had the impudence to act thus, practically without his knowledge. The Sahib was exceedingly annoyed with Sashibhushan and extremely pleased with the Manager, whom he was *dukkhit* to have given *dandobidhan* in a fit of temper. The Sahib had recently won a prize in a Bengali examination, hence he was given to speaking in high-flown book language with all and sundry.

The Manager averred that parents sometimes punished their children in anger, at others drew them into their affectionate embrace, so that there was no occasion for either the parents or the children to feel sorry.

Whereupon, after distributing adequate largesse to all the Joint Sahib's servants, Harakumar went to the moffussil to see the Magistrate Sahib. After hearing all about Sashibhushan's arrogant behaviour from him, the Magistrate remarked, "It struck me also as very strange that the Manager Babu whom I had always thought to be such a nice person, instead of informing me first and arranging for private compromise, should rush to bring a suit. The whole thing seemed so preposterous! Now I understand everything."

Finally he asked the Manager whether Sashibhushan had joined the Congress. Without turning a hair the latter calmly replied, "Yes".

The Sahib's normal ruling-race complex led him to perceive clearly that this was all the Congress' doing. The myrmidons of the Congress were secretly going about everywhere seeking for opportunities to engineer trouble and write articles in the *Amrit Bazar* picking a quarrel with the Government. The Sahib inwardly cursed the Government of India's weakness in not giving more summary powers to the Magistrates to crush these puny thorns underfoot forthwith. But the name of Sashibhushan the Congressman remained in the Magistrate's memory.

5

When the big things of life raise their powerful heads, the small things also are not deterred from spreading their hungry little network of roots and putting forward their claim in the affairs of the world.

When Sashibhushan was particularly busy with the Magistrate's annoying case, when he was collecting notes on law from various volumes, sharpening in his mind the points he would make in his speech, cross-examining imaginary witnesses, and trembling and perspiring every now and again at the mental picture of the crowded court-room and the future sequence of cantos in his war-epic—then his little pupil used to come regularly to his door, shabby reader and ink-stained exercise-book in hand, sometimes with flowers and fruit, sometimes with pickles, coconut-sweets and spiced home-made catechu with the fragrance of the *ketaki* from her mother's store-room.

The first few days she noticed that Sashibhushan was absent-mindedly turning over the pages of a huge forbidding-looking volume without pictures, but it did not seem as if he was reading it very attentively either. Sashibhushan used to try and explain to Giribala some portion at least of the books he read on other occasions—were there then not even a few words in that heavy black-bound volume which he could read out to her? And in any case, was that book so very important and Giribala so very insignificant?

At first, in order to attract her preceptor's attention Giribala began to spell and read her lessons out aloud in a sing-song tone, swaying the upper half of her body including her plait, violently to and fro. But she found this plan did not work very well. She became intensely annoyed in her own mind with that heavy black book, which she began to look upon as an ugly, hard, cruel human being. Every unintelligible page of that book took on the form of a wicked man's face and silently expressed its utter contempt of Giribala, because she was a little girl. If some thief could have stolen that book, she would have rewarded him with all the spiced catechu in her mother's store-room. The gods did not listen to all the unreasonable and impossible prayers she mentally said to them for the destruction of that book, nor do I think it necessary for my readers to hear them either.

Then the dejected girl gave up going to her tutor's home, lesson-book in hand, for a day or two. On coming to the path in front of Sashibhushan's room to see the result of these two days of separation, and glancing inside, she found that Sashibhushan, putting aside the black book, was standing alone and addressing the iron bars in some foreign language with gesticulations.

Probably he was experimenting on those irons how to melt the heart of the judge.

Sashibhushan the bookworm, ignorant of the ways of the world, thought it not altogether impossible even in these mercenary days to perform the wonderful feats of orators like

Demosthenes, Cicero, Burke, Sheridan, etc., who by the piercing arrows of their winged words had torn injustice to shreds, cowed down the tyrant, and humbled pride to the dust in the olden days. Standing in the small dilapidated house of Tilkuchi village, Sashibhushan was practising how to put to shame the arrogant English race flushed with the wine of victory, and make them repent for their misdeeds before the whole world. Whether the gods in heaven laughed to hear him or whether their divine eyes moistened with tears, nobody knows.

So he failed to notice Giribala. On that day the girl had no plums in her *sāri*-end. Having been caught once in the act of throwing plum-stones, she had become very sensitive with regard to that fruit, so much so that if Sashibhushan innocently asked some day—"Giri, are there no plums for me today?" she took it to be a veiled taunt and prepared to run away with the reproving exclamation "*jah!*" on her lips.

In the absence of plum-stones, she had to take recourse to a trick today. Suddenly looking at a distant point, she cried, "Swarna, dear, don't go, I shall be coming in a minute."

My masculine readers may think that these words were addressed to some distant companion, but my feminine readers will easily surmise that there was nobody in the distance and that the object aimed at was close at hand. But alas! the shot missed the blind man. Not that Sashibhushan had not heard, but he failed to perceive the purport of the call. He thought that the girl was really anxious to go and play and he had not the energy that day to draw her away from play to study, because he also was trying to aim his sharp arrows at somebody's heart. Just as the trifling aim of the girl's small hand missed the mark, so did the high aim of his practised hand, as my readers already know.

Plum-stones have this advantage that they can be thrown several times and if four miss the mark, then the fifth has a chance of hitting it. But however imaginary a person Swarna may be, she cannot be kept standing for long after one has told her "I am coming." If one treats her so, then people may naturally begin to entertain doubts as to her existence. So when this means failed, Giribala had to go without further delay. Still one did not notice in her steps that celerity which a sincere desire to join a distant companion would have warranted. It was as if she were trying to feel with her back whether anyone was following her or not; when she knew for certain that nobody was coming, then with a last feeble fraction of hope she looked round once, and not seeing anyone tore to pieces both that tiny hope and her loose-leaved lesson-book and scattered them on the road. If she could have found some possible means of returning the little knowledge that Sashibhushan had imparted to her, then probably she would have thrown it all down with a bang at Sashibhushan's door like the unwanted plum-stones, and come away. The girl vowed that before she met Sashibhushan next, she would forget all her lessons and not be able to answer any question he put to her—not one, not one, not even a single one! And then! Then Sashibhushan would be served right.

Giribala's eyes filled with tears. She derived some small comfort in her aching heart from thinking how deeply repentant Sashibhushan would feel if she forgot all her lessons, and a spring of pity welled up in her imagination for that future wretched Giribala, who would forget everything she had learnt, simply for Sashibhushan's fault.

Clouds gathered in the sky, as they do every day in the rainy season. Giribala stood behind a roadside tree sobbing for wounded pride. Such idle tears are shed every day by many a girl; it was nothing worthy of note.

6

My readers are aware of the reasons why Sashibhushan's researches into the law and his essays in oratory proved fruitless. The case against the Magistrate was suddenly withdrawn. Harakumar was appointed an Honorary Magistrate on the District bench and he used to go often to the district town in a soiled *chapkan* and greasy turban, to pay his respects to the Sahibs.

At long last Giribala's curses on that fat black book began to bear fruit—and it lay neglected, forgotten and exiled in a dark corner, collecting dust. But where was Giribala the girl who would have taken delight in this neglect?

The day when Sashibhushan closed his law-book and sat alone, he suddenly realized that Giribala had not come. Then he began to recollect the daily history of those few days, little by little. He remembered how one bright morning Giribala had brought a heap of *bakul* flowers wet with the new rains, tied in a corner of her *sāri*. When he did not raise his eyes from his book even on seeing her, her ardour became suddenly damped. Taking a needle-and-thread stuck in her *sāri*-end, she began to weave a garland of *bakul* flowers one by one, with bent head. She wove it very slowly, and it took a long time to finish; the day began to wear on, it was time for Giribala to go home, and yet Sashibhushan had not finished reading. Giribala left the garland on the plank bed, and sorrowfully went away. He remembered how her wounded feelings gradually gained in depth every day; how the time came when she gave up entering his room, and would appear now and again on the footpath in front and go away; and how at last the girl had even given up coming to the path—that too was now some days ago. Giribala's fit of pique never used to last so long. Sashibhushan sighed and remained sitting with his back against the wall like one bewildered and with nothing to do. In the absence of his little pupil, his books became distasteful to him.

He kept pulling one or two books towards him, then pushing them away again after reading two or three pages. If he began to write, his expectant eyes would throw an eager glance every now and again towards the lane and the house opposite, and his writing would be interrupted.

Sashibhushan was afraid Giribala had fallen ill. On making discreet enquiries, however, he learnt that his fears were groundless. Giribala did not go out of the house nowadays. A bridegroom had been settled for her.

On the morning following the day on which Giribala had strewn the muddy village lane with the torn leaves of her lesson-book, she was leaving the house early with quick steps, bearing various presents tied in her little *sari*-corner. Having passed a sleepless night owing to the intense heat, Harakumar was sitting outside with bared body, pulling at his *hookah*, since early morning. "Where are you going?" he asked Giri. "To Sashidada's house", she replied. "You needn't go to Sashibhushan's house", scolded Harakumar, "go back home." Saying which he spoke long and sternly to her anent the shameless behaviour of a grown-up girl about to enter her father-in-law's house. Since that day she had been forbidden to leave the house. This time she found no opportunity of humbling her pride and making it up with Sashibhushan. Mango-preserves, spiced catechu and pickled limes were relegated to their proper place on the store-room shelf. It went on raining, the *bakul* flowers went on falling, the guava-trees became laden with ripe fruit, and the ground beneath the plum trees became littered every day with succulent black plums dropped from the branches by pecking birds. Alas! even the loose-leaved lesson-book was no longer there.

7

On the day when the *sanai* was playing in the village for Giribala's wedding, the uninvited Sashibhushan was going to Calcutta by boat.

Since the withdrawal of the lawsuit the very sight of Sashibhushan had become a curse to Harakumar, for he was certain in his own mind that Sashibhushan looked down upon him with contempt. He began to discover a thousand imaginary proofs of this in Sashibhushan's looks and behaviour. All the other village-folk were gradually forgetting the history of his past indignity, only Sashibhushan was keeping alive its memory, he thought; hence he could not bear him. Whenever he met him, he used to feel a kind of shrinking shame, accompanied by a strong resentment. He vowed to himself that he would drive Sashibhushan out of the village.

It was not a very difficult task to constrain a person like Sashibhushan to leave the village. So the Manager Babu's desire was soon fulfilled. One morning Sashibhushan got into a boat with a load of books and a few tin boxes. The one happy tie that had bound him to the village, even that was being snapped today with great *éclat*. He had not fully realized before how firmly that delicate bond had entwined itself around his heart. Today when the boat set off, when the tops of the village trees and the sound of the wedding-music became gradually more and more indistinct, then suddenly a mist of tears spread over his heart and choked his voice, a rush of blood caused the veins in his forehead to throb with pain, and the whole panorama of the world seemed exceedingly hazy as if composed of shadowy illusion.

A strong wind was blowing from the opposite direction; hence the boat advanced slowly, though the current was favourable. At this juncture something happened on the river, which hindered Sashibhushan's journey.

A new steamer line had recently been opened from the station landing-place to the district town. Their steamer came noisily puffing along against the current, with its propellers working like wings and setting up waves on either side. The young Manager Sahib of the new line and a few passengers were on board, among whom were some inhabitants of Sashibhushan's village.

A money-lender's country-boat was trying to race the steamer from a little way off; at times it seemed about to catch up with her, and again kept falling behind. The boatman's spirit of rivalry was awakened. He put out a second sail on top of the first one, and even a third small sail atop of that. The tall mast bent low before the blast, and the parted waves danced madly with a loud splashing noise, on either side of the boat. The boat plunged forward like a horse with its reins snapped. At a certain point the path of the steamer took a slight bend, and here the boat outstripped it by taking a shorter cut. The Manager Sahib was leaning over the railing, eagerly watching this race. When the boat was flying along at top speed and had outstripped the steamer by about a yard, just then the Sahib raised his revolver and fired a shot at the swollen sail. In a moment the sail burst, the boat sank, and the steamer was hidden from sight round the bend.

Why the Manager acted thus, it is difficult to say. We Bengalees cannot always understand the workings of the Sahib's mind. Perhaps he felt the rivalry of an Indian sail to be intolerable; perhaps there is a fierce pleasure in putting a bullet through something broad and swollen in the twinkling of an eye; perhaps there is a certain ferocious and fiendish humour in putting the proud boat *hors de combat* in a second by making a few holes in its cloth. What the reason was I do not know exactly. But this I know for certain that the Englishman believed he would not be liable to be punished for this little joke, and he had an idea that the people whose boat was lost and who were in danger of losing their lives also could not be counted as human beings.

When the Sahib fired and the boat sank, Sashibhushan's boat had approached the place of occurrence. Sashibhushan was an eye-witness of the last scene. He hastened to the spot with his boat and rescued the boatmen. Only the man who was grinding spices for cooking in the kitchen could not be traced. The rain-swollen river flowed on swiftly.

The hot blood boiled in Sashibhushan's veins. The law was very dilatory—like a huge complex iron machine; it accepted proofs after weighing them, and apportioned punishment calmly—it did not possess the warmth of the human heart. But to separate food from hunger, desire from enjoyment, and anger from punishment appeared to Sashibhushan to be equally unnatural. There are many crimes which as soon as witnessed demand an immediate retribution from the witness' own hand, otherwise the god in him seems to sear the witness from within. At such a moment one feels inwardly ashamed to find comfort in the idea of the law. But the machine-made law and the machine-made steamer took the Manager further away from Sashibhushan. Whether the world was benefited in other ways, I cannot say, but this much is certain that Sashibhushan's Indian spleen was saved at this juncture.

Sashibhushan returned to the village with the boatmen who had survived. The boat had been laden with jute, which he appointed men to salvage, and tried to persuade the boatman to bring a police-case against the Manager.

But the boatman was unwilling to do so. He said the boat was sunk for good, but he was not prepared to sink with it. First of all, he would have to grease the palms, of the police; then he would have to give up all work and food and rest and wander about the law-courts; then God alone knows what trouble was in store for him and what the result would be if he prosecuted the Sahib. At last when he heard that Sashibhushan was himself a pleader, that he himself would pay all the costs of the suit and that there was every chance of his getting damages, he agreed. But the people of Sashibhushan's village who were present on board the steamer flatly refused to bear witness. "We didn't see anything, sir", they said to Sashibhushan, "we were at the back of the steamer, it was impossible to hear a gunshot for the throbbing of the machine and the lapping of the water."

Inwardly cursing his countrymen, Sashibhushan continued to conduct the case before the Magistrate.

No witnesses were required. The Manager admitted he had fired a shot. He said it was aimed at a flock of cranes flying in the sky. The steamer was then going at full speed and had just turned round the bend. So he could not possibly know whether a crow died or a crane died or the boat sank. Earth and sky contained so many things to aim at that no man in his senses would knowingly waste a pice-worth of shot on a dirty rag.

Acquitted on all charges, the Manager Sahib, puffing at a cigar, went to play whist at his club. The dead body of the man who was grinding spices in the boat was washed up on land nine miles farther off, and Sashibhushan returned to his village with frustration raging in his breast.

The day he returned, they were taking Giribala to her husband's home in a decorated boat. Though nobody had asked him, yet Sashibhushan came slowly to the riverside. The landing-place was crowded, so instead of going there he stood a little way off. When the boat left the landing-steps and passed in front of him, he caught a fleeting glimpse of the new bride, sitting with her *sari* drawn down over her bowed head. Giribala had long been hoping to see Sashibhushan somehow or other before leaving the village, but today she did not even know that her preceptor was standing there not very far away. She did not even raise her head once to look; only the tears coursed down both her cheeks in silent weeping.

The boat gradually receded and passed out of sight. The morning light glittered on the river; from the branch of a mango-tree nearby, a *papia* burst into rapturous song every now and then, seeking in vain to unburden the passion of its heart; the ferry-boat, laden with passengers, kept plying from one side of the river to the other; the women coming to the landing-steps to draw water, began discussing Giri's departure for her father-in-law's house in a loud babel of voices; and Sashibhushan, taking off his glasses and wiping his eyes, turned back and entered the small iron-grated room by the roadside. Suddenly it seemed as if he heard Giribala's voice calling "Sashidada!"

—Where, oh where?

Nowhere! Not in the room, not in the lane, not in the village—but in the midst of his own heart.

8

Sashibhushan again packed up his things and started for Calcutta. He had nothing to do in Calcutta, there was no particular object in going there; so instead of going by rail, he decided to travel all the way by boat.

At the height of the rainy season, a network of big and small zig-zag waterways had spread over the whole of Bengal. The veins and arteries of this green land seemed to be overflowing with sap on all sides into trees and plants, bushes and grass, corn and jute and sugarcane, in a mad exuberance of riotous youth.

Sashibhushan's boat proceeded to thread its way through all these narrow serpentine alleys of water, which had by then become level with the bank. The white-tufted grass and reeds and in some places the cornfields were under water. The bamboo-groves and mango-groves and fencing of the village had reached the very edge of the river, as if the daughters of the gods had filled with water to the brink the circular grooves around the tree-roots.

When he set out the woods were bright and smiling and glistening after their bath; but it soon clouded over and began to rain; whichever way one turned, it looked dismal and dingy. Just as during a flood, the cattle huddle together in their dirty, slushy, narrow byre and get drenched in the incessant showers of July, standing patiently with pathetic eyes; so was the harassed countryside of Bengal, dumb and sorrowful, being soaked continuously in its dense swamped and slippery jungles. The peasants were going about with their palm-leaf umbrellas; the women were going from one hut to another in the course of their daily household duties, getting drenched and shrinking from the cold wet wind and treading the slippery landing-stairs very cautiously to draw water from the river in their wet clothes. The men were sitting in their verandahs smoking, or if absolutely necessary, going out with *chaddar* wound round the waist, umbrellas over their heads and shoes in their hands. It is not one of our ancient and sacred customs to provide our long-suffering womenfolk with umbrellas in this sunburnt and rain-swept land of Bengal.

When the rain showed no signs of stopping, Sashi-bhushan began to get tired of the closed boat, and again decided to travel by rail. Arriving at a wide confluence of the river, he moored the boat and began to prepare for his midday meal.

It is the lame man's foot that falls into the ditch, as the saying goes. It is not the fault of the ditch alone, but the lame man's foot also has a special bent for falling into the ditch. On that day Sashibhushan furnished a good proof of this.

The fishermen had fixed bamboo-poles on either side of the confluence of two rivers and spread a huge net over them, keeping only room on one side for boats to pass. They had been doing this since a long time, and also paying rent for it. As ill luck would have it, this year the august District Superintendent of Police had suddenly deigned to come this way. Seeing his boat draw near, the fishermen warned his boatman beforehand in a loud voice and pointed out the passage at the side. But the Sahib's boatman was not in the habit of showing deference to any man-made barrier by taking a roundabout route, so he steered the boat clean through the net. The net stooped and made way for the boat, but its rudder became enmeshed and it took some time and trouble to disentangle it.

The Police Sahib got extremely red and angry, and had the boat moored. The four fishermen, seeing his threatening attitude, promptly decamped. The Sahib ordered his oarsmen to cut up the net, and the huge net, made at a cost of seven or eight hundred rupees, was cut to pieces.

After venting his wrath on the net, the Sahib finally sent for the fishermen. Unable to find the four runaway men, the constable caught hold of whichever four fishermen came to hand. They pleaded their innocence with folded hands supplicatingly. As the Police Bahadur was giving orders to his men to take the prisoners along with them, the bespectacled Sashibhushan with an unbuttoned shirt hastily thrown over his shoulders and his slippers pattering on the ground came in breathless haste to the police boat. In a quivering voice he said, "Sir, you have no right to cut up the net of these fishermen, and to harass these four men."

As soon as the Burra Sahib of the Police uttered a particularly offensive invective in Hindi, Sashibhushan sprang into the boat from the slightly raised river-bank, and throwing himself at once upon the Sahib, began to pummel him right and left like a child, like a madman.

After that he did not know what happened. When he awoke in the police-station, we are constrained to say that the treatment he received was conducive neither to his sense of dignity nor to his physical comfort.

9

Sashibhushan's father, with the assistance of pleaders and barristers, first got his son released on bail. Then preparations were set afoot for conducting the case.

The fishermen whose net had been destroyed belonged to the same holding and were under the same zemindar as Sashibhushan. When in difficulty, they used to come to him sometimes for legal advice. The men who had been seized and brought to the boat by the Sahib were also not unknown to him.

Sashibhushan sent for them in order to cite them as witnesses, but they were frightened out of their wits. If those who had to pass their daily lives with wife and children were to quarrel with the police, then where would their troubles end? How many lives were there in one man's body? The loss they had suffered was over and done with, now why this further trouble of a subpoena for bearing witness! "Sir, you have landed us in a great mess!" they all declared.

After much persuasion, they agreed to tell the truth.

In the meantime, when Harakumar took the opportunity of sitting on the bench to go and *salaam* the Sahibs, the Police Sahib said with a smile, "Manager Babu, I hear your tenants are ready to bear false witness against the police."

"Indeed! is such a thing possible?" said the startled manager, "that the sons of swine should have it in their bones to dare to do a thing like that!"

Readers of newspapers know that Sashibhushan's case had no legs to stand on.

One by one the fishermen came and deposed that the Sahib had not cut up their net, but had sent for them to the boat and taken down their names and addresses.

Not only that, but three or four of his village acquaintances stated that they were present at the place and time of occurrence, as members of a wedding-party, and had seen with their own eyes how Sashibhushan without any provocation had come forward and harassed the police constables.

Sashibhushan admitted that on being abused he had jumped into the boat and struck the Sahib; but the real reason for that was the destruction of the net and the ill-treatment of the fishermen.

Under the circumstances, that Sashibhushan should be punished could not be called unjust. But the sentence was somewhat severe. There were three or four charges— assault, trespass, interfering with police officers on duty, etc.—all of which were fully proved against him.

Leaving his beloved books in that small room, Sashibhushan went to jail for five years. When his father wanted to appeal, Sashibhushan repeatedly forbade him to do so. "Jail is welcome", he said, "iron bonds don't lie, but the freedom we have outside deceives us and gets us into trouble. And if you talk of good company, then the liars and cowards in jail are comparatively fewer, because there is less room—outside their number is much larger."

10

Soon after Sashibhushan went to jail, his father died. He had hardly any relatives to speak of. A brother of his had been holding a post in the Central Provinces since a long time, and could not make it convenient to come home very often; he had built a house for himself and settled there with his family. Whatever property he had in his village home was mostly appropriated by the manager Harakumar on various pretexts.

Fate so willed it that Sashibhushan had to undergo much more suffering in jail than usually fell to the lot of prisoners. Still the five long years passed.

Again one rainy day Sashibhushan came and stood outside the prison-walls with ruined health and vacant mind. He had gained his freedom, and that was all he had: he had no one and nothing to call his own. With no home, no relatives and no friends, he felt that the vast world was too big and loose for his solitary self.

While he was deliberating where to begin to pick up the broken threads of his life, a big carriage and pair came and stood in front of him. A servant alighted and asked him, "Is your name Sashibhushan Babu?" "Yes", he replied.

The man immediately held open the carriage-door and waited for Sashibhushan to get in. "Where am I to go?" he asked in surprise.

"My master has sent for you", replied the servant.

As the curious looks of the passers-by were getting intolerable, Sashibhushan jumped into the carriage without more ado. Surely there must be some mistake, he thought to himself. But he had to go somewhere in any case, and a mistake might just as well serve as the prelude to a new life.

On that day also sunshine and clouds were chasing each other all over the sky; and the rainwashed dark green corn-fields skirting the road were chequered with the lively play of sun and shadow. There was a huge chariot lying near the market-place, and from a grocer's shop nearby some Vaishnava mendicants were singing to the accompaniment of string instruments, drums and cymbals:

Come back, come back! O lord of my heart, Beloved, come back to this hungry,
> *parched and fevered breast.*

As the carriage advanced, the lines of the song could be heard growing fainter and still more faint in the distance:

O cruel one, come back! O soft and loving come!
Come back, O thou of the tender hue
                                   of the rain cloud!

The words of the song became gradually blurred and indistinct
and could no longer be followed. But its rhythm had set up
a turmoil in Sashibhushan's breast; he began humming to
himself and adding line after line to the song, and seemed
unable to stop:

O my joy, forever and forever my grief,
                                   come back!
O treasure churned from all my grief and joy,
                                   come to my heart.
O ever-desired, and ever-cherished one,
O thou fleeting, O thou everlasting,
                                   come to my arms.
Come to my bosom, to my eyes, in my sleep,
in my dreams, in the clothes and jewels I wear,
                                   to my whole world.
Come in the laughter of my lips, in the
                                   tears of my eyes,
My caresses, my wiles, my wounded pride,
In every remembrance and in forgetfulness.
In my faith and my work, my love's
                                   ardour and shyness,
In my life and my death, O come!

Sashibhushan's singing came to an end when the carriage
entered a walled garden and stopped in front of a two-
storeyed house.

Without asking any questions he followed the servant's
directions and entered the house.

The room in which he came and sat was lined on all sides
with big glass book cases filled with rows upon rows of books

of various colours and various bindings. At this sight his former life was set free from prison at once for the second time. These gilted and multi-coloured books seemed to him like familiar jewelled lion-gates at the entrance of the kingdom of joy.

There were some things lying on the table also. The short-sighted Sashibhushan bent forward and saw a cracked slate upon which were some old exercise books, a much torn arithmetic book, the Book of Fables and a Kashiram Das Mahabharata.

Upon the wooden frame of the slate was written in bold characters in Sashibhushan's hand—Giribala Devi. Upon the books and exercise books the same name was written in the same hand.

Now Sashibhushan knew where he had come. The blood coursed wildly in his veins. He looked out of the open window, and what did he see there? The small iron-barred room, the uneven village lane, the little girl in a striped *sāri*,—and his own carefree, quiet and peaceful daily life.

The happy life of those days was nothing wonderful nor extraordinary; day after day used to pass by unconsciously in trivial tasks and trivial joys, and the teaching of a little girl pupil was only one amongst those trifling things but that secluded life in a village corner, that circumscribed peace, those small joys, the face of that little girl—everything seemed to exist in a land of desire and shadowy imagination—in a heaven outside time and space and beyond his grasp.

All the scenes and memories of those bygone days, mingled with the soft light of this rainy morning and the *kirtan* song softly ringing in his ears, seemed to take on a new beauty of melodious sound and radiant light. The memory of the sad and hurt look on the face of the little neglected girl as he had last seen her in the jungle-girt muddy village lane was transformed on the canvas of his mind into a unique and wonderful picture full of deep pathos and a divine beauty. The sad tune of the *kirtan* blended with that picture, and it seemed to him that the ineffable sorrow at the heart of the universe had cast its shadow upon the face of that village maiden. Placing both arms on the slate and books upon the table, and hiding his face in them, Sashibhushan began after many years to dream dreams of long ago.

After a long time, hearing a slight noise Sashibhushan started and raised his head. He saw before him fruits and sweets on a silver salver, and at a little distance, Giribala standing and silently waiting. As soon as he looked up, Giribala, clad all in white in widow's garb, without a single ornament on her person, came and knelt before him, and took the dust of his feet.

She rose and looked at him—so emaciated and pale and broken in health—with her eyes full of sweet sympathy; and tears coursed down her cheeks.

Sashibhushan made an effort to ask her how she was, but could not find words to do so; stifled tears choked his utterance. The *kirtan* singers came and stood in front of the house in the course of their begging round and began to sing over and over again—

Come back, Beloved, come back!

Mahamaya

They met together in a ruined temple on the river bank:
Mahamaya and Rajib.

In silence she cast her naturally grave look at Rajib with
a tinge of reproach. It meant to say: "How durst you call me
here at this unusual hour today? You have ventured to do it
only because I have so long obeyed you in all things!"

Rajib had a little awe of Mahamaya at all times, and now
this look of hers thoroughly upset him: he at once gave up
his fondly conceived plan of making a set speech to her. And
yet he had to give quickly some reason for this interview. So,
he hurriedly blurted out, "I say, let us run away from this
place and marry." True, Rajib thus delivered himself of what
he had had in his mind; but the preface he had silently
composed was lost. His speech sounded very dry and bald—
even absurd. He himself felt confused after saying it, and had
no power left in him to add some words to modify its effect.
The fool! After calling Mahamaya to that ruined temple by
the riverside at midday, he could only tell her, "Come, let
us marry!"

Mahamaya was a *kulin's* daughter, twenty-four years old—
in the full bloom of her youth and beauty, like an image of
pure gold, of the hue of the early autumn sunlight; radiant
and still as that sunshine, with a gaze free and fearless as
daylight itself.

She was an orphan. Her elder brother, Bhavanicharan Chattopadhyay, looked after her. The two were of the same mould—taciturn, but possessing a force of character which burnt silently like the midday sun. People feared Bhavanicharan without knowing why.

Rajib had come there from afar with the Burra Sahib of the silk factory of the place. His father had served this Sahib, and when he died, the Sahib underook to bring up his orphan boy and took him with himself to this Bamanhati factory. In those early days such instances of sympathy were frequent among the Sahibs. The boy was accompanied by his loving aunt, and they lived in Bhavanicharan's neighbourhood. Mahamaya was Rajib's playmate in childhood, and was dearly loved by his aunt.

Rajib grew up to be sixteen, seventeen, eighteen, and even nineteen; and yet, in spite of his aunt's constant urging, he refused to marry. The Sahib was highly pleased to hear of this uncommon instance of good sense in a Bengali youth, and imagined that Rajib had taken him as his ideal in life. I may here add that the Sahib was a bachelor. The aunt died soon after.

For Mahamaya, too, no bridegroom of an equal grade of blue blood could be secured except for an impossible dowry. She steadily grew up in maidenhood.

The reader hardly needs to be told that though the god who ties the marriage knot had so long been ignoring this young couple, the god who forms the bond of love had not been idle all this time. While old *Prajāpati* was dozing, young *Kandarpa* was very much awake.

Kandarpa's influence shows itself differently in different persons. Under his inspiration Rajib constantly sought for a chance of whispering his heart's longings, but Mahamaya never gave him such an opportunity; her silent and grave look sent a chill of fear through the wild heart of Rajib.

Today he had, by a hundred solemn entreaties and conjurations, at last succeeded in bringing her to this ruined temple. He had planned that he would today freely tell her all that he had to say and thereafter there would be for him either lifelong happiness or death in life. Yet at this crisis of his fate Rajib could only say, "Come, let us go and marry", and then he stood confused and silent like a boy who had forgotten his lesson.

For a long while she did not reply, as if she had never expected such a proposal from Rajib.

The noontide has many undefined plaintive notes of its own; these began to make themselves heard in the midst of that stillness. The broken door of the temple, half detached from its hinge, began at times to open and to close in the wind with a low wailing creak. The pigeon, perched on the temple window, began its deep booming. The wood-pecker kept up its monotonous noise as it sat working on the *shimul* branch outside. The lizard darted through the heaps of dry leaves with a rustling sound. A sudden gust of warm wind blowing from the fields passed through the trees, making all their foliage whistle. Of a sudden the river waters woke into ripple and lapped on the broken steps of the *ghat*. Amidst these stray, languid sounds came the rustic notes of a cow-boy's flute from a far-off tree-shade. Rajib stood reclining against the ruinous plinth of the temple like a tired dreamer, gazing at the river; he had not the spirit to look Mahamaya in the face.

After a while he turned his head and again cast a supplicating glance at Mahamaya's face. She shook her head and replied, "No, it can't be."

At once the whole fabric of his hopes was dashed to the ground; for he knew that when Mahamaya shook her head it was through her own convictions, and nobody else in the world could bend her to his own will. The high pride of pedigree had run in the blood of Mahamaya's family for untold generations—could she ever consent to marry a Brahmin of low pedigree like Rajib? To love is one thing, and to marry quite another. She, however, now realized that her own thoughtless conduct in the past had encouraged Rajib to hope so audaciously; and at once she prepared to leave the temple.

Rajib understood her, and quickly broke in with "I am leaving these parts tomorrow."

At first she thought of appearing indifferent to the news; but she could not. Her feet did not move when she wanted to depart. Calmly she asked, "Why?" Rajib replied, "My Sahib has been transferred from here to the Sonapur factory, and he is taking me with him." Again she stood in long silence, musing thus: 'Our lives are moving in two contrary directions. I cannot hope to keep a man a prisoner of my eyes for ever.' So she opened her compressed lips a little and said, "Very well." It sounded rather like a deep sigh.

With this word only she was again about to leave, when Rajib started up with the whisper "your brother!"

She looked out and saw her brother coming towards the temple, and she knew that he had found out their assignation. Rajib, fearing to place Mahamaya in a false position, tried to escape by jumping out of the hole in the temple wall; but Mahamaya seized his arm and kept him back by main force. Bhavanicharan entered the temple, and only cast one silent and placid glance at the pair.

Mahamaya looked at Rajib and said with an unruffled voice, "Yes, I will go to your house, Rajib. Do you wait for me."

Silently Bhavanicharan left the temple, and Mahamaya followed him as silently. And Rajib? He stood in a maze as if he had been doomed to death.

2

That very night Bhavanicharan gave a crimson silk *sāri* to Mahamaya and told her to put it on at once. Then he said, "Follow me". Nobody had ever disobeyed Bhavanicharan's bidding or even his hint; Mahamaya herself was no exception to it.

That night the two walked to the burning-place on the river-bank, not far from their home. There in the hut for sheltering dying men brought to the holy river's side, an old Brahmin was lying in expectation of death. The two went up to his bedside. A Brahmin priest was present in one corner of the room; Bhavanicharan beckoned to him. The priest quickly got his things ready for the happy ceremony. Mahamaya realized that she was to be married to this dying man, but she did not make the least objection. In the dim room, faintly lit up by the glare of two funeral pyres hard by, the muttered sacred texts mingled with the groans of the dying as Mahamaya's marriage was celebrated.

The day following her marriage she became a widow. But she did not feel excessively grieved at the bereavement. And Rajib, too, was not so crushed by the news of her widowhood as he had been by the unexpected tridings of her marriage. Nay, he felt rather cheered. But this feeling did not last long. A second terrible blow laid him utterly in the dust; he heard that there was a grand ceremony at the burning *ghāt* that day as Mahamaya was going to burn herself with her husband's corpse.

At first he thought of informing his Sahib and forcibly stopping the cruel sacrifice with his help. But then he recollected that the Sahib had made over charge and left for Sonapur that very day; he had wanted to take Rajib with him, but the youth had stayed behind on a month's leave.

Mahamaya had told him "Wait for me". This request he must by no means disregard. He had at first taken a month's leave, but if need were he would take two months', then three months' leave and finally throw up the Sahib's service and live by begging, yet he would wait for her to his life's close.

Just when Rajib was going to rush out madly and commit suicide or some other terrible deed, a deluge of rain came down with a desolating storm at sunset. The tempest threatened to tumble his house down on his head. He gained some composure when he found that the convulsion in outer nature was harmonizing with the storm within his soul. It seemed to him that all Nature had taken up his cause and was going to bring him some sort of remedy. The force he wished to apply in his own person but could not was now being applied by Nature herself over earth and sky.

At such a time some one pushed the door hard from outside. Rajib hastened to open it. A woman entered the room, clad in a wet garment, with a long veil covering her entire face. Rajib at once knew her for Mahamaya.

In a voice full of emotion he asked, "Mahamaya, have you come away from the funeral pyre?"

She replied, "Yes, I had promised you to come to your house. Here I am, to keep my word. But, Rajib, I am not exactly the same person; I am changed altogether. I am the Mahamaya of old in my mind only. Speak now, I can yet go back to the funeral pyre. But if you swear never to draw my veil aside, never to look on my face, then I shall live in your house."

It was enough to get her back from the hand of Death; all other considerations vanished before it. Rajib promptly replied, "Live here in any fashion you like; if you leave me I shall die."

Mahamaya said, "Then come away at once. Let us go where your Sahib has gone on transfer."

Abandoning all his property in that house, Rajib went forth into the midst of the storm with Mahamaya. The force of the wind made it hard for them to stand erect; the gravel driven by the wind pricked their limbs like buck shot. The two took to the open fields, lest the trees by the roadside should crash down on their heads. The violence of the wind struck them from behind, as if the tempest had torn the couple asunder from human habitations and was blowing them away on to destruction.

3

The reader must not discredit my tale as false or supernatural. There are traditions of a few such occurrences having taken place in the days when the burning of widows was customary.

Mahamaya had been bound hand and foot and placed on the funeral pyre, to which fire was applied at the appointed time. The flames had shot up from the pile, when a violent storm and rainshower began. Those who had come to conduct the cremation quickly fled for refuge to the hut for dying men and shut the door. The rain put the funeral fire out in no time. Meantime the bands on Mahamaya's wrists had been burnt to ashes, setting her hands free. Without uttering a groan amidst the intolerable pain of burning, she sat up and untied her feet. Then wrapping round herself her partly burnt cloth, she rose half-naked from the pyre, and first came to her own house. There was no one there; all had gone to the burning *ghāt*. She lighted a lamp, put on a fresh cloth, and looked at her face in a glass. Dashing the mirror down on the ground, she mused for a while. Then she drew a long veil over her face and went to Rajib's house which was hard by. The reader knows what happened next.

True, Mahamaya now lived in Rajib's house, but there was no joy in his life. It was not much, but only a simple veil that parted the one from the other. And yet that veil was eternal like death, but more agonizing than death itself; because despair in time deadens the pang of death's separation, while a living hope was being daily and hourly crushed by the separation which that veil caused.

For one thing there was a spirit of motionless silence in Mahamaya from of old; and now the hush from within the veil appeared doubly unbearable. She seemed to be living within a winding sheet of death. This silent death clasped the life of Rajib and daily seemed to shrivel it up. He lost the Mahamaya whom he had known of old, and at the same time this veiled figure ever sitting by his side silently prevented him from enshrining in his life the sweet memory of her as she was in her girlhood. He brooded: 'Nature has placed barrier enough between one human being and another. Mahamaya, in particular, has been born, like Karua of old, with a natural charm against all evil. There is an innate fence round her being. And now she seems to have been born a second time and come to me with a second line of fences round herself. Ever by my side, she yet has become so remote as to be no longer within my reach. I am sitting outside the inviolable circle of her magic and trying, with an unsatiated thirsty soul, to penetrate this thin but unfathomable mystery, as the stars wear out the hours night after night in the vain attempt to pierce the mystery of the 'dark Night with their sleepless winkless downcast gaze.'

Long did these two companionless lonely creatures thus pass their days together.

One night, on the tenth day of the new moon, the clouds withdrew for the first time in that rainy season, and the moon showed herself. The motionless moonlit night seemed to be sitting in a vigil by the head of the sleeping world. That night Rajib too had quitted his bed and sat gazing out of his window. From the heat-oppressed woodland a peculiar scent and the lazy hum of the cricket were entering into his room. As he gazed, the sleeping tank by the dark rows of trees glimmered like a polished silver plate. It is hard to say whether man at such a time thinks any clearly defined thought. Only his heart rushes in a particular direction—it sends forth an effusion of odour like the woodland, it utters a cricket hum like the night. What Rajib was thinking of I know not; but it seemed to him that that night all the old laws had been set aside; that day the rainy season's night had drawn aside her veil of clouds, and this night looked silent, beautiful and grave like the Mahamaya of those early days. All the currents of his being flowed impetuously together towards *that* Mahamaya.

Like one moving in a dream, Rajib entered Mahamaya's bedroom. She was asleep then.

He stood by her side and stooped down to gaze on her. The moonbeams had fallen on her face. But, Oh horror! where was that face known of old? The flame of the funeral pyre, with its ruthless greedy tongue, had utterly licked away a part of the beauty from the left cheek of Mahamaya and left there only the ravages of its hunger.

Did Rajib start? Did a muffled cry escape from his lips? Probably so. Mahamaya woke up with a start—and saw Rajib before her. At once she replaced her veil and stood erect, leaving her bed. Rajib knew that the thunderbolt was uplifted. He fell down before her—he clasped her feet, crying "forgive me!"

She answered not a word, she did not look back for a moment as she walked out of the room. She never came back. No trace of her was found anywhere. The parting left all the remaining days of Rajib's life branded with a long scar.

The Conclusion

Apurba had got his B.A. degree and was coming back home to his village. The river, which flowed past it, was a small one. It became dried up during the hot weather, but now in the July monsoon the heavy rains had swollen its current and it was full to the brim.

The boat, which carried Apurba, reached the *ghāt* whence the roof of his home could be seen through the dense foliage of the trees. Nobody knew that he was coming and therefore there was no one to receive him at the landing. The boatman offered to carry his bag, but Apurba picked it up himself, and took a leap from the boat. The bank was slippery, and he fell flat upon the muddy stair, bag and all.

As he did so, peal after peal of very sweet laughter rose in the sky, and startled the birds in the neighbouring trees. Apurba got up and tried to regain his composure as best as he could. When he sought for the source of his discomfiture, he found, sitting upon a heap of bricks lately unloaded from some cargo boat, a girl shaking her sides with laughter. Apurba recognized her as Mrinmayi, the daughter of their neighbour. This family had built their former house some distance away, but the river shifted its course cutting away into the land; and they had been obliged to change their quarter and settle down in the village only about two years ago.

Mrinmayi was the talk of all the village. The men called her 'madcap', but the village matrons were in a state of perpetual anxiety becuase of her untractable wildness. All her games were with the boys of the place, and she had the utmost contempt for the girls of her own age. The favourite child of her father, she had got into these unmanageable ways. Her mother would often complain to her friends of her husband's spoiling the child. But, because she was well aware that the father would be cut to the quick if he saw his daughter in tears, the mother had not the heart to punish the girl herself.

Mrinmayi's face was more like that of a boy than a girl. Her short crop of curly hair reached down to her shoulders, and her big dark eyes showed no sign of fear or shyness. When the boat, carrying the absentee landlord of the village, was moored at the landing stage, she did not share the feeling of awe which possessed the neighbourhood, but shook her curly mane and took up a naked child in her arms and was the first to come and take her observation of the habits of this strange creature.

Apurba had come in touch with this girl on former occasions, and he had got into the habit of thinking about her from time to time during his leisure, and even while at work. Naturally, therefore, this laughter, with which she greeted his arrival, did not please him, in spite of its musical quality. He gave up his bag to the boatman and almost ran away towards his house. The whole setting of things was romantic— the river bank, the shade of the trees, the morning sunshine with birds' songs, and his youth of twenty years. The brick heaps hardly fitted in with the picture, but the girl who sat on the top of them made up for all deficiencies.

2

The widowed mother was beside herself with joy when her son returned unexpectedly. She at once sent her men to all parts of the village to search for milk and curds and fish. There was quite a stir among the neighbours. After the midday meal, the mother ventured to suggest to Apurba that he should turn his thoughts towards marriage. Apurba was prepared for this attack, as it had been tried before, and he had then put it off on the plea of examinations. But now that he had got his degree, he could have no such excuse to delay the inevitable. So he told his mother that if a suitable bride could be discovered he could then make up his mind.

The mother said that the discovery had been already made, and therefore there was no further excuse for deliberation. But Apurba was of opinion that deliberation was necessary, and insisted on seeing the girl before consenting to marry her. The mother agreed to this, though the request seemed superfluous.

The next day Apurba went out on his marriage expedition. The intended bride lived in a house which was not far from their own. Apurba took special care about his dress before starting. He put on his new silk suit and a fashionable turban much affected by the Calcutta people. He did not forget to display his patent leather shoes and silk umbrella. His reception was loudly cordial in the house of his would-be father-in-law. The little victim—the intended bride—was scrubbed and painted, beribboned and bejewelled, and brought before Apurba. She sat in a corner of the room, veiled up to her chin, with her head nearly touching her knees, and her middle-aged maidservant at her back to encourage her when in trouble. Her young brother sat near closely observing Apurba—his turban, his watch-chain, his newly budding moustache.

Apurba solemnly asked the girl: "What text-books are you reading in your school?"

No answer came from this bundle of bashfulness wrapped in coloured silk. After repeated questionings and secret pushings in the back by the maidservant, she rapidly gave the names of all her lesson-books in one breath.

Just at this moment the sound of scampering feet was heard outside and Mrinmayi burst into the room very much out of breath. She did not give the least heed to Apurba, but at once caught hold of the hand of Rakhal, the young brother, and tried to drag him outside. But Rakhal was intently engaged in cultivating his faculty of observation and refused to stir. The maidservant tried to scold Mrinmayi, keeping the pitch of her voice within the proper limits of decorum. Aparba retained his composure and sat still and sullen, fondling the watch-chain with his fingers.

When Mrinmayi failed in her attempt to make Rakhal move, she gave the boy a sounding smack on the shoulder, then she pulled up the veil from the face of the intended bride, and rushed out of the room like a miniature tornado. The maidservant growled and grumbled and Rakhal began to laugh immoderately at the sudden unveiling of his sister. He evidently did not take ill the blow he had received, because they had with each other a running account of such amenities. There was once a time when Mrinmayi had her hair long enough to reach her waist, and it was Rakhal who had ploughed his scissors through it one day till the girl in disgust had snatched them from the boy's hand and completed the destruction herself, leaving a mass of curls lying upon the dust like a bunch of black grapes.

After this cataclysm, the business of the examination came to a sudden stop. The girl-bride rose from her seat and changed from a circle of misery into a straight line, and then disappeared into the inner apartment. Apurba got up, still stroking his moustache, only to discover that his patent leather shoes had vanished. A great search was made for them, but they were nowhere to be found. There was nothing else to do but to borrow from the head of the house a pair of old slippers, which were sadly out of keeping with the rest of his attire.

When Apurba reached the lane by the side of the village pool, the same peal of laughter rang through the sky which he had heard the day before; and while he stood shamefaced and irresolute, looking about him, the culprit came out of her ambuscade and flung the patent leather shoes before him and tried to escape. Apurba rushed after her quickly and made her captive, holding her by the wrist. Mrinmayi writhed and wriggled, but could not set herself free. A sunbeam fell upon her mischievous face through a gap in the branches overhead, and Apurba gazed intently into her eyes, like a traveller peering through the limpid water of a rushing stream at the glistening pebbles below. He seemed to hesitate to complete his adventure, and slowly relaxed his hold and let his captive escape. If Apurba had boxed Mrinmayi's ears in anger, that would have seemed more natural to the girl than this silent incompleteness of punishment.

3

It is difficult to understand why a young man of culture and learning like Apurba should be so anxious to reveal his worth to this slip of a village girl. What harm would there be, if, in her pitiful ignorance, she should ignore him and choose that foolish poor Rakhal as her companion? Why should he struggle to prove to her that he wrote a monthly article in the journal *Visvadip,* and that a manuscript book of no mean size was waiting for publication in the bottom of his trunk, along with his scent bottles, tinted note-paper, harmonium lessons, etc.

In the evening Apurba's mother asked him: "Have you approved of your bride?"

Apurba said with a slight hesitation: "Yes, I like one of the girls."

"One of the girls!" she asked, "why, what do you mean?"

After a great deal of beating about the bush she found out that her son had selected Mrinmayi for his bride. When she grasped this fact she greatly lost her respect for the B.A. degree. Then followed a long struggle between them. At last the mother persuaded herself that Mrinmayi was not wholly impervious to improvement. She began to suspect also that the girl's face had a charm of its own, but the next moment the cropped head of hair came to her mind and gave her a feeling of disgust. Recognizing, however, "that hair is more amenable to reason than human nature, she felt consoled, and the betrothal was made.

Mrinmayi's father got the news. He was a clerk in an office at a small distant river station of a steamship company. He was engaged all day in selling tickets and loading and unloading cargo, living in a small hut with a corrugated iron roof. His eyes overflowed with tears when he got the letter telling him what had happened. How much was pleasure and how much was pain would be difficult to analyse.

Ishan applied to the head office in Calcutta for leave of absence. The reason of the betrothal seemed insufficient to the English manager of the company and the application was rejected. Ishan then asked for a postponement of the marriage till the autumn holidays; but he was told by the mother of the bridegroom that the most auspicious day for the marriage that year fell in the last week of the current month. So Ishan went on selling tickets and loading and unloading cargo with a heavy heart—his petitions rejected from both sides. After this, Mrinmayi's mother and all the matrons of the village began to admonish the girl about the future household duties.

She was warned that love of play, quickness of movement, loudness of laughter, companionship of boys and disregard of good manners in eating would not be tolerated in her husband's house. They were completely successful in proving the terrible cramped constraint of married life. Mrinmayi took the proposal of her marriage as a sentence of life-imprisonment, with hanging at the end of it. Like an unmanageable little pony, she took the bit between her teeth and said, "I'm not going to be married."

4

But she had to marry after all. And then began her lesson. The whole universe shrank for her within the walls of her mother-in-law's household. The latter began at once her reformation duties. She hardened her face and said:

"My child, you are not a baby. The vulgar loudness of your behaviour won't suit our family."

The moral which Mrinmayi learnt from these words was that she must find some more suitable place for herself and she became invisible that very afternoon. They went on vainly searching for her till her friend Rakhal played the traitor, and revealed her hiding place in a deserted, broken down wooden chariot once used for taking out the image of the god for an airing. After this, the atmosphere of her mother-in-law's home became intolerably hot. Rain came down at night.

Apurba, coming close to Mrinmayi in his bed, whispered to her: "Mrinmayi, don't you love me?" Mrinmayi broke out: "No, I shall never love you!"

"But what harm have I done you?" said Apurba.

"Why did you marry me?" was the reply. To give a satisfactory explanation to this question was difficult, but Apurba said to himself: 'I must win, in the end, this rebellious heart.'

On the next day, the mother-in-law observed some signs of petulance in Mrinmayi and shut her up in a room. When Mrinmayi could find no way to get out, she tore the bed sheet to rags with her teeth in vain anger, and flinging herself on the floor burst out weeping and calling in agony: "Father, father!"

Just then somebody came and sat by her. He tried to arrange her dishevelled hair as she turned from side to side, but Mrinmayi angrily shook her head and pushed his hand away. Apurba (for it was he) bent his face to her ear and whispered:

"I have secretly opened the gate; let us run away by the back door."

Mrinmayi again violently shook her head and said: "No."

Apurba tried to raise her face gently by the chin saying: "Do look who is there." Rakhal had come and was standing foolishly by the door looking at Mrinmayi. But the girl pushed away Apurba's hand without raising her face.

He said "Rakhal has come to play with you. Won't you come?"

She said: "No!" Rakhal was greatly relieved to be allowed to run away from this scene.

Apurba sat still and silent. Mrinmayi wept and wept, till she was so tired that she fell asleep; then Apurba went out silently and shut the door.

The next day Mrinmayi received a letter from her father, in which he expressed his regret for not being able to be present at the marriage of his darling daughter. He ended with his blessings. The girl went to her mother-in-law and said: "I must go to my father."

A scolding began at once: "Your father! what a thing to ask. Your father has no decent house for himself—how can you go to him?"

Mrinmayi came back to her room in despair and cried to herself, "Father, take me away from this place! I have nobody here to love me. I shall die if I am left here."

In the depth of the night, when her husband fell asleep, she quietly opened the door and went out of the house. It was cloudy, yet the moonlight was strong enough to show her the path. But Mrinmayi had no idea which was the way to reach her father. She had a belief that the road, which the post runners took, led to all the addresses of all the men in the world.

So she went that way, and was quite tired out with walking when the night was nearly ended.

The early birds doubtfully twittered their greetings to the morning, when Mrinmayi came to the end of the road at the river-bank where there was a big bazaar. Just then she heard the clatter of the iron ring of the mail runner. She rushed to him and in her eager, tired voice cried: "I want to go to my father at Kushiganj. Do take me with you."

The postman told her hurriedly that he did not know where Kushiganj was and the next moment wakened up the boatman of the mail boat and sailed away. He had no time either to pity or to question.

By the time Mrinmayi had descended the landing stairs and called a boat, the street and the river-bank were fully awake. Before the boatman could answer, some one from a boat near at hand called out:

"Hallo, Mrinu! How on earth could you get here?"

The girl replied in all eagerness: "Banamali, I must go to my father at Kushiganj. Please take me in your boat!"

This boatman belonged to her own village and knew all about the wild untameable girl. He said to her: "You want to go to your father? That's good. I'll take you."

Mrinmayi got into the boat. The clouds thickened and the rain came down in showers. The river, swollen by the monsoon, rocked the boat, and Mrinmayi fell asleep. When she woke up, she found herself in her own bed in her mother-in-law's house.

The maidservant began scolding her the moment she saw her awake. The mother-in-law came next. As she entered, Mrinmayi opened her eyes wide and silently looked in her face. But when the mother-in-law made a reference to the ill-breeding of Mrinmayi's family, the girl rushed out of her room and entered the next and shut the door from the inside.

Apurba came to his mother and said: "Mother, I don't see any harm in sending Mrinmayi for just a few days to her father's house."

The mother's reply was to scold Apurba in unmeasured terms for selecting this one girl from all the suitable brides who might have been had for the mere asking.

5

In the middle of the night, Apurba awakened Mrinmayi and said: "Mrinmayi, are you ready to go to your father?" She clutched his hand and said: "Yes."

Apurba whispered: "Then come. Let us run away from this place. I have got a boat ready at the landing. Come."

Mrinmayi cast a grateful glance at her husband's face, and got up and dressed, and was ready to go. Apurba left a letter for his mother, and then both of them left the house together hand in hand.

This was the first time that Mrinmayi had put her hand into her husband's with a spontaneous feeling of dependence. They went on their journey along the lonely village road through the depth of the night.

When they reached the landing stage, they got into a boat, and in spite of the turbulent joy which she felt Mrinmayi fell asleep. The next day—what emancipation, what unspeakable bliss it was! They passed by all the different villages, markets, cultivated fields, and groups of boats at anchor near some *ghāt*. Mrinmayi began to ply her husband with questions about every little trifle: where were those boats coming from, what were their cargoes, what was the name of that village?— questions whose answers were not in the text-books which Apurba studied in his college. His friends might be concerned to hear that Apurba's answers did not always tally with the truth. He would not hesitate for a moment to describe bags of sesame as linseed, and the village of Panchbere as Rainagar, or to point out the district magistrate's court as the landlord's office. Whatever answer she got, Mrinmayi was fully satisfied, never doubting its accuracy.

The next day the boat reached Kushiganj. Ishan, seated on his office stool, in his hut dimly lighted with a square oil-lantern, was deep in his accounts before his small desk, his big ledger open before him, when this young pair entered the room. Mrinmayi at once called out:

"Father!"

Such a word, uttered in so sweet a voice, had never sounded before in that corrugated iron room. Ishan could hardly restrain his tears and sat dumb for a moment, vainly seeking for some greeting. He was in great confusion how fitly to receive the young married couple in his office, crowded with bales of jute and piled up ledgers, which had also to serve him for a bedroom. And then about the meals—the poor man had to cook for himself his own simple dinner, but how could he offer that to his guests? Mrinmayi said, "Father, let us cook the food ourselves."

And Apurba joined in this proposal with great zest. In this room, with all its lack of space for man and food, their joy welled up in full abundance, like the jet of water thrown up all the higher because the opening of the fountain is narrow.

Three days were passed in this manner. Steamers came to stop at the landing stage all day long with their noisy crowd of men. At last, in the evening, the river-bank would become deserted and then—what freedom! And the cooking preparations in which the art of cookery was not carried to its perfection—what fun it was! And the jokes and mock quarrels about the mock deficiencies in Mrinmayi's domestic skill—what absurd carryings on! But it had to come to an end at last. Apurba did not dare to prolong his French leave, and Ishan also thought it was wise for them to return.

When the culprits reached home, the mother remained sulkily silent. She never even blamed them for what they had done so as to give them an opportunity to explain their conduct. This sullen silence became at last intolerable, and Apurba expressed his intention of going back to college in order to study Law. The mother, affecting indifference, said to him: "What about your wife?"

Apurba answered: "Let her remain here."

"Oh, no, no!" cried the mother, "you should take her with you."

Apurba said in a voice of annoyance: "Very well."

The preparation went on for their departure to the town, and on the night before leaving Apurba, coming to his bed, found Mrinmayi in tears. This hurt him greatly and he cried:

Mrinmayi, don't you want to come to Calcutta with me?"

The girl replied: "No!"

Apurba's next question was, "Don't you love me?" But the question remained unanswered. There are times when answers to such questions are absolutely simple, but at other times they become too complex for a young girl to answer.

Apurba asked : "Do you feel unwilling to leave Rakhal behind?"

Mrinmayi instantly answered: "Yes". For a moment this young man, who was proud of his B.A. degree, felt a needle prick of jealousy deep down in his heart, and said:

"I shan't be able to come back home for a long time." Mrinmayi had nothing to say. "It may be two years or more," he added. Mrinmayi told him with coolness, "You had better bring back with you, for Rakhal, a Roger's knife with three blades."

Apurba sat up and asked:

"Then you mean to stay on here?"

Mrinmayi said:

"Yes, I shall go to my own mother."

Apurba breathed a deep sigh and said:

"Very well: I shall not come home, until you write me a letter asking me to come to you. Are you very, very glad?"

Mrinmayi thought this question needed no answer, and fell asleep. Apurba got no sleep that night.

When it was nearly dawn, Apurba awakened Mrinmayi and said:

"Mrinu, it is time to go. Let me take you to your mother's house."

When his wife got up from her bed, Apurba held her by both hands and said:

"I have a prayer to make to you. I have helped you several times and I want to claim my reward."

Mrinmayi was surprised and said:

"What?"

Apurba answered:

"Mrinu, give me a kiss out of pure love."

When the girl heard this absurd request and saw Apurba's solemn face, she burst out laughing. When it was over, she held her face for a kiss, but broke out laughing again. After a few more attempts, she gave it up. Apurba pulled her ear gently as a mild punishment.

7

When Mrinmayi came to her mother's house, she was surprised to find that it was not as pleasant to her as before. Time seemed to hang heavily on her hands, and she wondered in her mind what was lacking in the familiar home surroundings. Suddenly it seemed to her that the whole house and village were deserted and she longed to go to Calcutta. She did not know that even on that last night the earlier portion of her life, to which she clung, had changed its aspect before she knew it. Now she could easily shake off her past associations as the tree sheds its dead leaves. She did not understand that her destiny had struck the blow and severed her youth from her childhood, with its magic blade, in such a subtle manner that they kept together even after the stroke; but directly she moved, one half of her life fell from the other and Mrinmayi looked at it in wonder. The young girl, who used to occupy the old bedroom in this house, no longer existed; all her memory hovered round another bed in another bedroom.

Mrinmayi refused to go out of doors any longer, and her laughter had a strangely different ring. Rakhal became slightly afraid of her. He gave up all thought of playing with her.

One day, Mrinmayi came to her mother and asked her: "Mother, please take me to my mother-in-law's house."

After this, one morning the mother-in-law was surprised to see Mrinmayi come and touch the ground with her forehead before her feet. She got up at once and took her in her arms. Their union was complete in a moment, and the cloud of misunderstanding was swept away leaving the atmosphere glistening with the radiance of tears.

When Mrinmayi's body and mind became filled with womanhood, deep and tender, it gave her an aching pain. Her eyes became sad, like the shadow of rain upon some lake, and she put these questions to her husband in her own mind—'Why did you not have the patience to understand me, when I was late in understanding you? Why did you put up with my disobedience, when I refused to follow you to Calcutta?'

Suddenly she came to fathom the look in Apurba's eyes when, on that morning, he had caught hold of her hand by the village pool and then slowly released her. She remembered, too, the futile flights of that kiss, which had never reached its goal, and was now like a thirsty bird haunting that past opportunity. She recollected how Apurba had said to her that he would never come back until he had received from her a message asking him to do so; and she sat down at once to write a letter. The gilt-edged notepaper which Apurba had given her was brought out of its box, and with great care she began to write in a big hand, smudging her fingers with ink. With her first word she plunged into the subject without addressing him:

Why don't you write to me? How are you? And please come home.

She could think of no other words to say. But though the important message had been given, yet unfortunately the unimportant words occupy the greatest space in human communication. She racked her brains to add a few more words to what she had written, and then wrote:

This time don't forget to write me letters and write how you are, and come back home, and mother is quite well. Our black cow had a calf last night—

Here she came to the end of her resources. She put her letter into the envelope and poured out all her love as she wrote the name: Srijukta Babu Apurbakrishna Roy. She did not know that anything more was needed by way of an address, so the letter did not reach its goal, and the postal authorities were not to blame for it.

It was vacation time. Yet Apurba never came home. The mother thought that he was nourishing anger against her. Mrinmayi was certain that her letter was not well enough written to satisfy him. At last the mother said to her daughter-in-law, "Apurba has been absent for so long that I am thinking of going to Calcutta to see him. Would you like to come with me?"

Mrinmayi gave a violent nod of assent. Then she ran to her room and shut herself in. She fell upon her bed, clutched the pillow to her breast, and gave vent to her feelings by laughing and excited movements. When this fit was over, she became grave and sad and sat up on the bed and wept in silence.

Without telling Apurba, these two repentant women went to Calcutta to ask for Apurba's forgiveness. The mother had a son-in-law in Calcutta, and so she put up at his house. That very same evening, Apurba broke his promise and began to write a letter to Mrinmayi. But he found no terms of endearment fit to express his love, and felt disgusted with his mother tongue for its poverty. But when he got a letter from his brother-in-law, informing him of the arrival of his mother and inviting him to dinner, he hastened to his sister's house without delay.

The first question he asked his mother, when he met her, was: "Mother, is everybody at home quite well?"

The mother answered: "Yes, I have come here to take you back home."

Apurba said that he thought it was not necessary on her part to have taken all this trouble for such a purpose, and he had his examination before him, etc., etc.

At dinner his sister asked him why he had not brought his wife with him when he returned to Calcutta this time. Apurba began to say very solemnly that he had his law examination to think of, etc., etc.

The brother-in-law cut in smiling:

"All this is a mere excuse: the real reason is that he is afraid of us."

His sister replied: "You are indeed a terrifying person! The poor child may well get a shock when she sees you."

Thus the laughter and jokes became plentiful, but Apurba remained silent. He was accusing his mother in his mind for not having had the consideration to bring Mrinmayi with her. Then he thought that possibly his mother had tried, but failed, owing to Mrinmayi's unwillingness, and he felt afraid even to question his mother about it; the whole scheme of things seemed to him full of incorrigible blunders.

When the dinner was over, it came on to rain and his sister said, "*Dada,* you sleep here."

But Apurba replied, "No, I must go home. I have work to do."

The brother-in-law said, "How absurd! You have no one at home to call you to account for your absence, and you needn't be anxious."

Then his sister told him that he was looking very tired, and it was better for him to leave the company and go to bed. Apurba went to his bed-room and found it in darkness. His sister asked him if he wanted a light, but he said that he preferred the dark. When his sister had left, he groped his way to the bedstead and prepared to get into bed.

All of a sudden a tender pair of arms, with a jingle of bracelets, were flung round his neck, and two lips soft as flower petals almost smothered him with kisses wet with tears.

At first it startled Apurba greatly, but then he came to know that those kisses, which had been obstructed once by laughter, had now found their completion in tears.

The Parrot's Training

Once upon a time there was a bird. It was ignorant. It sang all right, but never recited scriptures. It hopped pretty frequently, but lacked manners.

Said the Raja to himself: 'Ignorance is costly in the long run. For fools consume as much food as their betters, and yet give nothing in return.'

He called his nephews to his presence and told them that the bird must have a sound schooling.

The pundits were summoned, and at once went to the root of the matter. They decided that the ignorance of birds was due to their natural habit of living in poor nests. Therefore, according to the pundits, the first thing necessary for this bird's education was a suitable cage.

The pundits had their rewards and went home happy.

A golden cage was built with gorgeous decorations. Crowds came to see it from all parts of the world.

"Culture, captured and caged!" exclaimed some, in a rapture of ecstasy, and burst into tears.

Others remarked: "Even if culture be missesd, the cage will remain, to the end, a substantial fact. How fortunate for the bird!"

The goldsmith filled his bag with money and lost no time in sailing homewards.

The pundit sat down to educate the bird. With proper deliberation he took his pinch of snuff, as he said: "Text-books can never be too many for our purpose!"

The nephews brought together an enormous crowd of scribes. They copied from books, and copied from copies, till the manuscripts were piled up to an unreachable height.

Men murmured in amazement: "Oh, the tower of culture, egregiously high! The end of it lost in the clouds!"

The scribes, with light hearts, hurried home, their pockets heavily laden.

The nephews were furiously busy keeping the cage in proper trim.

As their constant scrubbing and polishing went on, the people said with satisfaction: "This is progress indeed!"

Men were employed in large numbers, and supervisors were still more numerous. These, with their cousins of all different degrees of distance, built a palace for themselves and lived there happily ever after.

Whatever may be its other deficiencies, the world is never in want of fault-finders; and they went about saying that every creature remotely connected with the cage flourished beyond words, excepting only the bird.

When this remark reached the Raja's ears, he summoned his nephews before him and said: "My dear nephews, what is this that we hear?"

The nephews said in answer: "Sire, let the testimony of the goldsmiths and the pundits, the scribes and the supervisors, be taken, if the truth is to be known food is scarce with the fault-finders, and that is why their tongues have gained in sharpness."

The explanation was so luminously satisfactory that the Raja decorated each one of his nephews with his own rare jewels.

The Raja at length, being desirous of seeing with his own eyes how his Education Department busied itself with the little bird, made his appearance one day at the great Hall of Learning.

From the gate rose the sounds of conch-shells and gongs, horns, bugles and trumpets, cymbals, drums and kettle-drums, tomtoms, tambourines, flutes, fifes, barrel-organs and bagpipes. The pundits began chanting *mantras* with their topmost voices, while the goldsmiths, scribes, supervisors, and their numberless cousins of all different degrees of distance, loudly raised a round of cheers.

The nephews smiled and said: "Sire, what do you think of it all?"

The Raja said: "It does seem so fearfully like a sound principle of Education!"

Mightily pleased, the Raja was about to remount his elephant, when the fault-finder, from behind some bush, cried out: "Maharaja, have you seen the bird?"

"Indeed, I have not!" exclaimed the Raja, "I completely forgot about the bird."

Turning back, he asked the pundits about the method they followed in instructing the bird.

It was shown to him. He was immensely impressed. The method was so stupendous that the bird looked ridiculously unimportant in comparison. The Raja was satisfied that there was no flaw in the arrangements. As for any complaint from the bird itself, that simply could not be expected. Its throat was so completely choked with the leaves from the books that it could neither whistle nor whisper. It sent a thrill through one's body to watch the process.

This time, while remounting his elephant, the Raja ordered his State Earpuller to give a thorough good pull at both the ears of the fault-finder.

The bird thus crawled on, duly and properly, to the safest verge of inanity. In fact, its progress was satisfactory in the extreme. Nevertheless, nature occasionally triumphed over training, and when the morning light peeped into the bird's cage it sometimes fluttered its wings in a reprehensible manner. And, though it is hard to believe, it pitifully pecked at its bars with its feeble beak.

"What impertinence!" growled the *kotwal*.

The blacksmith, with his forge and hammer, took his place in the Raja's Department of Education. Oh, what resounding blows! The iron chain was soon completed, and the bird's wings were clipped.

The Raja's brothers-in-law looked black, and shook their heads, saying: "These birds not only lack good sense, but also gratitude!"

With text-book in one hand and baton in the other, the pundits gave the poor bird what may fitly be called lessons!

The *kotwal* was honoured with a title for his watchfulness and the blacksmith for his skill in forging chains.

The bird died.

Nobody had the least notion how long ago this had happened. The fault-finder was the first man to spread the rumour.

The Raja called his nephews and asked them: "My dear nephews, what is this that we hear?"

The nephews said: "Sire, the bird's education has been completed."

"Does it hop?" the Raja enquired.

"Never!" said the nephews.

"Does it fly?"

"No."

"Bring me the bird," said the Raja.

The bird was brought to him, guarded by the *kotwal* and the sepoys and the sowars. The Raja poked its body with his finger. Only its inner stuffing of book-leaves rustled.

Outside the window, the murmur of the spring breeze amongst the newly budded *asoka* leaves made the April morning wistful.

The Trial of the Horse

Brahma, the creator, was very near the end of his task of creation when a new idea struck him.

He sent for the Store-keeper and said: "O keeper of the stores, bring to my factory a quantity of each of the five elements. For I am ready to create another creature."

"Lord of the universe," the Store-keeper replied, "when in the first flush of creative extravagance you began to turn out such exaggerations as elephants and whales and pythons and tigers, you took no count of the stock. Now, all the elements that have density and force are nearly used up. The supply of earth and water and fire has become inconveniently scanty, while of air and ether there is as much as is good for us and a good deal more."

The four-headed deity looked perplexed and pulled at his four pairs of moustaches. At last he said: "The limitedness of material gives all the more scope to originality. Send me whatever you have left."

This time Brahma was excessively sparing with the earth, water and fire. The new creature was not given either horns or claws, and his teeth were only meant for chewing, not for biting. The prudent care with which fire was used in his formation made him necessary in war without making him warlike.

This animal was the Horse.

The reckless expenditure of air and ether, which went into his composition, was amazing. And, in consequence, he perpetually struggled to outreach the wind, to outrun space itself. The other animals run only when they have a reason, but the horse would run for nothing whatever, as if to run out of his own skin. He had no desire to chase, or to kill, but only to fly on and on till he dwindled into a dot, melted into a swoon, blurred into a shadow, and vanished into vacancy.

The Creator was glad. He had given for his other creatures habitations—to some the forests, to other the caves. But in his enjoyment of the disinterested spirit of speed in the Horse, he gave him an open meadow under the very eye of heaven.

By the side of this meadow lived Man.

Man has his delight in pillaging and piling things up. And he is never happy till these grow into a burden. So, when he saw this new creature pursuing the wind and kicking at the sky, he said to himself: "If only I can bind and secure this Horse, I can use his broad back for carrying my loads."

So one day he caught the Horse.

Then Man put a saddle on the Horse's back and a spiky bit in his mouth. He regularly had hard rubbing and scrubbing to keep him fit, and there were the whip and spurs to remind him that it was wrong to have his own will.

Man also put high walls round the Horse, lest if left at large in the open the creature might escape him.

So it came to pass, that while the Tiger who had his forest remained in the forest, the Lion who had his cave remained in the cave, the Horse who once had his open meadow came to spend his days in a stable. Air and ether had roused in the horse longings for deliverance, but they swiftly delivered him into bondage.

When he felt that bondage did not suit him, the Horse kicked at the stable walls.

But this hurt his hoofs much more than it hurt the wall. Still some of the plaster came off and the wall lost its beauty.

Man felt aggrieved.

"What ingratitude!" he cried. "Do I not give him food and drink? Do I not keep highly-paid men-servants to watch over him day and night? Indeed he is hard to please."

In their desperate attempts to please the Horse, the men-servants fell upon him and so vigorously applied all their winning methods that he lost his power to kick and a great deal more besides.

Then Man called his friends and neighbours together, and said to them exultingly: "Friends, did you ever see so devoted a steed as mine?"

"Never!" they replied. "He seems as still as ditch water and as mild as the religion you profess."

The Horse, as is well known, had no horns, no claws, nor adequate teeth, at his birth. And, when on the top of this, all kicking at the walls and even into emptiness had been stopped, the only way to give vent to his feelings was to neigh.

But that disturbed Man's sleep.

Moreover, this neighing was not likely to impress the neighbours as a paean of devotion and thankfulness. So Man invented devices to shut the Horse's mouth.

But the voice cannot be altogether suppressed so long as the mistake is made of leaving any breath in the body. Therefore a spasmodic sound of moaning came from his throat now and then.

One day this noise reached Brahma's ears.

The Creator woke up from his meditation. It gave him a start when he glanced at the meadow and saw no sign of the Horse.

"This is all your doing," cried Brahma, in anger to Yama, the god of death: "You have taken away the Horse !"

"Lord of all creatures!" Death replied: "All your worst suspicions you keep only for me. But most of the calamities in your beautiful world will be explained if you turn your eyes in the direction of Man."

Brahma looked below. He saw a small enclosure, walled in, from which the dolorous moaning of his Horse came fitfully.

Brahma frowned in anger.

"Unless you set free my Horse," said he: "I shall take care that he grows teeth and claws like the Tiger."

"That would be ungodly," cried man: "to encourage ferocity. All the same, if I may speak plain truth about a creature of your own make, this Horse is not fit to be set free. It was for his eternal good that I built him this stable—this marvel of architecture."

Brahma remained obdurate.

"I bow to your wisdom," said Man: "but if, after seven days, you still think that your meadow is better for him than my stable, I will humbly own defeat."

After this Man set to work.

He made the Horse go free, but hobbled his front legs. The result was so vastly diverting that it was enough to make even a frog burst his sides with laughter.

Brahma, from the height of his heaven, could see the comic gait of his Horse, but not the tragic rope which hobbled him. He was mortified to find his own creature openly exposing its divine maker to ridicule.

"It was an absurd blunder of mine", he cried, "closely touching the sublime."

"Grandsire," said Man with a pathetic show of sympathy, "what can I do for this unfortunate creature? If there is a meadow in your heaven, I am willing to take trouble to transport him thither."

"Take him back to your stable!" cried Brahma in dismay.

"Merciful God!" cried Man, "what a great burden it will be for mankind!"

"It is the burden of humanity," muttered Brahma.

Old Man's Ghost

At the time of the Old Man Leader's death, the entire population wailed, "What will be our lot when you go?"

Hearing this, the Old Man himself felt sad. 'Who indeed,' thought he, 'will keep these people quiescent when I have gone?'

Death cannot be evaded, however. Yet the gods took pity and said: "Why worry? Let this fellow go on sitting on their shoulders even as a ghost. Man dies but a ghost does not."

The people of the country were greatly relieved.

For, worries come if only you believe in a future. Believing in ghosts you are freed from burden, all the worries enter the ghost's head. Yet the ghost has no head, so it does not suffer from headaches either, not for anybody's sake.

Those, who out of sheer wrong habit still attempt to think for themselves, get their ears boxed by the ghost. From this ghostly boxing you can neither free yourself nor can you escape it; against it is neither appeal nor any judgement at all.

The entire population, ghost-ridden, now walks with eyes shut. "The most ancient form of movement, this, with eyes shut," the philosophers assure them, "moving like blind fate, we call it. Thus moved the first eyeless amoeba. In the grass, in the trees, this habit of movement is still customary."

Hearing which, the ghost-ridden land feels its own primitive aristocracy. And it is greatly delighted.

The Ghost's *nayeb* is the inspector of the prison. The walls of the prison-house are not visible to the eye. And so it is impossible to imagine how to pierce those walls and get free.

In the prison-house one has to slave at turning the oil-press night and day but not even an ounce of oil is produced which is marketable; only the energy of men goes out in extracting the oil. When their energy goes out, men become exceedingly peaceful. And thus in that ghost's realm whatever else there might not be—food, or clothing or health—tranquillity remains.

How great is the tranquillity is proved by one example: in other lands excessive ghostly tyranny makes men restless and seek for a medicine-man. Here such a thought cannot arise. For the medicine-man himself has already been possessed by the ghost.

Thus the days would have passed; nobody would have questioned the ghostly administration. Forever they could have taken pride that their future, like a pet lamb, was tied to the ghost's peg; such a creature neither bleated nor baa'd, it sprawled dumb on the dust, useless as dust.

Only, for a slight reason, some little trouble arose. It was that the other countries of the world were not ghost-ridden. Their oil-presses turned so that the extracted oil might be used for keeping the wheels of men's chariots moving forward, not for crushing the heart and pouring heart's blood into the paws of the ghost. So, men there have not yet been completely pacified. They were terribly wakeful.

All over the ghostly empire: *the baby sleeps; quiet is the neighbourhood.*

That is comforting for the baby, and for the baby's guardian too; as to the neighbourhood, we have already seen how it is.

But there is the other line, *"the invaders enter the land."*

Thus the rhythm is completed—otherwise for lack of one foot, this history would have been crippled.

The pedants and pundits are asked: "Why is it thus?"

They toss their heads together and say: "Not the ghost's fault this, nor of the ghost-ridden land: the fault lies with the invader. Why does the invader come?"

"How right!" they all admit. And everyone feels exceedingly comforted.

Whosever the fault might be, near the back-door of the house loiter the ghost's emissaries, and in the open street outside everywhere roam the non-ghost's emissaries; the householder can hardly stay in his house, to stir out of doors is also impossible. From one side they shout "pay the taxes?" and from the other also they shout "pay the taxes!"

Now the problem is, *"how to pay the taxes?"*

Up to now, from north, south, east and west, *bulbulis* of all species have come in large flocks, and gorged themselves with the corn, nobody was mindful. With all those who are mindful, these people avoid contact, lest they have to do *prāyashchitta* for contamination. But those other folk who are mindful have a way of coming suddenly very near to them indeed and they do not observe any penance either.

The pedants and pundits open the text and say: "Pure are the unmindful, and impure the mindful ones; so be indifferent to these latter. Remember the sacred words, 'awake are those who sleepeth.'"

And hearing this the people are hugely delighted.

But, in spite of this, the query cannot be stopped, *"how to pay the taxes?"*

From the burning-ground, from the burial-ground the wild winds bring the loud answer: "Pay the taxes with the price of your modesty, with your honour, with your conscience, with your heart's blood."

The trouble with questions is: when they come they do not come singly. So, another question has arisen: "Will the ghostly reign itself remain for ever?"

Hearing this, all the lullaby-singing aunts and uncles put their hands on their ears in horror and exclaim: "Perdition! Never in our fathers' life have we heard of such a thing! What will then have happened to our sleep, the most ancient sleep, the sleep which is earlier than all awakening?"

"That I see", the questioner persists: "but these most modern flocks of *bulbulis* and these very much present invaders—what about *them*?"

"To the *bulbulis* we shall repeat the name of Krishna," assert the aunts and uncles, "and so shall we do to the invaders."

The ignorant youths get impertinent and bluster out; "Drive the ghost out we shall—whatever the means."

The ghost's *nayeb* rolls his eyes in anger and shouts, "Shut up! The oil-press hasn't stopped grinding. No, not yet."

Hearing which the baby of the land falls silent, and then turns to sleep.

The great fact is, the Old Man is neither alive nor dead, but is a ghost. He neither stirs the country up nor ever relaxes his grip.

Inside the country,. one or two men—those who never utter a word in daytime for fear of the *nayeb*—join their palms together and implore: "Old Man Leader, is it not yet time for you to leave us?"

"You fool," answers the Old Man, "I neither hold, nor let go; if you leave, then I have also left."

"But we are afraid, Old Man Leader!"

"That is where the ghost enters,"—comes the answer.

Great News

Said Kusmi "You would give me all the big news—so you promised, didn't you, *Dādāmashāy* How else could I get educated?"

Answered *Dādāmashāy:* "But such a sack of big news there would be to carry—with so much of rubbish in it."

"Why not leave those out?"

"Little else would remain, then. And that remainder you will think as small news. But that would be the real news."

"Give it to me—the real news."

"So I will."

"Well, *Dādāmashāy* let me see what skill you have. Tell me the great news of these days, making it ever so small."

"Listen."

Work was proceeding in peace.

In a *mahājani* boat there started a row between the sail and the oars.

The oars came clattering to the court of the Boatman, and said: "This cannot be endured any longer. That braggart sail of yours, swelling himself, calls us *chhoto lok*. Because we, tied night and day to the lower planks, must toil, pushing the waters as we proceed, while he moves by whim, not caring for the push of any one's hand. And so he is a *bara lok*. You must decide who is more worthy. If we are *chhoto lok* the inferior ones, we shall resign in a body. Let us see how you make your boat move."

The Boatman, seeing danger ahead, called the oars aside and whispered secretly: "Do not give ear to his words, brothers. He speaks an empty language, that sail. If you strong fellows did not work away, staking life and death, the boat would lie inert altogether. And that sail—he sits there in hallow luxury, perched on the top. At the slightest touch of stormy wind he flops, folds himself up, and lies low on the boat's thatch. Then all his vain flutterings are silenced, not a word from him at all. But in weal and woe, in danger and in crisis, on the way to the market and the ghat, you are my constant support. It is a pity that you have to carry that useless burden of luxury, to and fro. Who says you are *chhoto lok?*"

But the Boatman was afraid, lest these words be overheard by the sail. So he came to him and whispered into his ear: "Mr. Sail, none ever can be compared with you. Who says that you drive the boat, that is the work of labourers. You move at your own pleasure, and your pals and comrades follow you at your slightest gesture and bidding. And whenever you feel out of breath, you would flop down easefully, and rest. Do not lend your ear, friend, to the parleying of those low-bred oars; so firmly have I tied them up, that splutter as they might, they cannot but work as slaves."

Hearing this, the sail stretched himself, and yawned mightily.

But the signs were not good. Those oars are hard-boned fellows, now they lie aslant but who knows when they will stand up straight, slap at the sail and shatter his pride into shreds. Then the world would know that it is the oars who make the boat move, come storm come tornado, whether it be upstream or at ebb-tide.

Queried Kusmi: "Your big news, is it so small as this? You are joking."

Said *Dādāmashāy*: "Joking it seems to be. Very soon this news will become big indeed."

"And then?"

"Then your *Dādāmashāy* will practise keeping time with the strokes of those oars."

"And I?"

"Where the oars creak too muck, you will pour a drop of oil."

Dādāmashāy continued: "True news appears small, like the seeds. And then comes the tree with its branches and foliage. Do you understand now?"

"So I do," said Kusmi. Her face showed that she had not understood. But Kusmi had one virture, she would not easily admit it to her *Dādāmashāy* that she would not understand. That she is less clever than *Iru Māshi* is better kept concealed.

SHESH LEKHA

For My Parents

(Translator's dedication)

Preface

Rabindranath Tagore wrote most of these poems on his death bed, during the last few weeks before he died on 7th August 1941. The book *Shesh Lekha*, where all these fifteen untitled poems appeared, was published posthumously in 1942. What strikes one immediately on reading these poems about death and renewal is the sense of serene melancholy that informs the diction, a rich and sensuous understanding of the tones and textures of mortality. Studied in the context of his later work, it shows how the four last books *Prantik* (1938), *Rogsajya* (1940), *Arogya* (1941) and *Shesh Lekha* (1942) despite their apparent contradictions cohere to form one intricate experience, disquietingly simple, reiterating the triumphant theme that in death there is nothing to fear.

This book contains the poem Tagore dictated the morning of the operation from which he never regained consciousness. And the poem which he chose to be sung at his commemoration service. These poems all show a new certainty that surfaced after he passed through a critical illness in 1937 from which he never really recovered in full. They reveal a deep and sensitive understanding of man's relation to the universe. Quiet poems of short focus and understatement but of great perspective in their untroubled contemplation of what death can mean. They show that the whole universe is life, shaped with a love over which death has no power. Words are gently and precisely orchestrated to highlight each separate tone and facet and the total effect is a devastating confrontation with death. All the more powerful because it is so quiet and supremely confident. The message is almost haunting in its simplicity: death is but a new birth of the spirit into the great unknown.

Pritish Nandy

1

Before me stretches the ocean of peace:
helmsman, launch me.
Be my eternal companion,
take me in your arms.
The road to eternity will be lit
by the pole star.

Bestower of freedom,
your forgiveness, your mercy
shall sustain me forever
as I journey towards eternity.

May mortal bonds decay,
may the great universe embrace me
and in my heart know without fear
the great unknown.

Shantiniketan: 3 December 1939

2

Death like Rahu
casts shadows only
but cannot sap life's divine ambrosia:
entrapped by this material world
this I know for sure.

The eternal value of love
cannot be stolen
by any plunderer lurking
in secret caves of the universe:
this I know for sure.

What I found as most true
hid inherent falsehood in guise:
this disgrace of life
the laws of universe will not bear,
this I know for sure.

Everything moves by the ceaseless force of change:
this is the law of time.
Death appears changeless
and cannot therefore be true:
this I know for sure.

He who knows this world exists
realises himself,
as a witness of all that exists,
his truth is in the truth of that ultimate self:
this I know for sure.

Shantiniketan: 7 May 1940

3

Bird,
why do you forget your song at times?
Why not sing on?
A songless dawn is futile:
are you not aware of this?

The first touch of dawn
trembles on green trees:
in that tremor is your song
that wakes amongst the leaves.
You are the one this morning loves:
are you not aware of this?

The goddess of awakening is there:
she waits for me
her anchal spread:
are you not aware of this?

Do not deprive her
of the gift of your song.
After the dreams of a sorrowful night
your morning song
brings the message of a new life:
are you not aware of this?

Shantiniketan: 17 February 1941

4

The sun flames
on this lonely afternoon.
I stare at the vacant chair.
I find no consolation there.
In its breast
echoes the haunting voice of despair.

The voice of emptiness is filled with pity:
the message escapes.
Like the tragic eyes of a dog without its master

laments a heart that cannot understand
what happened and why.
All day and night its eyes search in vain.
The chair speaks with greater sorrow,
the dumb pain of the void
spreads in this room without you.

Shantiniketan: 26 March 1941

5

If I can once again
I shall find that chair
in whose embrace remains
the loving message of a distant land.

Escaped dreams of the past
shall crowd there again,
their half-heard murmurs
shall build a nest again.
Recalling pleasant memories,
making awakening sweet,
the flute that is now silent
shall bring back its melodies.

Arms outstretched near the window,
on the fragrant path of spring,
the footsteps of that great silence
shall be heard at night.

With the love of a distant land
she who has waited for long

will sustain her nearness forever,
her whispers resound in my ears.

She, whom words failed,
who spoke only with her eyes,
this chair will keep awake forever
memories of her tristful voice.

Shantiniketan: 6 April 1941

6

There comes the man supreme:
the world is thrilled,
grassblades quiver,
conches resound in the heavens,
gongs of victory sound on earth.
This sacred moment brings the great birth.

The forts of the moonless night
are ruins today.
On the hilltops dawn echoes:
fear not, fear not.
Hopes of a new life emerge.
Hail the new man:
the cosmos reverberates with this cry.

Shantiniketan: 1 Baisakh 1348

7

Life is sacred I know:
but its actual form I have never grasped.
From some mysterious fountainhead

it breaks
and travels down some wandering route
I cannot trace.
It gains a new purity each morning
from the dawn:
a million miles away
I fill this golden vessel with its lustre.

That life gave voice to the day and night:
it worshipped the unseen with wild flowers
and lit clay lamps
in the silent dusk.
My heart offered it
the first love of my life.
All routine loves
touched by its golden wand
are awake today:
my love for her,
for these flowers,
all these are its very own
by its touch.

At birth the book is brought, its pages blank:
it slowly fills with words each day.
Stringing bead after bead about oneself
the portrait emerges at day's end.
The painter recognises himself
by his own signature.
Then he lines through the words, the forms
with an indifferent stroke of black.
Only a few words in gold remain distinct:
they wake radiant beside the pole star.

Shantiniketan: 25 April 1941

8

In the fifth year of marriage
with the intimacy of an youth
full of mysteries,
secret juices ripen within the heart:
from the buds to clusters of fruit,
from stalk to fragile petal
spreads a golden glow.
A strange fragrance tempts guests in,
a restrained beauty
entrances the wanderer.
For five years the flowering creepers of spring
have filled with nectar the chalice of love:
drunk with honey
the garrulous black bee buzzes.
A serene joy welcomes the uninvited
and those who came when they heard.

In the first year of marriage
from all corners of the earth
the flute played the shahana raga,
the sound of laughter echoed everywhere.

Today a brief smile breaks on the face of dawn
in soundless humour.
The flute captures the resonance of the kannada
as the seven stars call for meditation.

In five years this dream of pleasure flowered
and brought a paradise of fulfilment in life.
The vasant pancham raga that played first
has now achieved fulfilment too.

As you walk the flowering forest bed
your anklets ring with the tremulous raga of spring.

Shantiniketan: 25 April 1941

9

Goddess of language:
I carve your image single minded
in this lonely courtyard.
Lumps of clay
lie scattered:
unfinished, voiceless,
they stare at the vacant
without hope.
At the feet of your proud image
they lie humbled,
not knowing why they are there.

Yet more pitiful than them are those
who had once found form
but as time passed
lost all meaning.
Where were you invited?
They cannot answer.
To build which dream
they bore the debt of dust
and came
to the door of mankind?
From which lost paradise
this portrait of Urvashi
did the poet want to capture
on this mortal canvas?

For this you were called,
kept with care in this gallery of paintings
and then forgotten one day.

The primeval dust you belong to
with supreme indifference claimed you
in its soundless chariot racing into the unknown.

This is good.
This tired acclaim,
crippled, waste today,
these routine humiliations
dog the steps of time
and interrupt its journey.
Spurned, insulted,
you find peace at last
when you become one with the dust again.

Shantiniketan: 3 May 1941

10

On this birthday I feel lost.
I want my friends to pledge
the touch of their hands,
this earth's ultimate love,
so that I can take with me life's supreme grace,
the last blessings of my fellow men.

My bag is empty today,
I have given away
all there was to give.

If something comes in return—
some love, some forgiveness—
I shall take them with me
when I set sail in my raft
towards that silent festival of the end.

Shantiniketan: 6 May 1941

11

On the bank of the Rupnarayan
I woke
and realised this world
was no dream.
With alphabets of blood
I saw my self defined.
I recognised my self
through endless suffering,
countless wounds.
Truth is cruel:
I love its cruelty
for it never lies.
Life is a tapasya of pain till death:
to gain the terrible value of truth,
settle all debts by death.

Shantiniketan: 13 May 1941

12

At this festival of gifts on your birthday
strange and colourful is this
courtyard of the early dawn.
With countless flowers and leaves

life offers its gifts with abandon.
Nature keeps a watch on her treasures
from time to time:
you are now a witness to her affluence.
When the giver and the taker are united,
a divine desire
is fulfilled today.
The poet of the universe, amazed,
blesses you:
as a witness for his verse, you have come
rain-washed
in this clear shravan sky.

Shantiniketan: 13 July 1941

13

The first day's sun
asked
the world's first emergence:
Who are you?
There was no answer.

Years passed.
The last day's sun
asked a final question
near the shores of the western sea
amidst the silence of dusk:
Who are you?
There was no answer.

Calcutta: 27 July 1941

14

Often the dark night of sorrow
has come to my door
armed with only one weapon:
the fearful visage of pain, macabre threats of terror—
deceptive in the dark.
Whenever I believed in that mask of terror
I suffered meaningless defeat.
This game of loss and victory, these apparitions of life:
stumbling ahead from childhood, dogged by this fear
I have heard the mockery of suffering.
This strange restless vision of terror:
crafted in the dark by the skilled hands of death.

Calcutta: 29 July 1941

15

You have riddled the path of your creation
with strange nets of deceit,
O deceitful one.
Snares of false beliefs you have skilfully laid
in our simple lives.
With such delusions you have marked the great:
for him you have not kept the secret night.
Your stars
light his way
towards his inner self,
a path for ever clear,
by his simple faith
made radiant all the way.
Apparently tortuous, he is actually simple:
and this is his pride.

Others think he is deluding himself.
But he finds truth
bathed in the inner light within himself.
Nothing can deceive him.
His last reward he carries
to his coffer.
He who can effortlessly bear your guiles
receives at your hand
his imperishable right to peace.

Calcutta: 30 July 1941

MY REMINISCENCES

Preamble

I do not know who has painted the pictures of my life imprinted on my memory. But whoever he is, he is an artist. He does not take up his brush simply to copy everything that happens; he retains or omits things just as he fancies; he makes many a big thing small and small thing big; he does not hesitate to exchange things in the foreground with things in the background. In short, his task is to paint pictures, not to write history. The flow of events forms our external life, while within us a series of pictures is painted. The two correspond, but are not identical.

We do not make time for a proper look at this inner canvas. Now and then we catch glimpses of a fragment of it, but the bulk remains dark, invisible to us. Why the painter ceaselessly paints, when he will complete his work, and what gallery is destined to hang his paintings, who can say?

Some years ago, someone questioned me on the events of my past and I had occasion to explore this picture-chamber. I had imagined I would stop after selecting a few items from my life-story. But as I opened the door I discovered that memories are not history but original creations by the unseen artist. The diverse colours scattered about are not reflections of the outside world but belong to the painter himself and come passion-tinged from his heart—thereby making the record on the canvas unfit for use as evidence in a court of law.

But though the attempt to gather a precise and logical story from memory's storehouse may be fruitless, it is fascinating to shuffle the pictures. This enchantment took hold of me.

As long as we are journeying, stopping only to rest at various shelters by the wayside, we do not see these pictures— things seem merely useful, too concrete for remembrance. It is when the traveller no longer needs them and has reached his destination that pictures start to come. All the cities, meadows, rivers and hills that he passed through in the morning of his life, float into his mind as he relaxes at the close of day. Thus did I look leisurely backwards, and was engrossed by what I saw.

Was this interest aroused solely by natural affection for my past? Some personal attachment there must have been, of course, but the pictures had a value independent of this. There is no event in my reminiscences worthy of being preserved for all time. Literary value does not depend on the importance of a subject, however. Whatever one has truly felt, if it can be made sensible to others, will always be respected. If pictures which have taken shape in memory can be expressed in words, they will be worthy of a place in literature.

So it is as literary material that I offer my memory pictures. To regard them as an attempt at autobiography would be a mistake. In such a light they would appear both redundant and incomplete.

Teaching Begins

We three boys were brought up together. Both my companions were two years older than I. When they were placed under their tutor, my teaching also began, but of what I learnt I can remember nothing now.

What recurs to me constantly is this. 'The rain patters, the leaf quivers.' I first heard it when I had just come to anchor after crossing the stormy region of the *kara, khala* series; it struck me then as the first poem by the ancestor of all poets. Whenever the delight of that day comes back to me, even now, I realise why rhyme is so vital in poetry. Because of rhyme words come to an end, and yet end not; the utterance finishes, but not its ring; and the ear and the mind go on with their game of tossing the rhyme back and forth. Thus did the rain patter and the leaves quiver in my consciousness again and again.

Another episode from this period of my early boyhood sticks fast in my mind.

We had an old cashier, Kailash by name, who was like one of the family. He was a great wit, and would constantly crack jokes with everybody, old and young—recently married sons-in-law and other newcomers into the family circle being the special butt of his humour. Even after his death we came to suspect that his humour did not desert him. Once my elders were engaged in an attempt to start a message service to the other world with a planchette. At one of the sittings the pencil scrawled out the name of Kailaṣh. He was asked what kind of life one led where he was. 'I had to find out the hard way, by dying,' came the reply. 'And now you survivors want a short cut. Nothing doing!'

Kailash used to rattle off for my special delectation a doggerel ballad composed by himself. The hero was myself, depicted awaiting in glowing anticipation the arrival of a heroine. She was so entrancing a bride that even fate was bewitched in her presence: her image burned brightly in my mind as I listened. The list of the jewllery which bedecked her from head to foot, and the unheard-of splendour of the preparations for the wedding, might have turned older and wiser heads; but what moved this boy, and set images of joy dancing before his eyes, was the jingle of the rhymes and the swing of the rhythm.

These two literary thrills still linger in my memory—and there is another, the nursery classic: 'The rain falls pit-a-pat, the tide comes up the river.'

The next thing I recall is the beginning of my school-life. One day I saw my elder brother, and my sister's son Satya, also a little older than myself, starting for school leaving me behind accounted unfit. I was yet to ride in a carriage or even go out of the house. So when Satya came back, full of unduly glowing accounts of his adventures on the way, I felt I simply could not stay at home. Our tutor tried to dispel my illusion with sound advice and a resounding slap: 'You're crying to go to school now, you'll have to cry a lot more later on to be let off.' I have no recollection of the name, face or character of this tutor, but the impression of his weighty advice and weightier hand has not yet faded. Never in my life have I heard a truer prophecy.

My crying drove me prematurely into the Oriental Seminary. What I learnt there I have no idea, but one of its methods of punishment I still bear in mind. A boy who was unable to repeat his lessons was made to stand on a bench with arms extended, and on his upturned palms were piled a number of slates. Let psychologists debate how far this method is likely to induce a better grasp of things.

I thus began my studies at an extremely tender age. My initiation into literature came around the same time, from the books that were in vogue in the servants' quarters. Chief among these were a Bengali translation of Chanakya's aphorisms, and the *Ramayana* of Krittivas. One particular day when I was reading this *Ramayana* comes back clearly.

The sky was cloudy. I was playing about in the long verandah overlooking the road. All of a sudden Satya, for some reason I do not remember, decided to frighten me by shouting, 'Policeman! Policeman!' My concept of the duties of a policeman was extremely vague. But of one thing I was certain: a person charged with a crime, once placed in a policeman's hands would, as sure as a wretch caught by a crocodile, go under and be seen no more. Not knowing how an innocent boy could escape such an unrelenting punishment, I bolted towards the inner apartments, shudders running down my back in blind fear of pursuing policemen. I broke the news of my impending doom to my mother, but it did not seem to disturb her much. Even so, I was not taking any chances; I sat down on the sill of my mother's door to read the dog-eared *Ramayana* with a marbled paper cover, which belonged to her old aunt. In front of me stretched the verandah running round the four sides of the inner courtyard, faintly aglow in the afternoon light of a cloudy sky. Coming upon me weeping over a sorrowful scene, my great-aunt took the book away from me.

Within and Without

Luxury was a thing almost unknown in my early childhood. The standard of living was then much plainer than it is now, as a whole. But it meant at least that the children of our household were entirely free from the fuss of being too much looked after. The fact is that for guardians the looking after of children may be an occasional treat; but for children being looked after is always an unmitigated nuisance.

We lived under the rule of the servants. To save themselves trouble they virtually suppressed our right of free movement. This was hard to bear—but the neglect was also a kind of independence. It left our minds free, unpampered and unburdened by all the usual bother over food and dress.

What we ate had nothing to do with delicacies. Our clothing, were I to itemise it, would invite a modern boy's scorn. On no pretext might we wear socks or shoes until we had passed our tenth year. In the cold weather a second cotton shirt over our first one was deemed sufficient. It never entered our heads to consider ourselves ill clad. Only when old Niyamat, the tailor, forgot to put a pocket into a shirt would we complain—for the boy has yet to be born who is so poor that he cannot stuff his pockets; by a merciful dispensation of providence, there is not much difference in wealth between boys whose parents are rich and poor. We used to own a pair of slippers each, but not always where we put our feet. The slippers were generally several moves ahead of us, propelled there by the following feet, their *raison d'être* thrown into doubt with every step we took.

Our elders in every way kept a great distance from us, in their dress and eating, coming and going, work, conversation and amusement. We caught glimpses of all these activities, but they were beyond our reach. Elders have become cheap to modern children, too readily accessible; and so have all objects of desire. Nothing ever came so easily to us. Many trivial things were rarities, and we lived mostly in the hope of attaining when we were old enough, the things that the distant future held in trust for us. The result was that what little we did get we enjoyed to the utmost; from skin to core nothing was thrown away. The modern child of a well-to-do family nibbles at only half the things he gets; the greater part of his world is wasted on him.

Our days were spent in the servants' quarters in the south-east corner of the outer apartments. One of our servants was Shyam, a dark chubby boy with curly locks, hailing from the district of Khulna. He would place me in a selected spot, trace a chalk line around me, and warn me with solemn face and uplifted finger of the perils of transgressing this circle. Whether the danger was physical or mental I never fully understood, but fear certainly possessed me. I had read in the *Ramayana* of the tribulations of Sita after she left the ring drawn by Lakshman, so I never for a minute doubted my ring's potency.

Just below the window of this room was a tank with a bathing ghat; on its west bank, along the garden wall, stood an immense banyan tree; and to the south was a fringe of coconut palms. Like a prisoner in a cell, I would spend the whole day peering through the closed Venetian shutters, gazing out at this scene as on a picture in a book. From early morning our neighbours would drop in one by one to take their baths. I knew the time of each one's arrival. I was familiar with the oddities of each one's toilet. One would stop his ears with his fingers while taking his regulation number of dips, and then depart. Another would not risk complete immersion but be content to squeeze a wet towel repeatedly over his head. A third would carefully flick the surface impurities away from him with rapid strokes of his arms, and then suddenly plunge in. Another would jump in from the top steps without any preliminaries at all. Yet another would lower himself slowly in, step by step, while muttering his morning prayers. Then there was one who was always in a hurry, hastening home as soon as his dip was over, and a second who was in no sort of hurry at all, following a leisurely bath with a good rub-down, changing from wet bathing clothes into clean dry ones with a careful adjustment of the folds of his waist-cloth, then ending with a turn or two in the outer garden and the gathering of flowers, after which he would finally saunter homewards, radiating cool comfort as he went. All this would go on till past noon. Then the bathing-place would become deserted and silent. Only the ducks would remain, paddling about and diving after water snails or frantically preening their feathers, for the rest of the day.

When solitude thus reigned over the water, my whole attention would focus on the shadows beneath the banyan tree. Some of its aerial roots, creeping down its trunk, had formed a dark complication of coils at its base. It was as if by some sorcery this obscure corner of the world had escaped the regime of natural laws, as if some improbable dreamworld, unobserved by the Creator, had lingered on into the light of modern times. Whom I saw there, and what those beings did, I am unable to express in intelligible language. It was of this banyan tree that I later wrote:

Day and night you stand like an ascetic with matted hair. Do you ever think of the boy whose fancy played with your shadows?

That majestic banyan tree is no more, alas, and neither is the tank that served as her mirror. Many of those who once bathed in it have departed too, merging with the shade of the great tree. And the boy, grown older, has put down roots far and wide and now contemplates the pattern of shadow and sunlight, sorrow and cheer, cast by this tangled skein.

To leave the house was forbidden to us, in fact we did not even have the run of the interior. We had to get our glimpses of Nature from behind barriers. Beyond my reach stretched this limitless thing called the Outside, flashes, sounds and scents of which used momentarily to come and touch me through interstices. It seemed to want to beckon me through the shutters with a variety of gestures. But it was free and I was bound—there was no way of our meeting. So its attraction was all the stronger. Today the chalk line has been wiped away but the confining circle is still there. The horizon is just as far away; what lies beyond it is still out of reach, and I am reminded of the poem I wrote when I was older:

> The tame bird was in a cage, the free bird was in the forest,
> They met when the time came, it was a decree of fate.
> The free bird cries, 'O my love, let us fly to the wood.'
> The cage bird whispers, 'Come hither, let us both live in the cage.'
> Says the free bird, 'Among bars, where is there room to spread one's wings?'
> 'Alas,' cries the cage bird, 'I should not know where to sit perched in the sky.'

The parapets of our terraced roofs were higher than my head. When I had grown taller and when the tyranny of the servants had relaxed, when, with the coming of a newly married bride into the house, I had achieved some recognition as a companion of her leisure, I would sometimes climb to the terrace in the middle of the day. By that time everybody in the house would have finished their meal and there would be an interlude in the business of the household; over the inner apartments would settle the quiet of a siesta, with wet bathing clothes hanging over the parapets to dry, the crows picking at the leavings thrown on a refuse heap in the corner of the yard; and in the solitude, the cage bird and the free bird would commune with each other, beak to beak.

I love to stand and look. My gaze fell first on the row of coconut trees at the far edge of our inner garden. Through these I could see the Singhi's Garden with its cluster of huts and its tank, and at the edge of the tank the dairy of our milkwoman, Tara; and beyond that, mixed up with the tree-tops, the various shapes and different levels of the terraced roofs of Calcutta flashing under the whiteness of the midday sun, stretching away and merging with the grayish blue of the eastern horizon. And some of these far distant dwellings, from which jutted out a covered stairway leading to the roof, seemed like upraised fingers signaling to me, with a wink, that there were mysteries below. The beggar at the palace door imagines impossible treasures in its strong-rooms. I can hardly describe the spirit of fun and freedom which these unknown dwellings seemed to me to suggest. In the farthest recesses of a sky full of burning sunshine I would just be able to detect the thin shrill cry of a kite; and from the lane adjoining the thin shrill cry of a kite; and from the lane adjoining the Singhi's Garden, past the houses dormant in noonday slumber, would float the sing-song of the bangle-seller—*chai churi chai*—at such times my whole being would float away too.

My father was constantly on the move, hardly even at home. His rooms on the third story remained shut up. I would pass my hands through the Venetian shutters, open the latch of the door and spend the afternoon lying motionless on his sofa at the south end. In the first place, a closed room is always fascinating; then there was the lure of stolen entry, with its savour of mystery; finally, there was the deserted terrace outside with the sun's rays beating upon it, which would set me dreaming.

And there was yet another attraction. The water-works had just started up in Calcutta, and in the first flush of triumphant entry it did not stint its supply even to the Indian quarters. In that golden age, piped water used to flow even to my father's third-storey rooms. Turning on his shower-tap I would take an untimely bath to my heart's content—not so much for the feel of the water, as to indulge my desire to do just as I fancied. The simultaneous joy of liberty and fear of being caught made that shower of municipal water seem like arrows of delight.

Perhaps because the possibility of contact with the outside was so remote, the excitement of it came to me much more readily. When things surround us at every hand, the mind becomes lazy, commissions others, and forgets that the joy of a feast depends more on nourishment by imagination than on external things. This is the chief lesson which infancy has to teach a human being. Then his possessions are few and trivial, yet he needs no more to be happy. For the unfortunate youngster who has an unlimited number of playthings, the world of play is spoilt.

To call our inner garden a garden is to go too far. It consisted of a citron tree, a couple of plum trees of different varieties, and a row of coconut trees. In the center was a paved circle, cracked and invaded by grasses and weeds waving their victorious standards. Only those flowering plants which refused to die of the gardener's neglect continued to perform their duties. In the northern corner was a rice-husking shed, where when need arose, the occupants of the inner apartments would congregate. This last vestige of rural life in Calcutta has since owned defeat and slunk silently away.

Nonetheless I have an idea that the Garden of Eden was no grander than this garden of ours, for Adam and his paradise were alike naked: they needed no embellishment with material things. Only since he tasted the fruit of the tree of knowledge, and until such time as he can fully digest it, has man's need for external trappings come to dominate him. Our inner garden was my paradise; it was enough for me. I clearly remember how in the early autumn dawn I would run there as soon as I was awake. A whiff of dewy grass and foliage would rush to meet me, and the morning, with cool fresh light, would peep at me over the top of the eastern garden wall from below the trembling tassels of the coconut palms.

Another piece of vacant land to the north of the house to this day we call the *golabari*. The name shows that in some remote past this must have been the barn where the year's store of grain was kept. In those days town and country visibly resembled each other, like brother and sister in childhood. Now the family likeness can hardly be traced. This *golabari* would be my holiday haunt when I got the chance. I did not really go there to play—it was the place itself that drew me. Why, is difficult to tell. Perhaps its being a deserted bit of waste land lying in an out-of-the-way corner gave it charm. Entirely outside the living quarters, it bore no stamp of functionality; what's more, it was as unadorned as it was useless, for no one had ever planted anything there. It was a desert spot. No doubt that is why it offered free rein to a boy's imagination. Whenever I saw a loophole in my warders' vigilance and could contrive to reach the *golabari*, I felt I had a real holiday.

Yet another region existed in our house and this I have still not succeeded in finding. A little girl playmate of the same age as I, called it the 'King's palace.' 'I have just been there,' she would sometimes tell me. But somehow the right moment for her to take me never turned up. It was said to be a wonderful place, with playthings as fabulous as the games that were played there. It seemed to me it had to be somewhere very near—perhaps in the first or second storey—but I never seemed able to reach it. How often did I say to my friend, 'Just tell me, is it really inside the house or outside?' And she would always reply, 'No, no, it's right here in this house.' I would sit and wonder: 'Where? Where? Don't I know all the rooms in the house?' I never cared to enquire who the King was; his palace remains undiscovered to this day; only this much is clear—it lay within our house.

Looking back at my childhood I feel the thought that recurred most often was that I was surrounded by mystery. Something undreamt of was lurking everywhere, and every day the uppermost question was: when, oh! when, would we come across it? It was as if Nature held something cupped in her hands and was asking us with a smile: 'What d'you think I have?' We had no idea there might be any limit to the answer.

I vividly remember a custard apple seed which I planted and kept in a corner of the south verandah, and used to water every day. The idea that the seed might actually grow into a tree kept me in a state of fluttering anticipation. Custard apple seeds today still have the habit of sprouting, but no longer to the accompaniment of that feeling of wonder. The fault lies not in the custard apple but in my mind.

Once we stole some rocks from an elder cousin's rockery and started a little rockery of our own. The plants we sowed in its interstices we cared for so excessively that only the stoicism of vegetables can account for their survival. Words cannot express the excitement this miniature mountaintop held for us. We were never in any doubt that our creation would be enigma of the earth and would not have been allowed to remain covered for very long.

The thought that behind every portion of the blue vault of the sky there reposed the secrets of the heavens also spurred our imaginations. When our pundit, wishing to illustrate some lesson in our Bengali science primer, told us that the sky was not a finite blue sphere, we were thunderstruck! 'Put ladder upon ladder,' he said, 'and go on mounting but you will never bump your head.' He must be mean with his ladders, I thought, and aloud said in a tone of rising indignation, 'And what if we put more ladders, and more and more?' When I grasped that to multiply ladders was fruitless I was dumbfounded. Surely, I concluded after much pondering, such an astounding fact must be part of the secret knowledge of schoolmasters, known to them and to no one else.

Servocracy

In the history of India the regime of the Slave Dynasty was not a happy one. In my own history I can find nothing glorious or cheerful to report about the reign of the servants. There were frequent changes of ruler, but never a variation in the code of restraints and punishments that afflicted us. At the time we had no opportunity to philosophise on the subject; we bore as best we could the blows that befell our backs, and accepted as one of the laws of the universe that it is the Big who hurt and the Small who get hurt. The opposite idea—that the Big suffer and the Small cause suffering—has taken me a long time to learn.

No hunter, whatever his intentions, looks at things from a bird's point of view. That is why the alert bird, which loudly warns the group before they are shot at, is shouted at severely. When we were beaten we howled, of which our chastisers strongly disapproved; in their eyes it was sedition against the servocracy. How well I recall their attempts to suppress our wailing by cramming our heads into nearby water-pitchers. Our outcry must have been most distasteful and inconvenient—that, no one can possibly deny.

Nowadays I sometimes wonder why such cruel treatment was meted out to us by the servants. I cannot admit that there was anything in our overall behaviour or demeanour to have put us beyond the pale of human kindness. The real reason must have been that the whole burden of us was thrown upon the servants, and that is something difficult to bear even by those who are nearest and dearest. If children are only allowed to be children, to run about and play and satisfy their curiosity, the burden becomes quite light. Insoluble problems are created only if one tries to confine children inside, keep them still or hamper their play. Then childishness becomes onerous and falls heavily on the guardian—like the horse, in the fable carried by bearers instead of being allowed to trot on its own legs: though money could procure bearers even for a horse, it could not prevent them from venting their anger on the unlucky beast at every step.

Of most of these tyrants of our childhood I remember only the cuffings and boxings, nothing more. Just one personality stands out. His name was Ishwar. Once he had been a village schoolmaster. He was a prim and prudent personage, sedately conscious of religious orthodoxy. The earth seemed too earthy for him, with too little water to keep it properly clean; he was engaged in constant warfare with its chronically soiled state. He would shoot his water-pot into the tank with a lightning movement so as to take his supply from an uncontaminated depth. It was he who, when bathing in the tank, continually thrust away the surface impurities until he took a sudden plunge, trying to catch the water unawares, as it were. When he walked, his right arm stood out at an angle from his body, as if, we like to think, he could not trust the hygiene of even his own garments. Day and night he carried himself like someone on perpetual guard against the infinite kinds of pollution that might slip through his defences and infect his contact with earth, water and air. That his body had contact with the world at all seemed insufferable to him.

His gravity of manner was unfathomable. With head slightly cocked he minced his carefully selected words in a sonorous voice. His literary diction was food for merriment to our elders behind his back, some of his high-flown phrases acquiring currency in our family repertoire of witticisms. But I doubt whether the expressions he used would sound as odd today; the literary and spoken languages, which used to be as sky from earth asunder, are now nearer to each other.

This erstwhile schoolmaster had discovered a way of keeping us quiet in the evenings. He would gather us around the cracked castor-oil lamp and read aloud stories from the *Ramayana* and *Mahabharata*. Some of the other servants would join the audience. The lamp would throw huge shadows of us right up to the beams of the roof, and also pick out the little house lizards catching insects on the walls and the bats doing a dervish dance round and round the verandahs outside, while we sat listening in silent, open-mouthed wonder.

I still remember the evening we came to the story of Kusha and Laba, in which those heroic lads looked set to pulverize the renown of their father and uncles; the silence of that dimly lit room was tense with anticipation. But already the hour was late and our prescribed period of wakefulness was almost up. Yet the story still had far to go.

At this critical juncture my father's old follower came to the rescue, and finished the episode for us at express speed to the quickstep of Dashuraya's verses. The soft slow chant of Krittivas' fourteen-syllabled *payar* measure was cast clean aside, and we were bowled over by the jingle of the alliteration and the jangle of the rhyme.

On some occasions these ancient texts gave rise to discussion and interpretation, which at length concluded with a profound pronouncement from Ishwar. Though he was only one of the children's servants, and therefore below many in domestic rank, like old grandfather Bhishma in the *Mahabharata* his seniority unfailingly asserted itself from his humbled seat below his juniors.

This high and principled guardian of ours had one weakness to which I feel bound to allude for the sake of historical accuracy. He used to take opium. It created a craving for rich food. So when he brought us our morning milk he was much attracted to it and, unlike us, not in the least repelled. If we gave the slightest hint of our natural repugnance, no sense of responsibility for our health could prompt Ishwar to press it on us a second time.

He also had severe doubts about our capacity for solid nourishment. We would sit down to our evening meal and a quantity of *luchis* heaped on a thick round wooden tray would be placed before us. He would gingerly drop a few on each platter—from a sufficient height to safeguard himself from contamination—like boons wrested from the gods in reward for human penance; there was never a hint of favouritism or over-indulgence in hospitality. Next would come an inquiry as to whether we should like any more. I knew the reply which would most gratify him, and could not bring myself to deprive him by asking for another helping.

Then again Ishwar was entrusted with a daily allowance for procuring our afternoon light refreshment. Every morning he would ask us what item we should like to have. We knew that to mention the cheapest would be accounted best, so we sometimes requested a light snack of puffed rice, and at other times an indigestible one of boiled *gram* or roasted ground-nuts. It is obvious that Ishwar was not as painstakingly punctilious with our diet as with our spiritual sustenance.

The Normal School

While at the Oriental Seminary I had discovered a way out of the humiliation of being a pupil. I had started a class of my own in a corner of our verandah. The wooden bars of the railing were my pupils, and I would act the schoolmaster, cane in hand, seated on a chair in front of them. I had decided which were the good boys and which the bad—I could even distinguish clearly the quiet from the naughty, the clever from the stupid. The bad rails had suffered so much from my constant caning that they would have longed to give up the ghost had they been alive. And the more scarred they got with my strokes the worse they angered me, till I knew not how to punish them enough. None of that poor dumb class remains to bear witness how tremendously I tyrannised over them. My wooden pupils have been replaced by cast-iron railings, and the new generation has not taken up their education in the old manner; if they were to try, they could never achieve the same results.

I have since realised how much easier it is to acquire the style than the substance of teaching. Without effort I had assimilated all the impatience, short temper, partiality and injustice displayed by my teachers, to the exclusion of the rest of their teaching. My only consolation is that I had not the power of venting these barbarities on any sentient creature.

Nevertheless, the difference between my wooden pupils and those of the Seminary does not stop my psychology from being identical with that of its schoolmasters.

I cannot have spent long at the Oriental Seminary, for I was still at a tender age when I joined the Normal School. The only one of its features which I remember is that before classes began all the boys had to sit in a row in the gallery and go through some kind of singing or chanting of verses—evidently an attempt to introduce an element of cheerfulness into the daily routine.

Unfortunately, the words were English and the tune quite as foreign, so that we did not have the faintest notion what sort of incantation we practised; neither did the meaningless monotony tend to make us cheerful. But this failed to disturb the serene self-satisfaction of the school authorities at having provided such a treat; they deemed it superfluous to ask the practical effect of their bounty; probably they would have called not being dutifully happy a crime. They were content to take the song as they found it, words and all, from the self-same English book that had furnished the theory.

The language into which this English resolved itself in our mouths is without doubt educative—to philologists at least. I can recall only one line: '*Kallokee pullokee singill mellaling mellaling mellaling.*'

After much thought I have been able to guess at the original of a part of it. *Kallokee* still baffles me but the rest I think was: '...full of glee, singing merrily, merrily, merrily'.

As my memories of the Normal School emerge from haziness and become clearer they are not the least sweet in any particular. Had I been able to associate with the other boys, the business of learning might not have seemed so intolerable. But that turned out to be impossible—so nasty were most of their manners and habits. So, in the intervals between classes, I would go up to the second storey and while away the time sitting near a window overlooking the street. I would count: one year—two years—three years and wonder how many such I would have to get through.

I remember only one of the teachers, whose language was so foul that I steadily refused to answer any one of his questions, out of sheer contempt for him. Thus I sat silent throughout the year at the bottom of his class, and while the rest of the class was busy I would be left alone to attempt the solution of many an intricate problem.

One of these, I remember, on which I cogitated profoundly, was how to defeat an enemy without having arms. My preoccupation with this question, amidst the hum of the boys reciting their lessons, comes back to me even now. If I could properly train up a number of dogs, tigers and other ferocious beasts, and put a few lines of these on the field of battle, I reckoned they would make an arresting sight with which to begin the fight. After that it would be up to the prowess of my army to achieve success. As I vividly visualized this wonderfully simple strategy, the victory of my side became assured beyond doubt.

As long as work had not yet come into my life I found it easy to devise short cuts to achievement; since I have been working I find that which is hard is hard indeed, and what is difficult remains difficult. This is less comforting, of course, but nowhere near so bad as the discomfort of trying to take short cuts.

When at last a year had passed in that class, we were examined in Bengal by Pandit Madhushudan Vachaspati. I got the largest number of marks of all the boys. The teacher complained to the school authorities that there had been favouritism. So I was examined a second time, with the superintendent of the school seated beside the examiner. This time, also, I got top place.

Versification

I could not have been more than eight years old at the time Jyoti, son of a niece of my father's, was considerably older. He had just gained access to English literature, and would recite Hamlet's soliloquy with great gusto. Why the idea entered his head that a mere child as I was should write poetry, I cannot tell but one afternoon he sent for me and asked me to try and make up a verse, after which he explained to me the construction of the *payar* metre of fourteen syllables.

Poems were things that up to then I had seen only in books—without mistakes inked out or visible sign of doubt or effort or human weakness. That any attempt of mine might produce a poem like these I could not even dare to imagine.

One day a thief had been caught in our house. Overpowered by curiosity yet trembling with fear, I had ventured to the spot to take a peep. He was just an ordinary man! When he was roughly handled by our door-keeper I felt real pity. My experience was similar with poetry.

After stringing together a few words at my own sweet will, I found them turned into *payar* verse and felt I had no illusions left about the glories of poetising. Now, when I see poor Poetry being mishandled, I feel pity. This has often moved me to restrain impatient hands, itching to assault her. Thieves have scarcely suffered as much as she, and from so many.

The first feeling of awe once overcome, there was no holding me back. I managed to get hold of a blue-paper manuscript book, courtesy of one of the officers of our estate. In my own hand I ruled it with pencil lines, at not very regular intervals, and began to write verses in a large scrawl.

Like a young deer which butts here, there and everywhere with its newly sprouted antlers, I and my budding poetry made a nuisance of themselves. More so my elder brother, whose pride in my performance impelled him to hunt about the house for an audience.

I recollect how, one day, as the pair of us were coming out of the estate offices on the ground floor after a conquering expedition against the officers, we came across the editor of the *National Paper,* Naba Gopal Mitra, who had just stepped into the house. My brother tackled him without further ado: 'Naba Gopal Babu! Rabi has written a poem. You must listen.' The reading following forthwith.

My works were not yet voluminous. The poet could carry all his effusions about in his pockets. I was writer, printer and publisher all in one; my brother, as advertiser, was my only colleague. I had composed some verses on 'The Lotus' which I recited to Naba Gopal Babu then and there, at the foot of the stairs, in a voice pitched as high as my enthusiasm. 'Well done!' he said with a smile. 'But what is a *dwirepha?*'

The word had the same number of syllables as *moumachhi,* the ordinary word for 'bee'. How I had got hold of *dwirepha* I do not remember. But it was the one word in the whole poem on which I had pinned my hopes. There was no doubt it had impressed our officers. But curiously enough Naba Gopal Babu did not succumb to it—on the contrary, he smiled! He could not be an understanding man, I was sure. I never read poetry to him again. I have added many years to my age since then, but I have not been able to improve upon my test of who is and who is not a connoisseur. However much Naba Gopal Babu might smile, the word *dwirepha,* like a bee drunk with honey, remained stuck in position.

Diverse Lessons

One of the teachers of the Normal School gave us private lessons at home too. His body was lean and dry, his voice sharp. He looked like a cane incarnate. His hours were from six to half-past nine in the morning. Our reading with him ranged from popular literary and science readers in Bengali to the epic of *Meghnadbadh*.

My third brother was very keen on imparting a variety of knowledge to us, so at home we had to go through much more than was required by the school course. We had to get up before dawn and, clad in loin-cloths, begin with a bout or two with a blind wrestler. Then without a pause we donned shirts over our dusty bodies, and started on our courses of literature, mathematics, geography and history. On our return from school our drawing and gymnastic masters would be ready for us. In the evening Aghore Babu came to give English lessons. It was nine o'clock before we were free.

On Sunday morning we had singing lessons with Vishnu. Then, almost every Sunday, came Sitanath Dutta to give us demonstrations in physical science. These last were of great interest to me. I remember distinctly the feeling of wonder which filled me when he put on the fire a glass vessel with some water and sawdust in it, and showed us how the lightened hot water rose up and the cold water went down, and how finally the water began to boil. I also felt a great elation the day I learnt that water is a separable part of milk, and that milk thickens when boiled because the water frees itself from the connexion as vapour. Sunday did not feel as if it were Sunday unless Sitanath Babu turned up.

There was also an hour when we would be told about human bones by a pupil of the Campbell Medical School, for which purpose a skeleton, with the bones fastened together by wires, was hung up in our schoolroom. And finally, time was also found for Pandit Heramba Tatwaratna to come and get us to learn rules of Sanskrit grammar by rote. I am not sure which of these, the names of the bones or the *sutras* of the grammarian, were the more jaw-breaking. The latter probably took the palm.

We began to learn English after we had made considerable progress in our education through Bengali. Aghore Babu, our English tutor, was attending the Medical College, so he taught us in the evening.

The discovery of fire was one of man's greatest discoveries so we are told. I do not dispute it. But I cannot help feeling how fortunate the little birds are that their parents cannot light lamps in the evening. They have their language lessons early in the morning—how gleefully everyone must have noticed. Of course we must not forget that it is not English they are learning!

This medical-student tutor of ours kept such good health that even the fervent and united wishes of his three pupils were not enough to cause his absence even for a day. Only once was he laid up, when there was a fight between the Indian and Eurasian students of the Medical College and a chair was thrown at his head. This regrettable occurrence was undoubtedly a blow for our teacher, but it struck us somewhat differently; in fact we thought his recovery was needlessly swift.

It is evening. The rain is pouring down in lance-like showers. Our lane is under knee-deep water. The tank has overflowed into the garden, and the shaggy tops of the bel trees are standing guard over the waters. Our whole being is radiating rapture like the fragrant stamens of the *kadamba* flower. Our tutor's arrival is already overdue by several minutes. But nothing is yet certain. We sit on the verandah overlooking the lane, waiting and watching with a pathetic gaze. All of a sudden our hearts seem to tumble to the ground with a great thump. The familiar black umbrella has turned the corner, undefeated even by such weather! Could it not be somebody else's? No, it could not! In the wide world there might be found another person, his equal in pertinacity, but never in this particular little lane.

Looking back on his period with us as a whole, I cannot say that Aghore Babu was a hard man. He did not rule us with a rod. Even his rebukes did not amount to scoldings. But whatever his personal merits, his time was *evening*, and his subject *English*! Even an angel, I am certain, would have seemed like a messenger of Yama, god of Death, to any Bengali boy if he had come to him at the end of a miserable day at school and lighted a dismally dim lamp to teach him English.

How plainly do I recall the day our tutor tried to impress on us the appeal of the English language. With great unction he recited to us some lines—prose or poetry we could not tell—from an English book. They had a most unlooked-for effect. We laughed so much that he had to dismiss us for the evening. He must have realised that he held no easy brief: that to get us to pronounce in his favour would entail a contest ranging over years.

Aghore Babu would sometimes try to bring the zephyr of outside knowledge to play on our arid schoolroom routine. One day he brought a paper parcel out of his pocket and said:

'Today I'll show you a wonderful piece of work by the Creator.' Then he untied the wrapping, produced a portion of the windpipe of a human being and proceeded to expound the marvels of its mechanism.

I still remember my shock. I had always thought the whole man spoke—had never even imagined that the act of speech could be viewed in this detached way. However wonderful the mechanism of a part may be, it is certainly less so than the whole person. Not that I put it to myself in so many words, but that was the cause of my dismay. Perhaps because the tutor had lost sight of this truth I could not respond to the enthusiasm with which he discoursed that day.

Another day he took us to the dissecting-room of the Medical College. The body of an old woman was stretched on the table. This did not disturb me overmuch. But an amputated leg lying on the floor upset me altogether. To view man in this fragmentary way seemed to me so horrid, so absurd, that I could not rid myself of the impression of that dark, unmeaning leg for many days.

After getting through Peary Sarkar's first and second English readers we embarked on McCulloch's *Course of Reading*. Our bodies were weary at the end of the day, our minds yearned for the inner apartments, the book was black and thick with difficult words, and the subject-matter could hardly have been less inviting, for it contained none of Saraswati, goddess of learning's maternal tenderness. Children's books then were not full of pictures as they are now. Moreover, at the gateway to every lesson an array of words stood sentinel, with separated syllables and forbidding accent marks like fixed bayonets barring the way to the infant mind. I repeatedly attacked their serried ranks in vain.

Our tutor would try to shame us by recounting the exploits of some other brilliant pupil of his. We felt duly contrite and also not well disposed towards that other pupil, but this feeling did not help to dispel the darkness which clung to that black volume.

Providence, out of pity for mankind, has instilled a soporific charm into all tedious things. No sooner did our English lessons begin than our heads began to nod. Sprinkling water into our eyes or taking a run round the verandahs were palliatives with no lasting effect. If by any chance my eldest brother happened to pass that way and caught a glimpse of our sleep-tormented condition, we would be let off for the rest of the evening. It did not take another moment for our drowsiness to be completely cured.

My First Outing

Once, when dengue fever was raging in Calcutta, a part of our extensive family had to take shelter in Chhatu Babu's riverside villa. We were among them.

This was my first outing. The bank of the Ganges welcomed me into its lap like a friend from a former birth. There, in front of the servants' quarters, was a grove of guava trees; my days would pass beneath their shade, sitting on the verandah gazing at the flowing current through the gaps between the trunks. Every morning, as I awoke, I felt the day somehow coming to me like a gilt-edged letter that would impart wonderful news upon my opening the envelope. So as not to miss any portion of it I would splash some water on my face and hurry to my chair outside. Every day there was the ebb and flow of the tide on the Ganges, the diverse movements of so many different boats, the shifting of the shadows of the trees from west to east, and, over the shady fringe of the woods on the opposite bank, the gush of golden life-blood through the pierced breast of the evening sky. Some days would be cloudy from early morning, the opposite woods black, black shadows moving over the river. Then with a rush would come vociferous rain blotting out the horizon; the dim line of the other bank would take its leave in tears; the river would swell with suppressed heavings; and the moist wind would frolic among the foliage of the trees.

I felt that walls, beams, joists and rafters, had given me new birth into the world. As I made fresh acquaintance with things, their dingy covering, fashioned from habit, seemed to drop away. I am sure that the sugar-cane molasses, which I used to have with cold *luchis* for breakfast tasted no different from the ambrosia quaffed by Indra, lord of the gods, in his heaven; for immortality is in the taster not in the nectar and will be missed by those who seek it elsewhere.

Behind the house was a walled-in enclosure with a tank and a flight of steps leading into the water from a bathing ghat. On one side of this ghat was an immense *jambolan* tree, and all round were various fruit trees, growing in thick clusters, in the shade of which the tank nestled in privacy. The veiled beauty of this retiring little inner garden had a wonderful charm for me, so different from the broad expanse of riverbank in front. It was like the bride of the house, in the seclusion of her midday siesta, resting on a many-coloured quilt of her own embroidering, murmuring the secrets of her heart. I spent many midday hours under that *jambolan* tree alone dreaming of the fearsome kingdom of the *yakshas* within the depths of the tank.

I had a great curiosity to see a village in Bengal. Its dwellings and shrines, lanes and bathing ghats, games and gatherings, fields and markets, its whole world as I saw it in imagination, strongly attracted me. Just such a village was now on the other side of our garden wall, but it was off-bounds to us. We had come out, but not into freedom. Formerly caged, we were now on a perch—but the chain was still there.

One morning two of our elders went out for a stroll into the village. I could not restrain my urge any longer, and, slipping out unperceived, followed them for some distance. As I went along the deeply shaded lane, with its close thorny *sheora* hedges, by the side of a tank covered with green water weeds, I absorbed picture after rapturous picture. I still remember a bare-bodied fellow occupied in a belated bath at the edge of the tank, cleaning his teeth with the chewed end of a twig. Suddenly my elders became aware of me behind them. 'Get back, go back at once!' they scolded. They were scandalised. My feet were bare, I had no scarf or upper garment over my shirt, I was not fit to come out—as if this was my fault! I had never been burdened with socks or superfluous apparel, so I not only went back disappointed that morning, but had no chance any other day of repairing the omission and being allowed out.

I was cut off from behind, but out front the Ganges freed me from all bonds. My mind could hop aboard any boat I saw sailing by and journey away, without charge, to lands not named in any geography.

This was forty years ago. I have not set foot in that *champak*-shaded villa garden since. The same old house and the same old trees must still be there, but I know the garden cannot be the same—for where am I now to recapture the freshness of wonder that made it what it was?

We returned to our Jorasanko house in town. And my days became like so many mouthfuls offered up and gulped down into the maw of the Normal School.

Practising Poetry

That blue manuscript book was soon filled, like the hive of some insect, with a network of variously slanting lines and the thick and thin strokes of letters. The eager pressure of the boy writer soon crumpled its leaves; and then the edges got frayed, and twisted up like claws as if to hold fast the writing within, till at last, by what river Baitarani I know not, its pages were swept away into merciful oblivion. At any rate they escaped the pangs of passage through the printing-press and need not fear birth into this vale of woe.

I cannot claim to have been a passive witness to the spread of my reputation as a poet. Though Satkari Datta was not a teacher of our class he was very fond of me. He had written a book on natural history—a fact that will not, I hope, provoke any unkind comment regarding his interest in me. One day he sent for me and asked: 'So you write poetry, do you?' I did not attempt to hide it. From that time on he would now and then ask me to complete a quatrain by adding a couplet of my own to one given by him.

Gobinda Babu was very dark, short and fat. He was the school superintendent. He sat in his black suit with his account books in an office room on the second story. We were all afraid of him, for he was the rod-bearing judge. Once I escaped into his room from some bullies, five or six older boys. I had no one to bear witness on my side—except my tears. I won my case, and after that Gobinda Babu kept a soft corner for me in his heart.

One day he called me into his room during the recess. I went in fear and trembling, but no sooner had I stepped before him than he accosted me with the same question as Satkari Babu: 'So you write poetry?' I did not hesitate to admit it. He commissioned me to write a poem on some high moral precept which I do not remember. The level of affable condescension involved in such a request can be appreciated only by those who were Gobinda Babu's pupils. When I handed him the verses next day, he took me to the highest class and made me stand before the boys. 'Recite,' he commanded. And I recited loudly.

The only thing praiseworthy about this poem was that it soon got lost. Its moral effect on that class was far from inspiring—and the sentiment it aroused was far from amicable. Most of them were certain that the poem was not my own composition. One said he could produce the book from which it was copied, but was not pressed to do so; to have to prove something is such a nuisance to those who want to believe. Finally, the number of seekers after poetic fame began to increase alarmingly; and the methods they chose were not among those which are recognised paths to moral improvement.

Nowadays there is nothing strange in a youth writing verses. The glamour of poesy is gone. I remember how the few women who wrote poetry in those days were looked upon as miraculous creations of the Deity. Today if one is told that some young lady does not write poems one feels sceptical. Poetry sprouts long before the highest Bengali class is reached; a modern Gobinda Babu would take no notice at all of the poetic exploit I have recounted.

Srikantha Babu

At this time I was granted a listener the like of whom I shall never have again. He had so inordinate a capacity for being pleased as to have utterly disqualified him for the post of critic on any of our monthly reviews. The old man was like a perfectly ripe Alfonso mango—not a trace of acid or coarse fibre in his composition. His tender clean-shaven face was rounded off by an all-pervading baldness; there was not the vestige of a tooth to worry the inside of his mouth; and his big smiling eyes gleamed with constant delight. When he spoke in his soft deep voice, his mouth and eyes and hands all spoke likewise. He was of the old school of Persian culture, and knew not a word of English. His inseparable companions were a hubble-bubble at his left, and a sitar on his lap; and from his throat flowed unceasing song.

Srikantha Babu had no need to wait for a formal introduction, for none could resist the natural claims of his genial heart. Once he took us to be photographed with him in some big English photographic studio. There he so captivated the proprietor with his artless story, in a jumble of Hindustani and Bengali, of how he was a poor man, but badly wanted this particular photograph taken, that the man smilingly allowed him a reduced rate. Nor did the sound of bargaining in that unbending English establishment sound at all incongruous, so naive was Srikantha Babu, so unconscious of any possibility of giving offence. He would sometimes take me along to a European missionary's house. There also, with his playing and singing, his caresses of the missionary's little girl and his unabashed admiration of the little booted feet of the missionary's wife, he would enliven the gathering as no one else could. Another behaving so absurdly would have been deemed a bore, but his transparent simplicity pleased all and drew them in to join his gaiety.

Srikantha Babu was impervious to rudeness or insolence. There was at the time a singer of some repute retained in our establishment. When he was the worse for drink he would rail at poor Srikantha Babu's singing in no very choice terms. The latter would bear this unflinchingly, making no attempt to retort. When at last the man's incorrigible rudeness brought about his dismissal Srikantha Babu anxiously interceded for him. 'He was not the cause, it was the drink,' insisted.

He could not bear to see anyone in sorrow or even to hear of it. So when any of the boys wanted to torment him they had only to read out passages from Vidyasagar's *Banishment of Sita*—and Srikantha Babu would become greatly exercised, thrusting out his hands in protest and begging and praying them to stop.

This old man was a friend of both my father, my elder brothers and us younger ones alike. He adjusted his age to suit each and every one of us. Just as any piece of stone is good enough for a freshet to dance and gambol around, so the least little stimulus would be enough to make Srikantha Babu beside himself with joy. I remember I once composed a hymn that did not stint the usual allusions to the trials and tribulations of this world. Srikantha Babu was convinced that my revered father would be overjoyed to hear such a gem. With his familiar unbounded enthusiasm he volunteered to acquaint him with it. Luckily I was not present at the time, but I heard later that my father was hugely amused that the sorrows of the world should have moved his youngest son so early to the point of versification. I am sure Gobinda Babu, the superintendent, would have shown more respect for my effort on so serious a subject.

In singing I was Srikantha Babu's favourite pupil. He had taught me a song: 'No more of Braja for me,' and would drag me about to everyone's rooms and get me to sing it to them. I would sing and he would thrum an accompaniment on his sitar and when we came to the chorus he would join in and repeat it over and over again, smiling and nodding his head at each one in turn, as if nudging them on to a more enthusiastic appreciation.

He was a devotee of my father. A hymn had been set to one of my father's tunes, 'For He is the heart of our hearts'. When he sang this to my father Srikantha Babu got so excited that he jumped up from his seat and twanged his sitar violently as he sang, 'For He is the heart of our hearts,' and then waved his hand about my father's face as he changed the words to 'For *you* are the heart of our hearts.'

When the old man paid his last visit to my father, the latter, by then bed-ridden, was at a riverside villa in Chunchura. Srikantha Babu, stricken with his last illness, could not rise unaided and had to push open his eyelids to see. In this state, tended by his daughter, he journeyed to Chunchura from his place in Birbhum. With a great effort he managed to take the dust of my father's feet and then return to his lodgings in Chunchura where he breathed his last a few days later. I heard afterwards from his daughter that he went to his eternal youth with the song '*how* Sweet is Thy mercy, Lord!' on his lips.

Our Bengali Course Ends

At school we were then in the class below the highest one. At home we had advanced in Bengali much further than the subjects taught in the class. We had been through Akshay Datta's book on popular physics, and had finished the blank-verse epic *Meghandhadh*. We read our physics without reference to physical objects, and so our knowledge of the subject was correspondingly bookish. In fact the time spent on it had been thoroughly wasted, much more so to my mind than if it had been wasted in doing nothing. The *Meghnadbadh*, also, was not a thing of joy to us. The tastiest titbit may not be relished when thrown at one's head. To employ an epic to teach language is like using a sword to shave—disrespectful to the sword, distressing to the cheek. A poem should be taught from the emotional standpoint; inveigling it into service as a grammar-cum-dictionary is not well-calculated to propitiate Saraswati, the goddess of learning.

All of a sudden our Normal School career came to an end, and thereby hangs a tale. One of our school teachers wanted to borrow a copy of my grandfather's life by Mittra from our library. My nephew and classmate Satya managed to screw up courage enough to mention this to my father. He had come to the conclusion that everyday Bengali would hardly do for the approach. So he concocted and delivered himself of an archaic phrase with such meticulous precision that my father must have felt our study of the Bengali language had gone a bit too far and was in danger of overreaching itself. The next morning, when our table had as usual been placed in the south verandah, the blackboard hung up on a nail in the wall, and everything was in readiness for our lessons with Nil Kamal Babu, we three were sent for by my father in his upstairs room. 'You need not do any more Bengali lessons,' he said. Our minds danced for joy.

Nil Kamal Babu was waiting downstairs, our books were lying open on the table, and the idea of getting us once more to go through the *Meghnadbadh* doubtless still occupied his mind. On one's death-bed the various routines of daily life are said to seem unreal: so, at that moment, everything, from the pandit down to the nail holding up the blackboard, became as empty as a mirage. Our sole difficulty was how to give this news to Nil Kamal Babu with due decorum. We did it at last with considerable restraint, while the geometrical figures on the blackboard stared at us in wonder and the *Meghnadbadh* looked blankly on.

The parting words of our pandit were: 'At the call of duty I may sometimes have been harsh with you—do not keep that in remembrance. You will learn the value of what I have taught you later on.'

I have appreciated that value. It was because we were taught in our own language that our minds quickened. Learning should as far as possible follow the process of eating. When the taste begins from the first bite, the stomach is awakened to its function before it is loaded, so that its digestive juices get full play. Nothing like this happens when the Bengali boy is taught in English, however. The first bite bids fair to wrench loose both rows of teeth—like an earthquake in the mouth! And by the time he discovers that the morsel is not of the genus stone, but a digestible bonbon, half his allotted span of life is over. While one is choking and spluttering over the spelling and grammar, the inside remains starved; and when at length the taste comes through, the appetite has vanished. If the whole mind is not functioning from the beginning its full powers remain undeveloped to the end. While all around was heard the cry for English teaching, my third brother was brave enough to keep us to our Bengali course. To him in heaven my reverential thanks.

The Professor

On leaving the Normal School we were sent to the Bengal Academy, a Eurasian institution. We felt we had gained an access of dignity, that we had reached the first storey of freedom. In point of fact that was the only progress we did make in that academy. What were taught there we never understood, neither did we make any attempt to learn, and it did not seem to make any difference to anybody. The boys there were annoying but not disgusting—which was a great comfort. They wrote 'Ass' on their palms and slapped it on to our backs with a jovial 'Hello!' They gave us a dig in the ribs from behind and looked innocently in another direction. They dabbed banana pulp on our heads and made off unseen. Nevertheless it was like coming out of slime on to rock—we were still harassed but we were not soiled.

This school had one great advantage for me. No one there cherished the forlorn hope that a boy of my sort could make any advance in learning. In a petty institution with an insufficient income, we had one supreme merit in the eyes of its authorities—we paid our fees regularly. This prevented even Latin grammar from proving a stumbling-block: the most egregious of blunders left our backs unscathed. Pity had nothing to do with it—the school authorities had spoken to the teachers!

Harmless the place might be, but it was still a school. The rooms were cruelly dismal, their walls on guard like policemen. The house was more like a pigeon-holed box than a human habitation. No decoration, no pictures, not a touch of colour, not an attempt to attract the boyish heart. The fact that likes and dislikes form a large part of the child mind was completely ignored. Naturally our whole being was depressed as we stepped through its doorway into the narrow quadrangle—and playing truant became chronic with us.

In this we found an accomplice. My elder brothers had a Persian tutor. We used to call him Munshi. He was of middle age and all skin and bone, as though dark parchment had been stretched over his skeleton without any filling of flesh and blood. He probably knew Persian well, his knowledge of English was fair, but his ambition lay in neither of these directions. His belief was that his skill in song was matched only by his proficiency in singlestick. He would stand in the sun in the middle of our courtyard and go through a wonderful series of antics with a staff—his own shadow being his antagonist. It need hardly add that his shadow never got the better of him, and when at the end he gave a great big shout and whacked it on the head with a victorious smile, it lay submissively at his feet. His singing, nasal and out of tune, sounded like a gruesome mixture of groaning and moaning coming from some ghost-world. Our singing master Vishnu would sometimes chaff him: 'Hold on, Munshi, you'll be taking the bread out of our mouths at this rate!' To which his only response would be a disdainful smile.

This shows that the Munshi was amenable to soft words; and whenever we wanted we could persuade him to write to the school authorities to excuse us from attendance. The school authorities took no pains to scrutinise these letters; they knew it would be all the same whether we attended or not, so far as educational results were concerned.

I have a school of my own now in which the boys are up to all kinds of mischief; for boys will be mischievous—and schoolmasters unforgiving. When any of us becomes unduly agitated at their conduct and is stirred into a resolution to deal out condign punishment, the misdeeds of my own schooldays confront me in a row and grin at me.

I clearly see that the mistake is to judge boys by the standard of grown-ups, to forget that a child is quick and mobile like a running stream, and that any imperfection need cause no great alarm, for the speed of the flow is itself the best corrective. When stagnation sets in, then there is danger. Thus it is the teacher, more than the pupil, who should beware doing wrong.

There was a separate refreshment room for Bengali boys to meet their caste requirements. This was where we struck up friendships with some of the others. They were all older. One of them is worth a digression.

His speciality was the art of magic, so much so that he had actually written and published a little booklet on it, the front page of which bore his name with the title of Professor. I had never before come across a schoolboy whose work had appeared in print, so that my reverence for him—as a professor of magic, I mean—was profound. How could I permit myself to believe that anything questionable could possibly find its way into the straight and upright ranks of printed letters? To be able to record one's own words in indelible ink—was that a slight thing? To stand uncovered yet unabashed, self-confessed before the world—how could one withhold belief in the face of such supreme self-confidence? I remember once that I got the type for the letters of my name from some printing-press, and what a memorable thing it was when I inked and pressed them on paper and saw my name.

This schoolfellow and author-friend of ours used to get a lift in our carriage. Soon we were on visiting terms. He was also great at theatricals. With his help we erected a stage on our wrestling ground, with painted paper stretched over a split bamboo framework. But a peremptory negative from upstairs prevented any play from being acted on it.

A comedy of errors was later played without any stage at all, however. Its author has already been introduced to the reader. He was none other than my nephew Satya. Those who see him now, calm and sedate, would be shocked to learn of the tricks he invented.

The event I am about to narrate happened a little later, when I was twelve or thirteen. Our magician friend had discoursed on things with such strange properties that I was consumed with curiosity to see them for myself. But the materials of which he spoke were invariably so rare or remote that one could hardly hope to get hold of them without the help of Sinbad the sailor. Once, though, the Professor forgot himself so far as to mention accessible things. Who could ever believe that a seed dipped and dried twenty-one times in the juice of a species of cactus would sprout and flower and fruit all in the space of an hour? I was determined to test this, without, of course, daring to doubt the assurance of a Professor whose name appeared in a printed book.

I persuaded our gardener to furnish me with a plentiful supply of the milky juice, and took myself one Sunday afternoon to our private mystery corner on the roof terrace, to experiment with the stone of a mango. I was quickly wrapped up in my task of dipping and drying—but the grown-up reader will probably not wait to ask me the result. In the meantime, I little knew that Satya, in another corner, had caused to root and sprout a mystical plant of his own creation all in the space of an hour. It was to bear curious fruit later on.

After my experiment the Professor rather avoided me, as I gradually came to perceive. He would not sit on the same side in the carriage, and seemed altogether to fight shy of me.

One day, all of a sudden, he proposed that each one should jump off the bench in our schoolroom in turn. He wanted to observe the differences in style, he said. Such scientific curiosity did not appear queer in a professor of magic. Every one jumped and so did I. He shook his head with a subdued 'Hmm.' No amount of cajoling could draw anything further from him.

Another day he informed us that some good friends of his wanted to make our acquaintance, and asked us to accompany him to their house. Our guardians had no objection, so off we went. The crowd in the room seemed full of curiosity. They expressed their eagerness to hear me sing. I sang a song or two. Mere child that I was, my voice was hardly likely to be a bull's bellow. 'Rather a sweet voice,' they all agreed.

When refreshments were put before us they sat round and watched us eat. I was shy by nature and not used to strange company; moreover the habits I had acquired while superintended by our servant Ishwar had left me a poor eater for good. They all seemed impressed with the delicacy of my appetite.

In the final act of this farce I received some curiously warm letters from our Professor that explained the whole situation. And here let the curtain fall.

I subsequently learned from Satya that while I had been practising magic on the mango seed, he had successfully convinced the Professor that I was dressed as a boy by our guardians merely to get me a better schooling, but that really this was only a disguise. To those who are inquisitive about imaginary science I should explain that a girl is supposed to jump with her left foot forward, and this is what I had done on the occasion of the Professor's trial. Little did I realise what a tremendously false step I had taken!

My Father

Shortly after my birth my father took to constant travel. So it is no exaggeration to say that in my early childhood I hardly knew him. He would now and then come back home all of a sudden, and with him came outsiders as servants with whom I felt extremely eager to make friends. Once he brought a young Punjabi servant named Lenu. The cordiality of the reception we gave him would have been worthy of Maharaja Ranjit Singh himself. Not only was he a foreigner, but a Punjabi too—this really stole our hearts away. We had the same reverence for the whole Punjabi nation as we did for Bhima and Arjuna of the *Mahabharata*. They were warriors, and if they had sometimes lost the fight, that was clearly the enemy's fault. It was glorious to have Lenu of the Punjab in our very home.

My sister-in-law had a model warship under a glass case which, when wound up, rocked on blue-painted silken waves to the tinkling of a musical box. I would beg hard for the loan of this to display its marvels to the admiring Lenu.

Caged in the house as we were, anything savouring of foreign parts had a peculiar charm for me. It was one of the reasons why I made so much of Lenu. It was also why Gabriel, the Jew, with his embroidered gaberdine, who came to sell *attars* and scented oils, stirred me so; and why the huge

Kabulis, with their dusty, baggy trousers and knapsacks and bundles, worked my young mind into a fearful fascination.

So when my father came, we would be content with wandering among his entourage and keeping the company of his servants. We did not reach his actual presence.

Once, while my father was away in the Himalayas, that old bogy of the British government, a Russian invasion, became a subject of agitated conversation among the people. Some well-meaning lady friend had enlarged on the impending danger to my mother with all the fancy of a prolific imagination. How could anybody tell from which of the Tibetan passes the Russian host might suddenly flash forth like a baleful comet?

My mother was seriously alarmed. The other members of the family possibly did not share her misgivings so, despairing of grown-up sympathy, she sought my boyish support. 'Won't you write to your father about the Russians?' she asked.

My letter, bearing the tidings of my mother's anxieties, was the first I wrote to my father. I did not know how to begin or end a letter, or anything at all about it. I went to Mahananda, the estate *munshi*. My resulting form of address was doubtless correct enough, but the sentiments could not have escaped the musty flavour inseparable from correspondence emanating from an estate office.

I had a reply. My father asked me not to be afraid; if the Russians came he would drive them away himself. This confident assurance did not seem to have the effect of relieving my mother's fears, but it served to free me from all timidity as regards my father. After that I wanted to write to him every day, and pestered Mahananda accordingly. Unable to withstand my importunity he would make out drafts for me to copy. But I did not know that there was postage to be paid for. I had an idea that letters placed in Mahananda's hands got to their destination without any need for further worry. It is hardly necessary to add that Mahananda was old enough to ensure that these letters never reached the Himalayan hill-tops.

After his long absences, when my father came home even for a few days, the whole house seemed filled with the gravity of his presence. We would see our elders at certain hours, formally robed in the *chogas,* passing to his rooms with restrained gait and sober mien, casting away any *pan* they might have been chewing. Everyone seemed on the alert. To make sure that nothing went wrong, my mother would superintend the cooking herself. The old retainer Kinu, with his white livery and crested turban, on guard at my father's door, would warn us not to be boisterous in the verandah in front of his rooms during his midday siesta. We had to walk past quietly, talking in whispers, and dared not even take a peep inside.

On one occasion my father came home to invest the three of us with the sacred thread. With the help of Pandit Vedantavagish he had collected the old Vedic rites for the purpose. For days at a time we were taught to chant in correct accents the selections from the *Upanishads,* arranged under the name of *Brahma Dharma,* by my father seated in the prayer hall with Becharam Babu. Finally, with shaven heads and gold rings in our ears, we three budding Brahmins went into a three-days' retreat in a portion of the third storey.

It was great fun. The earrings gave us a good handle to pull each other's ears with. We found a little drum lying in one of the rooms; taking this we would stand out in the verandah, and when we caught sight of any servant passing along in the storey below, we rapped a tattoo on it. This would make the man look up, only to avert his eyes and beat a hasty retreat at the next moment. We certainly cannot claim that we passed these days of our retirement in ascetic meditation.

I am convinced that boys like us must have been common in the hermitages of old. If some ancient document has it that the ten- or twelve-year-old Saradwata or Sarngarava spent the whole of his boyhood offering oblations and chanting mantras, we are not compelled to put unquestioning faith in the statement; because the book of Boy Nature is even older and is also more authentic.

After we had attained full Brahminhood I became very keen on repeating the *gayatri*. I would meditate on it with great concentration. It is hardly a text of which the full meaning may be grasped at that age. I distinctly remember what efforts I made to extend the range of my consciousness with the help of the initial invocation of 'Earth, firmament and heaven'. How I felt or thought it is difficult to express clearly, but this much is certain: that to be clear about the meaning of words is not the most important part of the process of human understanding.

The main object of teaching is not to give explanations, but to knock at the doors of the mind. If any boy is asked to give an account of what is awakened in him by such knocking, he will probably say something silly. For what happens within is much bigger than what comes out in words. Those who pin their faith on university examinations as the test of education take no account of this.

I can recollect many things which I did not understand, but which stirred me deeply. Once, on the roof terrace of our riverside villa, at the sudden gathering of clouds my eldest brother repeated aloud some stanzas from *The Cloud Messenger* by Kalidas. I could not understand a word of the Sanskrit, neither did I need to. His ecstatic declamation and the sonorous rhythm were enough for me.

Then, again, before I could properly understand English, a profusely illustrated edition of *The Old Curiosity Shop* fell into my hands. I went through the whole of it, though at least nine-tenths of the words were unknown to me. Yet, with the vague ideas conjured up by the rest, I spun out a variously coloured thread on which to string the illustrations. Any university examiner would have given me zero, but for me the reading of the book had not proved quite so empty.

Another time I had accompanied my father for a trip on the Ganges in his houseboat. Among the books he had with him was an old Fort William edition of Jayadeva's *Gita Govinda*, printed in Bengali script. The verses were not in separate lines, but ran on like prose. I did not know any Sanskrit then, yet because of my knowledge of Bengali many of the words were familiar. How often I read that *Gita Govinda* I cannot say. I particularly remember this line:

The night extinguished in solitary forest exile.

It roused a feeling of beauty in my mind. That one Sanskrit word *nibhrita-nikunja-griham,* meaning 'solitary forest exile', was quite enough for me.

I had to work out for myself the intricate metre of Jayadeva's poetry, because its divisions were lost in the clumsy prose form of the book. And this discovery gave me very great delight. Of course I did not fully comprehend Jayadeva's meaning. One could not even truthfully say that I grasped it partly. But the sound of the words and the lilt of the metre filled my mind with pictures of such grace that I was impelled to copy out the whole book for my own use.

The same thing happened, when I was a little older, with a verse from Kalidas' *Birth of the War God*. The verse really moved me, though the only words of which I gathered the sense, were 'the zephyr wafting the spray from the falling waters of the sacred Mandakini and trembling the deodar leaves.' They left me pining to taste the whole. When a pandit later explained to me that in the next two lines the breeze 'split the feathers of the peacock plume on the head of the eager deer-hunter', the thinness of the conceit disappointed me. I was much better off when I had relied only upon my imagination to complete the verse.

Whoever goes back to his early childhood will agree that his greatest gains were not in proportion to the completeness of his understanding. Our *kathakas* know this very well: when they give public recitals, their narratives always have a good proportion of ear-filling Sanskrit words and abstruse remarks calculated not to be fully understood by their simple hearers, but only to be suggestive.

The value of such suggestion is by no means to be despised by those who measure education in terms of material gains and losses. They insist on trying to tot up the account and find out exactly how much of a lesson can be rendered up. But children, and those who are not over-educated, dwell in that primal paradise where humans can obtain knowledge without wholly comprehending each step. Only when that paradise is lost comes the evil day when everything has to be understood. The road which leads to knowledge without going through the dreary process of understanding is the royal road. If that be barred, even though commerce may continue, the open sea and the mountaintop cease to be possible of access.

So, as I was saying, though at that age I could not realise the full meaning of the *gayatri*, something in me could do without a complete understanding. I am reminded of a day when, as I was seated on the cement floor in a corner of our schoolroom meditating on the text, my eyes overflowed with tears. Why they came I do not know; to a strict cross-questioner I would probably have given some explanation having nothing to do with the *gayatri*. The fact is that what goes on in the inner recesses of consciousness is not always known to the surface dweller.

A Journey with My Father

My shaven head after the sacred thread ceremony caused me one great anxiety. However partial Eurasian lads may be to the sacred Cow, their reverence for the Brahmin is definitely minimal. I expected that apart from other missiles, our shaven heads were sure to be pelted with jeers. While I kept worrying over this possibility I was summoned upstairs to my father. How would I like to go with him to the Himalayas? Away from the Bengal Academy and off to the Himalayas! How would I like it? Oh, I would have needed to rend the skies with a shout to give some idea of How!

The day we left home my father, as was his habit, assembled the whole family in the prayer hall for divine service. After I had taken the dust of my elders' feet I got into the carriage with my father. This was the first time in my life that I had a full suit of clothes made for me. My father had selected the pattern and colour himself. A gold-embroidered velvet cap completed my costume. This I carried in my hand, assailed as I was with misgivings about its impact atop my hairless head. As I got into the carriage my father insisted on my wearing it, so I had to put it on. Every time he looked away I took it off. Every time I caught his eye it had to resume its proper place.

My father was very particular in all his arrangements. He disliked leaving things vague or undetermined, and never allowed slovenliness or make-do. He had a well-defined code to regulate his relations with others and theirs with him. In this he was different from the generality of his countrymen. Among the rest of us a little laxity this way or that did not signify; in our dealings with him we therefore had to be anxiously careful. The size and significance of a task did not concern him so much as failure to maintain its required standard.

My father also had a way of picturing to himself every detail of what he wanted done. On the occasion of any ceremonial gathering at which he could not be present, he would think out and assign a place for each thing, a duty for each member of the family, a seat for each guest; nothing would escape him. After everything was over he would ask each one for a separate account and gain a complete impression of the whole for himself. So while I was with him on his travels, though nothing would induce him to interfere in how I amused myself, no loophole was left in the strict rules of conduct prescribed for me in other respects.

Our first half was to be at Bolpur for a few days. Satya had been there a short time before with his parents. No self-respecting nineteenth-century boy would have credited the account of his travels which he gave us on his return. But I was different, and had had no opportunity of learning to determine the line between the possible and the impossible. Our *Mahabharata* and *Ramayana* gave us no clue to it. Nor had we then any illustrated books to guide us. All the hard-and-fast rules that govern the world we learnt by knocking ourselves against them.

Satya had told us that, unless one was exceedingly expert, getting into a railway carriage was a terribly dangerous affair—the least slip, and it was all up. Once aboard, a fellow had to hold on to his seat with all his might, otherwise the tremendous jolt on starting might throw him off—there was no telling where to.

When we got to the railway station I was all a-quiver. So easily did we enter our compartment that I felt sure the worst was yet to come. And when, at length, we made an absurdly smooth start without any hint of adventure, I felt woefully disappointed.

The train sped on; the broad fields bordered by blue-green trees and the villages nestling in their shade flew past in a stream of pictures that melted away like a flood of mirages. It was evening when we reached Bolpur. As I got into the palanquin I closed my eyes. I wanted to preserve the whole of the wonderful vision to be unfolded before my waking eyes in the morning light. The freshness of the experience would be spoilt, I feared, by incomplete glimpses caught in the vagueness of twilight.

When I woke at dawn I was tremulously excited as I stepped outside. My predecessor had told me that Bolpur had one feature which was to be found nowhere else in the world. This was a path leading from the main buildings to the servants' quarters, which, though not covered over in any way, did not allow a ray of sun or a drop of rain to touch anybody passing along it. I started to hunt for this wonderful path, but the reader will perhaps not wonder at my failure to find it to this day.

Town boy that I was, I had never seen a rice-field and had a charming portrait of the cowherd boy, of whom we had read, pictured on the canvas of my imagination. I had heard from Satya that the Bolpur house was surrounded by fields of ripening rice, and that playing in these with cowherd boys was an everyday affair, of which the plucking, cooking and eating of the rice was the crowning feature. I eagerly looked about me. Where was the rice-field on all that barren heath? Cowherd boys might have been somewhere about, but how to distinguish them from any other boys was the question!

What I could not see did not take me long to get over—what I did see was quite enough. There was no servant rule, and the only ring which encircled me was the blue of the horizon, drawn around these solitudes by their presiding goddess. Within this I was free to move about as I chose.

Though I was still a mere child my father did not place any restriction on my wanderings. In the hollows of the sandy soil the rain water had ploughed deep furrows, carving out miniature mountain ranges full of red gravel and pebbles of various shapes through which ran tiny streams, revealing the geography of Lilliput. From this region I would gather in the lap of my tunic many curious pieces of stone and take the collection to my father. He never made light of my labours. On the contrary he was enthusiastic.

'Splendid!' he exclaimed, 'Wherever did you get all these?'

'There are many many more, thousands and thousands!' I burst out. 'I could bring as many every day.'

'That *would* be nice!' he replied. 'Why not decorate my little hill with them?'

An attempt had been made to dig a tank in the garden but, the water-table proving too low, the digging had been abandoned with the excavated earth left piled up in a hillock. On top of this my father used to sit for his morning prayer, and as he did so the sun would rise at the edge of the undulating expanse which stretched away to the eastern horizon in front of him. It was this hill he asked me to decorate.

I was very troubled, on leaving Bolpur, that I could not carry away my store of stones. I had not yet understood the encumbrance entailed and that I had no absolute claim on a thing merely because I had collected it. If fate had granted me my prayer, as I had dearly desired, and determined that I should carry this load of stones about with me for ever, today this story would be no laughing matter.

In one of the ravines I came upon a hollow full of spring water which overflowed as a little rivulet, where tiny fish played and battled their way up the current.

'I've found such a lovely spring,' I told my father. 'Couldn't we get our bathing- and drinking-water from there?'

'Perfect,' he agreed, sharing my rapture, and gave orders for our water-supply to be drawn from that spring.

I was never tired of roaming these miniature valleys and plateaus in hopes of alighting on something never before discovered. I was the Livingstone of this land which looked as if seen through the wrong end of a telescope. Everything there, the dwarf date palms, the scrubby wild plums and the stunted *jambolans,* was in keeping with the miniature mountain ranges, the rivulet and the tiny fish.

Probably to teach me to be careful my father placed some small change in my charge and required me to keep an account of it. He also entrusted me with the winding of his valuable gold watch. He overlooked the risk of damage in his desire to train me to a sense of duty. When we went out together for our morning walk he asked me to give alms to any beggars we came across. I could never render him a proper account at the end. One day my balance was larger than the account warranted.

'I really must make you my cashier,' observed my father. 'Money seems to have a way of growing in your hands!'

His watch I wound with such indefatigable zeal that very soon it had to be sent to the watchmaker's in Calcutta.

I am reminded of the occasions in later life when I used to tender the estate accounts to my father, who was then living in Park Street. I would do this on the second or third of every month. He was by then unable to read them himself. I had first to read out the totals under each heading, and if he had any doubts on any point he would ask for the details. If I made any attempt to slur over or conceal any item I feared he would not like, it was sure to come out. These first few days of the month were very anxious ones for me.

As I have said, my father had the habit of keeping everything clearly before his mind—whether figures of accounts, or ceremonial arrangements, or additions or alterations to property. He had never seen the new prayer hall at Bolpur, and yet he was familiar with every detail of it from questioning those who came to see him after a visit there. He had an extraordinary memory, and when once he got hold of a fact it never escaped him.

My father had marked his favourite verses in his copy of the *Bhagavadgita*. He asked me to copy these out for him, with their translation. At home I had been a boy of no account, but here, when these important functions were entrusted to me, I felt the glory of the situation.

By this time I was rid of my blue manuscript book and had got hold of a bound volume, one of Letts' diaries. I saw to it now that my poetising should not be lacking in outward dignity. It was not just writing poems, but holding a picture of myself as a poet before my imagination. When I wrote poetry at Bolpur I loved to do it sprawling under a young coconut palm. This seemed to me the true manner. Thus resting on the hard unturfed gravel in the burning heat of the day, I composed a martial ballad on the 'Defeat of King Prithvi'. In spite of its superabundance of martial spirit, it could not escape early death. That bound volume of Letts' diary followed the way of its elder sister, the blue manuscript book, leaving no forwarding address.

We left Bolpur and, making short halts on the way at Sahibganj, Dinapur, Allahabad and Kanpur, we stopped at last at Amritsar.

An incident *en route* remains engraved on my memory. The train had stopped at some big station. The ticket collector came and punched our tickets. He looked at me curiously as if he had some doubt that he did not care to express. He went off and came back with a companion. Both of them fidgeted about for a time near the door of our compartment and then again retired. At last the station-master himself came. He looked at my half-ticket and then asked: 'Is not the boy over twelve?'

'No,' said my father.

I was then only eleven, but looked older than my age.

'You must pay the full fare for him,' said the station-master.

My father's eyes flashed as, without a word, he took out a currency note from his box and handed it to the station-master. When they brought the change my father flung it disdainfully back at them, while the station-master stood abashed at this exposure of the meanness of his doubt.

The Golden Temple of Amritsar comes back to me like a dream. On many a morning I accompanied my father to this *gurudarbar* of the Sikhs in the middle of the lake. There the sacred chanting continually resounds. My father, seated amidst the throng of worshippers, would sometimes add his voice to the hymn of praise and, finding a stranger joining in their devotions they would welcome him most cordially, and we would return loaded with the sanctified offerings of sugar crystals and other sweets.

One day my father invited one of the chanting choir to our place and had him sing us some of their sacred songs. The man went away probably more than satisfied with the reward he received. Soon we had to take stern measures in self-defence, such was the insistent army of singers that invaded us. When they found our house impregnable, the musicians began to waylay us in the streets. As we went out for our walk in the morning, from time to time would appear a *tanpura*, slung over a shoulder; it made us feel like game birds that had spotted the muzzle of a hunter's gun. So wary did we become that the twang of a *tanpura,* even in the distance, would scare us away and fail utterly to bag us.

When evening fell, my father would sit out on the verandah facing the garden. He would summon me to sing to him. I can see the moon risen; its beams, passing through the trees, falling on the verandah floor; and I am singing in raga Behag:

O Companion in the darkest passage of life...

My father with bowed head and clasped hands listens intently. I recall the evening scene quite clearly.

I have already told of my father's amusement on hearing from Srikantha Babu of my maiden attempt at a devotional poem. I remember how, later, I had my recompense. On the occasion of one of our *Magh* festivals several of the hymns were of my composition. One of them was:

The eye sees thee not, who art the pupil of every eye.

My father was then bed-ridden at Chunchura. He sent for me and my brother Jyoti. He asked my brother to accompany me on the harmonium, and me to sing all my hymns one after the other, some of them twice over. When I had finished he said: 'If the king of the country had known the language and could appreciate its literature, he would doubtless have rewarded the poet. Since that is not so, I suppose I must do it.' With which he handed me a cheque.

My father had brought with him some volumes of the Peter Parley series from which to teach me. He selected *The Life of Benjamin Franklin* to begin with. He thought it would read like a story book and be both entertaining and instructive. But he found out his mistake soon after we began. Benjamin Franklin was much too business-like a person. The narrowness of his calculated morality disgusted my father. Sometimes he would become so impatient at Franklin's worldly prudence that he could not help using strong words of denunciation.

Until now I had had nothing to do with Sanskrit beyond learning some rules of grammar by rote. My father started me on the second Sanskrit reader at one bound, leaving me to learn the declensions as we went on. The advance I had made in Bengali stood me in good stead. My father also encouraged me to try Sanskrit composition from the very outset. With the vocabulary acquired from my Sanskrit reader I built up grandiose compound words with a profuse sprinkling of sonorous m's and n's, that made a most diabolical medley out of the language of the gods. But my father never scoffed at my temerity.

Then there were the readings from Proctor's *Popular Astronomy,* which my father explained to me in easy language and which I then rendered into Bengali.

Among the books which my father had brought for his own use, I often found myself gazing at a ten- or twelve-volume edition of Gibbon's *Rome.* They looked remarkably dry. I am only a helpless boy, I thought, I read many books because I have to. But why should a grown-up person, who doesn't have to read unless he pleases, give himself such bother?

In the Himalayas

We stayed about a month in Amritsar, and, towards the middle of April, started for the Dalhousie hills. The last few days in Amritsar seemed as if they would never pass, the Himalayas were calling me so strongly.

The terraced hillsides, as we went up in a *jhampan,* were aflame with flowering spring crops. Every morning we made a start after bread and milk, and before sunset took shelter in the next staging bungalow. My eyes had no rest the entire day, so much did I fear missing something. Wherever the great forest trees clustered together at a bend of the road into a gorge, a waterfall trickled out from beneath their shade, like a little daughter playing at the feet of hoary sages rapt in meditation and babbling over the black moss-covered rocks; there the *jhampan* bearers would put down their burden, and take a rest. Why had we ever to leave such spots, cried my thirsting heart. Why could we not stay on for good?

That is the great advantage of a first vision: the mind is not aware that there are many more to come. When this fact penetrates that calculating organ it promptly tries to make a saving in its expenditure of attention. Only when it believes something to be rare does the mind cease to be miserly. In the streets of Calcutta I sometimes imagine myself a foreigner, and only then do I discover how much is to be seen. The hunger to see properly is what drives people to travel in strange places.

My father left his little cash-box in my charge. He had no reason to imagine that I was the fittest custodian of the considerable sums he kept in it for use on the way. He would certainly have felt safer with it in the hands of Kishori, his attendant. So I can only suppose he wanted to instill in me the idea of responsibility. One day as we reached the staging bungalow, I forgot to make it over to him and left it lying on a table. This brought me a reprimand.

Every time we got down at the end of a stage, my father had chairs placed for us outside the bungalow and there we sat. As dusk came on the stars blazed wonderfully through the clear mountain atmosphere, and my father showed me the constellations or treated me to an astronomical discourse.

The house we had taken at Bakrota was on the highest hill-top. Though May had almost come it was still bitterly cold there, so much so that on the shady side of the hill the winter frosts had not yet melted.

My father was not at all nervous about my wandering freely even here. Some way below our house stretched a spur thickly wooded with deodars. I would go alone into this wilderness with my iron-tipped staff. What lordly trees, towering above me like giants! What vast shadows! What immense lives they had lived over the centuries! And yet this boy, born only the other day, crawled around between their trunks unchallenged. I seemed to feel a presence the moment I stepped into their shade like that of some ancient saurian whose cool, firm and scaly body was made of checkered light and shade on the leaf mould of the forest floor.

My room was at one end of the house. Lying on my bed I could see, through the uncurtained windows, the distant snow peaks shimmering dimly in the starlight. Sometimes, half-awake, at what hour I could not make out, I saw my father, wrapped in a red shawl, with a lighted lamp in his hand, softly passing by to the glazed verandah where he sat at his devotions. After dozing off, I would find him at my bedside, rousing me with a push before the darkness had yet passed from the night. This was the hour appointed for memorising Sanskrit declensions. What an excruciatingly wintry awakening from the caressing warmth of my blankets!

By the time the sun rose, my father, after finishing his prayers, joined me for our morning milk, and then stood with me, once more to hold communion with God by chanting the *Upanishads*.

Then we would go out for a walk. But how could I keep pace with him? Many adults could not! After a while, I would give up and scramble back home by some short cut over the mountainside.

Upon my father's return I had an hour of English lessons. At ten o'clock came a bath in ice-cold water. It was no use asking the servants to temper it with even a jugful of hot water without permission. To give me courage my father would tell of the unbearably freezing baths he had himself endured in his younger days.

Another penance was milk-drinking. My father was very fond of milk and could take quantities. But my appetite for it was grievously lacking, whether because I had failed to inherit it or because of my unfavourable early experiences with milk, I do not know. Unfortunately we used to have our milk together so I had to throw myself on the mercy of the servants, and to their human kindness (or frailty) I was indebted for my goblet being more than half full of foam.

After our midday meal lessons began again. This was more than flesh and blood could stand. My outraged morning sleep *would* have its revenge and I would be toppling over with uncontrollable drowsiness. But no sooner did my father take pity on my plight and let me off than my sleepiness was off likewise: the Lord of the mountains was calling!

Staff in hand I would often wander away from one peak to another, but my father did not object. To the end of his life, I have observed, he never stood in the way of our independence. Frequently I have said or done things repugnant to his taste and his judgement alike; with a word he could have stopped me but he preferred to wait until the prompting to refrain came from within. A passive acceptance of the correct and the proper did not satisfy him; he wanted us to love truth with our whole hearts; mere acquiescence without love he knew to be empty. He also knew that truth, if strayed from, can be found again, but a forced or blind adherence effectively bars access to it.

In my early youth I had conceived a fancy to travel the Grand Trunk Road, right up to Peshawar, in a bullock cart. No one else supported the scheme, and doubtless there was much to be urged against it as a practical proposition. But when I discoursed on it to my father he was sure it was a splendid idea—travelling by railway was not worth the name! And he forthwith proceeded to recount his own adventure on foot and horseback. Of any chance of discomfort or peril he had not a word to say.

Another time, when I had just been appointed secretary of the Adi Brahmo Samaj, I went over to my father at his Park Street residence and informed him that I did not approve of the practice of having only Brahmins conducting divine service to the exclusion of other castes. He unhesitatingly gave me permission to correct this if I could. Armed with the authorisation I found I lacked the power. I was able to discover imperfections but could not create perfection! Where were the men? Where was the strength in me to attract the right man? Had I the means to build in place of what I might break? Until the right man arrives, any form is better than none—

this, I felt, must have been my father's view. But not for a moment did he try to discourage me by pointing out these difficulties.

Just as he allowed me to wander the mountains at will, so he left me free to select my path in the quest for truth. He was not deterred by the risk of my making mistakes, neither alarmed at the prospect of my encountering sorrow. He held up a standard, not a disciplinary rod.

I could often talk to him of home. Whenever I got a letter from anyone there I immediately showed it to him. I believe I permitted him many a glimpse he could have had from no one else. My father also let me read letters to him from my elder brothers. It was his way of teaching me how I ought to write to him; for he by no means undervalued outward forms and ceremonial.

I remember how in one letter my second brother complained of being worked to death, tied by the neck to his post, expressing himself in somewhat Sanskritised language. My father asked me to explain briefly what was meant. I did so in my way, but he thought a different explanation better. In my overweening conceit I stuck to my guns and argued the point at length. Another person would have stopped me with a snub, but my father patiently heard me out and took pains to justify his view to me.

Sometimes he would tell me funny stories. He had many anecdotes of the gilded youth of his time. There were some exquisites for whose delicate skins the embroidered border of even Dacca muslins proved too coarse; among them, for a while, it was the tip-top thing to wear one's muslins with the borders torn off.

I was also highly amused to hear, first from my father, the story of the milkman suspected of watering his milk. The more men one of his customers detailed to supervise his milking the bluer the fluid became, until at last, when the customer himself interviewed the milkman and asked for an explanation, the man bluntly stated that if any more superintendents had to be satisfied the milk would be fit only to breed fish!

After I had spent a few months with him, my father sent me back home with his attendant Kishori.

My Return

The chains of the rigorous regime which had bound me had snapped for good when I had set out from home. On my return I acquired some rights. My very proximity to others ruled me out of mind before; by going away and coming back I came into focus.

I had a foretaste of appreciation while on my way back. Travelling alone except for my attendant, brimming with health and spirits, and conspicuous in my gold-worked cap, I was made much of by all the English people I came across in the train.

My arrival was not merely a homecoming, but also a return from exile in the servants' quarters to my rightful place in the inner apartments. Whenever the inner household assembled in my mother's room I now occupied a seat of honour. And she, who was then the youngest bride of our house, lavished on me a wealth of affection and regard.

In infancy the loving care of woman is to be had without the asking, and, being as much a necessity as light and air, is simply taken for granted. In fact children often fidget to free themselves from the web of feminine solicitude. But any creature who is deprived of it at its proper time is beggared indeed. This had been my plight after being brought up in the servants' quarters. So, when I suddenly came in for a profusion of womanly affection, I could hardly remain unconscious of it.

In earlier days, when the inner apartments were far away from me, they were the Elysium of my imagination. The *zenana*, which looks from the outside a place of confinement, for me was the abode of all freedom. Neither school nor pandit was there; nor, it seemed to me, did anybody have to do what they did not want to do. Its secluded leisure had something mysterious about it; one played about, or did as one liked and did not have to render an account of one's doings. This seemed especially so of my youngest sister, who attended Nil Kamal Pandit's class with us but appeared to be unaffected whether she did her lessons well or ill. While we had to hurry through our breakfast by ten o'clock and be ready for school, she her plait dangling behind, walked unconcernedly away withinwards, tantalising us to distraction.

And when the new bride, adorned with her necklace of gold, came into our house, the mystery of the inner apartments deepened. She, who came from outside and yet became one of us, who was unknown and yet our own, attracted me strangely: I burned to make friends. But if by much contriving I managed to draw near, my youngest sister would hustle me off with: 'What d'you boys want here? Keep away outside.' The insult, added to the disappointment, cut me to the quick. Through the glass doors of their cabinets one could catch glimpses of all manner of curious playthings, creations of porcelain and glass, gorgeous in colouring and ornamentation. We were not deemed worthy even to touch them, much less invited to play with them. These objects, rare and wonderful as they seemed to us, tinged the inner apartments with an additional allure.

Thus was I kept at arm's length by repeated rebuffs. The outside world was unavailable to me, and so, alas, was the inner. What little I saw of it impressed me like a series of paintings.

It is nine in the evening, for instance, and, my lessons with Aghore Babu over, I am retiring inside for the night. A murky flickering lantern hangs in the long Venetian-screened corridor leading from the outer to the inner apartments. At its end this passage becomes a flight of four or five steps, into which the light does not reach and down which I pass into the galleries running round the first inner courtyard. A shaft of moonlight slants from the eastern sky into the western section of these verandahs, leaving the rest in darkness. Within this patch of light the maids have gathered and sit on the floor close together, legs outstretched, rolling cotton waste on their thighs into lamp-wicks and chatting in undertones of their village homes.

Many such pictures are indelibly printed on my memory. Another is of the time after supper which begins with the washing of our hands and feet on the verandah before stretching ourselves on the ample expanse of our bed; whereupon one of the nurses, Tinkari or Shankari, comes and sits by our heads and softly croons to us the story of the prince travelling on and on over the lonely moor, and, as it reaches the end, silence falls on the room. With my face to the wall I stare at the black and white patches made by plaster that has fallen off here and there, faintly visible in the dim light; and I conjure many a fantastic image as I drop off to sleep. And sometimes, during the night, I hear in my half-broken sleep the calls of old Swarup, the watchman, going his rounds from verandah to verandah.

Then came the new order. From the inner dreamland known only in my fancies came all the recognition for which I had been pining, and more; when that which should have come naturally day by day was suddenly made good to me with accumulated arrears. I cannot say that my head was not turned.

The little traveller was full of his travels, and, with the strain of each repetition, the narrative got looser and looser until it utterly refused to fit the facts. Like everything else alas, a story also grows stale and the glory of the teller suffers likewise; that is why he has to add new colouring every time to maintain freshness.

After my return from the hills I was the principal speaker at my mother's open-air gatherings on the roof terrace in the evenings. The temptation to become famous in one's mother's eyes is as difficult to resist as such fame is easy to earn. While I was at the Normal School, when I first came across the information in some reader that the sun was hundreds and thousands of times bigger than the earth, I at once disclosed it to my mother. It served to prove that someone who looked small might yet have a certain grandeur. I used also to recite to her scraps of poetry used as illustrations in the chapter on prosody or rhetoric in our Bengali grammar. Now I retailed to her evening gatherings the astronomical tit-bits I had gleaned from Proctor.

My father's follower Kishori belonged at one time to a band of reciters of Dasharathi's jingling versions of the epics. While we were together in the hills he often said to me: 'Oh, my little brother, if I only had had you in our troupe we could have got up a splendid performance.' This would open up to me a tempting picture of wandering as a minstrel boy from place to place, reciting and singing. I learnt many of the songs in his repertoire, and these were in even greater demand than my talks about the photosphere of the sun or the many moons of Saturn.

But my greatest achievement in my mother's eyes was that while the rest of the inmates of the inner apartments had to be content with Krittivas' Bengali rendering of the *Ramayana,*

I had been reading with my father the original of Maharshi Valmiki himself, Sanskrit metre and all. 'Read me some of that *Ramayana,* do!' she said, overjoyed when I mentioned this.

Alas, my reading of Valmiki had been limited to the short extract from his *Ramayana* given in my Sanskrit reader, and even that I had not fully mastered. Moreover, on looking over it again, I found that memory had played me false and much of what I thought I knew had become hazy. But I lacked the courage to plead 'I have forgotten' to my eager mother awaiting the display of her son's marvellous talents; so in the reading I gave, Valmiki's intention and my explanation widely diverged. That tender-hearted sage, from his seat in heaven, must have forgiven the temerity of a boy seeking the glory of his mother's approbation—but not so the god whose role is to puncture pride.

My mother, unable to contain her feelings at my extraordinary exploit, wanted all to share her admiration. 'You must read this to Dwijendra,' she said.

Now I've had it! I thought, as I offered all the excuses I could think of, but my mother would have none of them. She sent for my eldest brother and as soon as he arrived greeted him with: 'Just hear Rabi read Valmiki's *Ramayana;* how splendidly he does it.'

It had to be done! But the god of pride relented and let me off with just a whiff of his power. My brother had probably been called away from his literary work and was preoccupied. He showed no enthusiasm to hear me render the Sanskrit into Bengali; as soon as I had read out a few verses he remarked simply, 'Very good,' and walked off.

Following my promotion to the inner apartments I found it all the more difficult to resume my school life. I resorted to all kinds of subterfuge to escape the Bengal Academy. Then they tried putting me at St Xavier's. But the result was no better.

My elder brothers, after a few spasmodic efforts, gave up all hope of me—they even ceased to scold me. My eldest sister one day said: 'We had all hoped Rabi would grow up to be a man, but he has been our biggest disappointment.' I felt that my value in the social world was depreciating distinctly; nevertheless I could not commit my mind to the eternal grind of school which, divorced as it was from all life and beauty, seemed such a hideously cruel combination of hospital and gaol.

One memory of St Xavier's I still hold fresh and pure. It concerns the teachers. Not that they were all of the same excellence. Among those who taught our class I could discern no particular dedication or humility. As a group they were in no wise better than the teaching-machine brand of school master. On its own, the educational engine is remorselessly powerful, but when the outward forms of religion are coupled to it like a stone mill, the heart of youth is truly crushed dry. This is the type of grindstone we had at St Xavier's. Yet, as I say, I possess one memory that elevates my impression of the teachers there to an ideal plane.

Father DePeneranda had very little to do with us—if I remember right he was a temporary replacement for one of the masters of our class. He was a Spaniard who seemed to have an impediment in speaking English. Perhaps for this reason the boys paid little heed to what he said. I felt that his pupils' inattentiveness hurt him, but he bore it meekly day after day. I do not know why, but my heart went out to him. His features were not handsome, but his face had a strange appeal. Whenever I looked on him his spirit seemed to be in prayer, a deep peace to pervade him within and without.

We had half an hour for writing our copy-books, a time when, pen in hand, I became absent-minded and my thoughts wandered hither and thither. One day Father DePeneranda was in charge of this class. He was pacing up and down behind our benches. He must have noticed more than once that my pen was not moving. All of a sudden he stopped behind my seat. Bending over me he gently laid his hand on my shoulder and tenderly inquired: 'Are you not well, Tagore?' It was only a simple question, but one I have never been able to forget.

I cannot speak for the other boys, but I felt in him the presence of a great soul, and even today the recollection of it seems to transport me into the silent seclusion of the temple of God.

There was another old Father whom all the boys loved, Father Henry. He taught the higher classes, so I did not know him well. But I remember one thing about him: he knew Bengali. He once asked Nirada, a boy in his class, the derivation of his name. Poor Nirada! He had long been supremely confident about himself—the derivation of his name never giving him the least pause for thought; he was utterly unprepared to answer this question. And yet, with a whole dictionary full of abstruse and unknown words to chose from, to be worsted by one's own name would be as ridiculous as getting run over by one's own carriage. So Nirada unblushingly replied: 'Ni—privative, rode—sun's rays; hence Nirode—that which causes an absence of the sun's rays!'*

---

* *Nirada* is Sanskrit for cloud. It is a compound of *nira*=water and *da*=giver. In Bengali it is pronounced 'nirode'.

Home Studies

Gyan Babu, son of pandit Vedantavagish, was now our tutor at home. When he found he could not secure my attention for the school course, he gave up the attempt as hopeless and tried a different tack. He took me through Kalidas' *Birth of the War-God,* translating it to me as he went along. He also read *Macbeth* to me, first explaining the text in Bengali and then confining me to the schoolroom till I had rendered the day's reading into Bengali verse. In this way he had me translate the whole play. I was fortunate enough to lose this translation and so am relieved of the burden of my karma to that extent.

It was Pandit Ramsarvaswa's duty to oversee our progress in Sanskrit. He likewise gave up the fruitless task of teaching grammar to his unwilling pupil, and read *Sakuntala* with me instead. One day he took it into his head to show my translation of *Macbeth* to Pandit Vidyasagar and took me over to his house.

Raj Krishna Mukherji had called at the time and was seated with him. My heart thumped as I entered the great pandit's study, packed full of books; nor did his austere visage help to revive my courage. Nevertheless, as this was the first time I had had such a distinguished audience, the desire to win renown was strong within me. I returned home, I believe, with some grounds for satisfaction. As for Raj Krishna Babu, he contented himself with admonishing me to be careful to keep the language and metre of the witches' parts different from that of the human characters.

During my boyhood Bengali literature was in meager supply, and I think I must have finished all the readable and unreadable books then extant. Juvenile literature as such had not evolved—but I am sure that did me no harm. The watery stuff served up to the young is a kind of diluted literary nectar that takes full account of them as children, but none of them as potential adults. Children's books should be such as can partly be understood by them and partly not. In my childhood I read every available book from one end to the other, and both what I understood and what I did not went on working within me. That is how the world itself reacts on a child's consciousness. The child makes his own what he understands, while that which is beyond him takes him on a step.

When Dinabandhu Mitra's satires came out I was not of an age for which they were suitable. A kinswoman of ours was reading a copy, but no entreaties of mine could induce her to lend it to me. She used to keep it under lock and key. Its inaccessibility made me want it all the more, and I decided I must and would read the book.

One afternoon she was playing cards, and her keys, tied to a corner of her sari, hung over her shoulder. I had never paid any attention to cards, in fact I could not stand card games. But my behaviour that day would hardly have borne this out, so engrossed was I in their play. At last, one side was about to make a score and in the excitement I seized my opportunity and hurriedly set about untying the knot which held the keys. I was not skilful, and so I got caught. The owner of the sari and of the keys took the fold off her shoulder with a smile, and laid the keys on her lap as she went on with the game.

Then I hit on a stratagem. My kinswoman was fond of *pan,* and I hastened to place some before her. In due course, she had to rise to get rid of the chewed *pan,* and, as she did so, her keys fell off her lap and were replaced over her shoulder. This time they were stolen, the culprit got away, and the book was read! Its owner tried to scold me, but the attempt was not a success, we both laughed so.

Dr Rajendra Lal Mitra used to edit an illustrated monthly miscellany. My third brother had a bound annual volume of it in his bookcase. This I managed to secure, and the delight of reading it through, over and over again, still comes back to me. Many a holiday siesta has passed with me stretched out on my bed, that square volume resting on my chest, reading about the narwhal or the curiosities of justice as administered by the Kazis of old, or the romantic story of Krishnakumari.

Why do we not have such magazines nowadays? We have philosophical and scientific articles on the one hand, and insipid stories, poetry and travels on the other, but no unpretentious miscellanies which the ordinary person can read with comfort—such as *Chambers'* or *Cassell's* or the *Strand* in England—offering a simple but satisfying fare of the greatest use to the greatest number.

I came across another little periodical in my young days called *Abodhabandhu* (The Common Man's Friend). I found a collection of its monthly numbers in my eldest brother's library, and devoured them day after day, seated on the door-sill of his study, facing a bit of terrace to the south. It was in the pages of this magazine that I made my first acquaintance with the poetry of Bihari Lal Chakravarti. His poems appealed to me the most of all that I read at the time. The artless flute-strains of his lyrics awoke within me the music of fields and forest glades.

Into these same pages I have wept many tears over a pathetic translation of *Paul et Virginie*. That wonderful sea, the breeze-stirred coconut forests on its shore, and the slopes beyond lively with the gambols of mountain goats—what a delightfully refreshing mirage the story conjured up for me on that terraced roof in Calcutta. And oh! the romance that blossomed along the forest paths of that secluded island, between the Bengali boy-reader and little Virginie with the many-coloured kerchief round her head!

Then came Bankim's *Bangadarshan* (The Mirror of Bengal), taking the Bengali heart by storm. It was bad enough to have to wait till the next monthly number was out, but to be kept waiting further till my elders had done with it was simply intolerable! Nowadays anyone who wishes may swallow the whole of *Chandrashekhar* or *Bishabriksha* at a mouthful But the process of longing and anticipating, month after month, of spreading over wide intervals the concentrated joy of each short reading, of revolving every instalment over and over in the mind while watching and waiting for the next; the combination of craving with satisfaction, of burning curiosity with its appeasement: those drawn-out delights, none will ever taste again.

The compilations from the old poets by Sarada Mitter and Akshay Sarkar were also of great interest to me. Our elders were subscribers, but not every regular readers of these series, so that it was not difficult for me to get at them. Vidyapati's quaint and corrupt Maithili language attracted me all the more because of its unintelligibility. I tried to make out his sense without the help of the compiler's notes, jotting down in my own notebook all the more obscure words with their context as many times as they occurred. I also noted down whatever grammatical peculiarities I perceived.

My Home Environment

One great advantage which I enjoyed in my younger days was the literary and artistic atmosphere which pervaded our house. I remember how, when I was quite small, I would lean against the verandah railings which overlooked the detached building comprising the reception rooms. These rooms would be lighted up every evening. Splendid carriages would draw up under the portico, and visitors would constantly come and go. What was happening I could not really make out, but I would keep staring at the rows of lighted casements from my place in the darkness. My physical distance from them was not great, but the mental gulf between them and my childish world was immense.

My elder cousin Ganendra had just had written a drama by Pandit Tarkaratna, and was having it staged in the house. His enthusiasm for literature and the fine arts knew no bounds. It was as if he and his group were striving to bring about in every area the renaissance which we see today. A pronounced nationalism in dress, literature, music, art and drama had been awakened in him and those around him. He was a keen student of the history of different countries, and had begun but could not complete a historical work in Bengali. He had translated and published the Sanskrit drama, *Vikramorvasi*, and composed many well-known hymns. He may be said to have given us the lead in writing patriotic poems and songs.

This was in the days when the Hindu Mela was an annual institution, and there his song, 'Ashamed am I to sing of India's glories,' used to be sung.

I was still a child when cousin Ganendra died in the prime of youth, but for those who once beheld him it is impossible to forget his handsome, tall and stately figure. He exerted an irresistible influence over others. He could draw men around him and keep them bound to him; and while they were in his physical presence, the bond was unbreakable. He was someone—a type peculiar to our country—who by their personal magnetism easily establishes himself in the centre of his family or village. In any other country, when important political, social or commercial groups are formed, such people naturally become national leaders. The capacity to organise a large number of men into a group involves a special kind of genius. In our country such genius runs to waste; a waste as extravagant, it seems to me, as that of plucking a star from the firmament instead of striking a match.

I remember still better his younger brother, my cousin Gunendra. He likewise kept the house filled with his personality. His large, gracious heart embraced relatives, friends, guests and dependants, alike. Whether in his broad south verandah, or on the lawn by the fountain, or at the tank-edge on the fishing platform, people gathered around him graced by a presence like benevolence personified. His wide appreciation of art and talent kept him radiant with enthusiasm. New ideas for festivity or frolic, theatricals or other entertainments found a ready patron, and with his help flourished and found fruition.

We were too young then to take any part in these doings, but the waves of merriments and life to which they gave rise came and beat at the doors of our curiosity. I remember how a burlesque composed by my eldest brother was once being rehearsed in my cousin's big drawing-room. From our place against the verandah railings of our house we could hear, through the open windows opposite, roars of laughter mixed with the sounds of a comic song, and would also occasionally catch glimpses of Akshay Mazumdar's extraordinary antics. We could not gather exactly what the song was about, but lived in hopes of being able to find out some time.

I recall how a trifling circumstance earned me the special regard of cousin Gunendra. I had never won a prize at school except once for good conduct. Of the three of us my nephew Satya was the best at his lessons. Once he did well in some examination and was awarded a prize. As we came home I jumped off the carriage to give the great news to my cousin who was in the garden. 'Satya has got a prize,' I shouted, as I ran to him.

He drew me to his knees with a smile. 'And have *you* not got a prize?' he asked.

'No,' said I, 'it's not mine, it's Satya's.' My pleasure at Satya's success seemed to touch my cousin. He turned to his friends and remarked on it as a very creditable trait. I remember how mystified I felt, for I had not thought of my feeling in that light. This prize for not getting a prize did me no good. There is no harm in making gifts to children, but they should not be rewards. It is not healthy for youngsters to be made self-conscious.

After the midday meal cousin Gunendra would attend the estate offices in our part of the house. The office room of our elders was a sort of club where laughter and conversation were freely mixed with matters of business. My cousin would recline on a couch, and I would seize some opportunity of edging up to him.

He usually told me stories from Indian history. I still recall my surprise on hearing how Clive, after establishing British rule in India, went back home and cut his throat: here was new history being made on the one hand and on the other a tragic chapter being hidden away in the darkness of a human heart. How could there be such brilliant success on the outside and such dismal failure within? This weighed heavily on my mind the whole day.

Some days cousin Gunendra would not be allowed to remain in any doubt as to the contents of my pocket. At the least encouragement out would come my manuscript book, unabashed. I need hardly state that my cousin was not a severe critic; in point of fact the opinions he expressed would have done splendidly as advertisements. Nonetheless, when my childishness became too obtrusive, he could not restrain his hearty 'Ha! Ha!'

One day it was a poem on 'Mother India', and as at the end of one line the only rhyme I could think of meant cart, I had to drag in a cart in spite of there not being a vestige of a road by which it could reasonably arrive, rhyme would not hear of any excuses from mere reason. A gale of laughter from cousin Gunendra greeted that cart and blew it back by the same impossible path it had come by, and it has not been heard of since.

My eldest brother was then busy with his masterpiece *Swapnaprayan* (Dream Journey), his cushion seat placed in the south verandah, a low desk before him. Cousin Gunendra would come and sit there for a time every morning. His immense capacity for enjoyment helped poetry to bloom like the breezes of spring. My eldest brother would go on alternately writing and reading out what he had written, his boisterous laughter at his own conceits making the verandah tremble. He wrote a great deal more than he finally used in his finished work, so fertile was his inspiration. Like the flowerets that carpet the feet of the mango groves in spring, the rejected pages of his *Dream Journey* lay scattered all over the house. Had anyone preserved them they would have made a basketful of blossoms to adorn today's literature.

Eavesdropping at doors and peeping round corners, we used to get our full share of this feast. My eldest brother was then at the height of his powers and from his pen surged, in wave after untiring waves, a tidal flood of poetic fancy, rhyme and expression, filling and overflowing its banks in an exuberant paean. Did we really understand *Dream Journey*? But then did we need to understand it absolutely in order to enjoy it? We might not have reached the wealth in the ocean depths—what could we have done with it if we had?—but we revelled in the surf on the shore; and how gaily, at its rise and fall, our life-blood coursed through every vein and artery!

The more I think of that period the more I realise that we no longer have the thing called a *majlis*. In our boyhood we beheld the dying rays of the intimate sociability characteristic of the last generation. Neighbourly feelings were then so strong that the *majlis* was a necessity, and those who could contribute to it were in much demand. Nowadays people call on each other on business, or as a matter of social duty, but not to foregather as a *majlis*. They have not the time, nor are there the same intimate relations! What comings and goings we used to see: how merry were the rooms and verandahs with the hum of conversation and the snatches of laughter! Our predecessors' faculty of becoming the centre of groups and gatherings, of starting and keeping up animated and amusing gossip, has vanished. Men still come and go, but those same rooms and verandahs seem empty and deserted.

In those days everything from furniture to festivity was designed to be enjoyed by the many; whatever pomp or magnificence there might have been did not savour of hauteur. Since then everything has become much grander, but hosts have become unfeeling, and have lost the art of indiscriminate invitation. The indigently clad, or even bare-bodied, no longer have the right to appear without a permit on the strength of their smiling faces alone. Those whom we nowadays seek to imitate in our house-building and furnishing have their own society, with its own wide hospitality. Our predicament, as I see it, is that we have lost what we had, but lack the means of building up afresh on the European standard, with the result that our home life has become joyless. We still meet for business or for politics but never for the pleasure of simply being together, with no purpose in mind than good fellowship—that has vanished. I can imagine few things more ugly than this social miserliness; and, when I look back on those whose ringing laughter coming straight from their hearts used to lighten the burden of our worldly cares, they seem like visitors from some other land.

Literary Companions

There came to me in my boyhood a friend whose literary help was invaluable. Akshay Chaudhuri was a school-fellow of my fifth brother. He was an MA in English literature, for which his love was as great as his aptitude. On the other hand, he had an equal fondness for the older Bengali authors and the Vaishnava poets. He knew hundreds of Bengali songs of unknown authorship, on which he would launch, with voice uplifted, regardless of tune, consequence, or the express disapproval of his hearers. Nor could anything, within him or without, prevent his loudly beating time to his own music, rapping the nearest table or book with his nimble fingers in a vigorous tattoo to help to enliven the audience.

He was also someone with an inordinate capacity for extracting enjoyment from all and sundry. He was as ready to absorb every bit of goodness in a thing as he was lavish in singing its praises. As a lightning composer of lyrics and songs of no mean merit he had an extraordinary gift, in which he took no personal pride. He had no concern for the future of the heaps of scattered paper on which his pencil had scrawled. He was as indifferent to his powers as his powers were prolific.

One of his longer poetic pieces was much appreciated when it appeared in the *Bangadarshan,* and I have heard his songs sung by many who knew nothing at all of their composer.

A genuine delight in literature is much rarer than erudition, and it was this unusual faculty in Akshay Babu which awakened my own literary appreciation. He was as liberal in friendship as in literary criticism. Among strangers he was like a fish out of water, but among friends discrepancies in wisdom or age made no difference to him: with us boys he was a boy. When he took his leave from the *majlis* of our elders late in the evening, I would buttonhole him and drag him to our schoolroom. There, seated on our study table, with undiminished geniality he would make himself the life and soul of our little gathering. Many times I have listened to him in rapturous dissertation on some English poem, engaged him in some appreciative discussion, critical enquiry, or heated dispute, or read to him some of my own writings and be rewarded in return with unsparing praise.

My fifth brother Jyotirindra was one of the chief helpers in my literary and emotional training. An enthusiast himself, he loved to evoke enthusiasm in others. He did not allow our difference in age to be any bar. This great boon of freedom which he allowed me, no one else would have dared to give; many even criticised him for it. His companionship made it possible for me to shake off my shrinking sensitiveness. It was as necessary to my soul after its rigorous repression as the monsoon after a fiery summer.

But for such snapping of my shackles I might have become crippled for life. Those in authority are never tired of holding forth the possibility of freedom's abuse as a reason for withholding freedom, but without that risk freedom would not really be free. The only way of learning how to use a thing properly is by misuse. For myself, at least, I can truly say that what little mischief resulted from my freedom always led on to the means of its cure. I have never been able to make my own anything which others tried to compel me to swallow by getting hold of me, physically or mentally, by the ears.

Nothing but sorrow has resulted except when I have been left freely to myself.

My brother Jyotirindra unhesitatingly let me loose in the fields of knowledge for better or worse, enabling me to put forth flowers or thorns, as my powers dictated. This experience has made me dread not so much evil itself, as tyrannical attempts to create goodness. Of punitive police, political or moral, I have a wholesome horror. The state of slavery which they induce is the worst form of cancer to which humanity is subject.

My brother would at one time spend days at his piano engrossed in the creation of new tunes. Showers of melody would stream from his fingers, while Akshay Babu and I, seated on either side, would busily fit words to the tunes as they grew in shape to help hold them in our memories. This is how I served my apprenticeship in song composition.

We cultivated music in our family from our early childhood. This had the advantage of allowing me to imbibe it into my whole being without effort. It also had the disadvantage of not giving me that technical mastery which learning step by step alone can produce. Of what may be called musical proficiency, I therefore acquired none.

Ever since my return from the Himalayas I had been getting more and more freedom. The rule of the servants came to an end; the bonds of my school life I deliberately loosened; neither did I give much scope to my home tutors. After taking me through *The Birth of the War-God* and one or two other books in a desultory fashion, Gyan Babu went off to take up a legal career. Then came Braja Babu. The first day he set me *The Vicar of Wakefield* to translate. I found that I did not dislike the book, but when this encouraged him to make more elaborate arrangement for my learning, I made myself scarce.

As I have said, my elders gave me up. Neither I nor they were troubled with any more hopes of my future so I felt free to devote myself to filling my manuscript book. And the writings which appeared in it were not better than might have been expected. My mind contained nothing but hot vapour, and vapour-filled bubbles frothed and eddied around a vortex of lazy fancy, aimless and unmeaning. No forms were evolved, there was only agitated movement: a bubbling up, followed by a bursting back into froth. What little substance was there was not mine, but borrowed from other poets. What belonged to me was the restlessness, the seething tension. When motion has been born, but a balance of forces has yet to be achieved, there is blind chaos indeed.

My sister-in-law was a great lover of literature. She read not to kill time like others, but to fill her whole mind. I was her partner in literary enterprise. She was a devoted admirer of the *Dream Journey*. So was I, the more particularly because, having been brought up in the atmosphere of its creation, its beauties had become intertwined with every fibre of my heart. Fortunately it lay entirely beyond my power of imitation, so the idea never occurred to me.

The *Dream Journey* may be likened to a superb palace of allegory, with innumerable halls, chambers, passages, corners and niches full of statuary and pictures of wonderful design and workmanship; and, in the grounds around, gardens, bowers, fountains and shady nooks in profusion. Not only do poetic thought and fancy abound, but the richness and variety of language and expression are also marvellous. It is not a small thing, this creative power which can bring into being so magnificent a structure complete in all its artistic detail, and that is perhaps why the notion of imitation never occurred to me.

At this time Bihari Lal Chakravarti's series of songs called 'Sarada Mangal' were coming out in the *Arya Darshan*. My sister-in-law was greatly taken with the sweetness of these lyrics. Most of them she knew by heart. She used often to invite the poet to our house, and had embroidered a cushion-seat for him with her own hands. This gave me the opportunity of making friends with him. He developed great affection for me, and I took to dropping in on his house at all times of the day, morning noon or evening. His heart was as large as his body, and a halo of fancy seemed to surround him like a poetic astral body—which was perhaps his true incarnation. He was full of artistic joy, and whenever I have been with him I have absorbed my share of it. Often I have come upon him in his little room on the third story, in the heat of noon, sprawling on the cool polished cement floor, writing his poems. Mere boy though I was, his welcome was always so genuine and hearty that I never felt the least awkwardness in approaching him. Then, rapt in his inspiration and forgetful of all surroundings, he would read out his poems or sing his songs to me. Not that he had much of the gift of song in his voice, but he was not altogether tuneless, and one could get a fair idea of the intended melody. When with eyes closed he raised his rich deep voice, his expression made up for what he lacked in execution. I still seem to hear some of his songs as he sang them. I would also sometimes set his words to music and sing them to him.

He was a great admirer of Valmiki and Kalidas. I remember how once after reciting a description of the Himalayas from Kalidas with all the strength in his voice, he said: 'The succession of long "a" sound here is not an accident. The poet has deliberately repeated this sound all the way from *Devatatma* down to *Nagādhirāja* as an aid to realising the glorious expanse of the Himalayas.'

The height of my ambition at the time was to become a poet like Bihari Babu. I might even have succeeded in working myself up into a belief that I was actually writing like him, but for my sister-in-law, his zealous devotee, who stood in the way. She would keep reminding me of a Sanskrit saying that the unworthy aspirant after poetic fame departs in jeers! Very possibly she knew that if my vanity was once allowed to get the upper hand it would be difficult afterwards to bring it under control. So neither my poetic abilities nor my powers of song readily received any praise from her; rather she would never let slip an opportunity of praising somebody else's singing at my expense, with the result that I gradually became quite convinced of the defects of my voice. Misgivings about my poetic powers also assailed me, but, as this was the only field of activity left in which I had any chance of retaining my self-respect, I could not allow the judgement of another to deprive me of all hope; moreover, so insistent was the spur within me that to stop my poetic adventure was a matter of sheer impossibility.

Publication

My writings so far had been confined to the family circle. Then the monthly *Gyanankur* (Seeds of Knowledge), started up and, as befitted its name, secured an embryo poet as one of its contributors. It began indiscriminately to publish all my ravings, and to this day a corner in my mind harbours the fear that when the day of judgement comes, some zealous literary detective will begin a search in the inmost *zenana* of lost literature, ignoring the claims of privacy, and expose these poems to the pitiless public gaze.

My first prose writing also saw the light in the pages of *Gyanankur.* It was a critical essay, and had a bit of a history.

A book of poems had been published entitled *Bhubanmohini Pratibha* (The Genius of Bhubanmohini). Akshay Babu in *Sadharani* and Bhudeb Babu in the *Education Gazette* hailed this new poet effusively. A friend of mine, older than me, whose friendship dates from this time, would come and show me letters he had received signed Bhubanmohini. He was one of those captivated by the book, and used frequently to send reverential offerings of books or cloth to the address of the reputed authoress.

Some of these poems were so wanting in restraint, both of thought and language, that I could not bear the idea of their having being written by a woman. The letters made it still less possible to believe that the writer was female. But my doubts did not shake my friend's devotion, and he went on with the worship of his idol.

Then I launched into a critique of the work of this writer. I let myself go, and held forth eruditely on the distinctive features of lyric and other short poems, my great advantage being that printed matter is unblushing; it does not betray the writer's real attainments. My friend turned up in a great passion and hurled at me the threat that a BA was writing a reply. A BA! I was struck dumb—like the time when I was younger and my nephew Satya had shouted for a policeman. I could see my triumphal pillar of argument, erected upon layers of nice distinction, crumbling before my eyes at the merciless assault of authoritative quotations, and the door effectually barred against my ever showing my face to the reading public again. Alas for my critique—under what evil star was it born! I spent day after day in the direst suspense. But, like Satya's policeman, the BA failed to appear.

Bhanu Singh

As I have said I was a keen student of the series of old Vaishnava poems being collected and published by Babus Akshay Sarkar and Sarada Mitter. Their language, well mixed with Maithili, I found difficult to understand, but for that very reason I took all the more pains to get at their meaning. My feeling towards them was the same eager inquisitiveness I felt towards an ungerminated sprout in a seed or the mysteries lying beneath the earth's surface. My enthusiasm was sustained by the hope of bringing to light some unknown poetical gems as I went deeper and deeper into the unexplored darkness of this treasure house.

While I was engaged in this, Akshay Chaudhuri happened to tell me the story of the English boy-poet Chatterton. What his poetry was like I had no idea; neither perhaps had Akshay Babu. Had we known, the story might have lost its charm. But the melodramatic element in it fired my imagination: the idea of Chatterton deceiving so many with his imitation of some ancient poet, followed by the unfortunate youth's taking his own life. Leaving aside suicide, I girded my loins to emulate young Chatterton.

One noon the clouds had gathered thickly. In the depths of this shady siesta I lay prone on the bed in my inner room and on a slate wrote *Gahana kusuma kunja majhe* ... I was highly pleased with my imitation Maithili poem, and lost no

time in reading it out to the first person I encountered. There
was not the slightest danger of his understanding a word of
it; consequently he could not but gravely nod and say, 'Good,
very good indeed!'

Later, I showed the poems to a friend and said: 'A tattered
old manuscript has been discovered while rummaging in the
Adi Brahmo Samaj library. I've copied some poems from it
by an old Vaishnava poet named Bhanu Singh.' Then I read
some of my imitation poetry to him. He was profoundly
stirred. 'These could not have been written even by Vidyapati
or Chandidas!' he rapturously exclaimed. 'I really must have
that manuscript so Akshay Babu can publish it.'

After that I showed him my manuscript book and proved
conclusively that the poems could not have been written by
either Vidyapati or Chandidas because the author happened
to be myself. My friend's face fell as he muttered, 'Yes, yes,
they're not half bad.'

When these poems of Bhanu Singh later appeared in
Bharati, Dr Nishikanta Chatterji was in Germany. He wrote
a thesis on the lyric poetry of our country comparing it with
that of Europe. Bhanu Singh was given a place of honour as
one of the old poets, such as no modern writer could have
aspired to. This was the thesis on which Nishikanta Chatterji
got his PhD!

Whoever Bhanu Singh might have been, had his writings
fallen into my hands I swear I would not have been deceived.
The language might have passed muster, for the old poets
always wrote in an artificial language variously handled by
different poets, not in their mother tongue. But there was
nothing artificial about their sentiments. Any attempt to test
Bhanu Singh's verse by its ring would have revealed base
metal. It had none of the ravishing melody of our ancient
pipes—only the cheap tinkle of a modern-day English barrel
organ.

Patriotism

Looked at from the outside, our family appears to have accepted many foreign customs, but at its heart flames a national pride that has never flickered. The genuine regard my father had for his country he never forsook through all the vicissitudes of his life, and in his descendants it took shape as a strong patriotic feeling. Such, however, was by no means characteristic of the times of which I am writing. Our educated men were then keeping at arms' length both the language and thought of their native land. My elder brothers had, nevertheless, always cultivated Bengali literature. On one occasion when some new connection by marriage wrote my father a letter in English it was promptly returned to the writer.

The Hindu Mela was an annual fair, which had been instituted with the assistance of our family. Babu Naba Gopal Mitra was appointed its manager. It was perhaps the first occasion dedicated to serving all India as our country. My second brother's popular national anthem, 'Bharater Jaya,' was composed for the Mela. The singing of songs glorifying the motherland, the recitation of poems about love for country, the exhibition of indigenous arts and crafts and the encouragement of national talent and skill were the features of this Mela.

On the occasion of Lord Curzon's Delhi *durbar* I wrote an essay, but at the time of Lord Lytton's it was a poem. The

British government of those days feared the Russians, it is true, but not the pen of a fifteen-year-old poet. So, although my poem lacked none of the fire appropriate to my age, there were no signs of consternation in the ranks of the authorities from commander-in-chief down to commissioner of police. Nor did any letter to *The Times* allude to apathy among the men on the spot in dealing with such impudence and go on in tones of sorrow more than anger to predict the downfall of the British Empire. I recited the poem under a tree at the Hindu Mela, and one of my hearers was Nabin Sen, the poet. He reminded me of this after I had grown up.

My fifth brother, Jyotirindra, was responsible for a political association of which old Raj Narain Bose was the president. It held its sittings in a tumble-down building in an obscure Calcutta lane. The proceedings were shrouded in mystery. This was its only claim to inspire awe, for there was nothing in our deliberations or doings of which government or people need have been afraid. The rest of our family had no idea where we spent our afternoons. Our front door would be locked, the meeting room in darkness, the watchword a Vedic mantra, our talk in whispers. These alone provided us with enough of a thrill, and we wanted nothing more. Though a mere child, I was also a member. We surrounded ourselves with such an atmosphere of hot air that we seemed constantly to be floating aloft on bubbles of speculation. We showed no bashfulness, diffidence or fear; our main object was to bask in the heat of our own ardour.

Heroism may have its drawbacks, but it has always maintained a deep hold on mankind. The literature of every country keeps alive this reverence. No matter where a man may find himself, he cannot escape the impact of this tradition. We in our association had to be content with responding to it as best we could, by letting our imaginations roam, talking tall and singing fervently.

There can be no doubt that to block all outlets to an urge so deep-seated in man and so prized by him, creates an unnatural condition favourable to degenerate activity. To leave open only avenues to clerical employment in any comprehensive scheme of imperial government is not enough; if no path is left for adventure men will pine for one, and secret passages will be sought, with tortuous pathways and ends unthinkable. I firmly believe that if the government had been suspicious and come down hard on us, then the comedy in the activities of our association's youthful members would have turned into grim tragedy. The play concluded, however; not a brick of Fort William is any the worse and we are now smiling at the memory.

My brother Jyotirindra began to busy himself with a costume for all India, and submitted various designs to the association. The dhoti was not deemed businesslike; trousers were too foreign; so he hit upon a compromise which detracted considerably from the dhoti while failing to uplift the trousers. That is to say, the trousers were decorated with the addition of a false dhoti-fold in front and behind. The even more fearsome thing that resulted from the combination of turban and *sola topee* even our most enthusiastic member would not have had the temerity to call an ornament. No person of ordinary courage could have dared to wear it, but my brother unflinchingly wore the complete outfit in broad daylight, passing through the house on an afternoon to the carriage waiting outside, indifferent alike to the stare of relation or friend, door-keeper or coachman. There may be many a brave Indian ready to die for his country, but there are few, I am certain, who even for the good of the nation will walk the streets in such pan-Indian garb.

Every Sunday my brother would get up a *shikar* party. Many of those who joined it, uninvited, we did not even know. There was a carpenter, a smith and others from all ranks of society. Bloodshed was the only thing lacking—at least I cannot recall any. Its other perquisites were so abundant and satisfying that we felt the absence of dead or wounded game to be a trifling omission. As we were out from early morning, my sister-in-law furnished us with a plentiful supply of *luchis* with appropriate accompaniments. Since our bag did not depend upon the fortunes of the chase we never had to return empty-bellied.

The neighbourhood of Maniktola has no lack of villa-gardens. We would turn into the bottom of any one of these, settle ourselves on the bathing platform of a tank and fling ourselves on the *luchis* in earnest. All that was left were the vessels used to carry them.

Braja Babu was one of the most enthusiastic of these blood-thirstless *shikaris*. He was the superintendent of the Metropolitan Institution and had also been our private tutor for a time. One day he had the happy idea of accosting the *mali* in charge of the garden into which we had trespassed with 'Hallo, has uncle been here lately?'

The *mali* lost no time in saluting respectfully before replying: 'No, sir, the master hasn't been lately.'

'All right, get us some green coconuts off the trees.' We had a fine drink after our *luchis* that day.

A small-time zamindar was among our party. He owned a villa by the riverside. One day we had a picnic there together, in defiance of caste rules. In the afternoon there was a tremendous storm. We stood on the steps leading into the water and shouted out songs. I cannot truthfully claim that all seven notes of the scale could be distinguished in Raj Narain Babu's singing, but he certainly sang as lustily as he could; and, as in the old Sanskrit works where the text is drowned by the notes, so the vigour of his limbs and features made up for his vocal performance. His head swung from side to side while marking time and the storm played havoc with his beard. It was late when we turned our hackney carriage homewards. The storm clouds had dispersed and the stars were twinkling. The darkness had become intense, the atmosphere silent, the village roads deserted, and the thickets on either side filled with fireflies like a carnival of sparks scattered by some ghostly revellers.

One of the objects of our association was to encourage the manufacture of lucifer matches and similar small industries. Each member had to contribute a tenth of his income for this purpose. Matches were wanted, but matchwood was hard to get; for though everyone knows about *Kangra* sticks and how fiercely a bundle is supposed to be wielded by an irate housewife, they inflame only bare backs and not lamp wicks. After many experiments we succeeded in making a boxful of matches. The patriotic fire that went into them was not their only value: the money we spent on them might have kept the family hearth burning for a year. Another little defect was that our matches would not burn unless there was a light handy to encourage them. If they could only have absorbed some of the patriotic spirit which conceived them, they might have been marketable even today.

News reached us of some young student who was trying to make a power-loom. Off we went to see it. None of us had any knowledge by which to judge the loom's practicality; but our capacity for believing and hoping was inferior to none. The poor fellow had got into debt over the cost of his machine, which we repaid for him. One day we found Braja Babu coming over to our house with a flimsy *gamcha* tied round his head. 'Made on our loom!' he shouted as he threw up his hands and executed a war-dance. Even then Braja Babu had grey hairs!

At last some worldly-wise people came and joined our society, made us bite the fruit of knowledge, and broke up our little paradise.

When I first knew Raj Narain Babu, I was not old enough to appreciate his many-sidedness. He combined many opposites. In spite of his hoary hair and beard he was as young as the youngest of us, his venerable exterior being simply a white mantle that kept his youth perpetually fresh. Even his extensive learning had been unable to do him any harm. He was absolutely transparent. To the end of his life his hearty laughter suffered no check, whether from the gravitas of age, ill-health, domestic affliction, profound introspection, or diversity of knowledge, all of which were his in ample measure. He had been a favourite pupil of Richardson, brought up in an atmosphere of English learning; but he had flung aside all obstacles created by his early habit and given himself up lovingly and devotedly to Bengali literature. The meekest of men, his inner fire flamed at its fiercest in his patriotism, as though to burn the shortcomings and destitution of his country to ashes. The memory of this saintly person—sweetly smiling, ever-youthful and unwearied by sickness or grief—is something worth cherishing by our countrymen.

Bharati

The period of which I am writing was one of ecstatic excitement for me as a whole. Many nights did I spend sleeplessly, not for any reason but from mere caprice, a desire to do the reverse of the obvious. I would stay up reading all alone in the dim light of our schoolroom; the distant church clock would chime the quarters as if each passing hour was being put up to auction; and now and then the bearers of the dead, passing along the Chitpur Road on their way to the Nimtollah cremation ground, would utter loud cries of 'Haribol!' Throughout moonlit nights in summer I would sometimes wander like an unquiet spirit among the patches of light and shadow made by the tubs and pots on the garden of the roof-terrace.

Those who are inclined to dismiss this as sheer poetising are wrong. The earth itself, in spite of its age, occasionally surprises us still by shifting from sober stability. In the days of its youth, when it had not become congealed and crusty, it was ebulliently volcanic and indulged in many wild escapades. The same is true of a young man. So long as the materials which go to make him have yet to acquire their final shape they are apt to be turbulent.

This was the time when my brother Jyotirindra decided to start *Bharati* with my eldest brother as editor, giving fresh food for our enthusiasm. I was then just sixteen, but I was

not left off the editorial staff. A short time before, with all
the insolence of youthful vanity, had I written a criticism of
Meghnadbadh. As acidity is characteristic of the unripe mango
so abuse is of the immature critic. When other powers are
lacking, the power to prick seems to become sharpest. Thus
had I sought to achieve immortality by leaving my scratches
on that immortal epic. This impudent criticism was my first
contribution to *Bharati*.

I also published a long poem called 'Kabikahini' (The
Poet's Story) in the first volume. It was a product of that age
at which a writer has seen practically nothing of the world
except an inflated image of his own nebulous self. Its hero
was naturally a poet, but not the writer as he really was, rather
as he thought he ought to be seen. Not that he desired to be
what he appeared, just that he wanted the world to nod
admiringly and say: 'Yes, here indeed is a poet—just the thing
to be.' The story made a great parade of universal love, pet
subject of budding poets, which sounds as important as it is
easy to talk about. While truth is yet to dawn upon one's
mind, and others' words are one's only stock-in-trade,
simplicity and restraint in expression are not possible. Instead,
in the endeavour to magnify that which is already big, a
grotesque and ridiculous exhibition becomes inevitable.

As I blush to read these effusions of my boyhood I am
struck with the fear that in my later writings too the same
distortion, wrought by straining after effect, may likely lurk
in a less obvious form. The loudness of my voice often drowns
the thing I would say, I cannot doubt; and some day or other
Time will find me out.

The 'Kabikahini' was the first work of mine to appear in
book form. When I went with my second brother to
Ahmedabad, an enthusiastic friend took me by surprise by
printing and publishing it and sending me a copy. I cannot
imagine this was a good idea, but the feeling it aroused in
me at the time was not that of indignation. He got his come-

uppance not from the author but from the public who hold the purse-strings. I have heard that a dead weight of these books lay heavy for many a day on the shelves of booksellers and the mind of the luckless publisher.

Writings done at the age I began to contribute to *Bharati* cannot possibly be fit for publication. There is no better way of ensuring repentance in maturity than to rush into print in youth. But it has one redeeming feature: the irresistible impulse to see one's writings in print exhausts itself early. Who are one's readers, what do they say, what printer's errors have remained uncorrected? These and like worries run their course as infantile maladies and leave one leisure in later life to attend to one's literary work in a healthier frame of mind.

Bengali literature is not old enough to have developed the internal checks which can serve to control its votaries. As he gains in experience, the Bengali writer has to evolve a restraining force from within himself. It is impossible for him to avoid creating a great deal of rubbish over a considerable length of time. His ambition to work wonders with the modest gifts at his disposal is bound to obsess him in the beginning, and spur him to transcend his natural powers at every step, and the bounds of truth and beauty therewith; this is always visible in early writings. To recover one's normal self, to learn to respect one's powers as they are, takes time.

That said, I have left much youthful folly to be ashamed of, besmirching the pages of *Bharati;* and this shames me not for its literary defects alone but for its atrocious cheek, its extravagance and its high-sounding artificiality. At the same time I recognise in the writings of that period a pervasive enthusiasm which I cannot discount. If error was natural, so was boyish hope, faith and joy. And if error was necessary for fuelling the flame, it has now been reduced to ashes leaving the good work done by the flame, which did not burn in vain.

Ahmedabad

When *Bharati* entered its second year, my second brother proposed to take me to England. My father gave his consent, and so, rather to my surprise, this further unasked favour of providence became a reality.

As a first step I accompanied my brother to Ahmedabad where he was posted as judge. My sister-in-law with her children was then in England, so the house was practically empty.

The judge's house is known as Shahibagh and was a palace of the Badshahs of old. At the foot of the wall supporting a broad terrace flowed the thin summer stream of the Sabarmati river along one edge of its ample bed of sand. When my brother used to go off to his court, I would be left all alone in the vast expanse of the palace, with only the cooing of the pigeons to break the midday lull. An unaccountable curiosity would keep me wandering about the empty rooms.

Into niches in the wall of a large chamber my brother had put his books. One of these was a gorgeous edition of Tennyson's works, with big print and numerous pictures. That book, for me, was as silent as the palace, and, in much the same way I wandered among its coloured plates. I could make nothing of the text, but it nevertheless spoke to me in inarticulate cooings rather than words. In my brother's library I also found a book of collected Sanskrit poems edited by Dr

Haberlin and printed at the old Serampore press. This too was beyond my understanding, but the sonorous Sanskrit words, and the march of the metre, kept me tramping among the 'Amaru Shataka' poems to the deep beat of their drum.

The upper room of the palace tower was my hermit cell, a nest of wasps my only companions. In unrelieved darkness I slept there alone. Sometimes a wasp or two dropped off the nest on to my bed; if I happened to roll on one, the encounter was displeasing to the wasp and distressing to me.

To pace back and forth across the extensive terrace overlooking the river on a moonlit night was one of my whims. It was while doing so that I first composed tunes for my songs. The song addressed to the rose-maiden was one of these, and it still finds a place in my published works.

Realising how imperfect was my knowledge of English I set to work reading English books with the help of a dictionary. From my earliest years my habit has been not to let any lack of complete comprehension obstruct the flow of reading, but to feel quite satisfied with the structure my imagination rears upon the bits that I do understand. I am reaping both the good and bad effects of this habit even today.

England

After six months in Ahmedabad we started for England. In an unlucky moment I began to write letters about my journey to my relatives and to *Bharati*. Now it is beyond my power to call them back. They were nothing but the outcome of youthful bravado. At that age the mind refuses to admit that its greatest cause for pride is in its power to understand, to accept, to respect; and that modesty is the best means of enlarging its domain. To admire and praise becomes a sign of weakness or surrender, and the desire to cry down and hurt and demolish with argument gives rise to a kind of intellectual fireworks. These attempts of mine of establish my superiority by revilement might have amused me today, had not their want of straightforwardness and common courtesy been too painful.

From my earliest years I had had practically no commerce with the outside world. To be plunged in this state, aged seventeen, into the midst of the social sea of England must have justified considerable doubt as to whether I would stay afloat. But as my sister-in-law happened to be in Brighton with her children I was able to weather the first shock under her shelter.

Winter was approaching. One evening as we chatted round the fireside, the children came running with the exciting news that it was snowing. We went out at once. The air was bitingly cold, the sky was bright with moonlight, the earth white with snow. This was not the face of Nature familiar to me, but something quite other—like a dream. Everything near seemed to have receded far off, leaving behind a still white ascetic in deep meditation. Such a sudden revelation of immense beauty on merely stepping through a door had never before happened to me.

My days passed merrily under the affectionate care of my sister-in-law and in boisterous romping with the children. They were greatly tickled by my curious English pronunciation; I failed to see the fun of this, though I joined wholeheartedly in the rest of their games. How could I explain to them that there was no logical means of distinguishing between the sound of 'a' in warm and 'o' in worm? I was forced to bear the brunt of ridicule more properly the due of the vagaries of English spelling.

I became quite adept at inventing new ways to keep the children occupied and amused. This art has stood me in good stead ever since, but I no longer feel in myself the same unlimited profusion of spontaneous invention. This was the first opportunity I had to give my heart to children, and it had all the freshness and overflowing exuberance of such a first gift.

However, I had not made this journey in order to exchange a home beyond the seas for the one on this side. The idea was that I should study law and come back a barrister. So one day I was put into a school in Brighton. The first thing the headmaster said after scanning my features was: 'What a splendid head you have!' This detail lingers in my memory because of the way that she in Bengal had enthusiastically taken it upon herself to keep my vanity in check, and impressed on me that, generally speaking, my cranium and features, compared with those of many another, were barely of average standard. I hope the reader will not fail to give me credit for implicitly believing her and inwardly deploring the parsimony of my Creator. On many other occasions, finding myself differently estimated by my English acquaintances from what she had accustomed me to, I began seriously to worry about the divergence in standards of taste between the two countries!

One thing in the Brighton school seemed truly wonderful: the other boys were not at all rude to me. On the contrary they would often thrust oranges and apples into my pockets and run away. I can only ascribe this uncommon behaviour to my being a foreigner.

I was not long in the school—but that was not its fault. Mr T arak Palit was then in England. He could see that this was not the way for me to get on, and prevailed upon my brother to let him take me to London, and leave me there in a lodging-house. The lodgings he selected faced Regent's Park—in the depths of winter. Not a leaf was to be seen on the row of trees out front whose scraggy snow-covered branches stood staring at the sky: the sight chilled my very bones.

For the newly arrived stranger there can hardly be a more cruel place than London in winter. I knew no one nearby, nor could I find my way about. Days in which I sat alone at a window, gazing at the outside world, returned to my life. But the new view was not attractive. There was a frown on its countenance; the sky was turbid, lacking luster like a dead man's eye; everything seemed turned in upon itself, shunned by the rest of the world. The room was scantily furnished, but there happened to be a harmonium which I used to play according to my fancy after the daylight came to its untimely end. Sometimes Indians would come to see me and, though my acquaintance with them was but slight, when they rose to leave I wanted to hold them back by their coat-tails.

While I lived in these rooms a man came to teach me Latin. His gaunt figure with worn-out clothing seemed no better able to withstand the winter's grip than the naked trees. I do not know what his age was, but he clearly looked older than his years. Some days, in the course of our lessons, he would suddenly be at a loss for a word, and look vacant and ashamed. His family thought him a crank. He had become possessed of a theory. He believed that in each age one dominant idea is manifested in every human society in all parts of the world; and though it may take different shapes under different degrees of civilisation, it is at bottom one and the same; nor does such an idea pass from one society to another by contact, for it holds even where no intercourse exists. This man's great preoccupation was the gathering and recording of facts to prove his theory. And while so engaged his home lacked food, his body clothes. His daughters had little respect for his theory, and were probably upbraiding him constantly for his infatuation. On occasion one could see from his face that he had lighted upon some new proof, and that his thesis had advanced correspondingly. Then I would broach the subject, and become enthusiastic for his enthusiasm. Other days he would be immersed in gloom, as if his burden was too heavy to bear. Then our lessons would stop at every step, his eyes would wander away into empty space, and his mind refuse to be dragged into the pages of the *First Latin Grammar.* I felt keenly for his poor starved body and theory-burdened soul and though I was under no delusion as to his capacity to assist me in learning Latin, I could not make up my mind to get rid of him. Our pretence of learning Latin lasted as long as I was at these lodgings. On the eve of my departure, when I offered to settle his dues he said piteously: 'I have done nothing, and only wasted your time. I cannot accept any payment from you.' With great difficulty I at last got him to take his fees.

Though my Latin tutor never ventured to trouble me with proofs of his theory, I still do not disbelieve it. I am convinced that men's minds are connected through some deep-lying continuous medium, and that a disturbance in one part is secretly communicated by it to other parts.

Mr Palit next placed me in the house of a coach named Barker. He lodged and prepared students for examinations. His mild little wife apart, not a thing about this household had beauty. One can understand how such tutors manage to attract pupils, for these unfortunate creatures do not often get the chance to make a choice. But it is painful to think of the conditions under which such men get wives. Mrs Barker had attempted to console herself with a pet dog, and so when Barker wanted to punish his wife he tortured the dog. Her dependence on this animal therefore made only for an extension of her own vulnerability.

From these surroundings I was only too glad to escape when my sister-in-law sent for me from Torquay in Devonshire. I cannot express how happy I was among the hills there, by the sea, in the flower-covered meadows, under the shade of the pine woods, and with my two restlessly playful little companions. Nevertheless I was sometimes tormented with doubts as to why, when my eyes were so surfeited with beauty, my mind so saturated with joy, and my leisurely days stretched to a limitless horizon of unalloyed happiness, poetry should refuse to call me. So one day I went forth along the rocky shore, armed with manuscript book and umbrella, to fulfil my poet's destiny. The spot I selected was of undoubted beauty, independent of my rhyme or fancy. A slab of rock hung over the waters as if perpetually eager to reach them; the sun slept smiling in the liquid blue below, rocked by the lullaby of the foam-flecked waves; behind, a fringe of pines spread its shadow like a garment slipped off by some languorous wood-nymph. Enthroned on my stony seat I wrote a poem, 'Magnatari' (The Sunken Boat). I might have believed it was good today, had I taken the precaution of drowning it then. But such consolation is not open to me, for the poem happens to exist and, though banished from my published works, a writ might yet cause it to be produced.

The call of duty was insistent, however. I returned to London. This time I found a refuge in the house of a Dr Scott. On a fine evening I invaded his home with bag and baggage. Only the white-haired doctor, his wife and their eldest daughter were there. The two younger girls, alarmed at the incursion of a strange Indian, had gone off to stay with a relative. I think they came back only after they received word that I was harmless.

In a very short time I became like one of the family. Mrs Scott treated me as a son, and the heartfelt kindness of her daughters was something rare even from one's relations.

One thing struck me when living in this family: human nature is everywhere the same. We are fond of saying, and I also then believed, that the devotion of an Indian wife to her husband is something unique, not to be found in Europe. But I at least was unable to discern any difference between Mrs Scott and an ideal Indian wife. She was entirely wrapped up in her husband. With their modest means there was no fussing about by too many servants; Mrs Scott herself attended to every detail of her husband's wants. Before he came home from work in the evening, she would arrange his armchair and woollen slippers before the fire. She never allowed herself for a moment to forget the things he liked, or the behaviour which pleased him. She would go over the house every morning with their only maid from attic to kitchen, and the brass rods on the stairs and the door knobs and fittings would be scrubbed and polished till they shone again. Over and above this domestic routine there were the many calls of social duty. After getting through her daily tasks she would join in our evening readings and music with zest; to add gaiety to the leisure hour being part of the duties of a good housewife.

Some evenings I and the girls took part in a table-turning seance. We would place our fingers on a small tea-table, and it would go capering about the room. Things reached the point where whatever we touched began to quake and quiver. Mrs Scott did not quite like all this. Sometimes she would gravely shake her head and say she had her doubts about its rightness. But she bore it bravely, not liking to put a damper on youthful spirits: until one day we put our hands on Dr Scott's chimney-pot hat to make it turn, and that was too much for her. She rushed up in a great state and forbade us to touch it. She could not bear the idea of Satan even momentarily having anything to do with her husband's headgear.

In all her actions her reverence for her husband was the one thing that stood out. The memory of her sweet self-abnegation makes it clear to me that the ultimate expression of all womanly love is to be found in reverence; that where no extraneous cause hampers its true development woman's love grows naturally into worship. Where the trappings of luxury are plentiful, and frivolity tarnishes both day and night, this love is degraded, and woman's nature does not get a chance of perfect expression.

I spent some months in this house. Then it was time for my brother to return home, and my father wrote to me to accompany him. The prospect delighted me. The light of my country, and its sky, had been silently calling me. When I said goodbye Mrs Scott took me by the hand and wept. 'Why did you come to us,' she said, 'if you must go so soon?'

That household in London no longer exists. Some of the doctor's family have departed to the other world, others have scattered to places unknown. But it lives still inside my head.

One winter's day, as I passed down a street in Tunbridge Wells, I saw a man standing by the roadside. His bare toes showed through his gaping boots, his chest was partly bare.

He said nothing to me, perhaps because begging was forbidden, but he looked up at my face just for a moment. The coin I gave him was perhaps more valuable than he expected, for after I had gone on a bit, he came after me, said, 'Sir, you have given me a gold piece by mistake,' and offered to return it. I might not have particularly remembered this, but for a similar thing which happened another time. When I first reached Torquay railway station a porter took my luggage to the cab outside. After searching my purse for small change in vain, I gave him half-a-crown as the cab started. Soon he came running after us, shouting at the cabman to stop. I imagined that finding me to be such an innocent he had hit upon an excuse to demand more. As the cab stopped he said: 'You must have mistaken half-a-crown for a penny, sir!'

I do not say I have never been cheated in England, but not in any way which it would be fair to hold in remembrance. What grew chiefly upon me, rather, was the conviction that only those who are trustworthy know how to trust. I was an unknown foreigner, and could easily have evaded payment with impunity—yet no London shopkeeper ever mistrusted me.

During the whole of my English stay I was mixed up in a farce I had to play out from start to finish. I happened to get acquainted with the widow of some high Anglo-Indian official. She was good enough to call me by the pet name Ruby. An Indian friend of hers had composed in English a doleful poem in memory of her husband. I need say nothing of its merit as poetry or of its felicity of diction. The composer, as ill-luck would have it, had indicated that the dirge was to be chanted in the *raga* Behag. One day the widow entreated me to sing it to her thus. Silly innocent that I was, I weakly acceded. Unfortunately no one present but I could realise the atrocious combination made by those absurd verses and the *raga* Behag. The widow seemed intensely touched to hear the

Indian's lament for her husband sung to its native melody. I thought the matter would end there, but this was not to be.

I met the widowed lady frequently at different social gatherings, and after dinner when we joined the ladies in the drawing-room, she would ask me to sing that Behag. Everyone clearly anticipated some extraordinary specimen of native music and added their entreaties to hers. From her pocket would emerge printed copies of the fateful composition, and my ears would begin to redden and tingle. At last, with head bowed and quavering voice I would have to make a stab at it—while only too keenly conscious that no one but me in the room would find the performance heartrending. Afterwards, amidst much suppressed tittering, would come a chorus of 'Thank you very much!' 'How interesting!' And in spite of its being winter I would perspire all over. Who would have predicted at my birth or at his death what a severe blow the demise of this estimable Anglo-Indian would be to me!

Then, for a time, while I was living with Dr Scott and attending lectures at University College, I lost touch with the widow. She was in the suburbs some way out of town, though I frequently got letters from her inviting me there. But my dread of the dirge kept me from accepting. At length I received a pressing telegram. It reached me when I was on my way to college. My stay in England was about to come to a close. I thought: I ought to see the widow once more before I leave, and so I yielded to her importunity.

Instead of coming home from college I went straight to the railway station. It was a horrible day, bitterly cold, snowing and foggy. My destination was the terminus of the line. So I felt quite easy in my mind and did not think it worthwhile to enquire about the time of arrival.

The station platforms were all coming on the right-hand side. I had ensconced myself in a right-hand corner seat reading a book. Outside it was already so dark that nothing was visible. One by one the other passengers got off. We reached and then left the station just before the last one. Then the train stopped again, but there was nobody to be seen, neither lights nor platform. A mere passenger has no means of divining why trains sometimes stop at the wrong times and places, so I decided to go on with my reading. The train began to move backwards. There seems to be no accounting for the eccentricity of railways, I thought, as I returned to my book. But when we came right back to the previous station, I could remain indifferent no longer. 'When are we getting to—?' I enquired.

'You are just coming from there,' was the reply.

'Where are we going now, then?' I asked, thoroughly flustered.

'To London.' And then it dawned on me that this was a shuttle. On enquiring about the next train to—I was told there were no more trains that night. And in reply to my next question I gathered there was no inn for five miles.

I had left home after breakfast at ten in the morning, and had eaten nothing since. When abstinence is the only choice, an ascetic frame of mind comes easily. I buttoned my thick overcoat up to the neck and, seating myself under a platform lamp, went on reading. The book I had with me was Spencer's *Data of Ethics,* then recently published. I consoled myself with the thought that I might never again get such an opportunity to concentrate so single-mindedly on such a subject.

After a short time a porter came and informed me that a special was running and would be ready in half an hour. I felt so cheered by the news that I closed the *Data of Ethics.* Where I had been due at seven I at length arrived at nine. 'What is this, Ruby?' asked my hostess. 'Whatever have you been doing with yourself?' I was unable to take much pride in the account I gave her of my adventures. Dinner was over; nevertheless, as my misfortune was hardly my fault, I did not expect condign punishment, especially from a woman. But all that the widow of the high Anglo-Indian official said was; 'Come along, Ruby, have a cup of tea.'

I was never a tea-drinker, but in the hope that it might partially allay my aching hunger I managed to swallow a cup of strong decoction with a couple of dry biscuits. When I finally reached the drawing-room I found a gathering of elderly ladies, and among them one pretty young American who was engaged to a nephew of my hostess and seemed busy going through the usual premarital love rites.

'Let us have some dancing,' said my hostess. I was in neither the mood nor condition for it. But it is the meek who achieve the seemingly impossible on this earth, and soon, although the dance was primarily for the benefit of the engaged couple, I found myself dancing with ladies of advanced years, with only tea and biscuits between myself and starvation.

But my sorrows did not end there. 'Where are you putting up for the night?' asked my hostess. This was a question for which I was not prepared. I stared at her, speechless, while she explained that since the local inn closed at midnight I had better betake myself thither without further ado. Hospitality was not entirely wanting, however, for a servant showed me the way to the inn with a lantern. At first I thought it might prove a blessing in disguise, and at once made enquiries for food: flesh, fish or vegetable, hot or cold, anything! I was told I could have drinks aplenty, but nothing to eat. When I then looked to slumber to forget my cares, there seemed to be no solace even in her world-embracing lap. My bedroom had a sandstone floor and was icy cold; an old bedstead and worn-out washstand were its only furniture.

In the morning the widow sent for me to breakfast. I found a cold repast spread out, evidently the remnants of last night's dinner. A small portion of this, lukewarm or cold, offered to me the previous night could not have hurt anyone, and might have made my dancing less like the agonised wrigglings of a landed carp.

After breakfast my hostess informed me that the lady for whose delectation I had been invited to sing was ill in bed, and that I must serenade her from the bedroom door. I was made to stand on the landing of the staircase. Pointing to a closed door, the widow said: 'That's where she is.' And I gave voice to that Behag dirge while facing the mysterious unknown on the other side. Of the consequent fate of the invalid I have heard nothing.

When I reached London I had to expiate in bed the results of my fatuous complaisance. Dr Scott's girls implored me, on my conscience, not to take this as a sample of English hospitality: it was surely the effect of India's salt.

Loken Palit

While I was attending lectures on English literature at University College, Loken Palit was my class-fellow. He was about four years younger than I. At the age I am writing these reminiscences a difference of four years is insignificant. But the gulf between seventeen and thirteen is difficult for friendship to bridge. Lacking weight in years, the older boy is always anxious to maintain the dignity of seniority. But this did not create any barrier in my mind in the case of Loken, for I could not regard him in any way as my junior.

Boy and girl students sat together in the college library for study. This was the place for our *tetê-à-tête*. Had we been fairly quite about it none need have complained, but my young friend was surcharged with high spirits that would burst forth as laughter at the least provocation. In all countries girls have a perverse degree of application to their studies, and I feel repentant as I recall the multitude of reproachful blue eyes which vainly showered disapproval on our merriment. I had not the slightest sympathy then with the distress of disturbed studiousness. By the grace of providence I have never had a headache in my life nor a moment of compunction on account of interrupted school studies.

With our laughter as an almost unbroken accompaniment we managed also to have some literary discussion, and though Loken's reading of Bengali literature was less extensive than mine, he made up with keenness of intellect. Among the subjects we discussed was Bengali orthography.

The way it arose was this. One of the Scott girls wanted me to teach her Bengali. As I took her through the alphabet I expressed my pride that Bengali spelling has a conscience, and does not delight in overstepping rules at every turn. I made clear to her how laughable the waywardness of English spelling would have been but for the tragic compulsion to cram it for examinations. But my pride took a fall. It became apparent that Bengali spelling was quite as impatient of bondage; force of habit had blinded me to its transgressions. I began to search for laws that regulated its lawlessness. I was quite surprised at the wonderful assistance Loken was able to offer.

After he had entered the Indian Civil Service and returned home, the work which had begun in University College library in rippling merriment flowed on in a widening stream. Loken's boisterous delight in literature was like the wind in the sails of my literary adventure. In the peak of youth I was driving my prose and poetry like a tandem at a furious rate, and Loken's unstinted appreciation kept my energies from flagging for a moment. Many an extraordinary flight of imagination began in his bungalow in the remote *mofussil*. On many occasions our literary and musical gatherings assembled under the evening star's auspices, finally to disperse beneath the morning star like lamps in the breezes of dawn.

Of the many kinds of lotus flowers that decorate the goddess Saraswati's feet the lotus of friendship must be her favourite. I have not been so lucky as to enjoy much of its golden pollen, but I cannot complain of any dearth of the aroma of good-fellowship.

'The Broken Heart'

While in England I began another poem, which I went on with during my journey home and finished after my return. This was published under the name of 'Bhagna Hriday' (The Broken Heart). At the time I thought it very good. Nothing strange in that, you may think, but it did not fail to attract appreciation from readers too. I remember how, after it came out, the chief minister of the late Raja of Tripura called on me solely to deliver the message that the Raja admired the poem and entertained high hopes of the writer's future literary career.

Let me set down here what I wrote about this poem of my eighteenth year in a letter when I was thirty:

When I began to write 'Bhagna Hriday' I was eighteen—neither in my childhood nor in my youth. This borderland age is not illumined by the direct rays of Truth; they are scattered here and there, and the rest is in shadow. And its imaginings are drawn-out and vague like twilight shades, making the real world seem like a world of fantasy. The curious part of all this is not that I was eighteen, but that everyone around me seemed to be eighteen also; we all flitted about in the same baseless, substanceless world of dream, where even the most intense joys and sorrows seemed insubstantial. There being nothing real against which to weigh them, the trivial did duty for the great.

This period of my life, from fifteen or sixteen to twenty-two or twenty-three, was one of utter disarray.

In the early life of the earth, before land and water had distinctly separated, giant malformed amphibians moved about the treeless jungles that flourished in the primeval ooze. The swirling passions of the immature mind are similar; twilit, misshapen and overblown, they haunt the trackless, nameless wilderness of the mind. They do not know what they are, nor why they wander, and, because they do not, they are inclined towards grotesque mimicry. For me it was an age of unmeaning activity when my undeveloped powers, unaware of and unequal to their real goals, jostled each other for an outlet, each seeking to assert superiority through hyperbole.

When milk-teeth try to push their way through, they work an infant into a fever. The agitation has no apparent justification until the teeth are out and have begun assisting the ingestion of food. Our early passions torment the mind in the same way, like maladies, until they realise their true relationship with the world.

The lessons I learned from my experiences at this time are to be found in every moral textbook, but are not therefore to be despised. Whatever confines our urges inside us, and checks their free access to the outside, poisons our life. Selfishness, for instance, refuses to give free play to our desires and so prevents them from working themselves through; that is why its close associate is always festering untruth. When our desires have a chance to be released in the form of worthwhile work the aberration is dispelled and a more natural condition asserts itself. That is the true state of human nature, and the joy of being human.

The immature condition of my mind that I have just described was fostered by the example and precept of the time, and I am not sure that the effects of these are not still lingering. Glancing back at that earlier period, I feel that English literature offered more stimulant than nourishment. Our literary gods were Shakespeare, Milton and Byron and the quality in their work which stirred us most was strength of passion. In English social life passionate outbursts are kept severely in check; for which very reason, perhaps, they so dominate English literature. Its characteristic is the suppression of vehement feelings to a point of inevitable explosion. At least this was what we in Bengal came to regard as the quintessence of English literature.

In the impetuous declamation of English poetry by Akshay Chaudhuri, who initiated us into English literature, there was the wildness of intoxication. The frenzy of Romeo's and Juliet's love, the fury of King Lear's impotent lamentation, the all-consuming fire of Othello's jealousy—these roused our admiration. Our restricted social life with its narrow field of activity was hedged in by such monotony that tempestuous feelings found no entrance; all was as calm and as quiet as could be. So our hearts naturally craved the life-bringing shock of emotion in English literature. This was not an aesthetic pleasure, but the jubilant welcome of a turbulent wave, even though it might bring to the surface the slime of the stagnant bottom.

In Europe, at the time when the repression of the human heart finally provoked the reaction known as the Renaissance, Shakespeare's plays were the equivalent of war-dances. The consideration of good and evil, beauty and ugliness was not their main concern. Man was consumed instead with an anxiety to break through all barriers to the inmost sanctuary of his being, there to discover an ultimate image of his own most violent desire. That is why we find such harshness, exuberance and wantonness in Shakespeare.

This spirit of bacchanalian revelry found a way into our demurely well-behaved social world, woke us up, and made us lively. Our hearts, smothered by ritual, pined for a chance to live, and we were dazzled by the unfettered vista revealed to us.

Something comparable happened in English literature when the slow measure of Pope's common time gave place to the dance rhythm of the French Revolution. Byron was its poet. His impetuosity pierced the veil that kept our hearts in virginal seclusion.

Thus did the pursuit of English literature sway the youth of our time, including me; a surf of excitement kept beating at me from every side. This first awakening was a time of quickening, not repression.

And yet our case was so different from that of Europe. There, excitability and impatience with shackles was a reflection of history in literature. It was an authentic exposure of feeling. The roaring of the storm was heard because a real storm was raging. But by the time it reached our world, it was little more than a gentle breeze. It failed to satisfy our minds, and our attempts to make it imitate the blast of a hurricane led us easily into sentimentality, a tendency that still persists and may not prove easy to cure.

The trouble is, English literature is a literature in which the reticence of true art is yet to appear. Passion is only one of the ingredients of literature and not its sum—which lies finally in simplicity and restraint. English literature does not fully admit this proposition.

Our minds are being moulded from infancy to old age by English literature alone. But other literatures of Europe, both classical and modern, which show the development of systematic self-control, are not subjects of our study and so, it seems to me, we are still unable to arrive at a correct perception of the true aim and method of literary work.

Akshay Babu, who made the passion in English literature came alive for us, was himself a votary of the emotional life. To comprehend truth seemed less significant to him than to feel it in his heart. He had no intellectual respect for religion, but songs of Shyama (the dark Mother) would bring tears to his eyes. He felt no call to search for ultimate reality; whatever moved his heart served him for the time being as the truth—even obvious coarseness not proving a deterrent.

Atheism was the dominant note of the English prose writings then in vogue—Bentham, Mill and Comte being favourite authors. Theirs was the reasoning in terms of which our youths argued. The age of Mill constitutes a natural epoch in English history. It represents a healthy reaction of the body politic: these destructive forces having been brought in, temporarily, to get rid of accumulated thought-rubbish. Our country adopted their letter, but not their spirit; we never sought to make practical use of them, employing them instead only as a stimulant to incite ourselves to moral revolt. For us atheism was mere intoxication.

For these reasons educated men fell mainly into two classes. One class would always thrust itself forward with unprovoked argument to cut all belief in God to pieces. Like the hunter whose hands itch to kill a living creature as soon as he spies it on a tree, these people, whenever they learn of a harmless belief lurking in fancied security, feel stirred to sally forth and demolish it. We had a tutor for a short time for whom this was a pet diversion. I was only a boy, but I could not escape his onslaughts. His attainments were not of any account, neither were his opinions the result of any enthusiastic search for truth, being gathered mostly from others' lips. But though I fought him with all my strength, I was no match and I suffered many a bitter defeat. Sometimes I felt so mortified I wanted almost to cry.

The second class consisted not of believers but religious epicureans, who found comfort and solace in gathering together and steeping themselves in pleasing sights, sounds and scents galore, under the garb of religious ceremonial; they luxuriated in the paraphernalia of worship. In neither of these classes were doubt or denial the outcome of the travail of their quest.

Though such religious aberrations pained me, I do not say I was entirely uninfluenced by them. With the intellectual impudence of youth I revolted. The religious services held in our family I would have nothing to do with, because I did not accept them. I busied myself in fanning a flame with the bellows of my emotions. This was only fire worship, the giving of oblations to increase the flame—with no other aim. And because my efforts had no purpose in mind they had no limit, always reaching beyond any prescription.

In religion and in my emotional life I felt no need for any underlying truth; excitement was everything. It brings to mind some lines by a poet of that time:

My heart is mine
    I have sold it to none,
Be it tattered and torn and worn away,
    My heart is mine.

In truth the heart need not worry itself so, for nothing compels it to wear itself to tatters. Sorrow is not truly to be coveted, but taken in isolation from life sorrow's poignancy may appear pleasurable. Our poets have often made much of this, forgetting the god they intended to worship. This is a childishness our country has not yet rid itself of. So today we often fail to see the truth of religion and indulge instead in aesthetic gratification. Equally, much of our patriotism is not genuine service of the motherland, but simply emotional gratification.

European Music

When I was in Brighton I once went to hear some *prima donna*. I forget her name. It may have been Madame Nilsson or Madame Albani. Never before had I heard such extraordinary command over the voice. Even our best singers cannot hide their sense of effort; nor are they ashamed to bring out, as best they can, top notes or bass notes beyond their proper register. The receptive portion of our audience have nothing against keeping the performance up to standard by dint of their own imagination. For the same reason they do not mind any harshness of voice or uncouthness of gesture in the exponent of a perfectly formed melody; on the contrary, they seem sometimes to believe that such minor external defects serve better to set off the internal perfection of the *raga*—like the outward poverty of the great ascetic Mahadeva, whose divinity shines forth naked.

This feeling seems entirely lacking in Europe. There, outward embellishment must be perfect in every detail, and the least defect stands shamed and unable to face the public gaze. In our musical gatherings no one minds if half an hour is spent in tuning up the *tanpuras,* or hammering into tone the drums, small and big. In Europe such duties are performed in advance, behind the scenes, for what appears out front must be faultless. There is no allowance for any weak spot in the singer's voice. In our country a correct and artistic exposition of the melody is the main object, all effort is concentrated upon it. In Europe the voice is the object of culture, and with it they perform impossibilities. Our connoisseurs are content if they hear the song; in Europe, they go to hear the singer.

That is what I saw in Brighton. It was as good as a circus. I admired the performance, but I could not appreciate the song. I could hardly keep from laughing when some of the *cadenzas* imitated the warbling of birds. I felt all the time that it was a misapplication of the human voice. When the turn came of a male singer I was considerably relieved. I especially liked the tenor voices, which had more flesh and blood in them, and seemed less like the disembodied laments of forlorn spirits.

After this, as I went on hearing and learning more and more of European music, I began to get into the spirit of it; but still I am convinced that our music and theirs abide in altogether different apartments, and do not gain access to the heart by the same door.

European music seems to be intertwined with the material life of Europe, so that the text of its songs may be as various as life itself. If we attempt to put our tunes to the same variety of uses they tend to lose their significance, and become ludicrous; for our melodies are meant to transcend everyday life and carry us deep into Pity, high into Aloofness: to reveal the core of our being, impenetrable and ineffable, where the devotee may find his ashram, or even the epicurean his paradise, but where there is no room for the busy man of the world.

I cannot claim that I felt the soul of European music but what little of it I came to understand from the outside attracted me greatly in one way. It seemed so romantic. To analyse what I mean by that word is somewhat difficult. What I have in mind is the diversity, the superfluity of waves on the sea of life, of the ceaseless play of light and shade over their undulations. There is the opposite aspect—of infinite extension, of the unwinking blue of the sky, of the silent hint of immeasurability in the distant circle of the horizon. Notwithstanding, let me repeat, lest I am not perfectly clear, that whenever I have been moved by European music I have said to myself: it is romantic, it translates into melody the evanescence of life.

Not that we wholly lack the same aim in some forms of our music, but it is less pronounced, less accomplished. Our melodies give voice to the stars that spangle the night, to the reddening sky of early dawn. They speak of the pervasive sorrow which lowers in the blackness of storm-clouds; the dumb intoxication of the forest-roaming spring.

Valmiki Pratibha

We had a profusely decorated volume of Moore's *Irish Melodies*. I often listened to their enraptured recitation by Akshay Babu. The poems combined with the pictorial designs conjured up a dream of Old Ireland. I had not then heard the original tunes, but had sung these Irish melodies to myself to the accompaniment of the harps in the pictures. I longed to hear the real tunes, to learn them, and sing them to Akshay Babu. Some such longings are unfortunately fulfilled, and die in the process. When I went to England I heard some of the Irish melodies and learnt them too, and that put an end to my keenness to learn more. They were simple, mournful and sweet, but they somehow did not fit the silent melody of the harp which filled the halls of the Ireland of my dreams.

When I came back home I sang the Irish melodies I had learnt to my family. 'What is the matter with Rabi's voice?' they exclaimed. 'How funny and foreign it sounds!' They even felt I spoke differently.

From this mixed cultivation of foreign and native melody was born *Valmiki Pratibha* (The Genius of Valmiki). The tunes in this musical drama are mostly Indian, but they have been dragged out of their classic dignity; that which soared in the sky has been taught to run on the earth. Those who have seen and heard it performed will, I trust, bear witness that the harnessing of Indian melodic modes in the service of the drama has proved neither demeaning nor futile. This conjunction is the only special feature of *Valmiki Pratibha*. The pleasing task of loosening the chains on melodic forms and making them adaptable to a variety of treatment completely engrossed me.

Several of the songs of *Valmiki Pratibha* were set to tunes originally severely classical in mode; some of the tunes were composed by my brother Jyotirindra; a few were adapted from European sources. The *telena* style of Indian modes specially lends itself to dramatic purposes, and has been frequently utilised in this work. Two English tunes served for the drinking-songs of the robber band, and an Irish melody for the lament of the wood-nymphs.

Valmiki Pratibha is not a composition which will bear being read. Its significance is lost if it is not sung and acted. It is not what Europeans call an opera, but a small drama set to music. That is to say, it is not primarily a musical composition. Very few of the songs are important or attractive in themselves; they serve merely as the musical text of the play.

Before I went to England we occasionally had gatherings of literary men in our house, at which music, recitations and light refreshments were served up. After my return one more such gathering was held, which happened to be the last. It was for this that *Valmiki Pratibha* was composed. I played Valmiki and my niece, Pratibha, took the part of Saraswati—a bit of history that is recorded in the drama's name.

I had read in some work by Herbert Spencer that speech takes on tuneful inflexions whenever emotion comes into play. It is a fact that the tone or tune is as important to us as the spoken word for the expression of anger, sorrow, joy and wonder. Spencer's idea that, through a development of these emotional modulations of voice, man found music, appealed to me. Why should I not try to act a drama in a kind of recitative based on this idea? The *kathakas* of our country attempt this to some extent, for they frequently break into a chant which, however, stops short of full melodic form. As blank verse is more elastic than rhymed, so such chanting, though not devoid of rhythm, can more freely adapt itself to the emotional interpretation of the text because it does not attempt to conform to the more rigorous canons of tune and time required by a regular melodic composition. The expression of feeling being the object, these deficiencies in form do not jar on the hearer.

Encouraged by the success of this new line in *Valmiki Pratibha*, I composed another musical play of the same class. It was called *Kal Mrigaya* (The Fateful Hunt). The plot was based on the story in the *Ramayana* of the accidental killing of a blind hermit's only son by King Dasharatha. It was played on a stage erected on our roof-terrace, and the audience seemed profoundly moved by its pathos. Afterwards, with slight changes, much of it was incorporated in *Valmiki Pratibha*, and the play ceased to be separately published in my works.

Much later, I composed a third musical play, *Mayar Khela* (The Play of *Maya*), an operetta of a different type. In this the songs were important, not the drama. In the other two a series of dramatic situations were threaded with a melody; here a garland of songs was threaded on the slimmest of plots. The play of feeling, and not action, was its main feature. While composing it I was indeed saturated with the mood of song.

The vigour which went into the making of *Valmiki Pratibha* and *Kal Mrigaya* I have never felt for any other work of mine. In these two works the musical ferment of the time found expression.

My brother Jyotirindra was engaged the livelong day at his piano, refashioning the classic melodic forms at his pleasure. And, at every turn of his instrument, the old modes took on unthought-of shapes and expressed new shades of feeling.

The melodic forms which had become habituated to their pristine stately gait, when compelled to march to more lively unconventional measures, displayed an unexpected agility and power, and moved us correspondingly. We could plainly hear the tunes speak to us, while Akshay Babu and I sat on either side fitting words to them as they grew out of my brother's nimble fingers. I do not claim that our libretto was good poetry, but it served as a vehicle for the tunes.

In riotous revolutionary joy were these two musical plays composed. They danced merrily to every measure, whether or not technically correct, indifferent as to whether the tunes were indigenous or foreign.

The Bengali reading public has on many an occasion been grievously exercised over some opinion or literary form of mine, but it is curious to find that the daring with which I played havoc among accepted musical notions did not arouse any resentment; on the contrary, those who came to listen departed pleased. A few of Akshay Babu's compositions found place in *Valmiki Pratibha,* along with adaptations of Bihari Chakravarti's 'Sarada Mangal' series of songs.

I used to take the leading part in the performance of these musical dramas. From my early years I had a taste for acting, and firmly believed that I had a special aptitude for it. I think I proved that my belief was not ill-founded. My earliest role was the part of Alik Babu in a farce written by my brother Jyotirindra. I was then very young, and nothing seemed to fatigue or trouble my voice.

In our house, at that time, a cascade of musical emotion was gushing forth day after day, hour after hour, its spray scattering into our being the whole gamut of colours. With the freshness of youth and energy, impelled by new-born curiosity, we struck out on paths in every direction. We felt we would try to test everything, and no achievement seemed impossible.

We wrote, we sang, we acted, we poured ourselves out on every side. This was how I stepped into my twentieth year.

Of the forces which pushed our lives along so triumphantly, my brother Jyotirindra was the charioteer. He was absolutely fearless. Once, when I was a mere lad and had never ridden a horse before, he made me mount one and gallop by his side. At the same age when we were at Shelidah (the headquarters of our estate) and news was brought of a tiger, he took me with him on a hunting expedition. I had no gun—if I had it would have been more dangerous to me than to the tiger. We left our shoes at the edge of the jungle and crept in on bare feet. At last we scrambled up into a bamboo thicket, partly stripped of its thorn-like twigs, where I somehow managed to crouch behind my brother till the deed was done, with no means of administering even a shoe-beating to the unmannerly brute had he dared to lay an offending paw on me!

Thus my brother gave me full freedom, inside and out, in the face of all dangers. No custom or convention restrained him, and so he was able to rid me of my shrinking diffidence.

Evening Songs

In the state of self-absorption of which I have been telling, I wrote a number of poems which have been grouped together, under the title of *Hriday Aranya* (The Heart-Wilderness) in Mohit Babu's edition of my works. In one of the poems subsequently published in a volume called *Prabhat Sangit* (Morning Songs), the following lines occur:

There is a vast wilderness whose name is Heart;
Whose interlacing forest branches dandle and rock darkness like an infant.
I lost my way in its depths.

From which came the name for this group of poems.

Much of what I wrote, when my life had no commerce with the outside, when I was engrossed in the contemplation of my own heart, when my imaginings wandered in many a disguise amidst causeless emotions and aimless longings, has been left out of that edition; only a few of the poems originally published in the volume entitled *Sandhya Sangit* (Evening Songs) are republished there, in the section Entitled 'The Heart-Wilderness'.

My brother Jyotirindra and his wife had left home travelling on a long journey, and their rooms on the third storey, facing the terraced roof, were empty. I took possession of these and the terrace, and spent my days in solitude. While left in communion with myself I do not know how I slipped out of the poetical groove into which I had fallen. Perhaps because I was cut off from those whom I sought to please and whose taste in poetry moulded the form I tried to give my thoughts, I freed myself naturally.

I began to use a slate for my writing. That helped in my emancipation. The manuscript books in which I had been indulging now bothered me. To make an entry in them seemed to demand a supply of poetic fancy commensurate with that of poets of renown. But to write on slate was clearly a matter of the mood of the moment. 'Fear not,' it seemed to say. 'Write just what you please, one rub will wipe all away!'

I wrote a poem or two, thus unfettered, and felt a real joy well up within me. 'At last,' said my heart, 'what I write is my own!' No one should mistake this feeling for pride. It was pride I had felt in my former productions, that being all the tribute I had to pay them. I refuse to call the sudden onset of self-confidence the same as the gratification of vanity. The joy of parents in their first-born is not due to pride in its appearance, but because it is their very own. If the child happens to be extraordinary they may also take pride in that—but that is another thing.

In the first flood-tide of that joy I paid no heed to the bounds of metrical form; just as a stream does not flow straight but winds as it lists, so did my verse. Before, I would have held this to be a crime, but now I felt no compunction. Freedom first breaks laws; then it makes laws that bring it under true self-rule.

The only listener to these erratic productions of mine was Akshay Babu. When he heard them for the first time he was as surprised as he was pleased, and with his approbation my path to freedom broadened.

The poems of Bihari Chakravarti were in a three-beat metre. Unlike the square-cut multiple of two this produces a globular effect. It rolls on easily, gliding as it dances to the tinkling of its anklets. I was once very fond of this metre. It felt more like riding a bicycle than walking. And to its stride I became accustomed. In the *Evening Songs*, without thinking of it, I somehow broke this habit. Neither did I fall under any other spell. I felt entirely free and unconcerned. I had no thought or fear of being taken to task.

The strength I gained by working freed from the trammels of tradition led me to discover that I had been searching in impossible places for something which was actually within myself. Nothing but want of self-confidence had stood in the way of my coming into my own. I felt as if I had risen from a nightmare to find myself unshackled. It cut extraordinary capers just to make sure I was free to move.

To me this is the most memorable period of my poetic career. *Evening Songs* may not have been worth much as poems, in fact they are fairly crude. Neither their metre, nor their language, nor their thought had taken definite shape. But for the first time I had written what I really meant, exactly as I felt. Even if the compositions have no lasting value, that pleasure certainly had.

An Essay on Music

I had been proposing to study for the bar when my father had recalled me home from England. Some friends, concerned at this curtailment of my career, pressed him to send me off again. This led to my starting on a second voyage towards England, this time with a relative as my companion. My fate, however, had so strongly vetoed my being called to the bar that this time I was not even to reach England. We disembarked at Madras and returned home to Calcutta. The reason was by no means as grave as the decision, but as the laugh was not against *me,* I refrain from setting it down here. Thus both my attempted pilgrimages to the shrine of Lakshmi, goddess of wealth, were scotched. I hope that the law-god, at least, will look on me with a favourable eye for not adding to the encumbrances on the bar-library premises.

My father was then in the Mussoorie hills. I went to him in fear and trembling. He showed no sign of irritation, but rather seemed pleased. He must have seen in my return the blessing of divine providence.

The evening before I started on this voyage I read a paper at the Medical College Hall on the invitation of the Bethune Society. This was my first public reading. The Reverend K.M. Banerji was the president. The subject was music. Leaving aside instrumental music, I tried to argue that the chief aim of vocal music was to bring out better what the words sought to express. The text of my paper was meager; instead I sang and acted songs throughout, illustrating my theme. The only reason for the flattering eulogy which the president bestowed on me at the end must have been the moving effect of my young voice, together with the earnestness and variety of its efforts. Today I must confess that the opinion I once voiced with such enthusiasm is wrong.

Vocal music has its own special features. When it happens to involve words the latter must not presume too much on the melody of which they are but the vehicle or seek to supersede it. If a song is great in itself, why should it wait upon words? It begins where mere words fail. Its power lies in the region of the ineffable; it tells us what the words cannot.

So the less a song is burdened with words the better. In the classic style of Hindustan the words are of no account, and leave the melody to make its appeal in its own way. Vocal music achieves perfection when the melodic form is allowed to develop freely, and carry our consciousness with it to its own wonderful plane. In Bengal, the words have always asserted themselves so much that our songs have failed to develop their full musical capabilities and have remained content to be handmaidens of poetry. From the old Vaishnava songs down to the songs of Nidhu Babu, the Bengali song has displayed her charms only in the background. She should follow the example of wives in our country who formally obey their husbands but actually rule them; music, while professedly in attendance on words, should in fact dominate them.

I have often felt this while composing my songs. As I hummed to myself and wrote the lines:

Do not keep your secret to yourself, my love,
But whisper it gently to me, only to me.

I found that the words by themselves had no means of reaching the region into which they were borne away by the tune. The tune told me that the secret, which I was so importunate to hear, had mingled with the green mystery of the forest glades, was steeped in the silent whiteness of moonlight night, was peeping out from behind the veil of illimitable blue at the horizon—and is the most intimate of all the secrets of earth, sky and waters.

In my early boyhood I heard a snatch of a song:

Who dressed you, love, as a foreigner?

This one line painted such wonderful pictures in my mind that it haunts me still. One day I sat down to set to words a composition of my own while full of this fragment of song. Humming my tune I wrote to its accompaniment:

I know you, O Woman from the strange land!
Your dwelling is across the Sea.

Had the melody not been there I do not know what shape the rest of the poem might have taken, but as it was it revealed to me the stranger in all her loveliness. It is she, said my soul, who comes and goes, a messenger to this world from the other shore of the ocean of mystery. It is she, of whom we now and then catch glimpses in the dewy autumn mornings, in the scented nights of spring, in the inmost recesses of our hearts— and whose song we sometimes strain skywards to hear. To the door of this charming stranger the melody wafted me, and to her were the rest of my words addressed.

Long after this, in a street in Bolpur, a mendicant Baul was singing as he walked along:

How does the unknown bird flit in and out of the cage!
Ah, could I but catch it, I'd ring its feet with my love!

I found this Baul to be saying the very same thing as my song. The unknown bird sometimes settles within the cage and whispers tidings of the infinite world beyond the bars. The heart eagerly desires to hold on to the bird for ever, but cannot. What else but melody can capture for us the comings and goings of the unknown bird?

That is why I am always reluctant to publish the words of my songs, for the soul will inevitably be lacking.

The Riverside

When I returned home from the outset of my second voyage to England, my brother Jyotirindra and sister-in-law were living in a riverside villa at Chandannagar and there I went to stay with them.

The Ganges again! Again those indescribable days and nights, languid with joy, piquant with yearning, attuned to the babbling of the river beneath the shade of its wooded banks. This Bengal sky full of light, this south breeze, this flow of the river, this right royal laziness stretching from horizon to horizon and from the green earth to the blue sky were all as food and drink to the hungry and thirsty. Indeed the place was like home, and these natural ministrations like that of a mother.

I am not speaking of very long ago, and yet time has wrought many changes. Our little riverside nests, sheltering in greenery, have been replaced by dragon-like mills which everywhere rear their hissing heads, belching forth black smoke. In the midday glare of modern life even our hours of mental siesta have been narrowed down to the lowest limits, and hydra-headed unrest has invaded every department of life. Maybe this is for the better, but I, for one cannot account it wholly to the good.

These riverside days of mine passed by like consecrated lotus blossoms floating in the sacred stream. Some rainy afternoons I spent in a veritable frenzy, singing old Vaishnava songs to my own tunes, accompanying myself on a harmonium. Other afternoons we would drift along in a boat, my brother Jyotirindra accompanying my singing on his violin. Beginning with *raga* Puravi, we went on varying our *ragas* with the declining day, and saw, on reaching *raga* Behag, that the western sky had pulled down the shutters on its storehouse of golden playthings, and the moon had risen in the east.

Then we would row back to the landing-steps of the villa and seat ourselves on a quilt spread on the terrace facing the river. A silvery peace by then rested on both land and water: hardly any boats were about, the fringe of trees on the bank was in deep shadow, and moonlight glimmered over the smooth flowing current.

The villa we lived in was known as Moran's Garden. A flight of stone-flagged steps led up from the water to a long, broad verandah which formed part of the house. The rooms were not regularly arranged, nor all on the same level, and some had to be reached by short flights of stairs. The big sitting-room overlooking the landing-steps had stained-glass windows with coloured pictures.

One of the pictures was of a swing hanging from a branch half hidden in dense foliage, and in the checkered light and shade of this bower two persons were swinging; and there was another of a broad flight of steps, leading into some castle-like palace, up and down which men and women in festive garb were coming and going. When light fell on the windows, these pictures shone wonderfully, putting me in a carefree mood. Some far-away, long-gone revelry seemed to coruscate silently in the light, and to animate the surrounding woods with some of the thrill of the couple swinging alone in the shadows of that unknown story.

The topmost room of the house was in a round tower with windows opening on every side. This was my poetry-writing room. Nothing could be seen from it save the tops of the trees, and the open sky. I was then busy with the *Evening Songs,* and of this room I wrote:

> Here, wherein the lap of limitless space clouds lie down to sleep,
> I have built my house for thee, O Poesy!

More about 'Evening Songs'

My reputation amongst literary critics at this time was that of a poet of broken cadence and lisping utterance. Everything about my work was dubbed misty, shadowy. However little I might have relished the charge, it was not wholly unfounded. My poetry did lack the backbone of worldly reality. How, amid the ringed-around seclusion of my early years, was I to get the necessary material?

But one thing I refuse to admit. Behind this charge of vagueness was the insinuation that it was a deliberate affectation. The fortunate possessor of good eyesight is apt to sneer at the youth with glasses, as if he wears them for ornament. While it may be permissible to reflect upon the poor fellow's infirmity, it is too bad to charge him with pretending not to see.

The nebula is a phase in creation, not something wholly outside the universe. To reject all poetry which has not attained definition would not bring us any closer to truth in literature. Any phase of man's nature that has found true expression is worth preserving—it may be cast aside only if it is not expressed truly. There is a period in a man's life when his feelings have the pathos of the inexpressible, the anguish of vagueness. His poetry cannot be called baseless—at worst it may be worthless, but it is not necessarily even that. Sin lies not in expressing a thing, but in failing to express it.

There is a duality in man. Of the inner person, beneath the outward flow of thoughts, feelings and events, little is known or heed taken; for all that, he cannot be ignored in living one's life. When the inner life fails to harmonise with the outer, this inner dweller is hurt, and his pain manifests itself outwardly in a manner to which it is difficult to give a name, or even describe; it is a cry more akin to an inarticulate wail than to words of precise meaning.

The pathos which sought expression in *Evening Songs* had its roots in my depths. Just as one's consciousness smothered in sleep wrestles with a nightmare in its efforts to awake, so the submerged inner self struggles to free itself from complexities and emerge into the open. These *Songs* are the story of that struggle. In poetry, as in all creation, there is opposition of forces. If the divergence is too wide, or the unison too close, there is no opportunity for poetry. When discord strives to attain and resolve itself into harmony, then words pour forth as poetry, like breath through a flute.

When *Evening Songs* first saw the light they were not announced by any flourish of trumpets, but nonetheless they did not lack admirers. I have told elsewhere the story of how when Bankim Babu arrived at the wedding of Mr Ramesh Chandra Dutt's eldest daughter, the host welcomed him with the customary garland of flowers. As I came up Bankim Babu eagerly took the garland, placed it round my neck and said: 'The wreath to him, Ramesh; have you not read *Evening Songs?*' And when Mr Dutt avowed he had not yet done so, the manner in which Bankim Babu spoke of some of them was ample reward.

Evening Songs gained me a friend whose approval, like the rays of the sun, stimulated and trained the shoots of my newly sprouted efforts. This was Babu Priyanath Sen. Just before this 'The Broken Heart' had led him to give up all hopes for me. I won him back with these *Evening Songs*.

Those who are acquainted with him know him as an expert navigator of all seven seas of literature, whose highways and byways he is constantly traversing in almost all languages, Indian and foreign. To converse with him is to gain glimpses of the most out-of-the-way scenery in the world of ideas. This experience proved of the greatest value to me.

He was able to give his literary opinions with full confidence, for he did not rely on his unaided taste to guide his likes and dislikes. His authoritative criticism assisted me more than I can tell. I used to read him everything I wrote, and, but for his timely showers of discriminating appreciation my early ploughings and sowings might not have yielded what they did.

Morning Songs

At the riverside I also did a little prose writing, not on any definite subject or plan, but in the way that boys catch butterflies. When spring comes within the mind, many-coloured short-lived fancies are born and flit about. Ordinarily they are unnoticed: it was probably mere whim of mine to collect those which came to me then. Or perhaps my emancipated self threw out its chest and decided to write just as it pleased. What I wrote was unimportant; the fact of writing was what mattered. These prose pieces were later published under the name *Bibidha Prabandha* (Diverse Essays), but they received no further lease of life in a second edition.

At this time, I think, I began my first novel, *Bouthakuranir Hat* (The Young Queen's Market).

After we had stayed for a time by the river my brother Jyotirindra took a house in Calcutta, on Sudder Street near the Museum. I remained with him. While I was writing the novel and *Evening Songs* here, a momentous revolution took place within me.

I was pacing the terrace of our Jorasanko house late in the afternoon. The afterglow of sunset combined with the wanness of twilight lent the approaching evening an unearthly wonder. Even the walls of the adjoining house grew beautiful. Could this lifting of the cover of triviality from the everyday world be some trick of the light? Never!

I could see at once that the evening had entered me; its shades had obliterated my *self*. While the self was rampant during the glare of day, everything was mingled with and hidden by it. Now that the self was in the background, I could see the world in its true aspect. That aspect has nothing trivial in it, but is full of beauty and joy.

Since this experience I have repeatedly tried the effect of suppressing my self deliberately and viewing the world as a mere spectator, and have invariably been rewarded with a sense of special pleasure. I remember I tried too to explain to a relative how to see the world in its true colours, and the lightening of one's sense of burden that follows such vision, without success I think.

Then I gained a further insight—one which has lasted all my life.

The end of Sudder Street, and the trees on the Free School grounds opposite, were visible from our Sudder Street house. One morning I happened to be standing on the verandah looking that way. The sun was just rising through the leafy tops of the trees. As I gazed, all of a sudden a lid seemed to fall from my eyes, and I found the world bathed in a wonderful radiance, with waves of beauty and joy swelling on every side. The radiance pierced the folds of sadness and despondency which had accumulated over my heart, and flooded it with universal light.

That very day the poem 'Nirjharer Swapnabhanga' (The Awakening of the Waterfall), gushed forth and coursed on like a cascade. The poem ended, but the curtain did not fall upon my joy. No person or thing in the world seemed trivial or unpleasing to me—not even, to my astonishment, the person who dropped in the next day or the day after.

He was a curious fellow who came to me now and then and asked all manner of silly questions. One day it was: 'Sir, have you seen God with your own eyes?' And on my having to admit that I had not, he averred that he had.

'What was it you saw?' I asked.

'He seethed and throbbed before my eyes!' was the reply.

Ordinarily one would not relish being drawn into the discussions of such a person. Moreover at the time I was entirely absorbed in my writing. Still, as he was a harmless sort of fellow, I did not like to hurt his susceptibilities and so tolerated him as best I could.

This time when he came I actually felt glad to see him, and welcomed him cordially. His mantle of oddity and foolishness had slipped off, and the person I hailed was the real man whom I felt to be in no wise inferior to myself and, furthermore, in close relationship with me. Finding in myself no trace of annoyance at the sight of him, nor any sense of my time being wasted, I was filled with an immense gladness and felt rid of some enveloping tissue of untruth which had been causing me needless discomfort and pain.

As I stood on the balcony, the movements, figures and features of each one of the passers-by, whoever they were, seemed extraordinarily wonderful as they flowed past—ripples on the ocean of the universe. From infancy I had been seeing only with my eyes, now I began to see with the whole of my consciousness. I caught sight of two smiling youths, walking nonchalantly, the arm of one on the other's shoulder, and I could not see it as of small moment; for in it I sensed the fathomless depths of the eternal well of joy, from which numberless sprays of laughter fly and scatter throughout the world.

I had never before marked the play of limbs and lineaments which accompanies even the least of man's actions; now I was spellbound by their variety on all sides, at every moment. Yet I saw them not as independent, separate, but as parts of the amazingly beautiful dance that always underlies the world of men, permeating every home and every multifarious human want and activity.

Friend laughs with friend, mother fondles child, cow sidles up to cow and licks its body—the immeasurability of these acts struck me with a shock that savoured almost of pain.

When I wrote of this period:

I know not how my heart flung open its doors of a sudden,
And let the crowd of worlds rush in, greeting each other—

it was no poetic exaggeration. Rather, I lacked the power to express all I felt.

For some time I remained in this state of self-forgetful bliss. Then my brother thought of going to the Darjeeling hills. So much the better, I thought. On the vast Himalayan tops I shall be able to look more deeply into what has been revealed to me in Sudder Street; at any rate I shall see how the Himalayas display themselves to my new gift of vision.

But victory lay in that little house in Sudder Street. After ascending the mountains, when I looked around, I was at once aware I had lost my new vision. My mistake must have been to imagine that still more truth could come from the outside. However sky-piercing the king of mountains may be, there was nothing for me in his gift; while He who is the Giver can vouchsafe a vision of the eternal in the dingiest of lanes, and in an instant of time.

I wandered about amongst the firs, I sat near the falls and bathed in their waters, I gazed at Kanchenjunga's grandeur against a cloudless sky, but there in what had seemed to me the likeliest of places I found *it* not. I had come to know it, but could no longer see it. While I was admiring the gem the lid had suddenly closed, leaving me staring at the casket. But, for all the high quality of its workmanship, there was now no danger of my mistaking it merely for an empty box.

Morning Songs came to an end, their last notes dying out with 'Pratidhani' (The Echo) which I wrote at Darjeeling. This proved such an abstruse affair apparently that two friends laid a wager as to its real meaning. My only consolation was that, as I was equally unable to explain the enigma to them when they came to me for a solution, neither had to lose any money over it. Alas, the days when I wrote thoroughly direct poems about 'The Lotus' or 'A Lake' had gone for ever.

But does one write poetry to explain something? It is a feeling within the heart that tries to find outside shape in a poem. When, after listening to a poem, someone says he has not understood it, I am nonplussed. If he were to smell a flower and say the same thing, the reply would be, 'There is nothing to understand, it is only a scent.' If he persisted, saying, '*That* I know, but what does it all *mean?*' then one either has to change the subject, or make it more abstruse by telling him that the scent is the form taken by universal joy in this particular flower.

That words have meanings is just the difficulty. That is why poets have to turn and twist them in metre and rhyme, so that meaning may be held somewhat in check and feeling allowed to express itself.

The utterance of feeling does not involve the statement of some fundamental truth or a scientific fact or a useful moral precept. Like a tear or a smile, a poem is only a picture of what is taking place within. If science or philosophy gain anything from it they are welcome, but that is not why it was written. If you catch a fish from a ferry-boat you are a lucky man, but it does not make the ferry-boat a fishing-boat; neither should you abuse the ferryman if he does not make fishing his business.

'The Echo' is a poem I wrote so long ago that I am now no longer called upon to render an account of its meaning.

Nevertheless, whatever its other merits or defects, I shall assure my readers it was not my intention in it to propound a riddle, or cleverly to impart some esoteric message. The fact of the matter was that a longing had been born within my heart, and I, unable to find any other name, had called the thing I desired an Echo.

When from the *fons et origo* of the universe streams of melody issue forth, their echo is reflected from the faces of those we love and the other lovely things around us into our hearts. What we love must be this echo, as I say, and not the things from which it happens to be reflected, for what we one day hardly deign to glance at may, on another day, be the very thing that claims our whole devotion.

I had viewed the world with external vision for so long I had been unable to see its universal aspects, its joy. When a ray of light suddenly found its way out from some innermost depth of my being, it spread everywhere and illuminated all things, which no longer appeared as discrete objects and events but were disclosed to my vision as a whole.

The stream which flows from the infinite towards the finite is Truth and Good; and it is subject to laws and definite in form. Its echo is Beauty and Joy, the very intangibility of which makes us beside ourselves. This is what I tried to say in 'The Echo' by way of a parable or song. That the result was not clear is not to be wondered at, for neither was the attempt clear to the attempter.

Let me set down here part of what I wrote in a letter at a more advanced age, about *Morning Song:*

> Nothing in the world truly exists, except my heart is a state of mind typical of a certain age. When the heart is first awakened it puts out its arms and tries to grasp the whole world, like a baby with new teeth which thinks everything is meant for its mouth. Gradually

it comes to understand what it really desires and what it does not. Then its nebulous urges narrow, acquire form, and may be kindled or themselves kindle. If one begins by wanting the whole world one gets nothing. When desire is concentrated with the whole strength of one's being upon any one object whatsoever it may be, then the gateway to the infinite becomes accessible. *Morning Songs* were the first projection of my inner self, and they consequently lack any sign of such concentration.

This first all-pervading outburst of joy has the effect of leading us in a more distinct direction—just as a lake eventually seeks an outlet as a river. In Mohit Babu's edition of my works, *Morning Songs* has been placed in the group of poems entitled 'Nishkraman' (The Emergence). In these poems was to be found the first news of my escape from the heart-wilderness into the open world. Since then, this pilgrim heart has made contact with that world, bit by bit, aspect by aspect, its woes as much as its joys, its shadows as much as its sunshine. And in the end, after gliding past a multitude of landing-ghats of ever-changing contour, it will reach the infinite—not a vague diffuseness, but the consummate perfection of Truth.

In my earliest years I enjoyed a simple and intimate communion with Nature. Each one of the coconut trees in our garden had a distinct personality. On coming home from the Normal School, when I saw behind the sky-line of our roof-terrace blue-grey water-laden clouds thickly banked up, the immense depth of gladness which filled me, all in a moment, I can recall clearly even now. When my eyes opened every morning, the blithely awakening world used to call me to join it like a playmate; the perfervid noonday sky, during the silent watches of the siesta hours, would spirit me away from workaday existence into the recesses of its hermit cell, and the darkness of night would open the door to phantom paths and bear me over the seven seas and across the thirteen rivers, past all possibilities and impossibilities, into its wonderland.

Then one day, with the dawn of youth, my hungry heart began to cry out for sustenance and a barrier to the interplay of inside and outside was set up. My whole being eddied round and round my troubled heart, creating a vortex in which my consciousness was confined. This loss of harmony as a result of the overriding claims of the heart, and the consequent constriction of the communion which had been mine, I mourned in my *Evening Songs*.

After that, in *Morning Songs*, I celebrated the sudden opening of a gate in the barrier as a result of some unknown shock—through which I regained my lost contact, not only as I knew it before but more deeply and fully by virtue of the intervening estrangement.

Thus the first book of my life came to an end with these chapters of union, separation and reunion. Actually, it is not true that it has come to an end. The same theme will continue, underpinning worse complexities and more elaborate solutions and leading towards a grander conclusion. Each of us comes along and completes one chapter only of a larger book, which is like a spoke on a wheel. At the circumference each spoke appears independent to a cursory glance but, in fact, it and every other spoke leads back to the self-same centre.

The prose writings of the *Evening Songs* period were published, as I have said, under the name *Bibidha Prabandha*. Others, which correspond to the time of my writing *Morning Songs*, came out under the title *Alochana* (Discussions). The different characteristics of these two collections are a good index of the change that had taken place within me meanwhile.

Rajendra Lal Mitra

It was about this time that my brother Jyotirindra had the idea of founding a literary academy by bringing together all the men of letters with a reputation. To compile authoritative technical terms for the Bengali language and in other ways to assist in its growth was to be its object—an idea very similar to that of the modern Sahitya Parishad (Academy of Literature).

Dr Rajendra Lal Mitra took up the notion with enthusiasm, and was in due time its president for the short interval it lasted. When I went to invite Pandit Vidyasagar to join it, he gave a hearing to my explanation of its aims and the names of the proposed members, then said: 'My advice to you is to leave us out—you will never accomplish anything with bigwigs; they can never be got to agree with one another.' Saying which he refused to come in. Bankim Babu became a member, but I cannot say that he took much interest in the work.

To be plain, so long as this academy lived Rajendra Lal Mitra did everything single-handed. He began with geographical terms. The draft list was compiled by Dr Rajendra Lal himself, and was printed and circulated for the suggestions of the members. We had an idea also of transliterating in Bengal the name of each foreign country as pronounced by itself.

Pandit Vidyasagar's prophecy was fulfilled. It proved impossible to get the bigwigs to do anything, and the academy withered away shortly after sprouting. But Rajendra Lal Mitra was an all-round expert, an academy in himself. My labours in this cause were more than repaid by the privilege of his acquaintance. I have met many Bengali men of letters in my time, but none who left an impression of such brilliance.

I used to go and see him in the office of the Court of Wards in Maniktola. I would go in the mornings, always find him busy with his studies and, with the inconsiderateness of youth, feel no hesitation in disturbing him. But I have never seen him the least bit put out on that account. As soon as he saw me he would put aside his work and begin to talk to me. It is a matter of common knowledge that he was somewhat hard of hearing, so he hardly ever gave me the occasion to ask a question. He would take up some broad subject and talk away upon it, and that was the attraction which drew me there. The conversation of no other person has given me such a wealth of ideas on so many different subjects. I listened enraptured.

I think he was a member of the textbook committee, and every book he received for approval he read through and annotated in pencil. Sometimes he would select one of these books as a text for discourses on the construction of Bengali or philology in general, that were of the greatest benefit to me. There were few subjects he had not studied, and anything he had studied he could clearly expound.

If we had relied not on the other members of the fledgling academy but left everything to Dr Rajendra Lal, the present Sahitya Parishad would doubtless have inherited the matters that now occupy it in a much more developed state.

Dr Rajendra Lal Mitra was a profound scholar, but he was also a striking personality, which shone through his features. Full of fire in public life, he could also unbend graciously and talk on the most difficult subjects to a stripling like me without being in the least patronising. I even took advantage of this to the extent of getting a contribution from him, 'Yama's Dog', for *Bharati*. I would not have ventured to take such a liberty with other great contemporaries of his; neither would I have met with such response if I had.

And yet when he was on the war-path his opponents on the Municipal Corporation or the Senate of the University were mortally afraid of him. In those days it was Krishna Das Pal who was the diplomat in politics, and Rajendra Lal Mitra who was the doughty fighter.

For the purposes of Asiatic Society publications and researches, he had to employ a number of Sanskrit pundits to do the mechanical work. I remember this gave certain envious and mean-minded detractors the opportunity to say that really everything was done by these pandits, while Rajendra Lal fraudulently appropriated all the credit. Today, too, we often find tools arrogating to themselves the lion's share of an achievement, regarding their wielder as a mere figurehead. If pens had minds they would certainly bemoan the unfairness of their getting all the stain and the writer all the glory!

Curiously this extraordinary man has been accorded no recognition from his countrymen even posthumously. One of the reasons may be that the national mourning for Vidyasagar, whose death followed shortly after, left no room for recognition of other bereavements. Another reason may be that since his main contributions lay beyond the pale of literature, he was unable to reach the heart of the people.

Karwar

Our Sudder Street party transferred itself next to Karwar on the western sea-coast. Karwar is the headquarters of the Kanara district in the southern portion of the Bombay Presidency. It is the tract of the Malaya hills of Sanskrit literature, where grow the cardamum creeper and the sandal tree. My second brother was then a judge there.

The little harbour, ringed by hills, is so secluded that there is nothing of a port about it. Its crescent-shaped beach flings out its arms around the open sea exactly as if eagerly striving to embrace the infinite. The edge of the broad sandy beach is fringed with a forest of casuarinas, broken at one end by the Kalanadi river, which flows into the sea after passing through a gorge flanked by rows of hills.

I remember how, one moonlit evening, we went upriver in a little boat. We stopped at one of Shivaji's old hill-forts, and stepping ashore found ourselves in the clean-swept little yard of a peasant's home. We sat in a spot lit by moonbeams glancing over the top of the outer wall, and there we dined off food we had brought with us. On our way back we let the boat glide. The night brooded over the motionless hills and forests and the silent flow of the Kalanadi, throwing its spell over all of them. We took a good long time to reach the mouth of the river, so, instead of returning by sea, we left the boat and walked home over the sands. The night was by then far advanced, the sea without a ripple, and even the murmur of the ever-troubled casuarinas had ceased. Their shadow hung motionless along the edge of the vast expanse of sand, and the ring of blue-grey hills around the horizon slept calmly beneath the heavens.

In this still and limitless whiteness we walked along with our shadows without a word. When we reached home my urge to sleep was lost in something deeper. The poem I wrote is mingled inextricably with the night on that distant seashore. I do not know how it will strike a reader without those memories. This doubt led to its omission from Mohit Babu's edition of my works. I trust that my reminiscences may be deemed its fit home:

Let me sink down, losing myself in the depths of midnight.
Let the earth leave hold of me, let her free me from the
    obstacle of dust.
Keep your watch from afar, O stars, drunk though you be with
    moonlight, and let the horizon hold its wings still around
    me.
Let there be no song, no word, no sound, no touch; nor sleep,
    nor awakening, but only the moonlight like a swoon of
    ecstasy over the sky and my being.
To me the world seems like a ship with countless pilgrims,
    vanishing in the remote blue of the sky, its sailors' song
    becoming fainter and fainter on the air,
While I sink in the folds of the endless night, fading away
    from myself, dwindling to a point.

One needs to add here that just because feeling is brimming over when something is being written, does not ensure it is good. Rather, the utterance is likely to be thick with emotion. Just as a writer should not be entirely removed from the feeling to which he is giving expression, so also if he is too close to it the truest poetry does not result. Memory is the brush which best lays on authentic colour. Proximity may be too compelling, leaving the imagination insufficiently free. In all art, not only in poetry, the mind of the artist must attain a degree of aloofness—the *creator* within man must be allowed sole control. If the material at hand gets the better of the creation, the outcome is a mere replica of the event, not a reflection of it from the artist's mind.

'Nature's Revenge'

In Karwar I wrote the 'Prakritir Pratishodh' (Nature's Revenge), a dramatic poem. The hero was a sanyasi who was striving for a victory over Nature by cutting the bonds of desire and affection to arrive at a true knowledge of himself. A little girl brings him back to the world from communion with the infinite and into the bondage of human affection. Then the sanyasi realises that the great is to be found in the small, the infinite within the bounds of form, and the eternal freedom of the soul in love. Only in the aura of love does every limit merge with the limitless.

The sea beach at Karwar is certainly the ideal place to appreciate that the beauty of Nature is not a mirage of the imagination, but a reflection of the joy in the infinite which entices us to lose ourselves. It is not surprising if we miss this infinitude in the abstract expression of this universal joy. But when we see beauty in the meanest of things and the heart is put into immediate touch with immensity, is any room left for argument?

Nature transported the sanyasi to the presence of the infinite enthroned in the finite, by way of the heart. In 'Nature's Revenge' on one side were shown the wayfarers and the villagers, content with domestic routine and unconscious of anything beyond it; and on the other the sanyasi busy casting away his all, along with himself, into self-imagined infinitude. When love bridged the gulf between the two, and householder and hermit met, the apparent triviality of the finite and the apparent nullity of the infinite alike disappeared. This, in a slightly different form, was the story of my own experience of the entrancing ray of light which found its way into the depths of the cave in which I had retired away from all touch with the outer world, and brought me more fully in touch with Nature again. 'Nature's Revenge' may be seen as an introduction to the whole of my future literary work or, rather, to the subject on which all my writings have dwelt: the delight of attaining the infinite within the finite.

On our way back from Karwar I wrote some songs for 'Nature's Revenge' on board a ship. The first one filled me with great gladness as I sang and wrote it sitting on the deck:

> Mother, leave your darling boy to us,
> And let us take him to the field where the cattle graze.

The sun has risen, the buds have opened, the cowherds are going to pasture; and they cannot allow the sunlight, the flowers, and their play in the grazing grounds to be empty. They want their Shyama (Krishna) to be with them there, in the midst of all these. They want to see the infinite in all its carefully adorned loveliness; they have turned out early because they want to join in frolics amid ghat and field and forest and mountain—not to admire from a distance, neither to be spellbound by majesty. Their requirements are of the slightest. A simple yellow garment and a garland of wild-flowers are all the raiment they need. For where joy reigns on every side, to search for it earnestly, or with pomp and ceremony, is to miss it.

Shortly after my return from Karwar, I was married. I was then twenty-two years old.

Pictures and Songs

Chhabi o Gan (Pictures and Songs) is the title of a book of poems, most of which were written at this time.

We were then living in a house with a garden on Lower Circular Road. Adjoining it on the south side was a large *busti*. I would often sit near a window and watch the goings-on in this populous settlement. I loved to see the inhabitants work, play and rest, and come and go multifariously. To me it was like a story come alive.

A faculty of many-sightedness possessed me at this time. Each separate picture I ringed with light from my imagination and joy from my heart and infused with a pathos of its own. The pleasure of demarcating each picture was much the same as that of painting it; both were the outcome of a desire to apprehend with the mind what the eye sees, and to see with the eye what the mind imagines.

Had I been a painter I should doubtless have tried to keep a record of the visions and creations of that period when I was so alert and responsive. But that instrument was not available to me. What I had was words and rhymes, and even with these I had not yet learnt to draw firm strokes or to colour without overflowing. Still, like a boy with his first paint-box, I passed an entire day creating pictures out of the many-coloured fancies of youth. If these pictures are viewed today, with the fact that I was twenty-two when I made them kept in mind, some worthwhile features may be discerned even through the crude execution and blurred colouring.

I have remarked that the first book of my literary life came to an end with *Morning Songs*. The same subject was then continued under a different title. Many pages at the start of this book are of no value, I know. New beginnings inevitably require much in the way of superfluous preliminaries. Had these been leaves on a tree they would have duly dropped off. Unfortunately, leaves of a book cling on even when they are no longer wanted. The feature of these poems was the close attention they paid even to trifling things. *Pictures and Songs* seized every opportunity of giving value to trivia by saturating them with colours straight from the heart.

That does not really do justice to the process of composition. When the mind is properly tuned, all parts of the universal song awaken its sympathetic vibrations. This music, roused within me, was the reason why nothing felt trivial to me as I wrote. Whatever my eyes fell upon prompted a response inside. Like children who play with sand or stones or shells or whatever they can find (for the spirit of play is within them), so we, when filled with youth, become aware that the universe is a harp of many thousand tunes, any one of which may serve for our accompaniment; there is no need to seek afar.

An Intervening Period

Between *Pictures and Songs* and *Kari o Komal* (Sharps and Flats) a child's magazine called *Balak* sprang up, flourished and died like an annual plant. My second sister-in-law felt the want of an illustrated magazine for children. Her idea was that the young people of the family would contribute to it, but as she felt that alone would not be enough, she took up the editorship herself and asked me to help by contributing.

After one or two numbers of *Balak* had come out I happened to go on a visit to Raj Narain Babu at Deoghar. On the return journey the train was crowded, and as there was an unshaded light just above the only berth I could get, I could not sleep. I thought I might as well take this opportunity of thinking out a story for *Balak*. In spite of my efforts a story eluded me, but sleep came to my rescue. In a dream I saw the stone steps of a temple stained with the blood of victims of sacrifice—and a little girl standing there with her father, asking him in piteous accents: 'Father, what is this, why all this blood?' and the father, inwardly moved, trying to quiet her questioning with a show of gruffness. When I awoke I felt I had got my story. Many of my stories have been given in dreams—and other writings too. This dream episode I made part of the annals of King Gobinda Manikya of Tripura and created out of it a short serial story, *Rajarshi* (The Royal Sage) for *Balak*.

Those were days of utter freedom from care. Nothing seemed to be anxious to express itself through my life or writings. I had not yet joined the throng of travellers on the path of life, but was a mere spectator at the window. Many wayfarers passed me by on various errands as I gazed out, and the seasons entered unasked and stayed with me like visitors in a foreign land.

Not only the seasons either. Men of all kinds, curious types floating about like boats adrift from their anchors, periodically invaded my little room. They sought to further their own ends at the cost of my inexperience with many an extraordinary device. They need not have taken such pains to get the better of me. I was entirely unsophisticated, my own wants were few, and I was not at all clever at distinguishing between good and bad faith. I have often imagined that I was assisting persons with their school fees to whom such fees were as irrelevant as books.

Once a long-haired youth brought me a letter from his 'sister' in which she asked me to take under my protection this brother of hers who was suffering from the tyranny of a stepmother (as imaginary as herself). That the brother was not imaginary was enough for me; his sister's letter was as unnecessary as expert marksmanship to bring down a bird that cannot fly.

Another young fellow came to inform me he was studying for the BA, but could not take the examination as he was afflicted with brain trouble. I was concerned, but since I was far from proficient in medical science, or in any other science, I was at a loss for advice. He, however, went on to explain that he had seen in a dream that my wife had been his mother in a former birth, and that if he could but drink some water which had touched her feet he would be cured. 'Perhaps you don't believe in such things,' he concluded with a smile. My belief did not matter, I said, but if he thought he could be cured, he was welcome; and so I procured him a phial of water supposed to have touched my wife's feet. He felt immensely better, he said. Beginning with water, in the natural course of evolution he came to solid food. Then he took up his quarters in a corner of my room and began to hold smoking parties with his friends, till I had to take refuge in flight from the smoke-laden air. He gradually proved beyond doubt that though his brain might have been diseased, it certainly was not weak.

After this experience I needed no end of proof before I could bring myself to put trust in children of previous births. My reputation must have spread though, for I received a letter now from a distressed daughter. Here, I gently but firmly drew the line.

Throughout this time my friendship with Babu Shrish Chandra Majumdar ripened apace. Every evening he and Priya Babu would come to my little room and we would discuss literature and music far into the night. Sometimes a whole day would be spent in this way. The fact is my *self* had not yet been moulded and nourished into a strong and definite personality, and so my life drifted along as lightly and easily as an autumn cloud.

Bankim Chandra

This was the time when my acquaintance with Bankim Babu began. My first sight of him was a matter of long before. The alumni of Calcutta University had started an annual reunion, of which Babu Chandranath Basu was the leading spirit. Perhaps he entertained a hope that in the future I might become one of them; anyhow I was asked to read a poem. Chandranath Babu was then quite a young man. I remember he had translated some martial German poem into English which he proposed to recite himself on the day, and came to us to rehearse it, full of energy. That a warrior poet's ode to his beloved sword was once his favourite poem will convince the reader that even Chandranath Babu once was young; and what's more, that those times were indeed peculiar.

While wandering about in the crush at the students' reunion, I suddenly came across a figure which struck me as distinguished beyond that of any other and who could not possibly have been lost in any crowd. The features of this tall fair personage shone with radiance and I could not contain my curiosity about him: he was the only person whose name I felt concerned to know that day. When I learnt he was Bankim Babu I marvelled all the more because it seemed a wonderful match of creator and creation. His aquiline nose, compressed lips, and keen glance betokened immense intellect. With his arms folded across his breast he seemed to walk as one apart, towering above the ordinary throng—that was what struck me most. On his forehead he had the mark of a true prince among men.

A small incident in that gathering is indelible. In one of the rooms a pandit was reciting some Sanskrit verses of his own composition and explaining them in Bengali to the audience. One of the allusions was not exactly coarse, but somewhat vulgar. As the pandit proceeded to expound this Bankim Babu, covering his face with his hands, hurried out. I was near the door and can still see his shrinking, retreating figure.

After that I often longed to see him, but I could not get the opportunity. At last, when he was deputy magistrate of Howrah, I made bold to call on him. We met, and I tried my best to make conversation. But I somehow felt greatly abashed while returning home, as if I had acted like a raw, bumptious youth in thrusting myself upon him unasked and unintroduced.

Quite soon, within a year or two, I attained a place as the youngest of the literary men of the time; but my position in order of merit remained uncertain. The reputation I had acquired was mixed with plenty of doubt and not a little condescension. It was then the fashion in Bengal to assign each man of letters a place by comparing him with a supposed compeer in the West. Thus one was the Byron of Bengal, another the Emerson and so forth. I began to be styled the Bengal Shelley. This was insulting to Shelley and only likely to get me laughed at.

My established cognomen was the Lisping Poet. My attainments were few, my knowledge of life meagre, and in both poetry and prose the sentiment exceeded the substance. There was nothing on which anyone could base praise with any degree of confidence. My dress and behaviour were of the same anomalous description. I wore my hair long and indulged in what was probably an ultra-poetical refinement of manner. In a word, I was eccentric and could not fit myself into everyday life like an ordinary man.

At this time Babu Akshay Sarkar started his monthly review, *Nabajiban* (New Life), to which I used occasionally to contribute. Bankim Babu had just closed a chapter in his editorship of the *Bangadarshan* and was absorbed in theological writing, for which purpose he had started the monthly *Prachar* (The Preacher). I contributed a song or two to this and an effusive appreciation of Vaishnava lyrics.

Now I began constantly to meet Bankim Babu. He was living in Bhabani Dutt's street. I visited him frequently, true— but there was not much conversation. I was then of an age to listen, not talk. I fervently wished we could warm up into discussion, but my diffidence got the better of my conversational powers. Some days his elder brother Sanjib Babu would be there reclining on his bolster. The sight would gladden me, for he was a genial soul. He delighted in talking, and it was a delight to listen. Those who have read his prose must have noticed how gaily and airily it flows like the sprightliest conversation. Very few have this gift in speech; and fewer still the art to translate it into writing.

This was the time when Pandit Sashadhar rose into prominence. I first heard of him from Bankim Babu. If I remember right, Bankim Babu also was responsible for introducing him to the public. His curious attempt to revive the prestige of Hindu orthodoxy with the help of western science soon spread all over the country. Theosophy had been preparing the ground for some time previously. Not that Bankim Babu even thoroughly identified with the new cult. No shadow of Sashadhar fell on his exposition of Hinduism in *Prachar*—that would have been inconceivable.

I was then coming out of my seclusion, as my contributions to these controversies show. Some were satirical verses, some farcical plays, others letters to newspapers. I descended into the arena from the clouds of sentiment and began to spar in right earnest.

In the heat of the fight I happened to fall foul of Bankim Babu. The history of this remains recorded in *Prachar* and *Bharati* of those days and need not be repeated here. At the close of this period of antagonism Bankim Babu wrote me a letter, which I unfortunately lost. Had I not, the reader could have seen with what consummate generosity Bankim Babu took the sting out of that regrettable episode.

The Steamer Hulk

L ured by an advertisement in some paper, my brother
Jyotirindra went off one afternoon to an auction and on
his return informed us that he had bought a steel hulk for
seven thousand rupees; all that was now required being an
engine and some cabins to make a full-fledged steamer.

My brother must have thought it a great shame that our
countrymen had set their tongues and pens in motion, but
not a single line of steamers. I have narrated earlier how he
tried to light matches for his country, but that no amount of
rubbing would make them strike. He also wanted to operate
power-looms, but after all his travail only one little *gamcha*
was born and then the loom stopped. Now he wanted Indian
steamers to ply and so bought this empty old hulk. In due
course it was filled not only with engines and cabins but with
loss and ruin too.

The latter fell on him alone while the experience benefited
the whole country. These uncalculating, unbusinesslike spirits
sow and water the country's field of business with their
activities. Though the flood subsides as rapidly as it comes,
it leaves fertilising silt behind to enrich the soil. When the
time for reaping arrives no one thinks of these pioneers; but
they who have cheerfully staked and lost their all in life, are
not likely in death to mind a further loss—that of being
forgotten.

On one side was the British-run Flotilla Company, on the other my brother Jyotirindra. How tremendously the battle of the fleets was waged, the people of Khulna and Barisal may still remember. Under the stress of competition, steamer was added to steamer, loss piled on loss, while income dwindled until printing tickets ceased to be worthwhile. A golden age dawned between Khulna and Barisal: not only were the passengers carried free of charge, but they were offered light refreshments *gratis*! Then a band of volunteers formed up who, with flags and patriotic songs, marched the passengers in procession to the Indian line of steamers. So while there was no dearth of passengers, every other kind of want began to multiply apace.

The accounts were uninfluenced by the fervour. While patriotic enthusiasm mounted higher and higher, three times three continued steadily to make nine on the wrong side of the balance-sheet.

One of the misfortunes which always pursues the unbusinesslike is that, while they are as easy to read as an open book, they never learn to read the character of others. And since it takes them a lifetime and all their resources to discover their weakness, they never get the chance to profit by experience. Others certainly gained—the passengers with free refreshments, the staff who showed no sign of starvation— but it was my brother who gained most, by facing his ruin so valiantly.

The daily bulletins of victory or disaster which arrived from the scene of action kept us in a fever of excitement. But one day came the news that the steamer *Swadeshi* had fouled the Howrah bridge and sunk. My brother had now completely overstepped the limits of his resources, and there was nothing for it but to wind up the business.

Bereavements

In the meantime death made its appearance in our family. Until now I had never met it face to face. When my mother died I was a child. She had been ailing for quite a long time, and we did not even know when her malady took a fatal turn. As we grew up, she used to sleep on a separate bed in the same room with us. Then in the course of her illness she was taken for a boat trip on the river, and on her return a room on the third storey of the inner apartments was set apart for her.

On the night she died we were fast asleep in our room downstairs. At an hour I could not tell, our old nurse ran in weeping, crying: 'Oh my little ones, you have lost your all!' My sister-in-law rebuked her and led her away, to save us the sudden shock at dead of night. Half awakened, I felt my heart sink but could not make out what had happened. When we were told of her death in the morning, I did not realise all it meant for me.

We came out into the verandah and saw my mother lying on a bedstead in the courtyard. Nothing in her appearance showed death to be terrible. The aspect it wore in that morning light was as lovely as a calm and peaceful sleep, and the gulf between life and absence of life was not brought home to us.

Only when her body was taken out through the main gateway and we followed the procession to the cremation ground did a storm of grief pass through me at the thought that Mother would never return by this door and again take her accustomed place in the affairs of the household. The day wore on, we returned from the cremation, and as we turned into our lane I looked up towards my father's rooms on the third storey. He was still sitting in the front verandah, motionless in prayer.

She who was the youngest daughter-in-law took charge of the motherless little ones. She saw to our food and clothing and all other wants, and kept us constantly near, so that we might not feel our loss too keenly. One of the attributes of the living is the power to heal the irreparable, to forget the irreplaceable. This power is strongest in early life, so that no blow penetrates too deeply, no scar is permanent. Thus the first shadow of death which fell upon us left no darkness behind; it departed as softly as it came, only a shadow.

In later life, wandering like a madcap at the first coming of spring with a handful of half-blown jessamines tied in a corner of my muslin scarf, as I stroked my forehead with the soft, rounded, tapering buds the touch of my mother's fingers would come back to me; and I clearly sensed that the tenderness dwelling in the tips of those fingers was the very same as the purity that blossoms every day in jessamine buds. And I felt that this tenderness is on the earth in boundless measure. whether we know it or not.

The acquaintance I made with Death at the age of twenty-three was a permanent one, and its blow reverberates with each succeeding bereavement in ever-expanding wreaths of tears. An infant can skip away from the greatest of calamities, but with the coming of age evasion is not so easy. The shock of that day I had to face full-on.

That there could be any gap in life's succession of joys and sorrows was something of which I had no idea. I had seen nothing beyond life, and accepted it as the ultimate truth. When death suddenly came, and in a moment tore a gaping rent in life's seamless fabric, I was utterly bewildered. All around, the trees, the soil, the water, the sun, the moon, the stars, remained as immovably true as before, and yet the person who was as truly there, who, through a thousand points of contact with life, mind and heart, was so very much more true for me, had vanished in an instant like a dream. What a perplexing contradiction! How was I ever to reconcile what remained with that which had gone?

The terrible darkness disclosed to me through this rent, continued to lure me night and day as time went by. I would constantly return to it and gaze at it, wondering what was left to replace what had departed. Emptiness is a thing man cannot bring himself to believe in: that which is *not*, is untrue; that which is untrue, is not. So our efforts to find something where we see nothing are unceasing.

Just as a young plant confined in darkness stretches itself, on tiptoe as it were, to reach the light, so the soul, when death surrounds it with negation, tries and tries to rise into affirmatory light. What sorrow is deeper than to be trapped in a darkness that prevents one from finding a way out of darkness?

Yet amid unbearable grief, flashes of joy sparkled in my mind on and off in a way which quite surprised me. The idea that life is not a fixture came as tidings that helped to lighten my mind. That we are not for ever prisoners behind a wall of stony-hearted facts was the thought that kept unconsciously rising uppermost in rushes of gladness. What I had possessed I was made to let go—and it distressed me—but when in the same moment I viewed it as freedom gained, a great peace fell upon me.

The all-pervading pressure of worldly existence is compensated by death, and thus it does not crush us. The terrible weight of eternal life does not have to be endured by man—this truth came over me that day as a wonderful revelation.

With the loosening allure of the world, the beauty of Nature took on a deeper meaning. Death had given me the correct perspective from which to perceive the world's full beauty, and as I saw the universe against this background, it entranced me.

At this time I had a recrudescence of eccentricity in thought and behaviour. I was being called upon to submit to the customs and fashions of the day as if they were something soberly and genuinely real; instead they made me want to laugh. I could not take them seriously. The burden of stopping to consider what other people might think of me was completely lifted from my mind. I have been about in fashionable book-shops with a coarse sheet draped round me as my only upper garment and a pair of slippers on my bare feet. In heat, chill and wet I used to sleep out on the verandah of the third storey. There the stars and I could gaze at each other, and no time was lost in greeting the dawn.

This phase had nothing to do with any ascetic feeling. It was more like a holiday spree occasioned by discovering the schoolmaster Life with his cane to be a myth, and being thereby able to shake myself free from the petty regulations of his school. If, on waking one fine morning, we were to find gravitation reduced to only a fraction of itself, would we still demurely walk along the main road? Wouldn't we rather skip over multi-storeyed houses for a change, or on encountering some monument take a flying jump and not have the trouble of walking round it? So, with the weight of worldly life no longer dragging at my feet, I could not adhere to the usual conventions.

Alone on the terrace at night I groped like a blind man trying to find some device or sign upon the black stone gate of death. In the morning, the light falling on my unscreened bed as I opened my eyes made me feel that the haze enveloping my brain was really transparent; just as when mist clears, hills, rivers and forests shine anew, so the dew-drenched picture of existence spread before me seemed refreshingly beautiful.

The Rains and the Autumn

According to the Hindu calendar, each year is ruled by a particular planet. So, in each period of my life, a particular season has assumed special importance. When I look back to my childhood I recall the rainy days best. I can see the wind-driven rain flooding the verandah floor; the row of doors into the rooms all closed; Peari, the old scullery maid, coming from the market, basket laden with vegetables, wading through the slush and drenched with the rain. And for no rhyme or reason I am careering about the verandah in ecstasy.

Something else comes back to me: I am at school in a class held in a colonnade with mats tied across the pillars as screens; cloud after cloud has rolled up during the afternoon, and they are now piled across the sky. As we watch, the rain falls in a dense sheet, the thunder rumbles at intervals long and loud; some mad woman with nails of lightning seems to rend the sky from end to end. The mat walls tremble under the blasts of wind as if they will be blown in. We can hardly see to read for the darkness; the pandit gives us leave to close our books. Letting the storm romp and roar on our behalf, we swing our dangling legs, and my mind flies right away across a distant plateau without end over which the prince of the fairy tale passes.

I remember, too, the depth of night in the month of *Shravan*. The pattering of rain, infiltrating my slumber, produces in me a restfulness more profound than deep sleep. In my waking intervals I pray that morning may see the rain continue, our lane under water, and the bathing platform of the tank submerged to the last step.

But at the age of which I was earlier speaking, autumn, not the rainy season, is on the throne beyond doubt. My life may be seen spread leisurely beneath the clear transparent sky of *Ashwin*. And in the molten gold of autumn sunshine softly reflected from the fresh dewy green outside, I pace the verandah and compose, in the raga Jogiya, the song:

In this morning light I know not what my heart desires

The day wears on, the gong in the house sounds twelve noon, the mode changes; but my mind remains full of music, leaving no room for work or duty. I sing:

What idle play is this, my heart, in the listless hours?

Then in the afternoon I lie on the white sheet on the floor of my small room, trying to draw in a sketch-book—by no means an arduous pursuit of the muse, just a toying with the wish to make pictures. The most important part remains in the mind; not a line of it is put on paper. And in the meantime the serene autumn afternoon filters through the walls of my room, filling it, like a cup, with intoxicating gold.

I do not know why, but all my days at that time I see as if under this autumn sky, lit by this autumn light: the autumn that ripened my songs as it ripens corn for the cultivators; the autumn that filled my granary of leisure with radiance; the autumn that flooded my unburdened mind with unreasoning joy and fashioned song and story.

The great difference between the rainy season of my childhood and the autumn of my youth is that in the former, Nature closely hemmed me in, entertaining me with her numerous troupe, her variegated make-up and her medley of music; while in the latter the festivity is within me. The play of cloud and sunshine has receded into the background, and murmurs of joy and sorrow have occupied the mind. It is these that lend the blue of the autumn sky its wistful tinge and invest the breath of the breezes with poignancy.

My poems had now reached the doors of men's minds. No longer could they come and go as they liked; there was door after door, chamber within chamber. How many times must we return with only a glimpse of light in a window, only the sound of pipes somewhere within the palace gates—some flute or *shehnai*—lingering in our ears! Mind has to treat with mind, will come to terms with will and many obstacles be surmounted before there can be true intercourse. The cascade of life dashes round these obstacles, splashing and foaming with laughter and tears, dancing and whirling in eddies and never allowing one to form a definite estimate of its course.

Sharps and Flats

Kari o Komal (Sharps and Flats) is a serenade from the streets before the dwelling-place of Man, a plea to be allowed entry and position within that house of mystery.

This word is sweet—I do not want to die.
I want to live within the stream of humanity.

This is the individual's dedication of himself to life.

When I started on my second voyage to England, on board ship I made the acquaintance of Ashutosh Chaudhuri. He had just taken his MA degree from Calcutta University and was on his way to England to join the bar. We were together only the few days the steamer took from Calcutta to Madras, but it became evident that depth of friendship does not depend upon length of acquaintance. Within this short time he so drew me to him by his natural simplicity of heart that our friendship seemed always to have been there.

When Ashu returned from England he became one of the family. He had not then had time or opportunity to pierce all the barriers that hedge in his profession and become completely immersed in it. The moneybags of his clients had not yet entirely loosened the strings holding their gold, and Ashu was still an enthusiastic gatherer of honey from various literary hives. The spirit that infused him had none of the mustiness of library morocco, but was fragrant with the scent of unknown exotics from over the oceans. At his invitation I enjoyed many a springtime picnic in those distant glades.

He had a special taste for French literature. I was then writing the poems later published as *Sharps and Flats*. Ashu discerned resemblances between many of them and old French poems. The common element, according to him, was the appeal made to the poet by the play of life, which found varied expression in each and every poem. An unfulfilled yearning to join this larger life was the vital force in both cases.

'I will arrange and publish these poems for you,' said Ashu, and the task was accordingly entrusted to him. The poem beginning 'This world is sweet' was the one he considered the keynote of the series, and so he placed it at the beginning.

He was very possibly right. In childhood, when I was confined to the house, I looked wistfully through the openings in the parapet of our inner roof-terrace and offered my heart to Nature. In my youth it was the world of men that exerted a powerful attraction upon me. I was an outsider, and looked out upon it from the wayside. My mind, on the brink of life, called out to a ferryman sailing away across the waves, as it were, with an eager waving of hands. For my life longed to begin its journey.

It is not true that my marked isolation acted as a bar to plunging into the social stream. I see no sign in those of my countrymen who have been in the thick of society all their lives that they enjoy any more than I do a life-giving touch from such intimacy. The social existence of our country has its lofty banks, its flights of steps, and its cool dark waters shadowed by antique trees from whose leafy branches the *koel* coos its ancient ravishing song. But, for all that, the water is stagnant. Where is its current, where are its waves, when does the high tide rush in from the sea?

Did I receive an echo of the triumphant paean of a river rising and falling in wave after wave, cutting its way through walls of rock to the sea when I looked at the neighbourhood beyond our lane? No! In my solitude I simply fretted for lack of an invitation to the place where the world's festival was being held.

Man may be overcome by profound depression in voluptuously lazy seclusion if deprived of commerce with life. From such despondency I have always struggled painfully to break free. My mind refused to respond to the cheap intoxications of political movements, devoid as they were of any national consciousness, completely ignorant of the country, and supremely indifferent to real service of the motherland. I was tormented by a furious impatience, an intolerable dissatisfaction with myself and all around me. Much rather, I told myself, were I an Arab Bedouin!

In other parts of the world there is no end to the movement, clamour and revelry of life. We, like beggar-maids, stand outside and look longingly on. When have we had the wherewithal to deck ourselves and join in? Only in a land where an animus of divisiveness reigns supreme, and innumerable petty barriers separate one from another, must this longing to express a larger life in one's own remain unsatisfied. I strained to reach humanity in my youth, as in my childhood I yearned for the outside world from within the chalk-ring drawn around me by the servants: how unique, unattainable and remote it seemed! And yet if we cannot get in touch with it, if no breeze can blow from it, no current flow out of it, no path be open to the free passage of travellers, then the dead things accumulating around us will never be removed but continue to mount up until they smother all vestige of life.

During the rains there are only dark clouds and showers. In the autumn there is the play of light and shade in the sky; but there is something else too—the promise of corn in the fields. The rainy season of my career was similarly vaporous and moist with puffy sentiment; my message was misty, my rhythm incoherent. But with my autumnal *Sharps and Flats* not only could colours be seen in the clouds but clearly crops were rising from the ground. There was a definite attempt in variety of both language and metre to establish contact with the real world.

And so another chapter closes. The light-hearted days of mixing freely with the world at will are over. My journey has now to be completed through the dwelling-places of men. And the good and evil, joy and woe which it thus encounters may not be viewed as pictures. What tumult is going on here! What construction and destruction, conflict and conjunction!

I do not have the power to disclose and describe the supreme art with which my Guide joyfully leads me past all obstacle, antagonism and crookedness towards fulfillment of my life's innermost meaning. And if I cannot clarify this mystery, whatever else I may attempt to explain is sure to mislead at every step. To analyse an image is to gather only dust, not the spirit of the artist.

So, having escorted you to the door of my sanctuary, I take leave of my readers.